STATUS AND SACREDNESS

STATUS
AND SACREDNESS

A General Theory of
Status Relations and
an Analysis of Indian Culture

MURRAY MILNER, JR.

New York   Oxford
OXFORD UNIVERSITY PRESS
1994

Oxford University Press

Oxford   New York   Toronto
Delhi   Bombay   Calcutta   Madras   Karachi
Kuala Lumpur   Singapore   Hong Kong   Tokyo
Nairobi   Dar es Salaam   Cape Town
Melbourne   Auckland   Madrid

and associated companies in
Berlin   Ibadan

Copyright © 1994 by Oxford University Press, Inc.

Published by Oxford University Press, Inc.,
200 Madison Avenue, New York, New York 10016

Oxford is a registered trademark of Oxford University Press

Library of Congress Cataloging-in-Publication Data
Milner, Murray.
Status and sacredness:
a general theory of status relations and
an analysis of Indian culture /
Murray Milner, Jr.
p.   cm.   Includes bibliographical references.
ISBN 0–19–508334–2
ISBN 0–19–508489–6 (pbk.)
1. Social status.   2. Social structure.
3. Sociology—Philosophy.
4. Religion and social status.
5. Sociology, Hindu.
6. Caste—India.
I. Title.   HM136.M52   1994
305.5'122'0954—dc20   93–20052

2 4 6 8 9 7 5 3 1

Printed in the United States of America
on acid-free paper

This book is dedicated to
my colleagues, students and friends
in Patna, Bihar, India, 1976–1977
and to Sylvia, Helene, and Catherine
who shared this experience

Preface

This is a book about social theory; it is also an empirical analysis. The empirical focus is the Indian caste system and Hinduism—though comparisons are made with other societies. While the analysis contains much detailed information about Hindu India, no previous knowledge of this culture is assumed. In many respects I depart from recent interpretations of India that stress its cultural uniqueness. The aim is to systematically explain the most prominent social and cultural features of Hindu India in a way that makes sense to both the novice and the specialist.

These explanations are primarily based on a typology of power and a general theory of status relations. The typology and theory are used to explain why social relationships take the form that they do when status is an important social resource. For example, explanations are offered for the tendencies toward limiting mobility, regulating marriage and eating, elaborating the norms governing styles of life, and social stability and conservatism—not just in India, but in all social situations where status is an especially crucial resource. I also argue that legitimation and sacredness are special forms of status. Hence the theory of status relations is used to analyze political legitimation and religious phenomena such as worship, doctrines of salvation, and beliefs about the world-to-come.

This theory of status relations is a special example of a more general theoretical approach that I call resource structuralism. It is posed as an alternative to some of the major perspectives of contemporary social theory—for example, rational choice theory, the theories of practice associated with Anthony Giddens and Pierre Bourdieu, and more unqualified forms of structuralism such as those of Claude Lévi-Strauss, Louis Althusser, and Peter Blau. I also try to show that the choice between methodologies emphasizing causal propositions and those emphasizing more interpretive and hermeneutical forms of understanding is a false one.

The political intent of the book is to critique certain forms of materialism and rationalism that have impoverished humankind both intellectually and morally.

The book is written for several audiences, and some hints about what will be of interest to whom may be helpful. Subsequent chapters build on what has gone before; therefore, something is lost when chapters are read out of context. Nonetheless, this is a long book, and some will not want to read all of it. Those who are South Asian specialists and have no particular interest in social theory may want to start with Chapter 3, skip Chapter 4, read Chapter 5, and then proceed to the chapters on their particular area of interest. Those interested in religious studies may want to start with the section of Chapter 2 entitled "Types of Power and Types of Social Formations," read through Chapter 5, and then skip to Chapters 12–15. Sociologists need to start at the beginning and read through Chapter 10; hopefully, the usefulness of the perspective will be apparent by that point.

Charlottesville, Va.   M.M.
March 1993

Acknowledgments

It has taken approximately twelve years to complete the research and writing of this book. I have incurred numerous debts, both intellectual and personal. To name each individual—the list runs to nearly a hundred—would require far too much space. While many of them will be critical of what I have produced, I am especially indebted to some four dozen South Asian scholars who have engaged me at one point or another in extended discussions. Several sets of people at the University of Virginia have been important to this process. First, the faculty, graduate students, staff, and visiting lecturers at the Center for South Asian Studies have taught me much of what I know about India. Second, my various deans, my sociology colleagues, my students, and the department's secretarial and support staff have been supportive and showed commendable patience—most of the time acting as if they actually believed I would complete this book. Careful editing by Marion Borg and Karin Peterson, and manuscript preparation by Joan Snapp were invaluable. Research leaves at The Delhi School of Economics, Clare Hall of Cambridge University, and the London School of Economics were especially productive periods. Numerous colleagues at these institutions were stimulating and helpful. The gracious hospitality of the late M. S. A. Rao, then Chair of the Department of Sociology at the Delhi School of Economics, requires special mention. I received research funding from the National Science Foundation through the American Institute of Indian Studies, and from the Center for Advanced Studies of the University of Virginia.

A great debt is owed to two South Asian scholars, Jonathan Parry and David White. Their ability and willingness to offer both probing criticism and moral support has been crucial to the completion of this work. They have given thoughtful responses to various drafts of most chapters. On theoretical matters early conversations with Jonathan Turner and later ones with Gianfranco Poggi have been very helpful. Careful critiques by André Béteille, Lewis Coser, Pauline Kolenda, and David Lockwood were important in making the final revisions.

In 1976 and 1977, I spent an academic year as a Fulbright Fellow teaching in the graduate Department of Sociology at Patna University, Bihar, India. My actual research and writing on India did not begin until several years later, but undoubtedly this experience played a crucial role in shaping my interest and thinking.

Contents

A Note on Foreign Words

I have italicized foreign words only when they first appear in the text. There are three exceptions to this pattern: italics are retained in quoted material; with proper names of specific texts (e.g., the *Bhagavad Gita*); and with the word *brahman*, which refers to the impersonal neuter form of the deity or being, to distinguish it from the masculine form, Brahman, which is the proper name of the priestly caste.

India has a more than fifteen major indigenous languages. I have followed the custom of using the Sanskrit form of words in scholarly writings when possible. Some words, however—often those taken from ethnographies of particular areas in India—are from other Indian languages.

The most important and frequently used foreign words are defined in the glossary.

All words from South Asian languages in Roman script have, of course, been transliterated from other alphabets. While there is now a supposedly standard method for doing this, the procedures guiding such transliterations have varied over time and by the particular translator. The result is that there are multiple English spellings of the same Indian word—for example, sakti and shakti, Siva and Shiva, pakka and pukka. When quoting others I have used the form found in the quoted text. Where I thought alternative spellings might cause confusion, I have tried to indicate the common alternatives in the glossary. Diacritical marks have been omitted.

STATUS AND SACREDNESS

1

Introduction

"The study of the caste system is both useful for our knowledge of India, and is an important task of general sociology." This is the opening sentence of *Homo Hierarchicus*, Louis Dumont's classic study of caste (1980:xiv). Karl Marx and Max Weber also thought the analysis of India was important—both in its own right and as a contribution to general sociological understanding (Marx 1968, 1983; Madan 1979; Weber 1958b, 1968). I share this conviction.

This is a book about India, but it is also a book about status relationships and process in all societies. The scope of the analytical task is even broader in two respects. First, I claim that sacredness is, in part, a special form of status. Hence many of people's relationships to sacred entities can be understood with the same analytical tools used to understand status relationships and processes. Second, the focus on status and sacral relationships is a means of considering the general problem of how variations in social resources affect the development and structuring of social formations and groups.

Before these issues are taken up directly, some comments are needed about the intellectual context.

Contemporary Social Theory

Perhaps the most famous sentence in social theory is Marx's epigram in *The Eighteenth Brumaire of Louis Bonaparte*: "Men [and women] make their own history, but they do not make it just as they please; they do not make it under circumstances chosen by themselves, but under the circumstances directly found, given and transmitted from the past" (Marx 1978:595). It expresses one of the central problems in social theory: How do we accurately portray the degree to which humans shape their own destiny and the degree to which it is shaped by factors beyond their control—especially the past history of their own actions? In other terms, to what degree is history the result of human agency and to what degree is it a matter of contingency?

On the whole, sociology has emphasized the second half of Marx's formula— partly as a reaction against the strong emphasis on "free choice" that has been characteristic of capitalist ideology in general, and utilitarianism and economics in particular. In contemporary social theory, this emphasis is most often expressed in various kinds of structuralism: how the residues of past actions shape subsequent behavior. An aspect of this endeavor is to show how the different parts of these structural residues are interrelated; for example, how the way work is organized affects family life. This broad tradition includes the enormously influential work of Lévi-Strauss (1963), the structural Marxism of Althusser (1990), the work of Blau (1977) inspired by the formal structuralism of Simmel, the Durkheimian structuralism of Black (1976) applied to the analysis of law, and various forms of structuralism linked to mathematical models (e.g., White 1976; Mayhew 1980; Burt 1982).[1] As different as these various perspectives are, they all have two things in common. First, they focus on the properties of collectivities and emphasize macro analysis. Second, they treat social phenomena as relatively objective social facts that can be usefully analyzed independently of the subjectivity or behavior of individuals.

The first part of Marx's formulation was not completely abandoned by sociology. It remained like the retarded child too beloved to be deserted but too troublesome to be admitted to the front parlor. Blumer's symbolic interactionism (1986) Goffman's dramaturgical analysis (1959), Garfinkel's ethnomethodology (1967), and Collins's conflict sociology (1975) all attempted to move the action of individuals more to the center of sociological analysis. It was, however, Berger and Luckmann's *The Social Construction of Reality* (1967) that most systematically attempted to integrate the two sides of the Marxian coin, though this was filtered through the lens of Alfred Schutz's phenomenology. (Aspects of this formulation are considered in more detail later.)

In the 1980s two additional critiques of structuralism emerged. One is rational choice theory, which attempts to extend some of the insights of economics to the analysis of social behavior in general. A major concern of this approach is to explain the emergence and variations of macro structures as the aggregate outcome of the relatively rational choices made by individuals. Hechter's (1987) theory of group solidarity and Coleman's *Foundations of Social Theory* (1990) are the most significant examples of this approach.

The other major alternatives to structuralism are theories of practice, which have also been influential in anthropology (see Ortner 1984). The most notable examples are the structuration theory of Anthony Giddens and the work of Pierre Bourdieu.[2] Giddens and Bourdieu are dissatisfied with the objectivism assumed by both structuralism and rational choice theory, and with the subjectivism character- istic of the earlier critiques of structural-functionalism such as symbolic interaction- ism, ethnomethodology, phenomenology, and Berger and Luckmann's social construction of reality perspective.[3] Their goal is a perspective that explains how concrete practices result in "constituting" (Giddens) or "reproducing" (Bourdieu) the structures of collectivities, *and* how these structures in turn shape subsequent behavior. They draw on a linguistic model: in the relationship between the speech of individuals and the structure of a language, the latter is both the result of the former and the medium of subsequent speech. But both Bourdieu and Giddens would strongly stress that, this process is not automatic or mechanical but involves considerable human agency, hence creativity and use of strategy. The structure of language and society limits, but does not determine, what people say and do; humans could always have said and done otherwise.[4]

While I am broadly sympathetic to the attempts to transcend the limits of structuralism, I believe the current efforts to do this—both rational choice theory and theories of practice—are too ambitious to give adequate guidance to most empirical research. The scope of the problems considered and the elaborateness and abstractness of the categories formulated are more enervating than stimulating. The goals of integrating micro and macro analysis, and (for theories of practice) transcending subjectivism and objectivism seem beyond the immediate reach of social science.[5] Most social scientists acknowledge that the behavior of individuals and the historically created structures of social systems are dialectically related. Each is the source of the other; the actions of individuals produce and reproduce social systems, and individuals can be created and sustained only in such systems. But this does not mean that our best chance for increased understanding lies in analyzing this full set of interrelationships.

The history of modern biology—the science that specializes in self-reproducing organic systems—is instructive in this respect. One of the earliest developments was in taxonomy, the ability to systematically distinguish and relate different whole organisms. Next came progress in anatomy and physiology, that is, in understanding the interrelationship between macro structures of relatively complex organisms. During the nineteenth century, a number of insights were developed about cell structure and microorganisms. In the middle of that century came Darwin's breakthrough in understanding the long-term transformation of species—which was built primarily on the comparative anatomy of relatively complex organisms. With Mendel's work and the development of population genetics, some hypotheses and assumptions—the theory of genes—developed about how similarities and variations were transmitted over generations. But significant progress in understanding the interrelationship between macro and micro levels of organisms was not made until the middle of the twentieth century and the development of molecular biology. Of course, biologists realized all along that organisms sustained and reproduced themselves and that the life cycle, changes between generations, and the evolution of species were rooted in the details of the micro processes. Not much progress in understanding the fundamental micro processes was made, however, until the discipline had matured and legitimated itself largely on its accomplishments in understanding relatively macro structures and processes.

My point is not that sociological research should be modeled after the historical patterns in biology; there are important differences between the natural and social sciences (see Giddens 1984, especially chap. 6). I do, however, question whether analyzing the extremely complex social processes whereby micro behavior produces macro structures is currently the best strategy for increasing our knowledge. We tend to resort to extremely abstract models based on debatable simplifying assumptions (rational choice theory) or to largely abandon attempts at systematic generalization (theories of practice). Consequently, devoting our primary attention to the complex processes by which structures are produced may be a serious distraction or a cul-de-sac.

The preceding extremely selective, condensed account of contemporary social theory is intended not to adequately summarize it but simply to serve as a contrast to the approach I will suggest.

A Theoretical Strategy

Bourdieu's approach to the dialectical relationship between structure and practice has been called "generative structuralism" (see Harker et al. 1990). This apt phrase indicates that at the center of analytical concerns is the ambitious search for a way to understand the generation of structure. But if our goals should be more modest, perhaps so should our labels. Hence I want to advocate a *provisional structuralism*. This form of structuralism would fully recognize that units of observation—structures and their interrelationship—are abstractions rooted in the practice of individuals. But it would also recognize that individuals are also abstractions drawn from ongoing sequences of practice rooted in structures. Where possible, attempts would be made to draw links between micro and macro levels of analysis and to give accounts of how structures are constituted. But explanatory arguments that were unable to make such connections would not be discounted simply because of this. This approach would also involve a more relaxed view about the necessity of integrating objectivism and subjectivism. There is nothing new about such an approach; it is, I believe, the implicit perspective of the vast majority of sociologists and anthropologists who attempt to analyze and provide explanations of empirical data.[6]

To indicate the provisional nature of the structuralism I am advocating, and to show how it can inform the other types of analysis and vice versa, in Chapters 9 and 10, I shift to something approximating a theory of practice perspective, and I build the analysis of Chapter 11 on a version of rational choice theory.

Simply advocating a provisional structuralism leaves open an important question: What kinds and aspects of structure are most important? I believe it will be especially fruitful to focus upon variations in the nature of resources, for example, whether wealth, force, or status are especially important in a given situation. I will refer to this approach as *resource structuralism*. People have agency but only to the degree that they have power and resources to make a difference in social outcomes. Obviously the *amount* of power that a particular person or group has will affect the degree to which they can have an impact on their social world. Less obvious, but perhaps even more important, the *type* of power and resources that people have can profoundly shape the nature of social relations. The society that has virtually no weapons is likely to be very different from the society that has nuclear arms—quite independently of how these are distributed. Moreover, the nature of the weapons available is likely to have a profound impact on the way they are distributed. It seems doubtful that a society would last very long if anyone could purchase a nuclear device at the neighborhood hardware store. Hence analyses of variations in the types of resources characteristic of different social contexts are likely to help us better understand the nature of social organization.

This was, of course, Marx's key insight about the relationship between the means and modes of production. Lenski's (1966) organization of our knowledge about stratification systems is an important example of this type of analysis in contemporary sociology; he shows that the level and type of technology available in a society has a profound influence on the level and type of social stratification.

Variations in material resource bases are of crucial importance. The more critical task for social theory, though, is to improve our conceptualization and understanding of variations in *nonmaterial or symbolic resources.* This is a prerequisite to a clearer understanding of how variations in resources shape variations in the organization of social life.

Types of Resources and Types of Social Structures

Two of the key tasks of sociology are to explain (1) why in particular historical circumstances some types of social formations are especially prominent, and (2) why a particular kind of social formation has the characteristics that it does. Most of the classics in sociology have considered some version of these problems. Marx focused on the formation of social classes and the conflicts that developed between them as the key dynamic that explained the course of history. Underlying Marx's argument was an assertion that the nature of social formations were tied to resources available to people. According to Marx, the means of production shape the way production activities are organized, which in turn shape most other features of a social order, including the crucial feature of class formation. Differences in people's relationship to the means of production—especially the differences between owners and laborers—produced the fundamental social divisions and conflicts. Marx on occasion overstated this effect and implied a technological determinism. Often he did not give adequate attention to the reverse causal relationship, that is, the way social and cultural factors determine the available resources. He also understated the independent effects of political power and the state.

Max Weber has been regarded as the primary alternative and antidote to Marx's strong emphasis on material factors, economic organization, and class formation. Perhaps the most influential single essay in the sociological literature is the section in Weber's *Economy and Society* entitled "Class, Status, and Party" (1968:926–39). It is the embryo of what has come to be known as a multidimensional approach to social analysis. Weber's concern in this essay was to avoid conflating or confusing different forms of power that served as the bases for different types of social formations. Generally serving as a warning against the oversimplification of social analysis, the essay has also served as a model of how to develop concepts and propositions for cross-cultural and historical analysis. It has inspired a number of important contributions to the sociological literature, and has been the inspiration for this endeavor as well.[7] I am aware of the criticisms of Weber's work on India,[8] but I believe his conceptualization of caste as an extreme form of status group is still the most fruitful means of relating the study of India to general sociology.

Of course, the Weberian perspective has not been limited to the analysis of caste. A long tradition of studies inspired by Weber emphasizes the significance of nonmaterial resources and types of social formations other than social class.[9] In my judgment these efforts, exemplary as they are individually, have been less extensive and less satisfying than those inspired by the Marxian tradition. Falling broadly within the latter are the work of Tilly (1974), Lenski (1966), Moore, Jr. (1967), Wallerstein (1974, 1980, 1989), Paige (1975), Skocpol (1979), Burawoy (1985), and Wright (1985). Together they have set an intellectual agenda and have inspired sustained macro sociological research in a way that the works from the Weberian tradition have not. Whatever the limitations of Marx's arguments, it is now a truism that variation in the means and mode of production will have crucial implications for social formations, and hence the structure of a society.[10] Marx did not talk primarily about "resources," "the distribution of power," and "social formations," but more concretely about historic forms of the means of production and class conflict. This concreteness has been the basis of much of the tradition's strength: its conceptualization was specific enough to identify important changes in the material basis of social life and the social formations this produced. In general, analyses focusing on nonmaterial resources have been less clear about their concepts and assertions and less impressive in their results.

In the last twenty-five years, important attempts have been made to elaborate and clarify how we might conceptualize nonmaterial resources more adequately. Most prominent has been the development of the notion of human capital, which refers to education and skill in the broadest sense of these words. The enormous literature on human capital, associated with such economists as Bowman (1962), Schultz (1963), and Becker (1964), has made important contributions to our understanding of the significance of nonmaterial resources. In addition to identifying knowledge and skills as an important type of social resource, this literature suggests that human capital is growing in importance relative to physical capital. Numerous arguments have developed over the eventual impact of this trend. Daniel Bell (1973) coined the phrase "postindustrial society" to characterize the broad consequences of this change. With respect to the specific effect on class formation, a debate developed over whether a new class is emerging whose power is based on knowledge rather than the control of physical capital. In addition to Bell, such names as Kristol (1972), Bruce-Briggs (1979), Berger (1979), and Gouldner (1979) are associated with this debate. The economists' use of the concept of human capital has been rightfully criticized for ignoring the significant effects of social stratification (see, e.g., Collins 1979; Bourdieu 1986). Nonetheless, the concept and its implications have made an important contribution to our understanding of human behavior.

Symbolic Capital

Beginning with the publication of Bourdieu and Passeron's *Reproduction in Education, Society and Culture* (1977), increasing attention has been turned to what has variously been called cultural capital, symbolic capital, status capital, and social capital. This line of thought has produced considerable discussion, a sizable scholarly literature, and some important studies of brilliance and insight (see, e.g., Bourdieu 1977, 1984; Collins 1979; Dimaggio 1979, 1982; Gouldner 1979; DiMaggio and Mohr 1985; Coleman 1986, 1990; Zukin and DiMaggio 1990). Here I will give primary attention to the work of Bourdieu because it has been widely discussed in both sociology and anthropology.

The basic idea is that certain kinds of skills, knowledge, dispositions, and social contacts serve as vital resources in the competition for power and privilege. Special attention has been given to three areas: educational credentials (Bourdieu and Passeron 1977; Collins 1979); the advantages of having "high culture"—knowledge about classical music, art, literature, "proper" accent, "taste" in food, clothing, and furnishings (DiMaggio 1982; Bourdieu 1984); and exchange processes in pre-modern societies (Bourdieu 1977). The key notion is that both the placement of individuals and the ability of privileged groups to reproduce themselves cannot be understood without taking into account these various nonmaterial forms of resources. Bourdieu recognizes that the various forms of symbolic capital are an important form of power that tends to be overlooked or discounted by traditional Marxism; he wants to remedy this inadequacy. Nonetheless, for Bourdieu the various forms of symbolic capital are ultimately economic power "misrecognized." Moreover, all social relationships involve the calculative pursuit of interests—and in that sense are exchange relationships (see, e.g., 1977:171– 83, 1986:252–55). In precapitalist societies and some sectors of capitalist societies, the nature of the calculations are hidden and disguised from the actors themselves, but power is ultimately rooted in material factors.

Notions of symbolic capital have stimulated much discussion, but in many respects the expected gains have not ensued. This is due, in part, to the imprecise way the concept has been used. As DiMaggio commented about Bourdieu's early work:

> [C]apital becomes less a potent and precise analytic tool than a weak figure of speech. Capitals proliferate: in addition to economic, cultural, and symbolic capital, we have linguistic capital, social capital, academic capital, scholastic capital, credentialed cultural capital, capitals of authority and of consecration, university, scientific, and artistic capital. No doubt there are others. The meanings of some—for example, social, cultural, and symbolic—seem to vary with their use. The status of others, whether they are subtypes of some other kind of capital or instead form markets of their own, is indeterminate. As the number of capitals increases, the metaphorical currency undergoes inflation and its value declines accordingly. (1979:1468–69)

Since these comments, Bourdieu has attempted to clarify his conceptualization of the "forms of capital" (1986). For Bourdieu, like Marx, capital is accumulated labor embodied in objects or the skills and dispositions of humans. It becomes capital when appropriated privately, thereby giving its "owners" the ability to appropriate the subsequent labor and products of others.[11] As previously indicated, he departs from Marx in his focus on various kinds of nonmaterial capital. In addition to the notions of physical capital and human capital used by economics, Bourdieu discusses cultural capital and social capital.

Cultural capital can exist in three forms: in the *embodied* state, i.e., in the form of long-lasting dispositions of the mind and body; in the *objectified* state, in the form of cultural goods (pictures, books, dictionaries, instruments machines, etc.) which are the trace or realization of theories or critiques of these theories, problematics, etc.; and in the *institutionalized* form of objectification [such as educational credentials]. (1986:243 [emphasis in original])

Social capital refers to the resources that linked social networks make available to individual members or to portions of the network. This process may be a relatively informal one such as borrowing from friends, or a formal coordination that mobilizes the resources of the network as a whole to some collective end. As Bourdieu notes:

Every group has its more or less institutionalized forms of delegation which enable it to concentrate the totality of the social capital . . . in the hands of a single agent or a small group . . . to represent the group, to speak and act in its name and so with the aid of this collectively owned capital, to exercise a power incommensurate with the agent's personal contribution. (1986:251)

Coleman (1988, 1990) also develops a concept of social capital that in essence refers to the same set of notions. In sum, Bourdieu draws distinctions between cultural and social capital, and among embodied, objectified, and institutionalized forms of cultural capital. Supposedly these categories are in contrast to physical and economic capital.

There are several problems with Bourdieu's conceptualization of capital. His categories rarely seem to be mutually exclusive, and it is unclear whether this imprecision is intended or not. For example, both physical and symbolic resources must have a cultural component for them to be of any value. If people are indifferent to nuclear weapons, tractors, impressionist paintings, or Shakespeare's plays, neither the physical possession of such items or knowledge about them are very valuable. Even if the term "cultural capital" is restricted to "high culture," it is not clear whether ownership or physical possession—of art objects, for example—is included or whether the focus is restricted to learning and dispositions. How distinctive the valued items are to a specific culture varies; gold is valued in many more cultures than are Bach's fugues. In sum, "cultural capital" is a highly ambiguous term that in the broad sense includes both physical and symbolic capital.

Moreover, it is unclear whether the three subtypes of cultural capital—embodied, objectified, and institutionalized—are unique to cultural capital or not, and whether they are mutually exclusive or not. The key example Bourdieu gives of institutionalized cultural capital is standardized educational credentials. Yet the same process of standardization and institutionalization occurs for physical resources. Obvious examples include property titles for real estate, automobiles, and patents. To make things even more complicated—though he does not say so explicitly—both physical and symbolic capital can also be social capital. If social capital is drawing on the resources of others through social networks—the core meaning for both Bourdieu and Coleman—this process can operate for either physical or symbolic resources. A merchant's credit at banks and a general's authority over his soldiers are social capital. Hence, while the notion of social capital may be useful for certain analytical purposes, it is important not to confuse this idea with the attempt to distinguish physical or economic capital from symbolic capital. In short, Bourdieu is still working with rather imprecise and vague categories. In fairness, he points out that the development of his concepts has been guided by the needs of particular empirical analyses, and hence they have been subject to continuing refinement.

More fundamental than lack of clarity and precision is Bourdieu's reductionist tendency to see symbolic forms of capital ultimately as ways of disguising and legitimating material forms of power. While I certainly agree that people often attempt to convert various forms of symbolic power into material power, I reject Bourdieu's assumption that this is always the disguised and "misrecognized" motive. Instead I will argue that people often have good reasons for seeking nonmaterial forms of power for their own sake. People can be concerned about their honor as an important source of power even if it has a negative impact on their material resources. In short, I want to break more fundamentally with Marxist materialist assumptions about the nature of power. Power can be rooted not only in forms of production but also in forms of consumption, not only in labor but also in play and worship—and these are more than "misrecognized" ways of controlling labor and the means of production. This is not, of course, to reject the obvious point that power is frequently, even usually, rooted in control of material means of production.

This book attempts to remedy some of these shortcomings in our understanding of symbolic capital. My approach is to narrow the focus of the analysis to one aspect of symbolic capital: social status. Though Weber's work provides the starting place for the analysis, many of his ideas about status and status groups remain implicit or inadequately developed. Hence one of my main efforts will be to produce a more developed theory of status relationships and status groups. More specifically, I will attempt to identify the distinctive characteristics of status that influence the organization of social life. The core of the analysis will trace out the consequences of these characteristics of status for patterns of interaction and group formation. This orientation is in contrast to most of the literature, which focuses on demonstrating how a previously undetected type of resource plays a subtle role in reproducing a particular historical form of inequality. This latter approach has been characteristic of much of Bourdieu's work and DiMaggio's early work (DiMaggio 1982; DiMaggio and Mohr 1985) as well. In contrast, my first concern will be to explain the key structural features of status inequality and group formation in contrast to other historical forms. Only then will my attention turn to the mechanisms for maintaining and reproducing status groups.

Status, Legitimacy, and Sacredness

If Weber's concepts of status and status group have had a seminal impact on sociology, perhaps this is even more true of his concept of legitimation and the types of legitimate authority. Yet the logical and empirical relationship between the concepts of status and legitimation remains largely underdeveloped. I will argue that for certain purposes it is useful to consider legitimation as a special type of status and that accordingly, understanding the sources of status can help to improve our understanding of the means of developing legitimacy.

Durkheim's notion of sacredness has been at least as seminal as Weber's discussion of status.[12] I have long been struck by the absence of any extended discussion on the connection between Durkheim's concept of the sacred and notions of social status, when obviously they were closely related. As already indicated, a major aim of my work is to remedy this lacuna by developing a theoretical framework that allows us to see status and sacral relationships as variations on a common theme.

For Weber and Durkheim the sociology of religion was at the core of sociology. In an indirect sense the sociology of religion was also central to Marx.[13] However, as Robert Wuthnow has noted, "the sociology of religion . . . appears to have become increasingly removed from the rest of the discipline" (1987:2). I hope to demonstrate that this separation is detrimental to the sociology of religion and to the discipline as a whole.

The Analytical Strategy

The formulation of my research question has been inspired by Marx, and the direction of an appropriate answer is suggested by Weber. My analytical strategy, though, is modeled after Emile Durkheim's *The Elementary Forms of Religious Life* (1965): I study a crucial case in order to identify general principles relevant to a variety of social situations. Durkheim selected the Australian aborigines because he thought theirs was the simplest human society, the ideal place to identify the elementary forms of religion. I have selected India for the opposite reason: it has the most elaborate and complex status system of any known society. In this respect my analytical strategy parallels that of Marx in *Capital* (1967). He constructed his general model of capitalism by focusing on England as the most advanced example of this type of society. My hope is that the intensity and extensiveness of status mechanisms in India will enable us more easily to identify the principles that underlie these processes in all social groups.[14]

Imagining India

If India is to be a critical case for theoretical analysis, an obvious question is: On whose version of India should we rely? There is no easy or simple answer; the nature of social reality is always contested in varying degrees. When it comes to characterizing even one's own society, the first person's common sense is often the next person's nonsense. When the society is complex and radically different from the one in which you grew up, the problems multiply rapidly.

To use the imagery suggested by Ronald Inden (1990): How should we imagine India?[15] In his extensive critique of past scholarship on India, Inden claims that it has produced distorted images, because of both the epistemological assumptions of Western scholarship and the political biases inherent in the "imperial formations" of which this scholarship was a part. At the core of Inden's analysis is an attack on the notion of essences: attempts to reduce the complexities of human life to a few factors that serve as the key to understanding a social reality. His main objection to the search for such essences is that they eliminate human agency. History becomes the playing-out of various kinds of supposedly ageless forces—whether it be caste society, the Hindu mind, the Asiatic mode of production, Oriental despotism, or whatever—rather than the outcome of the historical actions of complex human agents. Moreover, such essentialism tends to depoliticize human life rather than seeing it as a continual political struggle—in the broadest sense of politics. Drawing on the work of R. G. Collingwood, Inden suggests an alternative conceptualization of social reality that discards the notion of system, allows for overlapping rather than mutually exclusive social categories, and places human agency at the center of the analysis. There is considerable merit in much of Inden's critique. Ironically, though, he seems to turn past scholars into the hapless tools of various imperial formations, denying them the very agency he is so eager to restore to Indians.

How much agency we are to attribute to human actors is not simply a matter of a metatheoretical decision on the part of the analyst. Certainly our theoretical categories must not screen out all human agency, but neither should they exaggerate or glorify people's desire or ability to consciously "make their own history." One of my purposes is instead to examine how actors perceive their own levels of agency, and in turn how they attempt to manipulate both the perception and the reality of such agency.

The epistemological questions Inden raises are extremely complex, and to deal with them would require a different book. I will simply say that, in my opinion, the alternatives he proposes create as many problems as they solve. Like the projects of Giddens and Bourdieu discussed earlier, such goals are too ambitious for our present circumstances. We search for essences because we have no alternative; we select and abstract because we would otherwise be overwhelmed with complexity.

There are, however, two things we can do to avoid some of the pitfalls of such simplification. First, we can try to be explicit about what simplifying assumptions we are making—though doing this is an infinite regress that at some point we must lay aside in order to get on with both analysis and life. Second, we can attempt to minimize the degree to which we reify the results of our analyses; that is, we can try to avoid confusing the picture that we have drawn with the full-fledged reality.[16] Such pictures or models are always shaped by our own biases and preoccupations, not only by what we have studied. (As Inden says, "knowledge is underdetermined by reality" [1990:264]; hence we must also be extremely cautious when we use such models as guides to action—a use not relevant to this book per se; I offer no prescriptions about what Indians should do.)

As I have indicated, the notion of caste as a status group guides my analysis, with the implication that similarities exist between Indian caste and other forms of status groups. The recent literature on caste, in contrast has tended to emphasize India's total otherness. For example, the title of Dumont's book, *Homo Hierarchicus* (1980), implies that Indians are a special species, though, of course, he does not mean this literally. He sees the ideology and values of India as fundamentally different from those of the West. The work of McKim Marriott (1976,

1989), the early work of Inden (1976), and their joint work (1974, 1977) are even more adamant about this otherness, and they attack Dumont primarily for his over-reliance on Western categories. This emphasis on India's otherness has helped to overcome the ethnocentrism of Western scholarship. But in my opinion this has created an opposite ethnocentrism in at least certain forms of area studies. These contrasting forms of ethnocentrism and other limitations of Western scholarship about other cultures have been called "Orientalism" (Said 1979; Inden 1990)—though I am skeptical that such labeling does much to improve the problem.

In the India I will attempt to portray, what people do is not much different from or more mysterious than what people do in most places—when we take into account the particular configuration of resources they have available to them.[17] While most Indians are not Western bourgeois merchants endlessly calculating profit and loss, neither are they yogi mystics operating in some completely different realm of reality.

I must admit that this similarity is purchased at the price of a certain type of se-lectivity. When we look at Indian society through a theory of status relations, certain features are played up—"foregrounded" or "privileged," in the current intellectual jargon—and others are ignored. As the distinguished French Indologist Madeleine Biardeau says, "One cannot hope to make a system of Hindu culture as a whole, *without any remainder*" (1989:3 [emphasis in original]). But my selectivity is not a matter of "Orientalism." An analysis of capitalist societies that focuses on the central importance of the commodification of goods and services is going to leave out a lot of things that are important about those societies; most scholars would readily acknowledge this. But such selectivity also enables us to see a connection between phenomena that may initially appear unrelated. Computer dating services, children's allowances, funerals and weddings in commercial "chapels," the expan-sion of psychotherapy and professional counseling, the debate over the ownership and distribution of human organs, the increased participation of women in the labor force, the expansion of the nursing home industry, the im-portance of fast food restaurants—these are all rooted in the increased importance of economic exchange as the means of acquiring needed services and social relationships. The aim of my analysis is to point to connections in Indian society, fully acknowledging the selec-tivity involved. What results is not "the real" India. It is rather, I hope, one useful way of imagining India.[18]

Status, Sacredness, and the Modern World

Why Marx studied capitalism is obvious: it was the emerging economic system destined to replace virtually all previous forms of economic organization. (As indicated by the collapse of the socialist regimes in the Soviet Union and Eastern Europe, capitalism has no serious competitor as a mode of production.)

What is the practical significance of studying the Indian caste system? It certainly is not the wave of the future. Nor was the intent of the study to offer advice about how to eliminate, sustain or transform the caste system in India, though perhaps some of the conclusions are relevant to this issue. Rather, I envisioned the study as germane to the problems of developed societies and the modern world-system as a whole.

What is the relevance of a form of stratification that appears to be an eccentric anachronism of the past? In the twentieth century the one thing that virtually all societies have agreed upon has been the desirability of economic growth. As a result, status has increasingly come to be rooted in economic power. In a relatively anonymous urban world, where what people know about each other is often limited, status is more directly based on a few publicly visible attributes such as occupation and the possession of consumer commodities (and income and wealth, to the extent that these are known). A parallel process has been an ever increasing desacralization of the world, including not only historical social institutions but the entire cosmos. All aspects of the universe are treated as resources to be used in pursuing the desires and goals of modern humans.

Undoubtedly the closer linkage of status and economic resources has had some beneficial effects. Certainly the desacralization of many arbitrary and historically contingent human institutions has reduced some forms of human misery. Yet, many aspects of modern society are troubling: crime, child neglect and abuse, high divorce rates, an unproductive and alienated underclass, ethnic conflict, high population growth in poor countries, a large and sometimes increasing gap between rich and poor nations, a banal popular culture tied to the mass media, the increasing importance of worldwide markets that are often unstable and unpredictable—to list some widely discussed social problems. Even if these concerns are dismissed as the alarmism of liberals or the nostalgia of conservatives, another problem, in its broad outlines, is less debatable: the threat to the environment. Acid rain, polluted air, damage to the ozone layer, and toxic waste are all closely tied to the enormous value people have placed upon material consumer commodities and to the desacralization of the cosmos.

Whatever the disagreements among analysts like Weber (1958a), Tawney (1926), Polanyi (1957), and Hirschman (1977) over the origins of capitalism, they all see the productive capacity of the modern world as closely tied to a transformation of the status order. The modern world evolved from a system that treated merchants and bankers as near pariahs, and held asceticism in considerable regard, into one where these values were reversed. In the developed worlds, the activities of economic elites now have the presumption of legitimacy, those in the governmental sector are suspect and even derided, and most kinds of asceticism are considered bizarre. The cosmos, which had been respected and even worshipped as a divine creation, came to be seen as the result of contingent physical processes, an object having no meaning or value except as a material resource. In the terms of Weber's *The Protestant Ethic and the Spirit of Capitalism* (1958a), the modern world was founded not only on a new level of technology, but also on a new "ethic" and a new "spirit."

I am convinced that a successful transition to a postmodern world will require a similar transformation. A world culture in which status is so closely tied to economic success and consumer commodities is not likely to succeed in coping with the threat to the earth's ecology. Similarly, I am doubtful that the environment (and human beings themselves) can be adequately protected in a completely desacralized world. Undoubtedly, technological innovations that lower damage to the environment can and must play a role, but they seem unlikely to be enough as long as people's sense of self-worth is so closely tied to the possession of material objects. I am not advocating a return to the asceticism of the monk and nun, or to the good old days of traditional society. I am convinced that the consumerism of the contemporary United States, as it spreads to the rest of the world, is destroying much of value, in both the environment and various cultural traditions. In my opinion, the kind of transformation we need would require much greater insulation between economic and political power, on the one hand, and status, on the other. Social worth and value cannot remain so closely tied to economic power.

I am not, however, sanguine about the prospects of such a transformation. Much of the ideology associated with the environmental movement, not to speak of "New Age" beliefs, is at best superficial and naive. Even such notions as the Gaea hypothesis, which argues that the planet Earth is a single organism—so that to seriously damage a part threatens to destroy the whole—seems, at best, a crude metaphor. The difficulties of delegitimizing the materialism of the modern world (not to speak of the enormous complexities that would emerge were this to happen) are only beginning to be grasped. How do we make it possible for people to value something other than more goods and services, and to treat the cosmos with reverence—and if we do, what will happen?

Strange as it may seem, the culture of premodern India becomes relevant here: it has been relatively successful over a long period of time in insulating status from economic and political power. The spiritualism and nonmaterialism of India has frequently, perhaps even typically, been exaggerated. Nonetheless, status and moral worth have been less directly dependent upon economic and political power than in most other complex societies.

This does not mean that I see India as a model for the future. Clearly a reversion to traditional society will not do, nor will Gandhian utopianism suffice. Rather I see India as a warning about the considerable difficulties and contradictions inherent in delegitimating materialism and insulating status from material and economic power. And if we do not look unflinchingly at the potential difficulties, we are not likely to bring about the needed transformation.

To many people, of course, there is no need for such a transformation of the status order. To some, the notion that economic productivity must be devalued—at least relatively speaking—would seem at best unsophisticated. Some will advocate other forms of transformation that value material productivity even more. In my opinion, such strategies are likely to meet the same end as modern Marxism and socialism, for many of the same reasons. As strange as the idea of a world that limits economic growth and partially resacralizes the cosmos may seem, it is no more strange than the prospect of the modern world would have seemed to the medieval person. To the fourteenth-century noble, the thought that mere merchants would replace him at the top of the status hierarchy would have seemed ludicrous; it probably seemed almost as absurd to the merchant. But human actions and historical process have a strange way of transforming the absurdity of today into the reality of tomorrow.

Fortunately, the value of this study does not depend on readers agreeing with the argument sketched out in this section. The substance of the work—an identification of the patterns and processes characteristic of status and sacral relationships—should be of interest to social analysts whatever their visions and hopes for the future.[19]

2

Theoretical Concepts

Symbols, Agency, Contingency, and Structure

Humans are different from rocks. People are affected not only by material forces, but also by *symbolic* communication.[1] The most eloquent speech will leave a rock unaffected, whereas even children are influenced primarily by talk, rituals, and other forms of symbolic communication. Furthermore, people, but not rocks, attempt to influence their environment. They are not simply objects affected by external forces; humans are also subjects who have *agency*. They have power to affect their environment in a conscious and intentional way.[2] Of course, in some respects humans are objects affected by forces outside of themselves.[3] Often these forces are unpredictable, mysterious, and beyond control. Stated another way, humans are susceptible to considerable *contingency*.[4] Some of these forces are solely physical—for example, the weather or earthquakes. They affect both humans and rocks through the same mechanical causal processes. The weather is as indifferent to the presence of subjectivity in humans as it is to the absence of subjectivity in rocks. The forces that most shape humans are not of this kind, but are rather the result of the actions of other human subjects who have agency. Compared to that of other animals, human behavior is highly variable, preprogrammed by physical genetic codes only to a limited degree. Thus, humanly created forces can also be unpredictable, involving significant degrees of contingency.

Humans find high levels of contingency and unpredictability threatening, even terrifying; under such conditions they cannot control or even make sense of what is happening to them.[5] Hence they attempt to create social orders:[6] relatively predictable *structures* of relationships with other human subjects.[7] Social orders vary in the degree to which they see people as sheltered from contingency; some emphasize the significance of luck and fate, others stress initiative and responsibility. But in all social orders humans are seen both as having agency and as subject to contingency.

Structures are both enabling and constraining.[8] They expedite individual action by reducing the need to decide everything de novo. By cooperative efforts they make possible what would be impossible for the individual. That is, they create additional forms of agency. But they also limit alternatives. Most structures precede the existence of any particular human being and thus shape that person's identity and social opportunities. Therefore, for any given individual, structures create additional forms of contingency: some will speak English, some will speak Chinese; some are born to be kings, some to be slaves. Thus, while all structured social orders create both agency and contingency, they differ in their degree of emphasis on these two features.

This recognition of the human tendency to create social structures is not to assume that people prefer complete order, nor that social stability is better than social change. The issue of stability versus change is analytically separate from the issue of order versus entropy; a state of entropy can be stable over time, and a state of order can be dynamic over time.

Separation, Combination, and Linking

Structure can be conceived of as human subjects ordering their action and having their actions ordered through three general processes: *separation*, *combination*, and *linking*.[9] Social differentiation into distinct roles or groups is an example of separation. Social integration of disparate roles, individuals, or groups into more unitary social units is an example of combination.[10] The processes are also relevant on the symbolic level. Abstraction is the process of selecting and separating out certain elements of what is perceived; categorization is the process of combining similar abstracted elements and giving them a common name and identity. However, typically what happens, on the level of both actions and symbols, is not complete separation or complete combination, but rather separation, combination, and linking. The separate identities formed through separation and combination do not exist in a vacuum isolated from one another, but are sustained by ongoing ties and relationships. Subgroups form through separating dissimilar people and combining similar people, but typically such subgroups remain linked to each other through various kinds of communication, exchange of resources, authority relations, and social mobility—especially rites of passage. On the symbolic level, separate categories are created, but the meaning of any one term is specified largely by drawing parallels and contrasts with other terms (as dictionaries do) and by its place in sentences and larger bodies of discourse, that is, linking is crucial to meaning.

The pattern of separated, combined, and linked roles, individuals, and groups can be referred to as social structure. The pattern of separated, combined, and linked symbolized abstractions can be referred to as culture. Durkheim argued in *The Elementary Forms of the Religious Life* (1965) that the fundamental categories of knowledge, and by implication of culture in general, are often modeled after the differentiations in the social structure. While this is sometimes true, the relationship between these two realms is by no means simple—a problem we shall return to at several points.

As indicated earlier, this combining, separating, and linking is, of course, an aspect of the actions of human subjects. Structures are the products of the previous actions of individuals; individual agents are the product of structured social orders. Neither has logical, historical, or analytical priority. To use Hegelian-Marxian language, they are dialectically related. Both structured orders and individual agents must be continually reproduced. The variations over time in the specifics of the roles, individuals, and groups that are separated, combined, and linked can be called social change or history.[11]

Social Formations

One key consequence of this process of separation, combination, and linking is the production of social formations. A central focus of sociology is explaining the production, reproduction, and transformation of various kinds of social formations: families, friendships, lineages, tribes, churches, business firms, strata, classes, social movements, political parties, racial and ethnic groups, regions, nations, international alliances, and so forth. Some of these social formations may be little more than categories of the analyst, for example, all children in the world under the age of five. Others may serve as the base for important social movements and political action groups—for example, people in the United States over sixty-five years old. Others may be well-organized communities like the Black Muslims in Washington, D.C., in 1990. Social formations vary significantly in the degree to which they have well-developed patterns of social interaction, a common culture (or subculture), and social solidarity—in other words, the extent to which they are a group or community. Thus I use the term "social formation" to cover the full array of social identities produced by combination and separation. I use such terms as "group," "organization," and "community" to suggest higher levels of interaction and solidarity.

Some Elementary Forms of Formation

Two primary bases of social formations are social solidarity and social inequality. The first is a key mechanism of combination, bringing people together, while the second is a key mechanism of separation, setting them off from others. A brief review is required of some of the standard sociological theories about the sources of solidarity and inequality.

According to Durkheim (1965), religion is a crucial source of social solidarity, drawing people together and renewing their commitment to a common set of norms and values. Religious ritual is the mechanism that renews and reproduces this solidarity. But such ritual is relevant only in relationship to a belief in the sacred— that which is set apart and defined as other than the profane. Stated in its simplest terms, the combination of people into cohesive religious groups is rooted in the commonality they have because of their separation from something else: the sacred. They are equal in their otherness from the sacred.[12]

In his essay "An Analytical Approach to the Theory of Stratification," Talcott Parsons (1954) develops a very closely related argument, but takes it in the opposite

direction. He sees the elementary source of social stratification as rooted in differential conformity to commonly held social norms and values. Instead of focusing on
how solidarity is produced by setting members off from a sacred other, Parsons
focuses on how differentiation is produced because of consensus and solidarity.[13]
Parsons has been widely criticized for placing too much emphasis on value
consensus and social solidarity and for ignoring the crucial role of social conflict in
social life.

One of his most severe critics has been Ralf Dahrendorf (1958, 1959). In his
essay "On the Origins of Inequality Among Men," Dahrendorf (1968) offers an
explanation of the elementary forms of social stratification that can be summarized in
three points:

1. The very existence of society assumes social norms and sanctions to enforce them.
2. Differential conformity to norms and the resulting differential sanctions are the origin
of social inequality.
3. Norms are always the norms of the ruling class and biased in their favor to serve their
interests.[14]

Surprisingly, the first two points are essentially the Parsonian argument: a
commonality of norms is the baseline from which social inequality begins.[15]
Dahrendorf departs from Parsons in his third point, which is a restatement of
Marx's famous argument in "The German Ideology" (Marx and Engels 1978:
146–200). The difference is not over the centrality of common norms, but the extent
to which such norms are rooted in consensual solidarity: for both Dahrendorf and
Marx, norms typically arise from imposition and manipulation.

This difference is also reflected in divergent concepts of the sacred. Marx
recognized that social solidarity is often created by a human community seeing
themselves as one in contrast to the otherness of the sacred, and like Feuerbach, he
saw this as a form of alienation and reification. But in his "Theses on Feuerbach,"
Marx (1978) rejected the notion that this is a universal, not to mention necessary,
condition of the human situation. For Marx the sacred was not the symbol of the
solidarity and moral authority of the society as a whole, but was a feature of the
ideology of the ruling class, a means of maintaining solidarity under the conditions
of exploitation.

Whether the creation of the sacred is primarily a source of consensual solidarity
or a form of manipulated false consciousness is not my concern here;[16] the relevant
point is that one kind of separation—the setting off of the sacred—is closely related
to another kind of separation—the emergence of social stratification. Durkheim has
written at some length about what he meant by the elementary forms of religion.
But what are the elementary forms of inequality? Parsons and Dahrendorf suggest,
and the comparative study of societies confirms (Lenski 1966; Lenski and Lenski
1974), that ranked status differences are the first type of social inequality. They
appear before significant differences in wealth or political power, and their appearance seems to be closely related to the differentiation of the sacred and the profane. This is so because status and sacredness are, in part, two different forms of the
same thing: more accurately, sacredness is a special form of status. Moreover, the
processes that create status and sacredness are central to the production of social

formations, especially those with relatively high levels of solidarity and consciousness. Hence we can expand and sharpen our understanding of group formation by looking at the relationship between status and sacredness.

Empirical Variations

The identification of elementary forms of social phenomena is primarily a means to an end. The more fundamental goal is to explain empirical variations, from the elementary to the complex. As indicated in Chapter 1, two of the key tasks of sociology are to explain (1) why some types of social formations are especially prominent in particular historical circumstances, and (2) why a particular kind of social formation has certain typical characteristics. Following the Marxian tradition, I will argue that in large measure these outcomes are shaped by the nature of the resources that are available and dominant in a given historical situation. Following the Weberian tradition, I will argue that we need to explore more systematically the significance of nonmaterial resources in general and status in particular. My strategy will be to identify the distinctive characteristics of status that influence the organization of social life and consequently the type of social formation.

Before we systematically consider the characteristics of status as a resource, in Chapter 3, we must be define status and clarify its relationship to other forms of human resources.

Types of Power and Types of Social Formations

Agency distinguishes acting subjects from mere objects; it is a defining attribute of humanness. The concept of agency is closely linked to the concept of power. As Giddens says:

> [A]gency implies power. . . . Agency concerns events of which an individual is the perpetrator, in the sense that the individual could, at any phase in a give sequence of conduct, have acted otherwise. Whatever happened would not have happened if that individual had not intervened. . . . An agent is . . . able to deploy (chronically, in the flow of daily life) a range of causal powers, including that of influencing those deployed by others. (1984:9, 14)

But how do people go about intervening in the world and more specifically in the social world? What are the concrete means by which subjects exercise agency and power?[17]

Commands and Sanctions

The first step in exercising power is usually a special form of symbolic communication that can be referred to as commands or requests. Randomly beating people or handing them thousand-dollar bills is not a very effective way to exercise power. The desired result is more likely if you tell people what you want and then give the money to those who comply and beat those who do not. Because symbolic communication usually requires much less energy than exercising force or acquiring the goods needed to pay people, the use of commands greatly increases the efficiency of exercising power.

The command does not literally have to precede each and every sanction. Instead of posting no hunting signs, the feudal lord may simply execute the first poacher he catches, as a form of communication to others rather than retribution. However implicit, some form of command is usually crucial to the exercise of power.[18]

Commands by themselves are seldom effective for long; they need to be backed up by sanctions: the ability to reward or punish someone. There are three primary types of sanctions, hence three primary sources and types of power. First, when we want to exercise power over people, we can use force against them.[19] The exercise of force must be broken into two important subcategories. The first involves treating others primarily as objects. Examples include executions, battles in which the goal is to kill everyone on the other side, the physical restraint of insane persons or infants, physically moving unconscious people. This means of affecting people is physical causation rather than social interaction. The intention is not to elicit a particular response from another subject but to control or destroy an object. In such situations commands play a greatly diminished role. The second subcategory involves social interaction and thus has as a component symbolic communication. Force may be used without an explicit command but with the intent to motivate the other to perform some action: flee, surrender, confess, obey, show deference, and so on. Obviously the line between these two subcategories is not clear-cut, but as we shall see, the distinction is important for analytical and theoretical purposes. Most typically, force takes the form of violence—that is, it is intended to produce bodily harm or pain. There is, however, nonviolent force, as when we restrain a child or an insane person to prevent them from harming themselves.[20]

Second, we can attempt to influence people by giving or withholding valued objects and services. In the simplest case, people exchange such objects and services by barter. In complex societies money becomes a symbol that stands for such objects and services and thus is an intermediate element in exchange. This type of sanction has, of course, been studied most extensively by the discipline of economics.[21]

The third way we influence people is by expressing approval and disapproval. Generally people seek praise and avoid censure; accordingly, we can exercise influence over them by giving or withholding praise or censure. This process is analogous to the exercise of economic power by giving or withholding payments.[22] But just as our level of economic capital greatly affects our ability to influence people through economic exchange, a crucial factor affecting the potency of approvals and disapprovals is the status of the person who offers them. An undergraduate student's criticism of a professor's writing may not be pleasant, but it rarely has a significant impact upon the professor's career, while expressions of approval (or disapproval) from a highly respected figure in one's field can have crucial consequences.

One's own status, honor, and prestige (here used synonymously) are primarily composed of the accumulated praise and censure received from people who know you or know about you. Typically such approvals and disapprovals become generalized, stereotyped, and crystallized. "Sally wrote a good paper" becomes "Sally is a good student." In complex societies, the relatively standardized symbols of status called credentials are often used to evaluate actors, and "knowing" or "knowing about" you may mean no more than that someone has seen your resume or standardized test scores. These accumulated stereotyped approvals and disapprovals then become a capital resource if they are generally positive, or a debt and liability if they are negative.[23] They will determine the potency of one's subsequent expressions of approval and disapproval toward others. While I have phrased the argument in terms of individual persons, the same conceptualization can apply to other types of actors—for example, organizations or nation-states. In sum, the three fundamental types of sanctions are force, goods and services, and expressions of approval and disapproval.[24]

Indifference to Sanctions: Asceticism

Another source of power does exist: power rooted in being oblivious to the sanctions of others. Nearly everyone is indifferent to some potential sanctions; most adults have had to make an unpopular decision knowing some would express disapproval; few people are tempted to commit major crimes by an offer of insignificant petty rewards; most parents would not sell their children for even very large rewards.

In addition to these common levels of indifference, some actors try to be systematically indifferent to the sanctions of others. This is usually referred to as asceticism.[25] The various forms of asceticism typically involve a conscious and intentional effort—through poverty, fasting, nakedness, celibacy, nonviolence, silence, meditation, solitariness—to make oneself less sensitive to the three types of sanctions we have discussed, and to reduce or restrict social relations. Moreover, these practices often imply a criticism and sanctioning of more conventional forms of behavior. Ironically, the development of indifference to social sanctions is often perceived as a new form of power: otherworldly or spiritual power. In some cultures it can be converted into magical power that supposedly can be used to manipulate the physical and social world; the asceticism associated with shamanism is an example. In other cultures this indifference to the world may be solely a means to otherworldly salvation and irrelevant to worldly power.

Two digressions are now required for clarification, concerning knowledge, and the relations among power, agency and structure.

Knowledge

Knowledge is linked to power in a number of ways. The presence or absence of knowledge influences the effectiveness of sanctions. However, knowledge is not a distinctive type of sanction itself. For example, military intelligence provided by a spy may enable an army to use its available force to the best advantage, or to avoid the superior force of the enemy. That knowledge, however, is useless unless you have some capacity to attack, resist, or flee. A physician who warns you that your smoking is aggravating your ulcer is not sanctioning you; she is pointing out a cause-and-effect relationship. This information may *influence* your behavior, but she has not exercised power over you. She may simultaneously sanction you by expressing disapproval of your smoking habits, but the knowledge per se is not the sanction. If you are indifferent to her disapproval, her sanction will be ineffective, even though her causal prediction may be quite accurate. Even the knowledge of the blackmailer is not directly a sanction, but triggers the sanctions of third parties. The would-be lover who knows what gifts his beloved likes has an advantage over less knowledgeable competitors, but only if he has the money to buy presents. What the lover knows hints at a fundamental kind of knowledge: awareness of the social expectations relevant in a given social context. The distribution of such knowledge is a core feature of social structure.[26]

Knowledge is not an independent objective entity, but is socially produced and distributed. Hence, the content of knowledge can be biased or distorted to serve particular interests. Most people at one time or another have attempted to exaggerate their performance or hide their deviance—that is, distort social knowledge—in order to influence the rewards and punishments they receive. Another clear example of distorting knowledge is military deception. Both sides attempt not only to find out about the real intentions, strengths, and weakness of the enemy but also to mislead him about their own intentions and resources.

On a higher and more general level, we can think of *ideology* as biased knowledge intended to influence the exercise of power.[27] In some ways ideology resembles a modern organizational chart, which, with the rules and regulations that accompany it, forms a statement of how the organization is "supposed to" work from the point of view of its top elites. More accurately, it is what they are willing to proclaim in public about how the organization is supposed to work; even from the top elites' point of view, some of the formal organization is partly window dressing. Any sophisticated person who has worked in a modern complex organization knows that often considerable discrepancies exist between how things are "supposed to" work and how people actually behave. Such formal organizational statements make things look a lot simpler, neater, and fairer than they actually are. Incipient injustices and inefficiencies and the conflicts they produce are often studiously ignored and "left out of the picture." A key purpose of such ideology is to decrease the need to sanction people in order to gain compliance and/or to decrease the effectiveness of resistance. For example, if "common sense" defines male aggressiveness and dominance as an "inevitable" part of "human nature," then men are deferred to more often and women have a much harder time mobilizing power to resist such patterns. Ideologies are not usually blatantly inaccurate; patently false ideologies are seldom useful. As we shall see, if the discrepancies between the "official" picture and people's experience become too great, the ideology may be elaborated and qualified in order to explain away the contradictions.

A special case of the manipulation of knowledge is the use of *threats and promises*. Some analysts (e.g., Wrong 1980) have conceptualized the threat of force as a distinct type of power. I believe this is misleading. First of all, the use of threats is not restricted to force; an actor may be able to influence someone by threatening or promising to use any of the three types of sanctions I have outlined. The seducer's promise of marriage, the con man's promise of a lucrative return, the boss's threat of dismissal, the parent's threat to withhold love, are all used to affect behavior, and all involve the suggestion of a positive or negative sanction without its actual use. I see no reason, therefore, to treat the threat of force, or other threats and promises, as a distinct type of sanction. Like other ways of manipulating knowledge, they play a vital role in the exercise of power; their credibility is crucial to the structures of power. They are, in addition to commands, what transforms the social world from physical causation into symbolic interaction; not only do we communicate what we want others to do, we communicate, at least implicitly, how they will be sanctioned for obedience and disobedience.

There is, of course, a sense in which the knowledge of the spy, the physician, the blackmailer, the lover, and the ideologist can become a sanction: it can be converted into a good or service and exchanged for any of the three types of sanctions. The spy and the physician may refuse to share their information unless they are paid, and the blackmailer threatens to share his information if he is not paid. The lover may even decide that the money a competitor offers for his knowledge of his beloved is more attractive than his beloved. The campaign consultant or the priestly oracle may change masters if he gets a better offer. The other two types of sanctions, force and status, can also be converted into a good or service. Skilled warriors become mercenaries; prestigious persons endorse or advertise products; legislators sell their votes. But unlike force and status, knowledge cannot be used directly as a sanction.

Specialized and esoteric knowledge is often closely linked to status. Such knowledge is often respected, even if the extent to which it can be converted into economic and political power is limited. Consequently, the power of intellectuals— whether traditional religious elites, contemporary novelists, or modern scientists— is usually due to their status. To the degree that they exercise power, it is not usually because their esoteric knowledge gives them an advantage in how to best sanction others, or that they have accrued enough wealth to have significant economic power, but because their knowledge gives them status power. Albert Einstein had some political influence because of his status, not because his knowledge of physics increased his skill as a politician or made him a financial magnate. Again, the point is that while knowledge is linked to power in a number of ways, it is not a separate type of sanction.

Power, Agency, and Structure

An extensive literature has developed over how to conceptualize power. At the center of the debate is whether power should be defined as the ability of some actor to enforce his or her will in face of definite resistance—that is, power as manifest decisions and actions—or whether power is best thought of as latent structures that bias social outcomes in favor of some at the expense of others. The modern controversy begins with the power elite theorists (Hunter 1953; Mills 1956; Domhoff 1967), who relied largely on reputational methods to identify the supposed decision-making elite in American communities. Robert Dahl (1961) criticized these studies for not having actually observed whether the reputed kingpins in fact exercised the power attributed to them. He developed methodologies to remedy this purported defect and concluded that, at least in the community he studied, there was no consolidated power elite. Bachrach and Baratz (1962, 1970) in turn criticized

Dahl for focusing only on explicit policy decisions. According to them, a key means of exercising power was to keep things off the public agenda, and the "second face" of power was the ability to make something a "nondecision." The mere capacity to sanction others may make it unnecessary to do so; others conform to your wishes because they anticipate the consequences of not doing so. Power is seen as potential capacity. Steven Lukes (1974, 1977) extended these lines of thought. For him, the "third face" and ultimate form of power is the ability to shape people's desires and interests. Contrasting the concepts of power and structure, he sees the former as limited to episodic decisions that are acts of agency, and as often missing the more indirect and subtle structural mechanisms that shape social outcomes. A spate of writings has appeared attempting to clarify the relationships among the various aspects of power (Barry 1976; Foucault 1977, 1980; Wrong 1980; Giddens 1984; Mann 1986; Isaac 1987; Barnes 1988; Clegg 1988; Baldwin 1989; Gibbs 1989; Boulding 1990; Wartenburg 1990). With respect to the agency versus structure debate, I believe the most promising strategy is to treat both as aspects of power rather than to identify power exclusively with either.

The conscious and deliberate decisions of male employers to discriminate against women are an example of power as agency; the cultural assumption that it is "natural" for women to have primary responsibility for child care is an example of power as structure.[28] Men's higher level of experience in the labor force, in part the result of previous discrimination against women, is also structural power: it engenders pressure on employers to discriminate against women even if they do not want to do so.[29] Such structures of power are in part what enable men to exercise their agency to discriminate against women applicants and employees. Moreover, when cultural assumptions are taken for granted, men rarely have to exercise agency in order to perpetuate their power.

So power is not simply the episodic exercise of agency. It is also the accumulated residues of past actions, which provide the largely taken-for-granted structural context of subsequent actions. One way such structural contexts vary is in the type of sanction emphasized: the result is different types of power structures, which in turn produce different types of social formations.[30]

Types of Power and Social Formations

Each of the three types of sanction discussed earlier forms the basis for a different type of power structure. Force is the distinctive basis of political power; control of objects and services is the distinctive basis of economic power;[31] I will refer to the type of power that is based on approvals and disapprovals as "status power." (This term will seem a contradiction in terms to those who contrast status with power, but my point is that status is a form of power. When I do contrast "status" with "power," I will be referring to the distinction between status power and other forms of power.) Within each of the three realms—political, economic, and status—power takes the form of both acts of agency and biased structures.

In his famous essay "Class, Status, and Party," Weber (1968:926–40) focuses on how different types of power result in different types of social formations. Classes form around common positions in economic markets. Parties are formed from struggles over political power—assuming the existence of a modern nation-state.

Where no fully developed nation-state with a party system exists, we refer to the coalitions that form on the basis of political power as alliances, blocs, coalitions, caucuses, confederations, juntos, and so on; in some societies these are identical with kinship units such as lineages and clans. Weber uses the term "status group" to refer to the social formations based on common social honor and status (rooted in accumulated approvals and disapprovals).[32] The terms "class," "party," and "status group" usually refer to subgroups within larger macrosystems. We also have terms for these larger macrosystems that imply the type of power on which they are primarily based. "Economies" and "markets" indicate a system based on economic power. "The state" refers to an organized system of force. "Community," "nation," and "culture" imply primarily a sense of common identity and morality—and, in at least certain important respects, a common social status (see, e.g., Weber's discussions of "The Nation" [1968:357–58, 921–26]).[33]

Variations in the Importance of Resources

If changes in the means of production affect the way social life is structured, other differences in resources are also likely to have an effect. More specifically, we should expect social structure to vary with shifts in the relative importance of the three types of sanctions. In the American frontier, in the Lebanon of the 1980s, in early medieval Europe, and in most systems of slavery we would expect groups organized around the ability to use force to be more prominent in the social organization than in periods and locations where force was less crucial as a means of power.[34] Similarly, businesspeople and their ability to exercise economic power were more crucial in nineteenth-century England and in the 1980s United States than in fourteenth-century England and the 1960s United States.

This idea is certainly not new. To say that when a particular kind of sanction is important those who can use it will be more prominent is a near tautology. Can we go beyond such obvious statements? I believe the answer is yes: we can make systematic predictions about the nature of social structure from knowing something about the relative importance of the three types of sanctions. This is, of course, part of Weber's intent in "Class, Status, and Party" (1968). Initially, our efforts to identify systematic variations are likely to be more fruitful if we focus on situations where an emphasis on one resource or another is relatively extreme. Such situations hold constant important contextual variables that may affect the empirical relationships we are interested in. This analytic strategy is analogous to the way economists develop their theories by initially concentrating on situations that approximate perfect competition in the market place. In such situations the "laws" of supply and demand are more easily identified.[35]

This strategy requires two steps. First, we must be able to say something convincing about the relative importance of the three types of resources in a given setting. For example, is status more important in India than in most societies? Second, we must be able to specify how status shapes the social structure by identifying its special characteristics and its sources. We will take up the second set of questions first, and return to the first question in Chapter 5.

3

A Theory of Status Relationships: Key Elements

The Characteristics of Status as a Resource

Two characteristics typically receive special attention when any resource is analyzed: *amount* and *distribution*. For example, in the modern world two of our most crucial concerns are economic growth and the distribution of income and wealth. Underlying the ideas of amount and distribution are several related notions that are taken for granted. Implicit in the concept of amount is the notion of what I call *expansibility*: Can the amount be increased or decreased?[1] The preoccupation with economic growth only developed after people began to perceive that wealth could be systematically expanded rather than simply shifted from one individual or group to another.[2] Implicit in the concept of distribution is some notion of movability or *alienability*: for distribution to be a relevant concern, it must be possible to transfer resources from one social location to another. Until recently, no one was concerned with the distribution of human organs because they were an inalienable resource; they could not be transferred from one person to another.[3] With the development of organ transplants, complex and troubling issues have developed over the ownership and appropriate distribution of human organs. An inalienable resource cannot be exchanged or converted into something else; *exchange* or *convertibility* assumes alienability. Many societies have considered land inalienable. Most societies (but not all) have considered children to have inalienable ties to their parents—they could not be exchanged for something else. In contrast, girls and boys at puberty have often been exchanged through various sorts of marriage alliances.

Why does the inalienability and inexpansibility of resources vary? Obviously, there is a technical component: For example, the technical possibility of alienating, redistributing, and exchanging live organs did not exist until the last third of the twentieth century. Just as obviously, there is a component of historical and cultural contingency or arbitrariness. Cultures with similar levels of technical development may vary significantly with respect to the alienability and expansibility of different items, for example, land, children, women, serfs, and slaves. Between the level of technical possibility and historical contingency lies a third set of factors that arise from the core process of constructing social reality. Therefore, the social construction of reality perspective is a reasonable place to look for further insight about the inalienability and inexpansibility of resources. (Since I advocate what I call a provisional structuralism, which focuses on variations in resource bases, it may seem strange or even contradictory to root the basic categories of my analysis in the concepts of a social constructionist perspective. This strategy is a way of stressing the provisional nature of the structuralism I am advocating; the constructionist perspective has also proved more useful than the available alternatives for understanding variations in the nature of resources.[4])

As indicated in Chapter 1, Berger and Luckmann (1967) provide the classic exposition of this perspective. They describe the dialectical relationship between individuals and societies in terms of the three concepts of externalization, objectivation, and internalization. *Externalization* is the ongoing physical and mental activity of humans in the world; humans go beyond their internal subjective thoughts, emotions, and beliefs, and act upon an external world. Such external activity has consequences and leaves products, such as buildings, graves, written documents, shared memories. *Objectivation* is the process whereby the products of such activity come to be seen as objectlike; they appear to humans to have a reality and existence that no longer depends on immediate human wishes or actions. This can be true of physical objects or of social institutions that appear to be sacred, "natural," or "inevitable." *Internalization* is the appropriation by humans, especially the next generation, of some given, socially defined, objectified reality. Children and newcomers must learn what is taken for granted, natural, and inevitable. To become full members of the society they must incorporate these things into their subjective consciousness. As Berger says, "It is through externalization that society is a human product. It is through objectivation that society becomes a reality *sui generis*. It is through internalization that man is a product of society" (1969:4).[5]

These three concepts have implications for the inexpansibility and inalienability of resources. Action that has been objectivated in a physical object is much easier to alienate and redistribute than action that has been internalized in someone's mind. Conquerors can more easily appropriate gold than the respect of other people in the community. Similarly, knowledge can be moved much more easily than land. As we shall see, variations in inalienability and inexpansibility are in large measure a function of exactly how a resource is externalized, objectivated, and internalized. Now let us consider in more detail the characteristics of status as a resource.

Inalienability

Status is stereotyped approval (or disapproval), and is primarily "located" in other people's minds. To change your status or someone else's, you must change other people's opinions. Consequently, it is difficult to translate force or wealth directly into status; you can pay or force people to say good things about you and bad things about your enemies, but—short of long-term indoctrination—you cannot make them believe these things. Wealth and force can command ritualistic deference, but not status per se.[6] It is not possible to appropriate status the way property or social positions can be appropriated by means of force or wealth. Thus, status is a relatively inalienable resource.[7]

Physical objectivation, then, is relatively unimportant to status processes.[8] Status is sometimes symbolized by physical objects—blue ribbons, gold cups, laurel wreaths, diplomas, and military insignia are examples. The objects themselves are of little value, and the simple physical reproduction of such objects is either forbidden or sets off an inflationary spiral that makes the objects worthless. Physical symbols of status can be physically appropriated, but the approval and esteem of others cannot.

Inalienability places definite limits on the conversion of status into other forms of power. Attempts to gain status with force or wealth are, in the short run, self-defeating and even reduce one's prestige. Someone who purchases educational credentials from a degree mill is looked upon with contempt. Nor can the status of the established aristocrat be easily acquired by the nouveau riche or the conqueror. This points to one of the main purposes of status orders: to protect the privileged by providing them with a resource not easily taken or acquired by others. Such status orders frequently distribute negative status and thereby create underclasses and outcasts. The powerful usually define the negative characteristics of the subservient as inalienable—Untouchables are unclean, Negroes are less intelligent, ladies are more emotional—and thus they are supposedly incapable of meeting the norms of the dominant group. As long as such norms remain institutionalized, upward mobility requires redefining one's identity, that is, "passing."[9]

Obviously bribery, buying status symbols, and passing occur with some regularity. Not infrequently people "get away with" such activities, but in order for such exchanges to be successful they must be hidden or disguised. Few people brag about having purchased a phony degree or having paid someone to get their daughter invited to the debutante ball—this would destroy whatever status they might have gained. Not only are those who openly try to buy or coerce status held in derision, but so are those who respond to such incentives. To be obsequious and servile is degrading; to seek out such relationships in order to gain materially is reprehensible. Some of the most derisive terms in English characterize giving false praise—fawn, grovel, kowtow, wheedle, sweet-talk, truckle—and those who give it—sycophant, bootlicker, brownnose, toady, flatterer, yes man.

Nonetheless, such exchanges are an important part of social life. To be successful, however, they are rarely explicit quid pro quo transactions. The disinclined lover may be won over with flowers and gifts, but is insulted by an explicit offer of wealth for affection. Hourly wages with no job security may buy a laborer's time, but rarely his devotion and loyalty. There tend to be two types of implicit exchange in social situations where status or sacredness are important. In the first, the explicit concern of the giver is the nonmaterial resource of status or sacredness: association with and approval by those of high or sacred status are sought by offering gifts. The gifts of kings to various religious elites are the most obvious example. In the second, the explicit concern is obtaining services in the material world. The classic example is the granting of fiefs and benefices in feudal societies, in implicit exchange for commitment, gratitude, loyalty, and generalized deference. In either case, the explicit quid pro quo aspects are downplayed; to bargain too explicitly or suggest that approval or loyalty can be bought is counterproductive.

Not only is the exchange of praise for material payment morally suspect, but further, if the payment comes from a morally suspect source, this influences the legitimacy of accepting such gifts. For example, the church, university, or charity that accepts large donations from known gangsters loses prestige. Of course, one of the primary ways that conquerors and robber barons gain legitimacy is precisely by giving their ill-gotten gains to good causes, and charitable and religious institutions have historically depended on such questionable exchanges. The extent to which a gift from questionable sources affects the status of the giver and receiver also depends on the nature of the response. Issuing an honorary degree to a big donor improves the status of the giver more than issuing a cash receipt, but it further degrades the institution's status. This problem is not limited to institutions. The acceptability of gifts in general is conditioned upon the source, how the gift was acquired, and what is expected in return.

Even directly exchanging approval (or disapproval) is problematic. Mutual praise (or dispraise) is often discounted as being quid pro quo rather than genuine unbiased evaluation. The mutual adulation of lovers or the vitriolic exchanges between long-time enemies are seldom taken seriously as objective evaluation. In their ideal-type form, status processes are not exchange processes, but unbiased, freely given expressions of approval or disapproval.

Weber was, of course, well aware of the relative inalienability and inconvertibility of status, though he tends to restrict his discussion to the difficulties in transforming wealth into status, that is, class position into status group membership: "status honor need not necessarily be linked with a class situation. On the contrary, it normally stands in sharp opposition to the pretensions of sheer property" (1968:932). On the other hand, he points out: "Property as such is not always recognized as a status qualification, but in the long run it is, with extraordinary regularity" (1968:932). So immediate quid pro quo exchange is quite problematic, but long-term transformations are common. We shall consider how such a conversion is accomplished shortly.

In his discussion of Greek culture, Alvin Gouldner emphasizes another aspect of the inalienability of status:

> [The Greeks] saw that men grew old, infirm, became worn and haggard, and that all inevitably died; they saw that fortunes could change radically, leaving rich men poor and free men enslaved. While the Greeks knew what they wanted, they also knew that the things wanted were riddled with worms. . . . they thought to transcend the most tragic impermanence of all, life itself, by a quest for fame and repute. (1965:42)

Not only can you not "take it with you," but after death wealth and political power acquired in life are completely alienable and soon pass on to others. Because status is inalienable, one's reputation can live on after death and produce a form of worldly immortality.[10] If reputation is (1) culturally objectivated and (2) embodied in physical objects, and (3) these artifacts continue to exist and are understood by others, then one's status may even outlive one's own culture. Homer's writings immortalized Odysseus, as the pyramids did Tutankhamen and other pharaohs.[11]

My argument generalizes these various points and ties them to the basic concepts of a dialectical social construction of reality perspective. When we emphasize the relative inalienability of status and the difficulty of converting most resources into status quickly or easily, a whole array of phenomena are seen to be variations on a common theme.

An elaboration is needed concerning the relationships between knowledge and status. In some respects, knowledge is even more inalienable than status. Knowledge is only partly dependent upon a social consensus. There is an external world that, over the long run, places some limits on what passes for knowledge. Those who genuinely believe they can jump off cliffs or swim across oceans eliminate themselves from the debate about what constitutes knowledge. Stated another way, some types and aspects of knowledge do not in the long run depend solely upon the opinion of others. Thus, one's knowledge is less vulnerable to appropriation or destruction than one's status. The license of a physician or engineer can be revoked, severely damaging their professional and personal status, but the knowledge they have cannot be taken away from them.

Predictably, status groups often attempt to make their position even more secure by linking status to knowledge. Those with high levels of esoteric knowledge are admired: knowledge becomes a basis or source of status. To destroy a status order built on the possession of knowledge, it is necessary to change people's opinions both about what is and what ought to be. Obviously such changes can and have occurred, but to do this is much more difficult than either appropriating someone's wealth or political office, or even influencing their reputation by slander or favorable publicity. Consequently, we would expect status orders in which knowledge is one of the key sources of status to be especially stable; the more taken-for-granted and less dynamic the content of the knowledge, the more this will be the case.

My general theoretical point is that variations in the inalienability of resources are rooted in the objectivation and internalization process. One's status is tied to a community—what others have internalized about you. In contrast, knowledge is more internalized in the actor himself. The experiences of an actor and the information he has acquired by these experiences may affect his behavior or be used to shape his environment even if these are shared by no one else. In Bourdieu's (1986) and Coleman's (1988, 1990) terms, knowledge is less inherently a form of social capital than status. A refugee is rarely able to bring his community status with him when he flees his home, but he may be able to bring knowledge and skill relevant in his new situation. The extent to which he can bring wealth will depend on the form of objectivation; Swiss bank accounts (in the twentieth century) are more portable than gold, and gold is more portable than land. In short, variations in the inalienability of resources—that is, variations in the degree to which they can be appropriated, transported, and exchanged—are rooted in the particular forms in which externalized human action has been objectivated and internalized. While this book will focus on the implications for status, these notions are also quite relevant to the analysis of other types of resources.

Inexpansibility

Not only is status relatively immovable and stable, the amount of status available to a group is relatively inexpansible.[12] Stated another way, status is a relatively zero-sum or positional resource. One group or society can have ten or even a hundred times more per capita wealth or force than another society. No society, however, has a hundred, or even ten, times as much status per capita to distribute as another. Status is basically a matter of relative ranking. If a hundred Nobel Peace Prizes were awarded annually, each prize would be much less prestigious. Status is not, of course, absolutely inexpansible, but when status rewards are qualitatively expanded, inflation soon discounts the value of any given status position.[13] The more students get As, the less use they have have as a symbol of academic status.

Moreover, both participants and analyst sometimes confuse the redistribution of status with an expansion of the total amount of status available. The status distance between ranked groups can decrease without the actual rank order changing. This is a matter of redistribution. It is analogous to the upper class having 60 percent of the wealth and the lower class having 40 percent, rather than 80 percent and 20 percent, respectively. The first situation means less inequality but not necessarily more total resources. Similarly, status difference can be decreased and the relative status of many increased, but at a cost to those who previously had high status. Gouldner has emphasized the zero-sum nature of honor in the Greek contest system (1965:49–51). Patterson generalizes the argument somewhat:

> Few would disagree with Alvin Gouldner when he says that "a central, culturally approved value of Greek life, embedded in and influencing its systems of stratification is an emphasis on individual fame and honor," and that the contest for power and honor in ancient Greece, as in most honorific cultures, was largely a zero-sum game, "in that someone can win only if someone else loses." (1982:87)

I want to broaden the generalization: status is a relatively inexpansible resource in all societies—though the extent to which this is the case varies across cultures.[14]

The inexpansibility of resources has important implications for the rates and patterns of social mobility. Sociologists distinguish structural mobility from circulation mobility. Structural mobility is due to expanding resources or fundamental structural change. People move from blue-collar to white-collar jobs because the economy and the occupational structure use a higher proportion of white-collar workers than formerly. Or many people's annual income rises from $15,000 to $20,000 because the overall mean income has increased by $5,000. Circulation mobility refers to shifts in the social hierarchy over and above the amount produced by structural mobility. When circulation mobility occurs, someone must move down if someone else is to move up. If the total societal wealth does not increase, a richer person must become poorer if a poor person is to become richer.

This helps us to understand one of the key characteristics of status groups: Since status can be expanded to only a limited degree, in status groups most mobility is circulation mobility. If any significant number of people move up, a similar number must be demoted, or the overall status of the group will be eroded. Not surprisingly, status groups carefully restrict and limit upward mobility. This is characteristic of sororities and fraternities, exclusive clubs, the Social Register, honorary societies, aristocratic elites, and highly prestigious universities.

The relatively inexpansible nature of status is also related to the objectivation and internalization processes. Human actions externalized as labor can be stored in objects; each new tool or machine created is an additional usable resource. Labor can also be objectivated in military technology, thereby affecting the amount of force available. Force can also be stored, in a negative sense; once a soldier is killed he does not have to be killed again. Similarly, knowledge can be duplicated both in objectivation and internalization. Everybody can receive a textbook without this depleting the knowledge embodied in the book; as long as people have a need for the knowledge, the thousandth textbook is just as useful as the first one. Similarly, when the thousandth or millionth person internalizes the knowledge needed to read, the skill of the first person who learned to read is not diminished. To a significant degree the internalization of knowledge is independently accomplished by each actor.

In contrast, the status brought by literacy—or any competence—is very much affected by how many people have it. Literacy brings much less status when all can read and write than when only a small elite can. This is because the status symbols produced by objectivation, and the opinions produced by the internalization of values and norms, are inherently relational and social products. Status is a community project. It is social capital par excellence. If each member of a group has a different opinion about what is good, valuable, high, and low, there is no status order. In a sense, status must be objectivated and internalized by the community. Robinson Crusoe could objectivate his labor into additional goods. By reflection and study he could internalize new knowledge. What he could not do is create a status order—until Friday arrived.

In sum, status has two attributes crucial to understanding the characteristics of status groups. It is a relatively inalienable resource; therefore, once status orders become established they tend to be relatively stable and can be only indirectly affected by wealth and force.[15] It is a relatively inexpansible resource; therefore, those with high status have both the motivation and the ability to restrict and regulate mobility. The more important status is (especially if it is based on nonmaterial criteria) compared to other forms of power, the stronger these tendencies will be.

The Sources of Status

Having considered the attributes of resources per se, we now consider the mechanisms whereby social actors acquire status (positive or negative). The first source of status is the approval received for *conformity* to social norms,[16] or conversely, the disapproval received for nonconformity.[17] According to Weber, the crucial requirement to be a member of a status group is conformity to a prescribed lifestyle. "In content, status honor is normally expressed by the fact that above all else a specific style of life is expected from all those who wish to belong to the circle" (1968:932). Status groups, according to Weber, are based upon approved patterns of consumption. The approved lifestyle may also restrict certain kinds of economic activity, especially manual labor or "crass" forms of commercial activity.

To argue that conformity to norms is a key source of status is not to suggest that there is complete normative agreement. Whatever consensus does exist is often a tacit or practical consciousness with high levels of indexicality,[18] rather than an explicit articulated agreement.[19] In a complex differentiated society the norms, and thus what constitutes conformity, are more intricate. Complex societies may have multiple status orders precisely because differentiation produces multiple and often overlapping communities. Moreover, general societal norms tend to be associated with the interests of dominant groups. Norms specific to other strata are often counternorms that in some respects contradict the dominant ones; conformity to the norms of superior groups may necessarily mean deviance from one's own group. This deviance may not only be resented by old peers—"he thinks he's too good for us now"—but can be used as a rationale for rejection by superiors—"he's a pretentious upstart." To complicate matters, the highest levels of status are sometimes associated with innovation, which is of course a form of deviance. Even the ability to deviate from norms without getting caught may be admired and may contribute to one's status. For example, the ability of a noted politician to keep an extramarital affair out of the press may increase his prestige with other politicians. Hence conformity is not a simple matter. Such complexities do not negate the fact that conformity to norms is a key source of status and that, in even the most status-conscious differentiated societies, there are some generalized norms.

The second source of status is *associations*: the people, objects, and locations with which one comes in regular contact. Especially crucial are associations with other people in expressive—as contrasted to instrumental—relationships.[20] To associate with people in expressive, intimate relationships is to implicitly express approval of them; to refuse to associate implies disapproval. Thus relationships like marriage and friendship can dramatically affect one's status, and are carefully regulated when status is a crucial resource.

The significance of such regulation becomes even clearer if we recall that status is a relatively inexpansible resource. Associating with people of lower status raises their status and lowers ours. In addition, a ripple or multiplier effect results: when we then associate with those who have traditionally been our peers, our lowered status now lowers their status, reducing the amount of status available to the status group as a whole. Either the average status of group members will erode, or someone within the group will be moved downward. Of course, this does not occur in every instance of association between higher and lower status people. Nonetheless, crucial associations such as marriage, or the regularization of even casual associations, are likely to produce this result over the long run.

This effect is conditioned by the content of the relationship: the more egalitarian it is, the greater the impact on the actors' subsequent status. For example, if a woman from an outcast group is added to the king's harem, his status will be affected only marginally. If, however, the same woman becomes his first and only wife, her lower status will have a significant negative impact upon his status. On the other hand, the status of the outcast woman may increase enormously because of her association with a person of such high status—even in relatively demeaning circumstances. Obvious parallels exist in contemporary social life; for example, servants to very high status people often have a second career and develop limited fame by writing about their former employers.

The concepts of conformity and association are logically connected to the ideas of agency and contingency introduced in the preceding chapter. The notions of conformity and of expressing approval or disapproval assume some notion of agency; normally we reward and punish only those who "could have done otherwise" (Giddens 1984)—though of course cultures vary in the precise way agency and responsibility are attributed to individuals. While often we can choose with whom we associate, this is not always the case. Most importantly, we cannot choose our parents or our mother tongue; for the child these associations are solely matters of contingency. A person may have slightly more agency in defining their racial, gender, and national identities, yet these too are largely contingent. Until recent centuries, most social associations were ascribed, which means they were a matter of contingency rather than agency. Obviously this correlation between agency and conformity on the one hand, and contingency and association on the other, is imperfect. Nonetheless, as we shall see later, the parallel has significant ramifications for other aspects of social and cultural organization.

More immediately, however, each source of status—conformity and association—has implications for the subsidiary characteristics of status groups. Let us now consider these.

"Secondary" Elaboration, Editing, and Ritualization

A perennial tension exists between abstractions and the concrete reality they portray. On the one hand, it is essential to abstract and simplify reality in order not to be overwhelmed with complexity, and on the other hand, such abstractions are constantly in need of *elaboration* in order to "fit" them to the complex reality that they represent. This is true of relationships between individuals, as they try to adapt their personal expectations and cultural roles—friend, spouse, employee, and so on—to the concrete interpersonal relations that make up their lives. This is also true of scientific theories, ideologies, and normative and legal systems—that is, virtually any system of abstractions. For example, the more complex the social structure, the more laws and rules must be interpreted and elaborated if they are to remain legitimate. The more inaccurate or biased the abstractions (whether descriptive or imperative), the more interpretation and elaboration are needed to explain away the discrepancies. Ptolemaic astronomy required elaborate special theories to explain away the differences between the predictions of the main theory and what was observed. Legalized racial segregation in the United States required secondary legal doctrines such as "separate but equal" and "states' rights" to explain away the contradictions between the basic premises of the Constitution and the legal and empirical reality.

A related mechanism for handling discrepancies can usefully be referred to as *editing*: the embarrassing features of reality and routinely accepted deviations from supposedly honored ideals are studiously ignored, or at least not given the legitimacy of formal recognition. For example, the important contributions of blacks and women were left out of American history books. In short, abstractions, including norms and ideology, are elaborated and edited in order to relate the abstract to the concrete and especially to explain away discrepancies between the ideal and the actual. Since norms are central to a status system, we should expect to find these processes.

In addition to the processes characteristic of all systems of abstractions, status systems have additional sources of elaboration. If status groups want to restrict mobility, and if conformity to the group's norms is a key source of status, then status groups do not want simple norms anyone can follow. This can be remedied by elaboration: the more exclusive the group, the more elaborate and esoteric the norms are likely to become. Behaviors difficult for outsiders to learn will be emphasized—for example, accent, demeanor, taste, style, and esoteric rituals. Because these are difficult to learn unless you have grown up in the relevant social setting, they provide a reliable way to distinguish the established elite from upstarts.

In addition to serving as a screening mechanism, the elaboration of norms is a key form of institutionalization. According to Berger and Luckmann (1967:53–67) institutionalization originates in habituation: having to decide self-consciously what to do each time a given situation arises is stressful and inefficient. Habits help to reduce this problem, but personal habit is not enough. Institutionalization requires habits and expectations that are mutually reinforcing: "everyone knows that when X occurs we do Y." The more elaborated these habits and mutual expectations, the more firmly established will be the institution's fundamental assumptions. For example, the more elaborate and widely accepted kinship terms are, the more the existing kinship structure is likely to be taken for granted. The more elaborate capitalist markets and firms are, the more private ownership of the means of production is taken for granted: if property rights were to be drastically limited, most other things about capitalism would have to be changed.[21]

Supplementing and overlapping the process of elaboration is what I will call *ritualization*. Since ritual is, by definition, highly patterned and stereotypical behavior, "faking it" is difficult; outsiders are usually easy to detect. For example, it is easier for the average nonmember to blend into a Methodist or Presbyterian worship service or a neighborhood association meeting than into a pre–Vatican II high mass, a Pentecostal service, or a Masonic lodge meeting. The latter three require specific, detailed ritual knowledge and skills that are difficult to learn quickly or fake. Rituals may be elaborated for explicitly defined events, as in religious services, or for ritualized conformity to norms governing everyday life. Fraternities, sororities, lodges and clubs, debutante balls, and upper class social events in general have extensive rituals. So do otherworldly sects who wish to set themselves off from the conventional world that surrounds them. The key point is a simple one: the elaboration of norms and rituals helps to distinguish between insiders and outsiders and to increase the objectivated, routine, taken-for-grantedness of social institutions.

Somewhat paradoxically, where status-group membership is primarily ascribed, the elaboration of norms and rituals provides opportunities for achievement: the aristocrat can display his refined knowledge and careful conformity to "good manners." The initial contingency of birth is mitigated by means of the moral conformity of the responsible agent. As indicated earlier, all credible ideologies must give some credence to both agency and contingency. Such opportunities to display conformity and achievement (which nonmembers cannot match) contribute to legitimacy.

Especially significant for our analysis a particular type of elaboration and ritualization. I have found it useful to refer to this type of patterning as *secondary norms and rituals*. The concept can be illustrated by asking: How do groups insure adherence to important norms with a minimum of resistance? One way is to surround these norms with additional "layers" of norms, symbols, and rituals that buttress the primary norms. A simple example of this comes from the modern military. One of its central concerns is to train soldiers to follow orders, even in the face of injury or death. A related concern is to train them to act in coordinated unison so that the force a unit exerts is more than the sum of its individuals' actions. To accomplish this, the military institutes almost endless rules, symbols, and rituals of obedience and deference to authority—during training. Soldiers must salute and address superiors in deferential language. Minutely detailed rules govern their personal appearance and the orderliness of their quarters. They are taught to carry out orders, no matter how senseless, pointless, and burdensome: dig large holes and then fill them up. The soldier's body and bodily movements also become a symbol of discipline: for example, freshly pressed uniforms, shined shoes, standing rigidly at attention, turning and moving in a precise and specified way. To instill a highly developed proclivity to act in coordinated unison, they must learn to march and drill. The marching column, and especially the drill team, is a metaphor for the obedient, coordinated, and unified fighting unit. The military parade is a symbolic metaphor for the coordination not only of individuals, but also of military units. The emotional intensity stimulated by bands, flags, and the like simulates the emotional intensity required in combat.

Few, if any, of these activities are needed or used in combat situations. But these secondary norms, rituals, and symbols instill obedience and solidarity, and create latent social metaphors for the kinds of social units required in modern combat.[22] In the military example the connections between the primary and secondary norms are relatively transparent. We will take up more subtle cases later.

The secondary elaboration of norms and rituals seems to be especially characteristic of status groups; the "thickening" and objectivation of the social structure is particularly prevalent in such structures. This is partly because status, in contrast to wealth or military power, can be objectivated in physical objects only to a limited extent, hence symbolic rather than physical accumulation and storage is important. Another reason for such elaboration is because status systems rely primarily on expressions of approval and disapproval for sanctioning; the acceptance of norms and their supporting ideology needs to be more unquestioning than in systems that rely on force or material incentives. For these reasons, the elaboration of secondary norms and rituals is particularly important where status is an especially crucial resource.[23] In sum, because conformity to norms is a primary source of status, elaboration, editing and ritualization of the norms (and the ideologies which justify them) are common where status is a crucial resource. Now let us return to the implications of status through associations.

The Regulation of Mating and Eating

Status groups are especially concerned about the regulation of intimate expressive relationships. Such relationships are often symbolized by sex and eating together, for what seem to be several interrelated reasons. Mating and eating are the way humans are physically reproduced; eating reproduces the individual organism from day to day, and sex reproduces the species. In both cases, human actions become objectivated in objects we call bodies. These key activities for physical reproduction also become key symbols of social reproduction, in which actions become objectivated in subjects we call persons. To be a person is to have an "identity"—a word that has two almost contradictory meanings. One implies combination, that two or more entities are the same; the other refers to separation, those characteristics that distinguish a given entity from other entities. The social reproduction of human identities involves both of these. A distinctive person is created, who also has a sameness and commonality with other members of her society. Intimacy seems to be especially crucial to identity formation and maintenance; here humans are most vulnerable to and affected by one another.

In most if not all cultures, mating and eating are considered intimate activities. In both situations, something is shared and something crosses the boundary of one's body. The primal form of eating is a baby nursing. In both nursing and sex, a physical appendage of one body enters another body and provides satisfaction of a basic need—ideally for both parties. Whatever the biological or psychic sources, in most societies sexual relations and sharing a meal are key signs of social intimacy. Since social identities are most affected by intimate relationships, this is where the group must be most concerned about who is allowed to associate with whom.

Such relationships are even more significant if they are publicly visible and publicly acknowledged by the parties involved. The institution of marriage creates such visibility and acknowledgment. Predictably, while many status groups are concerned about the regulation of sexual relations in general, they are especially concerned with the regulation of marriage. A member of the elite may be excused for sowing his or her "wild oats," but they are likely to be excluded or degraded if they marry beneath their rank. Seeing that their children marry the "right kind of person" is a pivotal responsibility for high status families. Because marriage is the epitome of the intimate expressive relationship, and implies high levels of approval, it has a significant effect on the status of the two individuals and the two families. Accordingly, in most well-developed status groups marriages are carefully arranged, often by the families rather than the couple. Where the couple have the formal responsibility for choosing a mate, families are commonly concerned that their young people "run in the right circles." Elite schools, debutante balls, exclusive summer camps, and sororities and fraternities are all means of increasing the likelihood of appropriate matches.[24]

In contemporary American adolescent society, a parallel preoccupation with mating is apparent. Adolescents are often obsessed with who is dating or "going with" whom; it frequently is a crucial determinant of status-group membership for high school students. On occasion the status order that concerns parents is not the one their adolescent children see as important. The boy from the good family may date the cheerleader from across the tracks, or the upper class girl may become infatuated with a football hero—to the consternation of the parents. Whatever the disagreement between parents and children over who is an appropriate match, both see intimate expressive relationships as a key determinant of social status.

While less significant than marriage and dating, eating with someone also implies intimacy and mutual approval, and status groups are also concerned about who eats with whom. Executive dining rooms, officers' clubs, and Oxbridge high tables symbolize this concern. Who gets invited to whose dinner party is a characteristic preoccupation of modern upper and upper middle classes. The equivalents of fraternities at Princeton University are called eating or dining clubs, and the definition of membership in an Oxbridge college hinges on whether one has dining rights. Moreover, in most status groups the more intimate the form of eating, the more carefully regulated is the company. Your boss's boss may be invited to your daughter's wedding reception or a large cocktail party, though you realize he will probably decline, but to invite him over for a family meal on a weekday night would be presumptuous. The latter would imply more intimacy and approval than someone of such status is likely to grant. The concern is not limited to adults; among adolescents in the United States, a key locale for working out status relationships is the school cafeteria; who sits with whom is both a crucial sign and determinant of the distribution of status. If adolescents want their family's approval and want others to see that they are having a "serious" relationship, the girlfriend or boyfriend is invited home to dinner.

The elaboration of norms and rituals and the regulation of mating and eating are overlapping processes: many of the elaborated norms and rituals do concern the regulation of mating and eating, but the two processes are analytically independent.

Summary

By focusing on the characteristics of status as a resource—its inalienability and inexpansibility—and on the sources of status—conformity and association—we have been able to organize considerable information about status relationships. Such characteristics as relative stability, restrictions on mobility, and tendencies toward the regulation of marriage and eating can now be seen as parts of an overall logic of social organization, rather than as disparate elements or peculiarities of particular cultures.

Up to this point I have avoided mention of India, the caste system, or Hinduism in order to show the potential general relevance of my arguments. For now I will suspend the introduction of theoretical concepts and proceed to more empirical matters. Additional general theoretical elements will be introduced (especially in Chapters 8 and 12) as they become necessary to sustain the analysis.

4

Key Features of Indian Society: What Is to Be Explained

Having indicated the broad theoretical arguments that shape the analysis, our next task is to outline the phenomena to be explained.

What follows is an extremely summarized, rudimentary introduction to Indian society and culture, for the benefit of those who are unacquainted with South Asia. As in any analysis, the facts selected are constituted and shaped in part by my theoretical assumptions. I will focus on the core attributes of Hinduism, the caste system, patterns of political-economic dominance, and three sets of important cultural ideas: purity, sexual asceticism, and auspiciousness.

Hinduism: A Brief Sketch

Hinduism is the product of a religious heritage that is three thousand years old. Often a distinction is drawn between the earlier periods of this tradition, known as Brahmanism or Vedic religion, and later Hinduism proper. The former was the religion of the Aryans who invaded north India some time in the second millennium B.C.E.[1] This religion focused on sacrifices. Central to it was the maintenance of cosmic order (*rta*) through the generation and channeling of a kind of mystical heat (*tapas*) by means of sacrifices and the devotional fervor of the priests.[2] To simplify drastically, this heat was the fundamental source of power needed to either sustain or transform the various features of the cosmos. Because improperly conducted sacrifices could produce disaster, a high premium was placed upon proper ritual knowledge; thus learning has been a central value from the earliest periods of this tradition. The procedures and rationale for these sacrifices are outlined in four religious texts referred to as the Vedas—hence the phrase "Vedic religion." An even more extended set of sacrificial instructions is elaborated in a series of slightly later texts known as the Brahmanas. From the earliest times, an important element of Vedic and later ritual activity has been the recitation of *mantras*—formulaic prayers and incantations that are thought to influence gods or produce magical results.

At some time during the first millennium B.C.E., the notion that the soul (*atman*) of human beings went through an extended series of reincarnations (*samsara*) became widely accepted in India. Human experience was increasingly defined as suffering (*duhkha*); reincarnation only extended it. Now the aim of religious activity was to escape from worldly existence rather than to sustain the cosmos by ritual sacrifices. By the middle of the first millennium, Buddhism and Jainism had emerged as critiques of and alternatives to Brahmanism. Central to these traditions was the notion of nonviolence (*ahimsa*), which was in part a response to the political violence of the times and in part a criticism of ritual sacrifice. Within the Brahmanical tradition itself, sacrifice was increasingly conceived of as a more personal process, and various individual meditation techniques were substituted for the earlier elaborate priestly sacrifices. Tapas was now generated by asceticism—for example, fasting and celibacy—and meditation. The word "tapas" also came to refer not only to the result, that is, "heat," but to the means; when people or gods wanted to increase their power, it was said that they would go perform tapas. Tapas in this sense is a means of producing religious and magical power that has the potential for overriding all other forms of power. While tapas could give one power over relatively worldly matters, the goal of these techniques was increasingly release (*moksa*) from worldly suffering and the endless cycles of reincarnation. Anyone, from Untouchables to gods, can engage in tapas, but it is especially characteristic of Brahman sages (*rishis*). *Yoga* is the term applied to the best-known set of meditation techniques. This internalization of sacrifice and shift toward individual asceticism, meditation, and nonviolence was recorded in a set of texts known as the Upanisads. The effective use of these techniques required not only asceticism, but extensive knowledge (*jnana*): what had to be learned had changed, but knowledge continued to be central to Brahmanical religion. It was not a popular religion for the masses, but mainly a set of practices carried out by those who renounced the world and devoted their lives to learning the necessary techniques. These renouncers are most often referred to as *sannyasins*.

Partly in response to the competition from Buddhism and Jainism, what has been called the new Brahmanical synthesis gradually emerged between, roughly, 200 B.C.E. and 500 C.E., and is seen as the beginning of Hinduism proper. The main thrust of this synthesis was to reformulate the ideas of the Vedas and the Upanisads so that they were not only relevant to a small elite but could be adopted by the much larger number of Brahman householders—who nonetheless constituted a small proportion of the total population. A key element of this synthesis was a redefinition of the ancient concept of *karma*. In Vedic religion the word had referred primarily to the actions that constituted the elaborate sacrifices. Now it referred primarily to the ritual and practices of the household, and even more broadly to virtually all human behavior. Increasingly, the path to salvation was not ritual sacrifice or the knowledge and practice of esoteric meditation techniques, but proper action (karma) in one's day-to-day life. What constituted proper action was gradually explicated in a series of religious texts known as the Dharmasutras, a series of brief sayings or rules, and the Dharmasastras, a more extended set of treatises. As their name suggests, they focused on what was becoming the central concept of Hinduism, *dharma*. The word can be roughly translated as "law," and it has the dual connotations of the English word: on the one hand, the universal regularities that govern the cosmos, and on the other hand, the rules for human conduct. The second meaning gained prominence, and Hinduism came to be a religion—or perhaps more accurately, a way of life—that emphasized conformity to a complex set of norms that governed not only ritual but virtually all aspects of life. Since such an extensive and complex set of norms was not easily learned, Brahmans remained learned experts relative to the rest of the population—though the content of their knowledge had again shifted significantly.

Eventually, five key concepts become linked together: dharma ("law"), karma ("action"), atman ("soul"), samsara ("reincarnation"), and moksa ("release"). Whether one's actions (karma) are good or bad is determined by the degree to which one conforms to dharma. One's good and bad actions cling to the soul (atman) and determine the subsequent experiences one has, including the rank of one's reincarnation—Brahman, Sudra, Untouchable, animal, or even a worm. Ultimately, because of the operation of karma through repeated incarnations (samsara), good is rewarded and evil is punished; one's good deeds may go unnoticed and one's sins may escape punishment in this life, but over the course of repeated incarnations, virtue will be rewarded and evil punished. The supreme reward is escape (moksa) from the sufferings inherent in the endless rounds of samsara. Moksa is possible only if in the course of samsara the soul (atman) is purified by virtuous behavior ("good karma") that is in conformity with dharma. Especially important is conformity to one's *svadharma*, that is, the rules and actions appropriate for one's own caste. Religious texts repeatedly remind the Hindu that it is more meritorious to perform one's own svadharma poorly than to perform someone else's perfectly. Implicit in the notion of svadharma is the recognition that few humans can be concerned only about moksa most of the time. Moksa, then, is made the final goal in a broader set of goals of "Man," known as the *purusarthas*. The four classic purusartha of the Hindu man are *kama*—desire, especially sensual and erotic pleasure; *artha*—the pursuit of interest, especially material interests; dharma, which in this context emphasizes religious ritual duties; and finally, moksa. Each of these is a legitimate goal in the appropriate context. However, different social categories are especially associated with certain goals: the renouncer is especially concerned with moksa, the Brahman householder with dharma, and the king with artha.

With the new Brahmanical synthesis and revitalization, the core features of Hinduism were largely in place. Several additional developments were, however, of great importance. Especially significant was the codification of two additional sets of religious texts. First were the two great epics, the *Mahabharata* and the *Ramayana*, long epic poems about heroes somewhat similar to *Beowulf* and the Homeric epics. Originally these were primarily secular stories. Brahmans reworked them many times, and when they reached more or less final form, in the second or third century C.E., an array of more religious themes had been added. Among other things, these texts laid the foundation for the full deification of Krishna and Rama and the development of the cults that worship them.

The second set of important texts are the sixteen Puranas, which date from about the sixth to the sixteenth century. They typically contain myths concerning the cycles of creation and destruction of the cosmos, and the origin, genealogy, and exploits of various gods and sages (rishis). The scheme of cycles is rather complicated, but the essential notion is that over a period of millions of years the world goes through repeated cycles, each with four stages, or *yugas*. Each succeeding stage is more degenerate, the last and present stage being the *Kali Yuga,* in which corruption is increasingly apparent. At the end of this yuga the world will be destroyed; it will then be re-created, and the whole cycle begins again.

While many gods may be discussed, each Purana tends to emphasize one of the three high gods of Hinduism: Brahma, Visnu, and Siva. In relation to the cyclical yuga scheme, Brahma is the creator, Visnu the preserver, and Siva the destroyer, though the latter two have many additional functions and aspects. The key heroes of the epics, Krishna and Rama, are frequently conceived of as incarnations of Visnu. In addition to the three gods, there are numerous forms of the Goddess figure, Devi, who is often called "Mother." She is identified with power (*sakti*), which can be either destructive or positive, and accordingly she has both horrific and beneficent incarnations. In her beneficent form she is usually the wife or consort of Visnu, Siva, or Brahma; in her destructive form she is usually single and is commonly known as Durga or Kali.

Like the epics, the *Puranas* contributed to a greater emphasis on theism and the worship of a particular sectarian deity. A key characteristic of this theism (and of Hinduism in general) is the lack of a clear-cut line between gods and humans; Brahmans, kings, and to some degree all people contain elements of the divine. The central form of religious ritual became the *puja*, an adaptation of old rituals used to honor household guests. The essence of the puja is to honor a particular deity by reverently offering a set of services and gifts. The basic form of puja is the same for personal, household, and temple worship—though the degree of elaborateness can vary significantly. At the core of most pujas is the offering of food, which is "tasted" by the deity and then returned as *prasada*, literally "grace," to be eaten by the devotees.

The development of devotional (*bhakti*) movements in South India in about the seventh century accentuated the preexisting tendency toward theism. Some of these movements were, in part, protests aimed at orthodox Brahmanical dominance and the inequalities of the caste system. They emphasized the use of indigenous languages rather than Sanskrit, and most of all, they stressed a personal relationship between the devotee and the deity. Salvation was seen as primarily the result of the deity's grace,[3] and in response the devotee offered devotion (bhakti) and worship. While the rules of the Dharmasastras and the mediation rituals of the Upanisads were not completely rejected, they were deemphasized, and for most Hindus were no longer the primary means to salvation (moksa).

An important form of sectarianism that places special emphasis on the divinity and power of the human person, is Tantrism. It is expounded in various non-Vedic texts known as Tantras. It is closely associated with the worship of the Goddess, though there are important forms of Tantrism that focus on other gods. No one or two characteristics adequately define Tantrism, but it is primarily a form of secret spiritual discipline (*sadhanna*), learned from a guru, that seeks to give the devotee extraordinary powers in this world, including liberation (moksa) in this life. There are many different Tantric sects, and the details of their beliefs and practices vary enormously, but most are in principle open to all castes. They are typically defined

as anti-Vedic, and the rituals of some groups involve what, from an orthodox perspective, would be antinomian practices that emphasize impurity and sexuality. On
the other hand, many elements of Tantric practice have been incorporated into the
conventional forms of both the orthodox and bhakti forms of Hinduism.

Caste and the Social Structure

The earliest Aryan text, the *Rig Veda*, describes four ranked social categories, suggesting a prototype of the caste system. By 200 B.C.E., the ideology of the system
was well developed and elaborated in the most influential of the Dharmasastras, the
Manusmriti or *The Laws of Manu*. The caste system, like all human institutions, has
undergone numerous changes and has varied from one locality to another.
Nonetheless, considerable continuity and generality in the basic features of this institution is evident. It is to a description of these that we now turn.

Varna and Jati

According to the classical religious texts of Hinduism, the population is divided into
four ranked categories called *varnas*: the Brahmans, who are priests, the Kshatriyas,
who are warriors, the Vaisyas, who are farmers and merchants, and the Sudras, who
are laborers and servants. The first three categories are considered "twice born"
(*dvijas*) because they go through an initiation ceremony and are allowed to study
the sacred Veda texts. The Sudras are servants to the twice-born varnas. The
Manusmriti (Buhler 1964:1:91) says, "One occupation only the lord prescribed to
the Sudra, to serve meekly even these other three castes." In addition to these four
categories, there are the Untouchables, who are supposedly outside the system but
in fact are an integral part of it.[4]

The proportion of the population that falls into each varna varies greatly by region, but in most areas, none of the top three varnas constitutes as much as 10 percent of the population, and the total of these three is less than 30 percent.
Untouchables typically constitute at least 10 percent of the total. That is to say, in
most regions the bulk of the population are Sudras or some mix of Sudras and
Untouchables. The distribution of the population by varna varies greatly by locale,
and as we shall see, certain categories are unrepresented in some areas. Sudras,
women, and Untouchables are in principle forbidden to read the most ancient and
sacred religious texts referred to generically as the Vedas.

The link between the varna categories of the texts and later medieval and modern social structures is somewhat ambiguous. We do not know whether castes actually developed out of varnas, but it is clear that the varna scheme has long served as
a simplified indigenous model of the caste system. The actual society is organized
into thousands of specific castes that are each associated with a traditional occupation. Only in a few artisan and service castes such as washerman, barber, and goldsmith have most members earned their living by carrying out what is supposedly
their traditional occupation, though in rural areas many more have performed their
traditional functions on occasion. Most castes can and do participate in both agri-

cultural production and modern occupations. Castes are usually identified with one of the varna categories. There are hundreds, if not thousands of castes that are classified as Sudras: barbers, carpenters, blacksmiths, goldsmiths, oil seed pressers, farmers, potters, cowherders, flower growers, vegetable gardeners, grain parchers, tailors, weavers, and bangle makers—to mention only a few of the most common. The other varnas are associated with a smaller number of castes, which are still categories rather than actual social groups.

The caste structure in a given local region is composed of a small proportion of all of these possible categories. In most villages the number of castes represented ranges from five to twenty-five. There are nearly always some type of Brahman and an array of Sudra castes in a local area. Often groups claiming Kshatriya or Vaisya status are present, but in many areas these varnas are not represented.

The members of a particular caste in a village are linked to those in other villages by ties of kinship and marriage, forming regional caste units sometimes referred to as subcastes. These range in size from a few hundred to perhaps tens of thousands. A regional subcaste is a network of relatives or potential in-laws; members know each other directly or through trusted third parties. In this sense, these regional subcastes are the social groups that make up the system, though their boundaries are often fuzzy.

Usually these regional subcastes are endogamous; that is, husbands and wives are from the same subcaste (or closely allied ones of similar status), and their children will also be members. For contemporary Hindus, endogamy is the essence of the caste system. If there were no restrictions on cross-caste marriage, the caste system would cease to exist. Accordingly, the vast majority of marriages are arranged by the parents. Frequently there are several distinct endogamous subcastes in a local region that belong to the same caste category. For example, there are often more than one group of "cowherders" in a given area who do not intermarry or dine together, even though from the point of view of other people they belong to the same caste; from their own perspective, differences exist among them that are substantial enough to produce quite distinctive segments who neither intermarry or eat with one another. Accordingly, the referent of the word "caste" or *jati*, depends on the context in which it is used.[5] Most people in a village know the caste category of everyone else, but may not know everyone's particular subcaste. In a local area, jati groups are hierarchically ranked, with the Brahmans at the top and the Untouchables at the bottom. The exact ranking of groups is subject to dispute, but most of the disagreement is over whether a particular caste is just above or just below another local caste group, not over the general location of these castes in the local hierarchy.

Muslims make up about 11 percent of the Indian population, and Sikhs, Christians, Jains, and other minorities constitute about 6 percent; the representation of one these groups in any given area is enormously variable. In some areas of the Punjab, Sikhs constitute the overwhelming bulk of the population, while the same is true for Christians in a few areas of South India. In most of these non-Hindu groups, there is a strong tendency for marriages to be arranged only between strata or subgroups that are fairly close to one another in rank. While the castelike features within these religious minorities may be much less elaborate than for Hindus, there is often a strong proclivity toward endogamy and other characteristics typical of status groups.

Through the nineteenth century, a distinction between "right-handed" (*valangai*) and "left-handed" (*idangai*) caste was important in South India, referring to two coalitions of local caste groups that cut across the varna categories and caste rankings. The division between the two was partly related to sectarian religious differences, but the correlation was very imperfect. At certain periods, intense conflict erupted between such coalitions. This distinction is no longer manifest but is still an incipient cleavage.

Asrama

In the law books, or Dharmasastras, the varna distinctions are part of a broader social scheme known as the *varnasramadharma* system: the social categories and norms that outline the appropriate duties for twice-born men. Varna distinctions focus on the differences in the duties and functions of the different ranked social categories. *Asrama* refers to the life stages of twice-born men and the responsibilities appropriate for each one. The Dharmasastras describe a number of different versions of the asrama scheme but the more-or-less standard one includes the following four stages. First, as a student (*brahmacarin*), one's responsibility is to study the Vedas under the guidance of a guru. Second, as a householder (*grihastha*), one should marry, produce children, acquire wealth, and support those in other stages of life. This is the pivotal status of the village social structure. Being a householder does not exclude one from being a religious functionary; for example, a householder can be a priest to other households (*purohit*), a temple priest (*pujari*), or a scholar (*pandit*). In the third stage, that of forest-dweller (*vanaprastha*), the householder supposedly gives up his responsibilities and retreats to the forest with his wife to meditate and study. Few if any actually enter this largely hypothetical stage. Finally, the renouncer (sannyasin) severs his relationship with his family and society in general and becomes a wandering holyman, dependent on daily gifts of food to sustain himself. A small but significant number of individuals from all castes, not just twice-born men, do become sannyasins; as we shall see, they play an important role in Hindu society. Most twice-born Hindus, even Brahmans, only go through the first two stages, and for non-Brahmans the first brahmacarin stage may be brief and perfunctory. For the lower castes the asrama scheme is irrelevant.

Economic and Political Power: Control of Land and Labor

Local Elites and the Jajmani System

While caste rank is correlated with economic and political power, the correlation is by no means perfect. Typically, local political and economic structures are primarily controlled by a dominant caste or coalition. In most areas these controllers of land and labor are not Brahmans; frequently they are Sudras. Often the dominant caste or coalition is able to mobilize considerable physical force, should this become necessary to protect its interest. Members of this dominant group typically serve as *jajmans*—a term with a complex history. In modern India, jajman refers to an individual for whom Brahmans perform religious rites in return for gifts and fees. By extension, the term also refers to those for whom a variety of specialist castes provide various goods and services. In return for these services, they are given a portion of the jajman's grain at harvest time. Jajmans are usually members of the dominant landowning caste in a given area. In this system the integration of the division of labor at the village level is not carried out primarily by either market relationships or direct forms of coercion such as slavery or serfdom.

Kings and Chieftains

At most points in its history, India was divided into a multitude of relatively small kingdoms and, like most agrarian societies, was ruled by various coalitions of warrior elites. During some periods, rulers managed to extend their power over large sectors of the subcontinent. Typically, such a king was not the sole undisputed ruler of his whole realm but was the king of kings; lesser kings gave at least ritual and symbolic loyalty to more powerful rulers in their area. There were multilayered hierarchies of kings, with each level giving ritual deference to superior levels. A lower level may or may not have contributed significant economic or military resources to a higher level in the form of tribute, taxes, and military units; this varied considerably. Both higher and lower level kings were often considered incarnations or prime ministers of one of the major Hindu deities.

Below the level of kings were sundry hierarchies of chieftains who varied enormously in their titles, powers, and privileges. At the bottom of this hierarchy were the headmen of villages, who were typically members of the dominant caste or coalition in a local area. The degree of autonomy held by chieftains varied considerably. These linkages sometimes approximated a feudalistic model, in which local chiefs were near equals of their lords and had high levels of autonomy. In other periods and localities, chieftains were little more than glorified servants of their lord, approximating what Weber called patrimonialism rather than feudalism (both terms are used as only rough approximations). Of course, the line between chieftains and kings was by no means clear-cut. Able and ambitious chieftains frequently defeated and replaced their former masters or declared themselves kings.

At all levels, the links in this loose hierarchy could be reinforced by kinship and marriage. The king's brothers or sons were often the first among chieftains who ruled subareas of the kingdom. Simultaneously or alternatively, alliances could be strengthened by marriages between two previously independent ruling groups. As we shall see, it was at these upper levels of society that marriages most frequently occurred between families that differed in caste rank.

As in the jajmani system at the local level, the symbolic and ritual elements of these relationships among the ruling elite tended to be more highly elaborated and more crucial than in parallel relationships in most other agrarian civilizations. The institution of gifts was crucial to the establishment and maintenance of these and many other relationships; especially important were the type of gift known as *dana*. As in many premodern societies, most land belonged to the king (which is not to say that it was his private property in the modern sense). The king's land was granted to others in return for various kinds of payments or, much more commonly, for assorted services. In India these grants of land typically took the form of gifts.

But these were not gifts of absolute ownership. Rather recipients were given rights to use of the land and the income it generated. The services provided in return ranged from fielding units of armed soldiers to conducting temple rituals to sweeping public areas. Not infrequently, at the upper levels of these hierarchies, "gifts" were a matter of a king returning what he had recently conquered in exchange for ritual deference and some level of political acquiescence.

Land was by no means the only type of gift. Equally important were "honors" and privileges; especially crucial were various symbols, titles, and rights that indicated high rank and close association with the king. Gifts were not restricted to subordinates and retainers in the military-political hierarchy; gifts to Brahmans and various religious institutions such as temples and monasteries were the most important. Kings established and maintained their legitimacy largely through such gifts. As a consequence, Brahmans and various religious institutions became important controllers of land in some areas. Rich merchants are also recorded as giving numerous gifts to Brahmans and other religious and civic institutions, but they rarely competed openly for political power.

During some periods, of course, kings were often not Hindus. After the eleventh century, many of the most important kings were Muslims, as were the various Mogul emperors. Under Muslim rule, the lower levels of the hierarchies of kings and chieftains could be either Muslims or Hindus, and typically were some combination of the two—though the higher in the hierarchy one went, the more likely Muslims were to predominate. While the basic logic of kingly "ownership" and grants clearly operated in these situations too, it is much less clear to what extent the language and symbols typical of Hindu kingdoms were deemphasized or modified. There are, however, many records of Muslim rulers making Hindus subordinate kings and chieftains and providing significant gifts to Hindu religious institutions.

With the consolidation of British power in the middle of the nineteenth century, major changes in control of land and labor began to occur. Under what the British called "permanent settlement," vast portions of land were converted into private property and granted to various local elites. Land was now no longer held as a gift from a king but was owned outright, and usually was a commodity that could be bought and sold. Local landed elites became much more independent of higher levels of political organization. Similarly, there was a clear tendency for labor to become a commodity. The nearly absolute power of traditional land controllers over laborers was qualified, and in principle laborers could sell their labor to the highest bidder; this also meant that peasants and laborers could be dismissed when it was profitable to the landowners. The rate of these changes varied greatly by area, but they were universal in principle, if not in practice, by the time India became independent from Britain. The actual forms of the organization of production remain a complex mixture of precapitalist and capitalist forms of domination.

Cultural Ideologies and Codes

Two sets of cultural ideas are common themes in Indian thought and play a crucial role in tying together Hinduism, caste, and the political structure. These ideas are conscious ideologies used to explain and justify well-known patterns of behavior; they are also latent codes that communicate relationships that are more tacit, implicit, and unconscious.

Purity and Pollution

First, the notion of purity (*sauca*) is a central theme in Indian culture. According to Dumont (1980), differences in purity are the underlying basis of the caste system. Brahmans have the highest status because they are perceived to lead lives ritually and religiously purer than others'. Untouchables are at the bottom because they engage in activities that are highly defiling. In short, the gradations of the caste system are based on gradations of purity and impurity (*asauca*). Many, if not most, of the rules governing relationships between individuals and groups are rooted in this concern. Higher castes cannot eat with or marry those from lower castes because it would be polluting; they should minimize physical contact and social intercourse with low Sudras and Untouchables. In addition to their direct implications for caste relationships, notions of purity and pollution affect a wide array of daily activities, especially those having to do with cooking, eating, personal cleanliness, and worship. Similar notions are common in many other cultures; elites often claim superior moral and physical purity and see contact with the lower strata as polluting. Nonetheless, compared to most other cultures, Hindus are preoccupied with the notions of purity and pollution, and these concerns shape many of their day-to-day activities.

Sexual Asceticism

Purity is expressed in many cultures through sexual asceticism. In Hinduism the notion of control of sexuality—more concretely, the control and retention of male semen—has a broader symbolic role. Sexual asceticism expresses much more than simply one form of purity. It is an important form of austerity or tapas that is considered to be a key means of power.

Auspiciousness and Inauspiciousness

This set of cultural ideas focuses on the prospects for well-being. To what degree are happenings, events, times, or particular patterns of behavior and relationships propitious, opportune, felicitous, or favorable? For example, when is it propitious to begin the construction of a new house, and how should that house be laid out in order to maximize the chances that its residents will experience good fortune? The reverse idea, inauspiciousness, is concerned with the ominous, the threatening, the unlucky. Auspiciousness and inauspiciousness are primarily concerned with mundane well-being, and more abstractly with economic and political power.

Purity and impurity are the special concerns of the Brahman, while auspiciousness and inauspiciousness have been the special concern of the king or local dominant caste—though virtually all village Hindus are conscious of and affected by both sets of cultural ideas. Astrology plays an especially important role; it is a key means

of determining the auspiciousness or inauspiciousness of certain undertakings, relationships, and times. For example, the horoscopes of couples are matched to see if
their marriage will be auspicious and what time is most propitious for the wedding.
In addition to attempts to predict what is auspicious and what is not, elaborate rituals
are performed to improve the chances of an auspicious outcome. An important means
of reducing inauspiciousness is the giving of ritual gifts (dana).

These three sets of ideas—purity and impurity, sexual asceticism, and auspiciousness and inauspiciousness—play a key role in the day-to-day life of traditional
Hindus.

What Is to Be Explained

This book will offer a set of systematic explanations for many of the broad structural features of Hinduism and Indian society just described.
In sum, a partial list of the phenomena to be explained includes the following:

1. The key structural features of the caste system including why dharma is a central
   cultural category (Chapter 5).
2. The key social categories characteristic of Hindu society including the varna scheme
   (Chapter 6).
3. The major mechanisms of articulating the status and the economic-political orders and
   more specifically the means of political legitimation (Chapter 7).
4. The centrality and significance of the concepts of purity–pollution, sexual asceticism,
   and auspiciousness–inauspiciousness (Chapters 9 and 10).
5. The variations in the rules governing marriages (Chapter 11).
6. The basic structure and dynamics of the puja (Chapter 13).
7. The key variations in Hindu soteriology (Chapter 14).
8. The key features and variations in Hindu eschatology (Chapter 15).

My analysis attempts to explain this considerable array of phenomena with a general
theoretical framework that is relevant to any social situation in which status is a crucial resource. While the focus is on Indian society, I will also suggest how the same
theoretical ideas can both identify and explain parallel phenomena in other societies.[6]

5

Explaining the Key Features of Caste

Status and Power in India

One of the main arguments in Dumont's analysis of caste is that power and status are, in India at least, two separate phenomena, and that status is the crucial determinant of caste. A brief quote illustrates his position:

> For this ideal type of hierarchy to emerge it was necessary that the mixture of status and power ordinarily encountered (everywhere else?) should be separated, but this is not enough: for pure hierarchy to develop without hindrance it was also necessary that power should be absolutely inferior to status. (1980:74)

Dumont makes an absolute distinction between status and power, but to do so creates needless semantic and analytic confusion.[1] In contrast, the typology I have outlined in Chapter 2 defines status as a particular form of power, which is backed by sanctions rooted in the expressions of approval and disapproval. Hence, those who have high status have a particular form of power. Lower caste groups know that even poor Brahmans have a kind of power they do not.

They also know that this is not the same kind of power that their landlords or the police have; as Dumont points out, status is not a mere reflection of economic and political power. The extent to which one form of power can be converted into another is limited (at least in the short run)—specifically, economic and political power cannot be easily converted into status or vice versa. As Dumont points out, it is the exception when Brahmans are kings, and in most areas they are not even the key land controllers.

The status order of the caste system, then, cannot be reduced to control of economic or political power; yet it is analytically misleading to consider this phenomenon, as Dumont does, a unique Hindu ideology of hierarchy that produces a different kind of human mentality, that is, a *Homo hierarchicus*. It is more useful to conceptualize India as a culture that, *relatively speaking*, has been singularly able to insulate status power from the effect of other forms of power. (This insulation is only relative. Power based on religious status has been constantly vulnerable to other forms of power; we will explore some of the details of this later.)

This relative insulation of status from other forms of power is analytically important. It gives rise to a society in which status not based on other forms of power is exceptionally important; hence it provides a unique site for testing a general theory of status groups and status relationships. If that theory is correct, the proposed conceptualization of power (Chapter 2) and the general theory of status groups and relations (Chapter 3) should explain the key structural features of the Indian caste system.

What Is to Be Explained

I will begin by simply listing the key structural features of the caste system which are the explicandum of the analysis, that is, the initial "facts" to be explained.[2] These are

1. The relative long-term stability of the system, especially the Brahmans' continuous cultural prominence if not dominance.
2. The careful restriction of mobility, more specifically: (a) a person's central social status in the community is inalienable and, in principle, mobility across caste boundaries is prohibited, (b) caste position is in principle based solely on inheritance and ascription, and (c) enormous social and individual energies are devoted to differentiating and ranking caste groups and maintaining their boundaries and identities.
3. The extensiveness of detailed norms and elaborate rituals regulating day-to-day life and the centrality of the concept of dharma.
4. The cultural emphasis on the regulation of marriage and eating arrangements.
5. The pervasiveness of gift giving, especially what is known as dana, as a central feature of religious activity, statecraft, marriage arrangements, and ritual activity in general.

These features will be explained in terms of the theoretical concepts that have been presented in earlier chapters: the characteristics of status as a resource (inalienability and inexpansibility), and the sources of status (conformity and association).

Stability and Inalienability

During the nineteenth century, a near mythology developed about the timeless nature of Indian social structure: the image of an isolated village largely unaffected by macro political events and organized by the unchanging system of castes. C. T. Metcalfe represents a common British viewpoint:

> The village Communities are little Republics, having nearly everything they want within themselves, and almost independent of any foreign relations. They seem to last where nothing else lasts. Dynasty after dynasty tumbles down; revolution succeeds to revolution; Hindu, Pathan, Mughal, Maratha, Sikh, English, are masters in turn, but the village communities remain the same. (quoted in Spear 1978:189)

The last fifty years' scholarship has devoted considerable effort to drastically revising this image. Numerous studies have shown that the caste system and local Indian social structures in general are far more dynamic and subject to historical change than was thought. A recurrent conclusion of the village studies conducted by anthropologists is that power and privilege are constantly problematic and a major preoccupation of Indian villagers.[3] This more accurate view, however, should not cause us to overlook the element of truth in the old image. As the Indian sociologist S. C. Dube has said:

> Notwithstanding the passage of time, the village system in India still continues to have many of the characteristics described by Manu [ca. 200 B.C.E.]. . . . the division of labor in the community is governed to a very great extent by traditional caste occupations, and cooperative labor of a number of different castes is required not only for agricultural activities, but also for socio-religious life. (1955:2–4)

Indian culture's tendency toward stability is seen in Hinduism's most fundamental concept, dharma. Dharma is an extremely central and complex notion,[4] but as Robert Lingat, a renowned French scholar of classical Indian law, points out:

> The most general sense [of *dharma*] is provided by its root, *dhr*, which signifies the action of maintaining, sustaining, or supporting and which has produced *fre* in Latin (*fretus*, depending upon, daring to) and *fir* (*firmus*, strong in the physical and moral senses, whence solid, hard, durable). *Dharma* is what is firm and durable, what sustains and maintains. (1973:3)

Hence at the core of Indian thought is a concern with stability.

More important sociologically, the Indian caste system and related religious tradition is the oldest historically specific and identifiable human institution.[5] Elements of it can be traced to Vedic texts, that probably date from about the tenth century B.C.E. (e.g., *Rig Veda*, 10. 90. 12).[6] Between the second century B.C.E., and the second century C.E. the caste system was both well established—though not necessarily universal—and elaborately codified in the *Manusmriti,* and it has had an uninterrupted existence since then. As P. V. Kane, the great Indian scholar of the Dharmasastras, says:

> Our cultural history shows some central features. . . . The first is that there has been an unbroken religious tradition from the Vedic times almost to the present day. Vedic mantras are still employed throughout the whole of India in religious rites and ceremonies by all brahmanas and by a large number of the members of castes claiming to be Kshatriyas and Vaisyas. (1977:1622)

This is true of South Indian Dravidian regions as well as the more Aryan North. In his discussion of South Indian medieval kingship, David Shulman also recognizes Indian culture's striking continuities:

> I have no wish to suggest a nonexistent homogeneity either in historical, structural features or in the related symbolic systems. Nevertheless, there is, I believe, reason to posit an underlying cultural continuity, perhaps most obvious in the symbolic order articulated by our texts. South Indian social symbolism seems at times to be imbued with an

innate conservatism, especially when linked to a crystallized formally defined ideology. Indeed, the continuities may stretch as far back as the Vedic materials on kingship. (1985:8–9)[7]

This view is not limited to scholars; there are significant numbers of orthodox Hindus in India who would claim that the basic features of the caste system, as outlined in the *Manusmriti*, are and should be legitimate. Moreover, one can observe a significant degree of similarity between the codified rules and the actual stratification structure of contemporary Indian villages (of course, there are also drastic differences). In contrast, little if any continuity exists between ancient Egypt, Greece, Rome, Persia, and China and the contemporary societies that exist on these sites; for the first three, and probably the fourth, such continuity ceased more than a thousand years ago.[8] The ideological centrality of notions of durability, the historical continuity, and the relative stability of Indian social structure at the village level all call out for a sociological explanation. Perhaps such nonsociological factors as geographical location and climate, and the contingency and luck of history have played some role, but the primary explanation most likely lies in something relatively unique about the social structure and culture. My hypothesis is that this relative stability is due to the centrality of status as a form of power and to the relatively inalienable nature of status as a resource.

The centrality and inalienability of status means that other forms of power are not easily translated into a higher rank within the caste system. This is especially true once a status order has become firmly institutionalized, as it has in the Indian caste system. In order for a local caste group to change its relative status, it has to literally change the minds of the vast majority of people both above it and below it in the local caste hierarchy. In contrast, for example, as difficult as it might be for low caste groups to increase their wealth, to do so would not logically and inherently require the cooperation of upper caste groups.

A crucial corollary of the system's relative stability is the Brahmans' prominent and often dominant position as cultural and religious leaders over a long period. One source of this long tenure is the consistency with which they have rejected wealth and political power as a defining characteristic of membership. The earliest texts assign political power and economic activity to other groups—the Kshatriyas and Vaisyas, respectively—and this has continued to be the ideal, and frequently the actuality. Hence the many changes in political and economic dominance during the last three thousand years have not succeeded in eroding the fundamental basis of Brahmanical power—though it is likely that such an erosion is now occurring.

In sum, while the caste system has undergone great changes over the long period of its existence, it has been relatively stable compared to most human institutions. This relative stability is in no small part due to the centrality of status and its relative inalienability.

Mobility and Inexpansibility

From a conventional Western perspective, the central defining characteristic of a caste system is the absence of mobility: a person's central social status is inalienable and unchangeable, and in principle, mobility across caste boundaries is prohibited.[9] The lack of social mobility in South Asia has often been exaggerated (see, e.g., Silverberg 1968); moreover, it is important to be clear about what kind of mobility we are discussing.

Economic and political mobility has often been considerable, though its likelihood has varied by caste group. Variations in the economic and political fortunes of upper and middle castes have been a common feature of Indian society for a very long time, if not always. Some Brahmans are very rich and some are very poor. Merchant and landowning castes have frequently improved or declined economically and politically. Drastic upward or downward economic or political mobility among artisan castes—barbers, carpenters, blacksmiths, potters—has been uncommon, though not unheard-of. For the lowest castes, particularly for Untouchables, significant relative improvements in either economic or political conditions were rare in preindependence India.

Such economic and political mobility is not, however, the type of mobility that is the focus of my argument. Rather I am referring to status mobility.[10] It is usually linked to economic and political mobility but is distinct. It does occur in traditional India, but drastic change in ritual status, not to mention mobility across caste categories, is severely restricted.

The key mechanism for restricting mobility is ascription; for the overwhelming percentage of people, caste is inherited at birth and in principle cannot be changed. Of course changes do occur, but they must be disguised or defined so as to avoid violating the norm of ascription. Consequently, a significant change in caste status usually takes more than one generation and involves the transformation of the status of the local caste group or a segment of it, rather than an individual or household. Moreover, it typically occurs by disguising or redefining lower status origins. For example, upwardly mobile castes claim that they have been misclassified and that "originally" they were members of some higher caste—not surprisingly, the one to which they now aspire. Sometimes this does not involve a change in caste name per se, but an argument that their caste "really" belongs to a higher varna, usually Kshatriya or Vaisya rather than Sudra.[11] There is no ideological justification for caste-status mobility, but only for the restoration of the supposedly original state of things (again illustrating the cultural concern with stability). No one who claimed to be a member of a high caste would freely admit, much less brag about, his low caste origin.

My hypothesis is that the preoccupation with restricting mobility, and the consequent ascription and inalienability of caste identity, are rooted in the relative inexpansibility of status. To raise the status of some is to lower the status of others; to decrease the impurity of Untouchables has the long-term consequence of eroding the Brahman's extraordinary purity (see Dumont 1980:46–54). As indicated earlier, the tendency to restrict and regulate mobility is characteristic of most status groups; we would expect that the more central the status order is in the overall stratification system, the stronger this tendency would be. If castes are, as Weber claimed, the extreme form of status groups, we would expect a singular preoccupation with the restriction of mobility.

The obvious corollary to this hypothesis is that actors will be concerned about caste boundaries. Mobility, by definition, involves the crossing of such boundaries.

Hence if mobility is to be restricted, such boundaries must be carefully defined and maintained.[12] Therefore, we would expect the relative centrality and inexpansibility of status in India to lead to a great concern with the identification and maintenance of caste boundaries: careful genealogies, records or witnesses of marriages, exclusive rituals to make clear who is a member and who is not, and extensive social sanctions against those who violate or even question the identity and boundary of the group. These concerns are, of course, characteristic of caste groups in India, especially upper caste groups.

In sum, while earlier views of India may have overlooked the considerable mobility that occurs, nonetheless mobility that clearly violates caste boundaries is seldom defined as legitimate, and status mobility is much more restricted than in most societies. The root source of this inclination to restrict mobility is (1) the relative centrality of ritual status compared to other societies, and (2) its relative inexpansibility.

Conformity and the Elaboration of Norms and Rituals

The crucial norms of Indian lifestyle center on matters of ritual purity and impurity. Conformity to these norms is an important determinant of a local caste's status. For example, the caste that is vegetarian, does no manual labor, prohibits its widows from remarrying, is fastidious about the observance of daily and life-stage religious rituals, drinks no alcoholic beverages, and carefully regulates the behavior of its unmarried women is defined as living a relatively pure lifestyle. Accordingly, it has a higher status—other things being equal—than a caste that does not conform to this pattern. The rules that define purity and impurity vary somewhat from one locality to another, but such norms are highly salient in most of India.

The fact that Indian villagers are concerned about such conformity is the basis of what the anthropological literature terms "attributional" theories of caste rank, a perspective expounded by Stevenson (1954) and, to a significant degree, by Dumont (1980). According to this perspective, different levels of purity (or impurity) are attributed to a caste on the basis of its members' typical level of conformity to the norms governing ritual purity. However, once significant status inequalities between groups become established—by whatever means—the behavior of specific individuals has little effect on the caste status attributed to them. Rather, it is the attributions made by upper castes that most count. Moreover, lower castes are often coerced into accepting the lifestyle imposed upon them.

When conformity is a source of status, higher status groups tend to elaborate and complicate the norms in order to make it more difficult for those of lower status to conform. Probably in no other known society has this process been carried so far.

The central concept of dharma, as well as the long history of the development of Indian sacred texts, shows a strong proclivity toward the elaboration and codification of complex norms—both about how to conduct ritual processes and how to conduct one's day-to-day life.

As indicated in Chapter 4, dharma can be roughly translated "law," with the dual connotation of the universal regularities of the cosmos and the rules for human conduct. Vedic religion, preoccupied with the proper conduct of ritual sacrifices that were thought to literally sustain the cosmos, emphasized the first of these meanings. The proper conduct of such sacrifices was crucial; mistakes could bring disaster. But as the orthodox Brahmanical synthesis (Hopkins 1971; Brockington 1981) emerged around the beginning of the Christian era in the West—in response to Buddhism and other anti-Brahmanical religions—the concept of dharma increasingly focused on rules governing day-to-day conduct. As P. V. Kane says, "ultimately . . . [dharma's] most prominent significance came to be 'the privileges, duties and obligations of a man, his standard of conduct as a member of the Aryan community, as a member of one of the castes, as a person in a particular stage of life'" (1968:3). The notion of duty tends to be emphasized, typically in relationship to some recognized social role: one's duties as a father, as a worker in a certain occupation, as the member of a particular caste. While there is some implication of moral imperative—what one ought to do—equally central is a notion of acting out what is one's nature. Not to act according to dharma is a violation not simply of a social norm but of one's very essence and the cosmic order.

The codes that constitute dharma have been elaborated to an extreme. The four Vedas themselves are the codification of ritual procedures, but the elaboration process begins in earnest with the Brahmanas, an extensive set of priestly manuals that outline elaborate procedures and rules for conducting ritual sacrifices, as well as the purported reasons for such procedures. With the Upanisads, the focus shifts from literal sacrifices to the internalization of worship through meditation, but the tendency toward codification and elaboration continues; in these texts the elaborate procedures for yoga are first systematically laid out. The Dharmasutras, which are collections of pithy aphorisms, have an increased emphasis on rules governing the daily life of the householder. They receive even more emphasis in the Dharmasastras: these treatises are the archetypal example of the elaboration of norms by an established status group. These tendencies are less pronounced in the epics—the *Mahabharata* and the *Ramayana*—and the Puranas, but are not completely absent even there.

The tendency toward the elaboration of norms is not restricted to ancient sacred texts. The same process can be seen in the actual behavior of Hindu Indians: (1) the extensive norms and procedures regarding ritual purity—especially with respect to eating, food preparation, and personal cleanliness; (2) the complex rules concerning appropriate marriage partners, at least for upper castes; (3) the elaborate rituals that are conducted in homes each day by those who are pious; (4) the long list of holy days and periods in the calendar year that demand special forms of behavior and ritual; and (5) the elaboration of bureaucratic rules and procedures beyond what is commonly found in other societies.

India's long history of extensive elaboration and codification of norms is what the theoretical ideas presented earlier would lead us to expect. Where status is a crucial resource and conformity to norms a key source of status, there is a strong tendency toward the elaboration of norms—both those governing interpersonal relations and those relevant to ritual procedures. Such elaboration results both from the competition between those within the status group trying to set themselves off from their peers, and as a means of defending the status group against outsiders and upstarts. It might be added that the social history of contemporary India is, in large

measure, the history of the simplification of the rules that were the basis of traditional forms of status—especially those governing travel, eating, and marriage—
as the importance of traditional status declines relative to other forms of power.

Associations and the Regulation of Marriage and Eating

Two striking characteristics of the caste system are the elaborate restrictions on
marriage and eating. Marriages are arranged by parents and are a crucial source and
sign of a family's status. As Mandelbaum says:

> On all social levels, a marriage is a test of a family's status. Then more than any other
> time a family's alliances stand forth proven and personified by gifts and attendance;
> its status hinges on its strength in allies and clients. Hence a marriage provides the
> prime opportunity for demonstrating and validating family status. A family, like other
> social units in this society, is hierarchically appraised, judged by jati fellows and by
> fellow villagers as superior or inferior to other families. (1970:98)

Marriage is the time that the family is most under pressure to display its status, and is
also the time that caste boundaries are most important. Marriage is typically allowed
only within one's own local caste group or an allied caste of relatively similar status.
"Marriage is the relation that demarcates each jati most clearly. All marriages are supposed to be between a bride and groom of the same jati; no marriage may be made
outside of it" (Mandelbaum 1970:16). Anthropologists term this system "caste endogamy." The reality is more complex and flexible than this ideal, yet the vast majority of marriages does conform to the villagers' understanding of caste endogamy.
(The patterns of marriage alliances is analyzed in some detail in Chapter 11.)

Eating, like marriage, is an important indicator of social boundaries. In village
India, meals are usually shared only with members of one's own caste. The highly
orthodox may be even more restrictive, limiting their dining to closely related family members. As the theoretical discussion indicated, in status groups, the more intimate the form of eating, the more carefully regulated is the company, a gradation
seen in the North Indian distinction between *kacca* and *pakka* food. The actual
physical content of a kacca meal can vary significantly, but it always includes the
staples that are normally consumed in the context of the intimate family. To take a
kacca meal with someone is to imply intimacy and approval. In contrast, pakka food
is the food of the bazaar, the food that is eaten at public events and in public places.
In India this is customarily fried food. Traditionally such foods were fried in ghee,
butter that has been boiled and will not spoil at room temperature; like all products
of the cow, it is considered purifying because it comes from a sacred animal. The
indigenous explanation of why pakka food can be shared with a wider array of
people is that the ghee protects the food and those who eat it from impurities.
However, there are foods eaten at public events that are not fried in ghee—for example, various kinds of sweets. My interpretation of these facts is that the initial
concern is not the actual physical composition of the food, but rather the social context with which it is typically associated, and the level of intimacy it implies. One
concrete bit of evidence for this interpretation is the fact that, because of the high

price of ghee, much of the fried food defined as pakka is now fried in vegetable oil, which traditionally has no purifying properties—in fact, caste groups traditionally associated with its production were of rather low status because of the perceived impurity of their occupational activity.[13]

While the formal categories of pakka and kacca are less common in South India, there does seem to be a tendency for the type of food to vary as the intimacy and exclusiveness of the group sharing it varies. As suggested earlier, the tendency to regulate mating and eating patterns is characteristic of status groups, since intimate associations imply approval and equality. As Mandelbaum notes:

> Permanently, all in a household are ritual equals because of, and by means of, their intimate interaction. Similar ritual equality prevails more widely for all families among whom intermarriage may occur. Endogamy bounds the jati, which is kept as a firm unit by the strong taboo on marrying out of the jati. If we coin the term excest for this taboo, we can say that the horror of excest in village India is almost as powerful as the horror of incest. (1970:231)

If one associates with those of lower caste, especially in intimate expressive relationships such as eating and marriage, this will lower one's status. Perhaps more significantly, it in turn affects the status of other members of your family and caste. "Hence villagers hold that a regular and serious defilement of some in the jati inevitably spreads, by contact, to the whole—unless normal jati relations with the defiled ones are cut off" (Mandelbaum 1970:192–93).

That association implies approval is the implicit logic behind what are called "interactional" theories of caste ranking (Marriott 1959, 1960). This approach focuses on who is willing to accept food, water, and so on from whom as a sign of relative status. Those of lower rank are supposedly willing to accept food from those of higher rank, but not vice versa. In all likelihood, interactional approaches probably are more reliable in estimating rank than attributional theories alone; this is largely because it is easier for researchers to ask whether a member of one caste will accept food from the member of another than to observe how much various castes actually conform to the norms of ritual purity.[14] At any rate, attributional and interaction theories are not mutually exclusive alternatives: both conformity and association must be taken into account to adequately understand status groups and castes.

Gifts: Articulating Status and Material Resources

Humans cannot live by bread alone—nor by praise alone. Those who specialize in acquiring high status need to transform at least some of it into bread; those with lots of bread usually want some respect. While exchange may be necessary in a status order, it is also problematic. It risks destroying what it seeks to acquire. The open purchase of approval greatly diminishes its value to the buyer, and erodes the status of the seller—quite aside from any moral qualms the parties involved might have. Hence implicit modes of exchange are common, frequently taking the form of gifts.

The significance of gifts in premodern societies has long been recognized, and has been central to much of anthropological analysis since the work of Malinowski

(1922) and Mauss (1970). While most gifts seem to be linked to considerations of status and honor, I will not consider all the many theoretical and empirical issues associated with the analysis of gifts. I will restrict my analysis to gifts as a mode of articulating status and material resources in relatively complex societies.

As we saw in Chapter 3, in contrast to the direct quid pro quo exchange of the profane market, there are two types of gifts that, however self-interested, tend to have a more symbolic and sacral quality: (1) gifts directed toward superiors that solicit their approval and acceptance, and that implicitly involve the transfer of material resources to them, and (2) gifts directed toward subordinates that explicitly transfer material resources and honors to them, and implicitly attempt to elicit their commitment and deference.

If such gifts are characteristic of status orders in general, we should expect to find them in Indian culture. Trautmann identifies a parallel distinction in the Dharmasastra texts:

> The fundamental typology of exchange consists of the intersection of two oppositions: what we may call exchange sacred and profane, and exchange noble and ignoble. To put it a little more concretely, the first opposition is between the religious gift (giving upwards) and commerce (buying and selling), and the second opposition is between the lordly gift (giving downward what has been acquired by conquest) and dependency (service for wage). . . . In this formulation, the two forms of gift do not appear to be kinds of exchange at all. (1981:278)

A distinction is made "between fruits or ends that are 'seen' or apparent and those that are 'unseen' or invisible. . . . Only if the gift is made without this visible quid pro quo in prospect, among other things, can it be presumed that it incurs an invisible fruit, a transcendentally bestowed counter gift" (1981:281). Such gift giving is central in India to political legitimacy, the distribution of the village grain harvest (the jajmani system), the handling of inauspiciousness, marriage, and worship (each will be considered in some detail later).

It is apparent that a general theory of status relationships that focuses on the nature of status as a resource, and the sources of status, can explain some of the key features of the Indian caste system. The concatenated description I have provided shows important connections between the various elements of the system, and shows how the key features of caste are extreme examples of features characteristic of most status groups.

6

The Social Categories
of Traditional India

The Problem Defined

In Chapter 5, explanations for some of the key structural features of the caste system were sketched out. These features are closely associated with a set of interrelated indigenous social categories that also require analysis and explanation. These categories (introduced in Chapter 4) have been used by Hindus to describe and understand their society. For example, the varna scheme (Brahman, Kshatriya, Vaisya, and Sudra) has been an especially important model for the appropriate relationship between caste groups. Why are these categories more salient to the actors than other distinctions? And why does the importance of particular subcategories vary? Certainly the particular historical experiences and cultural traditions of India have played a crucial role in forming these categories, but that is only part of the story.

Drawing on the typology of sanctions, resources, and power developed in Chapter 2, I will argue that many of India's central cultural categories can be usefully understood as a particular variant of patterns that are common to most complex societies, because of the similarities in the types of power that are available in all societies. Conversely, the dissimilarities—the special emphasis some categories receive in Indian culture—are related to the particular (and in some respects relatively unique) features of India's traditional structures of power.

What Is to Be Explained

The analysis will focus primarily on the elements of the varnasramadharma scheme: the four varna categories and the life stages of twice-born upper caste males. I will attempt to show how these categories are structurally related to one another and to other categories such as Untouchables, bandits, right and left castes, and the four yuga periods. Some of the specific questions to be considered are

1. Why has the varna scheme, which in most periods only vaguely represents the actual social structure, been so persistent and prominent in Indian culture?
2. Why are there four (rather than three, five, etc.) categories in the varna scheme?
3. Why are Untouchables not included in the varna scheme?
4. Why is India famous for its Brahmans, holymen, and Untouchables rather than its merchants, bandits, kings, farmers, or numerous other social categories?
5. Why is the identity and composition of the Vaisya varna relatively ambiguous, in the earliest texts including merchants, farmers, and herders, making up the bulk of the population, but in the last thousand years referring primarily to merchant castes who compose a small percentage of the population?
6. How are the right and left castes related to the varna categories?
7. Why are Brahmans and Sudras found in virtually all local areas, while many areas have no castes that are identified as Kshatriyas or Vaisyas?
8. What are the typical tensions within each varna category, and what subdivisions are these likely to produce?

Each of these questions by itself has been of interest only to certain South Asian specialists, and some of these questions have been given rather standard answers. For example, one explanation for the four varna categories has been that the Aryans originally divided themselves into Brahman, Kshatriya, and Vaisya, and then added the fourth category of Sudra to distinguish the indigenous people they conquered when they invaded India (Thapar 1966). Assuming this is correct, it leaves unanswered the question of why the Aryans had three categories. Nor does it explain why the scheme remained largely unrevised for two to three thousand years, even though for most of that period it was a very poor representation of the empirical groups that made up the society. It is not sufficient to say that these are categories in the sacred texts; many of the categories represented in early texts have been either revised or ignored. Another explanation points out that there are several important fourfold schemes: four varnas, four stages of life, four goals of man, four yugas, four Vedas, and so on (Biardeau 1989:103). But other numbers, such as five, are used in various schema, and this explanation does not offer any particular insight into the categories' content.[1]

What I propose to do is to supplement the various ad hoc historical and cultural explanations with a more systematic set of sociological explanations: we can increase our understanding of these categories by asking how they are related to the different types of power introduced in Chapters 2 and 3.

Before preceding to a detailed analysis of key cultural categories, it is necessary to develop a general theoretical model of elites and specify the special characteristics of India relevant to this model. This will be outlined in the next three sections of this chaper.

Relationships Between the Different Types of Power

The different types of sanctions and power can be either mutually supportive, or antithetical, or both. For example, if goods are constantly appropriated by force, and workers are murdered and abused with impunity, the accumulation and exchange of goods and services are next to impossible. Therefore, force must be organized to repress the illicit use of force. Conversely, those who provide protection must have food, clothing, shelter, and other amenities that obviously require the production of goods and services. An orderly exchange of goods and services for protection (and vice versa) does not occur automatically; force and monopoly must be replaced by legitimate rules about the terms of exchange. Crude force is not very useful for motivating people to carry out complex production tasks. Conversely, withholding goods and services is ineffective for motivating wielders of force; they can simply take what they want. In other words, the exercise of force and the possession of goods and services are constantly problematic, unless they are recognized as legitimate. The actions of both protectors and producers are more efficient if they receive the approval of each other. Expressions of approval and disapproval are the basis of status. Hence, legitimation can be conceptualized as the status of a particular pattern of action, or of a particular actor's right to engage in that pattern of action.

Whose approval, though, creates legitimacy? Obviously, the wielders of force and the producers of goods and services have conflicting interests; typically (though perhaps not universally) the former want to get as much as they can for the protection they provide, and the latter want to pay as little as possible. An acceptable compromise usually requires the assistance of some relatively neutral third party—someone whose main source of power is rooted in neither force nor possession of goods and services. This is the classic role of religious elites and intellectuals. Their power is rooted primarily in the status derived from their conformity to norms not directly concerned with the control of force or material resources—typically the possession of esoteric types of knowledge, including ideologies. Such elites are usually experts in the "other world," or even if completely secular, are seen as living in "ivory towers." Somewhat ironically, this detachment gives them the power to provide approval and legitimation for the structures of this world. While they can be extremely useful in legitimizing the use of force or the possession of material resources, they are also dependent on these other types of power: they too need protection and material necessities. As in the relationship between protectors and producers, there is always the question of at what cost. In sum, the different types of power can be mutually supportive, but they also offer much potential for conflicts of interests.

Types of Elites and Their Antagonists: A General Model

The suggested relationship between the different types of power and sanctions implies the emergence of different types of elites with potentially common and conflicting interests. In turn, the notion of elites implies the category of nonelites. A very simple analytical model of the key social categories relevant to many complex societies can be based on three variables: (1) the distinction between elites and nonelites; (2) the differentiation among elites in terms of the three types of power; and (3) the differentiation within both nonelites and each type of elite, based on the strains inherent in the possession of a particular kind of power.[2]

The first distinction is between elites and nonelites. Most people have relatively low levels of political, economic, and status power. In the political and military realm, these nonelites take many more orders than they give, in the economic realm their income is primarily dependent upon their labor, and in the area of status they may be respectable, but they are not notables. Obviously, many strata and cleavages may exist within this broad category. The most fundamental cleavage separates the integral members of a society, who receive at least a minimum level of respect, from those excluded from the society. Most striking are outcast groups, but other examples include the lumpen proletariat, underclasses, political prisoners, slaves, and severely deprived racial, ethnic, and religious groups. The exclusion of such groups usually creates higher levels of solidarity between elites and respectable nonelites than would otherwise occur. Outcasts are a reminder to nonelites that their situation could be much worse; the recurring dilemma for respectable nonelites is whether their antipathies are best directed at elites or at outcasts.

There is also a contradiction within each type of elite. Experts in force have the potential to both protect and exploit. Warrior elites are often seen as little better than those they supposedly protect against; to rephrase Rogers and Hammerstein, they may "'protect' you out of all you own."[3] Telling the police-warrior from the robber-invader is sometimes difficult; to the degree that the distinction can be made, it is based on some concept of law. The legitimate use of force is thus tied to upholding the norms and traditions of the group, which frequently are embodied in some form of law. In modern societies, extralegal changes of regime have most often come about by military coup d'état; changes in agrarian regimes are often brought about by conquering invaders or peripheral robber bands. The ruler's dilemma is how to use force to achieve both elite and societal interests and at the same time to show restraint and respect for traditions and laws, in order to secure legitimacy. The dilemma of the ruled is whether the threats of outsiders and criminals are worse than the demands of political elites.

In the realm of material production, a cleavage often arises between economic elites who control alternative means of production. Typically, this involves a conflict between ascendant means of production and more traditional ones. In agrarian societies, those who control and manage land are threatened by those who specialize in more movable forms of resources, for example, merchants, traders, and bankers. (In contemporary industrial societies, much of the debate over class formation has been over whether a new class is emerging whose power is rooted in knowledge and human capital rather than in ownership of physical capital.) Ironically, those who control the dominant means of production in any given historical period usually need the assistance of those who control the new forms of production, and vice versa. The landed nobility and gentry of preindustrial societies needed the goods and services of commercial elites if they were to have anything but the most provincial of lives, and in turn, they were the main initial market for the luxury goods and money-lending of the commercial elites. While often in competition (both economically and in seeking the support of political and religious elites), the two elites also need each other. It is difficult for established elites to utilize the goods and services of rising elites without at the same time contributing to their legitimacy and wealth, and rising commercial elites face the reverse predicament. The dilemma of each group is how to develop terms of cooperation without harming their long-term interests. Rarely is there a solution; typically, old elites

make a series of short-term accommodations that eventually undercut their dominance (in specific historical circumstances other outcomes are, of course, possible).
As defined here, the cleavages between economic elites are not necessarily based on
old and new means of production, but can simply involve different means.
Examples include cleavages between farmers and herdsmen, or merchants and
bankers or local and long-distance traders.

In intellectual and religious elites, a cleavage often develops between those who
support and legitimate the worldly activities of other elites, and those who are more
critical of these. The ideal-typical distinction here is between priests and prophets
(or renouncers).[4] Priests focus on mediation between this-worldly and otherworldly
perspectives, and normally their primary efforts are toward the legitimation of
worldly structures. In contrast, prophets tend to criticize existing structures or to re-
nounce them as irrelevant and of no value. Intellectuals and religious elites too involved in political and economic structures forfeit an independent basis of status
and legitimacy; professors who become cabinet members soon have their objectiv-
ity questioned, and medieval bishops who became knights and rulers, compromising
their sacral status, were violently dispatched by their enemies like any other feudal
lord. Conversely, complete detachment and rejection of the world makes religious
and intellectual elites' status largely irrelevant to worldly matters, restricting it to
"cloisters" and "ivory towers." Hence intellectuals and religious elites are constantly
under cross-pressures that frequently produce social cleavages in given historical
situations.

This simple model suggests that there are typically three types of elites and a
large population of nonelites, so that there is potential for cooperation and conflict
among these four categories and within each category. The degree to which these
differences have developed varies across societies, in two ways: (1) the degree of
actual functional differentiation varies, and (2) the degree of ideological differentiation varies—that is, the degree to which the "official" picture exaggerates or downplays the actual level of functional differentiation.

Applying the Model to India

Thus far, the argument has been that all complex societies have a tendency to develop four basic categories, which have internal tensions that potentially will produce a further differentiation of each—or a total of eight categories.[5] Particular historical circumstances, of course, will determine whether all the categories are fully
differentiated, and will influence their relative importance.[6] The next step is to specify how the particular historical circumstances of India distinguish it from complex
societies in general. This added information will help us predict and explain (1) why
the four main categories are so explicit and central to Indian cultural discourse, and
(2) which of the eight potential categories are likely to receive special emphasis and
prominence, and which will be more latent.

Clearly, a very large number of historical factors might be considered. One goal
of analysis, however, is parsimony: to account for as much of the data as possible
with the fewest number of explanatory variables. Accordingly, the explanation here

is based, first, on the general model already discussed, and second, on three additional historical characteristics of India: (1) for the period of concern, India has been an agrarian society; (2) relative to other agrarian societies, status in India has been an especially important resource; and (3) the classical social categories of India are largely ideological formulations of Brahmans.

While the general model predicts that eight social categories should be present in India in some form, these historical facts can suggest which categories are likely to be prominent. First, because until recently India has been an agrarian society, categories related to nonagrarian forms of production, such as trade or manufacturing, are likely to be less prominent and less clearly differentiated. Second, because of the relatively great importance of status in India, categories in which power (or powerlessness) is fundamentally tied to status, rather than political or economic power, should be especially prominent. Third, because of the long cultural dominance of Brahmans, categories are likely to have been elaborated and edited in order to make the Brahman category central, to repress the visibility of its competitors, and to explain away contradictions and discrepancies.

The last factor also helps to account for the explicitness and centrality of the varna scheme in Hindu culture.

The Genius of the Brahmans

The varna scheme is ideology, in the sense introduced in Chapter 2; that is, it is a simplified idealized picture of a particular social reality, from the point of view of some subgroup, usually an elite. In this case it is the idealized Brahmanical view of how Indian society is "supposed to be" organized, down-playing crucial conflicts and tensions. It employs editing—leaving out or deemphasizing important competitors and embarrassing facts—and elaboration—creating additional categories to explain away contradictions and inconsistencies. Why is the varna scheme so relatively visible and longstanding in Indian culture, compared to similar schemes in other cultures, when it only vaguely represents the actual social structure? Since the varna scheme represents the Brahmans' view of how the world should be socially organized, the answer lies in the long-term structural importance of Brahmans in this culture.

Between the Aryans' arrival in India (second millennium B.C.E.) and the new Brahmanical synthesis (200 B.C.E.–900 C.E.) represented in the Dharmasastras, the Brahmans made ritual status the core of their identity and the fundamental basis of their power. They were in principle committed to nonviolence (ahimsa), partly because violence was viewed as degrading, and thus compromised their religious purity. Accordingly, they formally assigned political and military power and economic activity to other varnas. Brahmans did, however, control land, often participated in the rule of the various kingdoms in which they found themselves, and on occasion even became warriors (see, e.g., Shulman 1985:110–11, 149–51). Their genius, though, was to avoid making the control of land and labor, or the control of force—the two are intimately related in agrarian societies—the primary basis of their power. These resources are the most alienable and easily appropriated by outside conquerors or upstart discontents, and in India's long and complex history frequently were; in contrast, a highly elaborated lifestyle, emphasizing ritual purity, among other things, was nearly impossible for outsiders to copy or appropriate.

The Brahmans had another genius: they rejected the notion that ritual purity required renunciation and lifelong otherworldliness. While they adopted many of the characteristics of ascetic renouncers, the key social position in the Brahmanical synthesis was the twice-born householder. This enabled the Brahman to combine in one social position the power of the exemplary religious life and active participation in the worldly affairs of an agrarian society. There were two other salutary consequences of their qualified renunciation. First, the Brahmans could biologically and socially reproduce themselves; outsiders did not have to be recruited to a monastic order or special "calling." Second, the religious elite could be geographically dispersed and made an integral part of the agrarian infrastructure. Consequently, conquerors who might be motivated to destroy this religious elite could not do so without the risk of disrupting the agrarian infrastructure on which their privileges ultimately depended. The lands of monasteries can be appropriated with relative ease without disrupting the infrastructure precisely because the nature of monasticism is to be physically and morally separated from the rest of society. Monasteries, while important in Hinduism, have not been as central as in Buddhism or even medieval Christianity. Accordingly Brahmanical Hinduism has been less vulnerable. As priests, Brahmans could demand gifts; at the same time, they could become landholders and thus not be solely dependent on the petty gifts of the masses.

Nonetheless, this attempt to live a relatively ascetic and nonviolent lifestyle "in the world" presented many dilemmas. For example, how could one's purity be maintained if one constantly had to serve as a temple priest for the masses? One of the results of this dilemma was considerable internal differentiation of function, lifestyle, and status among Brahmans, so that they could serve a wide variety of functions and clientele while preserving a common identity.

In short, the genius of the Brahmans was combining a highly regulated and esoteric lifestyle, which gave them an inalienable religious status, with a legitimate opportunity for many of their members to have significant local control over the crucial resources in an agrarian society—land and labor. Dumont is correct in saying that power was encompassed by and made inferior to status. A more accurate way to say this is that power based on religious status was fundamental—in the sense that it was the core of the Brahman's identity, both for himself and others.

I do not envision an ancient sage or group of elders who with unimaginable wisdom plotted out a strategy enabling them to win out over every competitor. Historical outcomes are the result of actors' agency, the opportunities the social structure makes available to particular groups in particular circumstances, and innumerable contingencies. But through some combination of agency and contingency, of genius and luck, the Brahmans developed a cultural tradition that tended to direct their economic, political, and moral interests into the structures outlined above. This tradition played an important role in their ability to maintain a social identity, and often cultural dominance, over three millennia. No group lasts so long on luck alone.[7] Nor can such persistence be due to the beneficence or contrivance of others who "really" had all the power. The key to the maintenance of this self-created role has been the formal assignment of primary political and economic power to others. This attitude and strategy have been generally maintained, at least in principle, well into the modern period.

It seems accurate to refer to this strategy as *ideological delegation*. Such a strategy is not unique to the Brahmans or to India; a primary structural feature of modern capitalism is the formal separation of economic power from political power and moral responsibility for the well-being of the broader society. Capitalists qua capitalists are supposed to pursue their own economic interests; the well-being of the society is supposed to be left to politicians and the Invisible Hand of the market. Under such conditions wealth tends to become the primary basis of status.

Kshatriyas and Sudras

Religious elites that limit or forgo direct involvement in force and political power run the risk of being unable to defend their interests against those who specialize in force and politics. The worldly power that the Brahmans do have is dependent upon the protection provided by kings and warriors. The Brahmans' dilemma is how to translate their religious status into other resources, including wealth, without undercutting that status, the fundamental basis of their power. The king's dilemma is how to get the religious elite to legitimize his political power without becoming too dependent upon them or having to reward them too handsomely. Heesterman has commented:

> [The Brahmin] is—like the renouncer—cut off from the king's world. Indeed, if he is to preserve his transcendent authority, the brahmin must shun the king and all his works, even his gifts and benefices. Yet he cannot live on his purity and transcendence. For his sustenance he is obviously, though contradictorily, dependent on the king whom he should avoid. So the king and brahmin need but cannot reach each other, because the brahmin must opt out of the necessary compact. (1985:201)

Of course, most Brahmans have not opted out completely. Moreover, the Brahman is not the only source of legitimation, and so the Indian king may decide to abandon the Brahman. In short, the Brahman–Kshatriya relationship is vital to both yet full of contradictions.

Contradictions also inhere in Brahmans' relationship with Sudras. Brahmans could not have led exemplary religious lives, requiring high levels of ritual activity, if they had to be self-sufficient in an agrarian society. They had families to support and could not live as frugally as ascetics. The obvious solution was to find or create a class of laborers and servants to relieve them of the more onerous aspects of production; this is one of the key roles of the Sudra varna. The Brahmans stabilized the availability of this labor by providing ritual services to at least the higher status segments of this class, and by enlisting the ruler's support in the demands for such service. However, these relationships make the Brahmans more dependent on the ruler, involve them in the morally ambiguous exercise of power, and bring them into regular contact with those who are less pure. In short, the exemplary lifestyle requires appropriating the labor of others, but ironically this involves Brahmans in relationships that undercut their purity.

Missing Categories

Some social categories that are clearly important in Indian culture are not part of the varna scheme.

Renouncers

Since Dumont's essay on renouncers (sannyasins), it has generally been conceded that they constitute a crucial social category for understanding Indian social structure and culture (Dumont 1980:app. B). In India, as in many societies, the highest religious status goes to renouncers, those who give up worldly comforts and security in their quest for salvation. Even among Brahman householders, the pandit scholar has a higher status than household priest (purohit) or temple priest (pujari), in part because the first most closely resembles the renouncer.[8] As Dumont (1980) and others have indicated, Brahmans have had a highly ambivalent relationship to renunciation. Some of their strongest competitors have been the renouncers and monks of Buddhism, Jainism, and numerous other anti-Brahmanical movements. On the other hand, all Brahmans ideally should become renouncers in the last stage of life, since being tied to the world (as householders necessarily are) is detrimental to one's spiritual well-being. Priestly activity by its nature involves mediating between the sacred and the profane and thus decreases the purity of the mediator. Moreover, to the degree that religious devotion is carried out with the intent of worldly reward, the status acquired from such devotion is seriously compromised. When religious elites are too blatant or rapacious, their followers become cynical, their status is thus lowered, and in turn the economic support they receive from their devotees is reduced. Of little use, then, in providing political legitimacy to warriors and rulers, they also become highly vulnerable to the force these groups wield.[9] The great dilemma for the Brahmans has been how to create a lifestyle that gives them religious virtue comparable to the renouncer's, without becoming asocial and otherworldly like these competitors. As White observes, "while they rejected the renunciant ideology as antisocial, the brahmins were in the process of co-opting many of its elements as a means to maintaining a social and ethical distance from which to exert their authority" (1991:110). The austere and otherworldly life of the renouncers has been both a serious competitive threat to Brahmans and a source of much of their creativity and capacity for religious renewal.[10]

Untouchables

While the classical texts are full of references to outcast groups such as Candalas, Svapaka, and Pulkasa, the Untouchable category is not part of the varna scheme. Outcasts are often associated with the wilderness; they are outside of, rather than part of, organized society (see White 1991:chaps. 4–5). Yet, like renouncers, they are a crucial structural category in the Indian social structure. First, as Dumont clearly argues, the extraordinary purity and status of the Brahmans is in part due to the extraordinary impurity of the Untouchables. This fits with the notion, introduced earlier, that status is a relatively zero-sum resource: if some are to have extraordinary purity, others must have extraordinary impurity. Second, as with all pariah groups, the existence of Untouchables both raises the social status of Sudras and warns them that, whatever their present discomforts, things could be far worse. Though many Sudras compete with Untouchables for employment as laborers, they are not inclined to identify with the lifestyle of those who are closest to them in the mode of production. There are very real, tangible advantages to being even a landless Sudra as compared to being an Untouchable. In conclusion, just as the renouncers are both a crucial and yet implicit rather than explicit category, so are Untouchables.

Bandits

Though it has received little attention in the scholarly literature on South Asia, the category of bandit is an integral element in the system of categories. The bandit is significant not only because he threatens the conventional social order, but because he has the potential to transform himself into a king, the chief guarantor of that order. Shulman's insightful comments on this category are based on South Indian materials, but the general thrust of his remarks seems relevant to all of India:

> [T]he early stage of "raw" power is associated both with banditry and the wilderness. The association is of fundamental importance to the symbolism of the South Indian state: the bandit stands as a basic symbol of unchecked power in its natural, seemingly marginal location. Nevertheless . . . the South Indian bandit also stands remarkably close to the king.
>
> Indeed, the bandit is marginal less because of any geographical considerations than by virtue of his relation to central values, and symbols. . . . [The king] must be seen either to control power through ascetic denial . . . or better still, to surrender it again and again [through gifts]. . . . Failing this, he will be tainted in the eyes of his Brahmin guarantors with the obscenity that always appears to accompany unchecked power. The bandit, on the other hand, has no such compulsion—until the moment he wishes to be king. In his natural, unreconstructed state, he enjoys a pleroma of violent power that he need not hesitate to use. (1985:343–44)

In contrast, the distinguishing characteristic of the king and the legitimate warrior is that he upholds dharma (Gonda 1969a:17–21). Indian culture, or at least the Brahmanical recounting of it, recognizes the ambiguity of the distinction: the king is always in danger of degenerating into the bandit,[11] and the bandit has the potential to become the king.[12]

In sum, renouncers, Untouchables, and bandits are the potential antagonists of Brahmans, Sudras, and Kshatriyas, respectively, but are also their alter egos. Many of the dynamics of Indian culture result from these inherent contradictions.

Ambiguous Categories

Vaisyas: The Anomalous Category

Compared with the other varnas, the Vaisya category is ambiguous and anomalous, in the following senses. First, the sacred texts suggest that a large portion, if not most, of the population falls into this category—yet empirically it contains the smallest number of people. Second, while in Vedic society most Vaisyas must have been farmers or herders, for at least a thousand years the category has referred primarily to merchant castes. Third, even in premodern India, many of those engaged in trading and commercial activity belonged to other varnas. These are anomalies within the culture itself. In addition, on the analytical level, the correspondence between the economic elites of the general model and the Vaisyas of the varna scheme is not very good. These anomalies suggest a need to explore in more detail the nature of economic elites.

Economic Elites in Agrarian Societies

The general model presumes that economic elites are as clearly differentiated as religious and political elites, and more or less on a par with them in terms of social significance. This differentiation, though, depends on a situation in which the means of production, the labor supply, and what is produced are all highly secure, so that some people can concentrate on production and distribution activities.

In several respects, this was not the case in agrarian societies in general, and India in particular. Until the twentieth century, India was an agrarian society, that is, one in which the overwhelming bulk of productive activity was directed toward agriculture and subsidiary activities, and the most characteristic mode of production was the use of the plow by family units to produce food crops. Land is a crucial resource in an agrarian society; and the protection and control of land and labor is continually problematic. The key means of production are physically dispersed: it is impossible to build a wall around all of a society's cultivated land to keep laborers in and marauders out. The population is also dispersed; people may live in protected villages, but these are necessarily scattered and relatively isolated. Farmers in a premodern agrarian society cannot assume that someone called "the police" or "the courts" will adequately protect their "private property." Those who organize and control force, then, will be the primary controllers of the means of production—perhaps sharing control with others, such as vassals, clients and tenants, in highly complex patterns of delegated authority. Accordingly, in agrarian societies, merchants and artisans, who deal in relatively concentrated goods and services that can be protected and transported with relative ease, are usually the only ones whose power is primarily economic, and who come close to being pure economic elites.

As early as the sixth century B.C.E., there were significant numbers of prosperous merchants in India, and between 200 B.C.E. and 300 C.E., they became an important and wealthy community (Thapar 1966:chap. 6). Nonetheless, their trading activities frequently had to be combined with the use of force. The most obvious examples were various merchant warrior groups. Some of these were also members of religious orders, a further indication of the relative lack of differentiation of "pure" economic elites (Cohen 1964; Mines 1984). Even these "mixed" groups are dependent on and vulnerable to political and religious elites, hence their status is usually, at best, ambiguous. They may accumulate great wealth, but they are typically looked down upon by other elites. This situation is reflected in the varna scheme.[13]

Moreover, the overlapping categories of merchant and Vaisya are not and perhaps never were the primary economic elites in Indian society.[14]

Right and Left Castes

If an economic elite is less developed in agrarian societies, differentiation within the Vaisya category is also likely to be less developed than in the other three varnas. Nonetheless, if our general model is a good one, we should find latent differentiation within the economic elite. I want to suggest that the distinction between right (valangai) and left (idangai) castes in South India is just such a differentiation, based in the means and modes of production.[15]

While this cleavage was only fully developed in parts of South India during certain time periods, it is latent and incipient in many parts of the subcontinent. From the tenth century C.E., *valangai* ("right") and related terms began to appear in Tamil inscriptions as a means of identifying certain groups. By the eleventh century, the contrasting term *idangai* ("left") was used in a similar matter. Both terms were used throughout much of Dravidian South India through the nineteenth century; in this century they have gradually fallen into disuse. From the seventeenth through the nineteenth century, they seem to have been especially salient terms to designate conflicting alliances of caste groups.

While clearly at times these terms were associated with sectarian religious disputes and other historically contingent conflicts, these do not seem to be the fundamental basis of the distinction. The contrast between right and left, obviously used in many societies (see Needham 1973), can symbolize a variety of social differentiations and concerns; in South India, it fundamentally refers to various caste groups' location in the relations of production. Right castes are nearly always the local controllers of land, and the castes that are closely allied with or dependent upon them. Left castes are typically artisan and merchant castes and others in conflict with the dominant land controllers. (In some historic situations, left castes are associated with urban settings; Mines [1984] has argued that in medieval times the left castes who were organized as warrior groups played a crucial role in providing economic integration between nucleated agrarian centers separated by unsafe wilderness areas; they provided the means of transporting and exchanging goods across regions.)

Compared to right castes, there is more variation in lifestyle, and less interaction, among the various left castes. Right castes have been referred to as "bounded," that is, tied to land controllers. In contrast, left castes have been referred to as "unbounded," reflecting their variation in social organization.[16] Brahmans (and, apparently, other highly literate castes, such as accountants) seem to be "above" the distinction and the related conflicts. At least during the first few centuries, "left" seems to be used also to designate new "outsider" groups that are being incorporated into Hindu agrarian society. Stated in theoretical terms, these outsider groups seem to be in the process of shifting from preagrarian modes of production into the lower strata of the expanding agrarian society. Stein (1980) emphasizes that right and left are usually coalitions that create regional and even broader alliances, rather than strictly local coalitions or factions.

In addition to differences in economic activity, and the nature of their alliances, dissimilarities in lifestyle and status criteria are apparent. Right castes tend to seek and admire the ability to associate with and dominate others. They are relatively earthy, materialistic, and demonstrative—especially in showing their anger and engaging in physical conflict. They have lavish displays at weddings and similar ceremonies. In some respects, they follow a diminutive version of the kingly model of status. Left castes show a reluctance to be associated with anyone other than their immediate family members and rarely seek to directly dominate others. Even if they are wealthy, they have a minimum number of servants who are kept at a distance. Their actions and demeanor are restrained and controlled. Tendencies toward asceticism, vegetarianism, and unorthodox forms of religion are common. Beck (1972) emphasizes that in contrast to the kingly model, the left castes seem to follow a more Brahmanical lifestyle and concept of status.

In the theoretical terms introduced in Chapter 3, each group uses a different strategy for obtaining and maintaining their status. Right castes emphasize association with higher groups, and the material resources this requires, as a source of status. Left castes emphasize conformity to norms. (As we shall see, this contrast is important at a number of points in differentiating between other categories.)

In contrast to Beck, Mines (1984) emphasizes that left castes do not necessarily follow the Brahmanical lifestyle, and that they tend to replicate within themselves the status differences of the right caste. The most obvious theoretical interpretation of this phenomenon is that groups who are rooted in alternative (and usually lower status) modes of production will use a variety of strategies to transform whatever economic and political power they have into status. In some cases this will involve adapting lifestyles counter to those of the dominant elites (such as land controllers) and in others, imitating their lifestyles. Which strategy is chosen probably depends on how much direct control the dominant groups exert over others' consumption patterns; where sumptuary laws or norms prevent imitation, alternative and counter-lifestyles will be adopted.

Categories of right and left were never explicit in North India, but these distinctions seem latent. As Beck notes, "throughout the subcontinent the artisan communities have attempted to counteract the power of the landed castes with the assertion of superior status on the grounds of the exclusiveness of their caste customs and the orthodoxy of their ritual" (1973:402). In addition, throughout North India the merchant castes are often relative outsiders in the place they live. Banias, Auroas, Agrawals, Marwaris, Bohras, and Khattris, all merchant caste groups, are usually thought to have originated in some specific region but are now widely dispersed in North India (as are Jain, Muslim, and Sikh merchants). Bayly (1983) has stressed the importance of the merchant and service castes' role in the major transformations that occurred in North India from the end of the eighteenth to the end of the nineteenth century under the British. These groups established important networks, despite the long dominance of local agrarian-based castes; while intracaste ties remained important, they were supplemented by extensive intercaste ties crucial to the development of wider markets and a money economy. These castes later were an important element of the middle classes so prominent in the independence movement. In short, while the concept of right and left castes never developed in North

India, the latent basis of such a distinction, rooted in largely nonagrarian modes of production, was certainly present.

Much of the conflict that developed between right and left castes in the South occurred over the honors and "shares" received during temple worship and the various processions associated with this. That is, conflict arose over the ability of these two groups to have their relative status publicly validated. This is probably one reason why in certain periods the right–left distinction has been linked to sectarian religious disputes. Perhaps the differentiation of the two groups remained more latent in the North because, in contrast to the South, temple worship never played as crucial a role in either religious activities or political integration.

In short, the left and right distinction seems to be primarily rooted in alternative modes of production, which are then often intertwined with other bases of conflict such as sectarian religious disputes. This is what our general model of elites would predict, and parallel phenomena are seen in many societies.

The Prominence of Certain Categories

As I have argued, most complex societies have some equivalent of priests, prophets (or renouncers), and at least quasi outcasts; nonetheless, these categories are more prominent in Indian culture than in most others. If you ask either foreigners or Indians what social categories are most distinctly Indian, the answer would not be bandits, merchants, farmers, or kings—nor the non-Brahman categories of the varna scheme. India is famous for Brahmans, holymen,[17] and Untouchables.

The greater salience of these three social categories is rooted in the unique importance in India of status as a source of power and powerlessness.[18] The pivotal role and decisive contribution of Brahmans has already been discussed. Ascetic holymen are common in many societies, but in India the tradition of renunciation has developed the techniques and importance of asceticism more elaborately than probably anywhere else. Central to this culture is the concept of tapas (heat generated by austerities) and the status the observance of these austerities confers. Many societies have despised groups—slave societies and modern concentration and labor camps have been more brutal, and underclasses in industrial societies may be even more disadvantaged economically, relative to average levels of well-being, than Untouchables in India. But nowhere else has such an extensive and indispensable outcast group developed whose exclusion is so dependent on negative religious status. Given the centrality of status, it is not accidental that India's lower social strata are "outcasts" rather than prisoners, slaves, paupers, or the unemployed.

The Presence and Absence of Varnas

The cultural prominence of a category is, at best, weakly related to its empirical occurrence. The cultural significance of unicorns is not due to their empirical frequency. It is the exception for castes from all four varnas to be found in the same local area, much less in the same village. The pattern of deviance from the classic scheme is not random, though; the Kshatriya and Vaisya categories are most likely to be unrepresented, while the vast majority of local areas (though not necessarily each village) have Brahmans and Sudras. Moreover, a Sudra caste is frequently the dominant local land controller (in pre-British and colonial India, such Sudra castes sometimes provided the local ruling king).

Why are two of the categories present in nearly every local area in India, while the other two are often unrepresented? In terms of our earlier theoretical discussion, the functions of the Kshatriya and Vaisya varnas are based on alienable resources that can be easily appropriated by others. Obviously, warriors and rulers can be defeated and replaced by other warriors, and in turn they can redistribute land and political offices to their followers. Moreover, in this part of the varna system, status is more directly based on material resources. The Kshatriya who does not rule or the Vaisya who has no property is easily dismissed as a pretender. Of course, the same is true for the Brahman who has no Vedic or ritual knowledge. The difference is that outsiders and upstarts are much more likely to be able to appropriate goods, land, or political control—and are generally much more interested in doing so—than ritual knowledge and religious status. Hence it is not surprising that, taking Indian history as a whole, the Kshatriya varna is a highly fluid one. In fact there are textual myths that depict the destruction of all Kshatriyas (see Shulman 1985:110–28). The specific jatis claiming to be Kshatriyas are highly variable from one region to another; many regions have few or no jatis with convincing claims to that varna. On the other hand (as noted in our discussion of bandits) it is very common historically for a Sudra jati to have successfully conquered an area and eventually claimed Kshatriya status (Mandelbaum 1970:452–55; Shulman 1985: chap. 7).

In South India, the absence of Kshatriyas in part reflects the fact that Brahmanism and its social categories came from the North. Such historical or diffusion explanations are, however, insufficient: they do not explain why Brahmans are virtually everywhere in the South and why important areas of the North (e.g., Bengal) have no Kshatriyas.

As already indicated, jatis claiming Vaisya status are relatively rare. Typically, they are merchants; only a few landholding agricultural castes claim to be Vaisyas. On the other hand, many of the merchants in India are not Vaisyas, but are from other varnas and non-Hindu religious groups. Just as warriors can be defeated, outsiders can acquire movable goods with relative ease and enter into trading.

It may be relatively easy for upstart groups to appropriate the functions of Kshatriyas and Vaisyas, but because status is relatively inalienable, appropriating their varna category is much more difficult. It requires the acquiescence of the other castes in an area, especially Brahmans. While in some cases lower castes have been successful in making such a transition, in many cases they have not, hence these categories are relatively underrepresented.

To summarize: Brahmans (and Untouchables) are nearly universal because their religious status is a relatively inalienable resource. The universality of Sudras is rooted in the indispensability of labor in an agrarian society.[19] In contrast, the resources required to carry out the functions of the Kshatriya and the Vaisya can be acquired through force or shrewdness by castes not in those varnas, most typically

Sudras. The consequences are manifold. In some historical situations, Kshatriyas and Vaisyas have disappeared from places where they were once important. In other situations, it was possible for Hinduism to become well established without these social categories, because jatis of other varnas carried out the functions of Kshatriyas and Vaisyas satisfactorily. In still other situations, those originally of other varnas took on these functions and then claimed to be Kshatriyas or Vaisyas. Thus, the distribution of jatis identified with the Kshatriya and Vaisya varnas is unstable and erratic compared to the near universality of Brahmans and Sudras.

Elaboration: Asramas and Yugas

What we have described so far is "editing"—the maintenance of ideological versions of reality by omitting some categories, keeping some ambiguous, and emphasizing others. Now we turn to "elaboration"—the creation of additional interpretations and categories. The asrama scheme (the four life stages of twice-born males) and the yuga scheme (the four stages of degeneration between the creation and destruction of the cosmos) can be seen as elaborated categories whose purpose is to explain away discrepancies and thus buttress the credibility of the primary categories.[20]

Not surprisingly, categories such as bandits and outcasts are studiously left out of the cardinal Brahmanical schemes; but other categories are too important to leave out, even if they sometimes point to embarrassing discrepancies or conflicts. The renouncers (sannyasins) are sometimes the Brahmans' chief critics and competitors, yet the category cannot be simply ignored or rejected, because the Brahmans' own ideals are in part rooted in the renouncers' asceticism and discipline. The creation of the varnasramadharma scheme, which relegates the role of sannyasin to the last of four (largely hypothetical) stages of life, thus incorporates the tradition of the renouncer into the Brahmanical varna scheme. It provides a rationale for how Brahmans can be both ascetic, celibate renouncers and householders, who own land and have families.

This elaboration creates a new discrepancy: very few Brahmans ever move beyond the householder (grihastha) stage to become sannyasins. Perhaps equally embarrassing, many renouncers are not Brahmans. This contradiction too has been dealt with by elaboration. In the scheme of yugas, the present is always seen as the last most degenerate stage, the Kali Yuga, in which humans are no longer capable of conforming to the divine categories like varna and asrama in the way they did in previous ages. Nonetheless, the categories and the relationships suggested are valid, since they are part of the very cosmos itself.

I am not implying that the process of elaboration literally occurred in the manner and sequence I have outlined, nor that the rationales I have given were the only ones operating. There were probably many motivations for creating the yuga and the varnasramadharma schemes; it seems likely, though, that the social pressures and mechanisms I have described played a role in the creation and maintenance of this particular structure of cultural categories.

Conclusion

In this chapter I have provided a particular kind of explanation of why some categories are present in the Indian culture and others are absent or latent, and of their variations in saliency and frequency. A second purpose of this chapter has been methodological and theoretical. Considerable scholarly effort has been devoted to various kinds of structural analyses of social categories. Structural anthropologists in general, and Lévi-Strauss in particular, have been leaders in this endeavor. Das's work (1982) is an excellent example of this technique applied to India. Shulman (1985) has also concentrated on social types, using a more eclectic "tool box" approach to the problem.[21] His work provides a much more detailed and richly textured discussion of some of the categories I have considered, and I have drawn on some of his ideas extensively. Perhaps even more seminal are the various essays by Heesterman (1985).

As useful as such analyses may be, our understanding can be further advanced by asking more explicitly about the connection between key social categories and the types of sanctions and patterns of resources that are characteristic of a society. This is not an argument for any kind of simple reductionism. The kind of analysis provided here is not the only legitimate way to analyze cultural categories; many categories have not been considered, and many important features of the categories considered have not been analyzed. What this type of analysis does provide is a systematic framework for identifying the kinds of categories likely to be important, and a tool for comparative analysis. These applications are suggested most clearly in the parallel drawn between the general model of elites/nonelites and the varna scheme, and in the analysis of right and left groups.

The same kind of analysis is relevant to other societies. For example, it is not accidental that in U.S. society the terms "politician" and "government official" (not to mention "government bureaucrat") have deeply rooted negative connotations. This is not the case for such terms as "businessman," "corporate executive," or even "capitalist." This distinction is clearly related to the relative importance and legitimacy attributed to different types of resources and power in American culture.

The point is obvious once it has been said, and many of the connections suggested in the analysis of Indian categories will be obvious to South Asianists. The "trick," however, is to fit these obvious points into a larger pattern of connections and understanding: that has been the goal of this chapter, and is a key aim of the book.

7

The Articulation of Status
and Material Resources:
Political and Economic Legitimacy

The Analytical Problem

Since this is a book about the nature of status and sacral relationships, an extensive analysis of India's enormously complex political and economic structures is beyond the scope of this endeavor. Rather, the task at hand is to indicate some of the key links between the status order and the organization of political and economic power. The essence of political and economic power in an agrarian society is the control of land and labor. This chapter considers the ways such control is dependent on the status order, and more specifically, how a theory of status relations can help us understand the mechanisms used to produce political legitimacy.

Because exercising force and controlling land and labor are so intimately related in agrarian societies, I will not usually differentiate between the political and the economic. The relevant contrast for the analysis that follows is between the status order and the material resources of the political (cum economic) structures. In part, this is an analytical simplification.[1] This simplification is, however, also present in Indian culture in the contrast between dharma and artha.[2] As we have seen, the first is concerned with right conduct and is especially associated with Brahmans. The second refers to the pursuit of material interests broadly conceived, and is especially associated with kings.

As I have stressed earlier, status and material forms of power, like the sacred and the profane, must to a significant degree be separated and insulated from one another. For certain purposes, though, they must be reunited and linked. In this sense, this chapter focuses on the articulation of these two types of resources. The aspect of such articulation that will receive primary attention is political legitimacy.

What Is to Be Explained

Even in considering political legitimacy, the analysis will be selective. I will concentrate on explaining the following features of premodern Hindu political structures:

1. Why the concept of *rajadharma*, the duties of the king, is so central to kingly legitimacy in India and why it creates pressures for other sources of legitimacy.
2. Why the form of the premodern Indian state varies from one locality and time period to another, and more specifically, why it has sometimes been characterized as a priestly theocracy, other times as an absolute monarchy, and yet other times as a clan monarchy or brotherhood of warriors.
3. Why implicit exchange in the form of gifts, and especially those gifts referred to as "dana," is a key mechanism for maintaining political legitimacy at virtually all levels of the society.
4. Why the recipients and types of gifts emphasized varies depending upon which of the three types of state mentioned above is dominant.
5. Why the mode of allocating the grain harvest referred to as the "*jajmani* system" has been a key mechanism for maintaining the legitimacy of local land controllers, and how this both reflects and diverges from the mechanisms of legitimacy used at higher levels of political dominance.

The Concept of Legitimacy

One way to conceptualize the effect of the status order on the political and economic orders is in terms of the concept of legitimacy. How is the political order and the control of economic resources transformed from a system of pure coercion and violence to one in which orders and laws are obeyed because they are believed to be valid and morally binding—or more typically, into something in between these two poles? Movement in the direction of this second state is what Weber referred to as "legitimacy." While a full discussion of Weber's use of this term and the literature it has stimulated would lead us on a protracted tangent, a brief quote will give the main import of his concept:

> An order which is adhered to from motives of pure expediency is generally much less stable than one upheld on a purely customary basis through the fact that the corresponding behavior has become habitual. . . . But even this type of order is in turn much less stable than an order which enjoys the prestige of being considered binding, or, as it may be expressed, of "legitimacy." The transitions between orientation to an order from motives of tradition or of expediency to the case where a belief in its legitimacy is involved are empirically gradual. (1968:31)

Weber's characterization of a legitimate order as one having prestige is significant. In my terminology, it is a regime receiving approval and hence a positive status.[3] Earlier I suggested sacredness is a special form of status. The same is true for legitimacy. Thus the process of gaining political legitimacy has parallels with the processes of gaining status.

Legitimacy can be usefully thought of as a preliminary or primary form of status; not necessarily approval of one's actions, but rather, approval of one's right to act in certain circumstances. An example may help to clarify this distinction. I was never a great admirer of Richard Nixon. Rarely did I approve of his actions as president. Nonetheless I acknowledged—even approved of—his right to be president, since he had been elected by apparently legal procedures. As far as I was concerned, there was a weak correlation between his status and his legitimacy. On the other hand, generalized status must fall within broad parameters for there to be political legitimacy. When the full scope of the Watergate scandal became apparent, I could no longer approve of even his right to be president. Even many of those who had been great admirers of Nixon reacted similarly, and accordingly, he lost his political legitimacy. In this sense, political legitimacy is logically a primary or preliminary form of status. This distinction is present in most societies, though the explicitness varies with historical context.

As we have seen, there are two primary ways to affect one's status: conformity and association. Thus we should expect these to be the main mechanisms for acquiring political legitimacy. Let us examine some of the ways these processes work in India.

Legitimacy as Conformity: Rajadharma

How does an Indian king or chieftain maintain his legitimacy? First and foremost, like virtually all rulers in agrarian societies, he has to be an effective organizer of military power, both to subordinate and protect his subjects. He is likely to stay in power longer and rule more effectively, however, if he gains some legitimacy. Discussions of legitimacy focus on relating the exercise of power, particularly the use of sanctions, to general principles—and in most historical contexts, to some notion of law (see, e.g., Giddens 1984:29–31; Poggi 1990:7–8). Legitimacy is supposedly increased by reducing blatant arbitrariness and contingency in the exercise of power. Stated another way, rulers are more likely to get subjects to conform to commands and norms if the state itself conforms to certain types of norms.

As we have seen, dharma is the key Hindu category relating to principles, norms, and laws. Perhaps the key subcategory of dharma is rajadharma, the duties of the king. In the Hindu tradition, the king is not the promulgator of laws, but their enforcer. The explication of the divine law is the task of the Brahman. The king's duties, as described in the sacred texts, are extensive and demanding. In addition to being a valiant and enthusiastic warrior, the king must be a wise judge (unrelenting in the punishment of evil and yet merciful), appoint honest and able ministers, be extremely shrewd in his relations with enemies and potential enemies, honor Brahmans, perform religious rituals regularly, provide extensive gifts to many, avoid excesses in drink and gambling, limit his sensuality, prevent the intermarriage of castes, make sure everyone follows his legitimate occupation and lifestyle (svadharma), and more generally protect and uphold the caste order (varnasramadharma). Last but not least, he is held responsible for good rains and the fertility of the land.[4] In short, he must be the very paragon of virtue, wisdom, and power. While many of the expectations outlined in the sacred texts are Brahman ideology, in part intended to keep the king on the defensive, Hindu culture actually expected much of its kings. Unsurprisingly, kings sought mechanisms of legitimacy other than conformity to the norms, since living up to the cultural ideal was virtually impossible.

Legitimacy by Association

The other key way to increase one's legitimacy is to create alliances. One tactic is to associate with those who have high status. The astute researcher who is submitting a funding proposal will persuade prestigious members of the profession to serve as consultants and to allow their names to be listed in the proposal. Such consulting has been known to involve a generous fee for modest and sometimes quite ritualistic levels of work. A variation on this tactic is to develop associations with prestigious elites from other sectors of society: business schools create advisory committees of important leaders from commerce and industry, English departments invite prestigious authors to be writers-in-residence, political science departments induce well-known politicians to lecture their students and faculty. Though both patterns involve upward association, one seeks out those who have similar functions and responsibilities, while the other aims at those who have different responsibilities. A second tactic for attaining legitimacy is to seek the support and appreciation of one's subordinates.[5] The instructor who does not get along with his departmental chairperson is more secure if his classes are heavily enrolled and he is beloved by his students. Such popularity requires some technical competence—that is, conformity to norms of one's discipline and institution. Equally important, though, is the careful management of one's associations with students; one can neither be too aloof nor too familiar.

The wise ruler also seeks such legitimating associations. Parallels are found in the Indian context and these require more extended discussion.

Alternative Coalitions: A Model

While coalitions and associations with Brahmans were the most common means by which Hindu kings gained legitimacy, other types of alliances were also important to producing both legitimacy and the material bases of power. A simple model captures the major possibilities and their consequences. Hindu kings or chieftains had primarily three potential categories of actors with whom they could build alliances: Brahmans, other more powerful kings, and other subordinate warriors. A strong emphasis on any one of these possibilities suggests three ideal-type state structures. A primary reliance on Brahmans moves things in the direction of a state in which priests are the power behind the throne. Perhaps Dharbhanga under the influence of the ancient and influential Maithila Brahmans, and in some periods even a Brahman king, approximates this model. The second alternative is to rely especially on subordinate warriors for support. Here legitimacy is rooted in a brotherhood of warriors, or a clan monarchy rooted in kinship and hypergamous marriages that links different strata of the warriors together. The small Rajput kingdoms of North India approximate this model. Brahmans were present, but were relatively poor and powerless compared to the Rajputs, or Brahmans in many other areas. This pattern was probably more common before the Moghol and British conquests (see Hutton 1963:95). The third alternative is a hierarchy of kings. Alliances are made with yet grander kings, not only to avoid their wrath or gain their political support, but also because this provides additional legitimacy. At the top of this hierarchy is the *chakravartin* king, who is the direct representative or even the incarnation of the great god Visnu; he adds legitimacy and splendor to all those who become associated with him. The South Indian kingdoms such as the Pallavas and the Cholas approximated this model.

Many of the debates over the nature of Indian kingship have in effect been arguing for the precedence of one of these models over the other.[6] I would argue that all three of these strategies were used in different times and places. Kings frequently used complex combinations of the three—plus other alliances. For example, while the Cholas claimed chakravartin status, Brahmans played a crucial role in secular as well as religious matters. In all three of these possible strategies, Brahmans, and by extension castes and renunciation, were important. Now that the model has helped to identify the main forms of legitimating associations, let us consider the key content of such linkages.

Kings and Gifts

Gifts are a central component of all three types of alliances just outlined. Whether gifts were more significant in Indian polity than in other agrarian polities is difficult to say, but probably they were. Unquestionably, they were a central feature of kingly rule in India and, as we shall see later, of local forms of dominance. The centrality and pervasiveness of gifts can hardly be overemphasized. Most of the inscriptions that form the primary sources for South Indian history are records of such gifts. Clearly, from as far back as the eleventh century, and possibly much earlier, gifts were a major means of establishing legitimacy for rulers.

Gifts are central because the desired goal is political legitimacy, a form of approval and status. As we have seen, "buying" this in any explicit way is self-defeating. Thus gifts are used as an aspect of implicit exchange relations. As we saw in Chapters 3 and 5, there are two types of exchange: what Trautmann (1981:278) contrasts in the Indian contexts as sacred and profane exchange and noble and ignoble exchange. Which type of implicit exchange receives emphasis depends upon which of the three types of alliances is being established or maintained. Now let us examine the types of gifts that are characteristic of each of these types of alliances.

Kings and Religious Elites

As the preceding chapter indicated, Brahmans and Kshatriyas tend to use different strategies for acquiring power and privilege.[7] Brahmans attempt to carefully maintain and improve their ritual purity, by meticulously following the norms that reduce pollution, and by being careful not to associate with those who are less pure. Often this practice limits the pursuit and maintenance of material resources.[8] In contrast to Brahmans, warrior-kings are supposed to be primarily concerned about the pursuit of material interests—in developing control of the key resources of an agrarian society—that is, land and labor. Accordingly, they created wide-ranging alliances with a variety of castes, including those of relatively low status. The nature of their control often required rather extensive interaction with others. While they were not unconcerned about their ritual and religious status, they were less finicky about the norms of purity and pollution. In fact the key function of their role, the exercise of force, necessarily involves them in pollution. So does any direct involvement in agricultural production, which inevitably includes such activities as plowing, cutting grain, castrating bullocks, and so on. In the Brahmanical view, these activities implicate one in violence. Warrior-kings' preoccupation with the pursuit of wealth and political power significantly limits their ritual status.

An obvious strategy for mitigating the material vulnerabilities of religious elites and the moral vulnerabilities of political elites is some form of alliance between them, in which material resources flow in one direction and moral approval flows in the other. This is a key aspect of the relationship between Brahmans and warrior-kings. Because of the need to keep such exchanges implicit, gifts play a central role.

As we have seen, the paradigmatic type of gift was directed toward Brahmans and related religious institutions. This is the first type of exchange discussed by Trautmann. Such gifts included donations for temples, monasteries, facilities for pilgrims, the cost of sacrifices, and the like. Brahmans are needed to carry out worship and other ritual activities properly. Rulers at nearly all levels of Hindu society devoted substantial resources to supporting Brahmans and their ritual activities. More was involved than simply winning favor. Gifts are part of a sacramental religious ritual, and many are a particular type of gift referred to as "dana." Dana contains the sin (*pap*) that rulers necessarily acquire in carrying out their activities. Only Brahmans have the purity to receive this sin and digest or transform it.[9] Nonetheless, in receiving such gifts, Brahmans inevitably compromise their own purity. Therefore, however avaricious their actual behavior, they usually profess a reluctance to accept gifts. Moreover, this eliminates any need to directly reciprocate, since to return such a gift would be to return the sin and inauspiciousness attached to it. These matters will be considered in Chapters 10 and 11. Now we shift our attention from relations between political elites and religious elites to relations among the political elite.

Relations Between Rulers

Gifts were also used to maintain relationships between different levels of rulers. Here we are dealing primarily with what Trautmann terms noble and ignoble exchange. As recent research has emphasized, multiple levels of kingship existed: little kings acknowledged the superiority of bigger kings, and they in turn gave deference to still greater kings (Richards 1981; Inden 1982; Dirks 1987). Dirks describes the basic form of this relationship:

> Like the relations of worship established in puja, the root political metaphor, political
> relations commence when a lesser king or noble offers service to a greater lord or
> king. They [the political relations] are "established" once the service is recognized in
> the form of gifts made by the superior to the inferior. Gifts [to the subordinate] in-
> clude titles, emblems and honors, rights to enjoy the usufruct of particular lands,
> and/or the privilege to rule on behalf of the superior over a particular area. (1987:47)

These gifts did not, however, involve a transfer of any kind of absolute ownership
or authority. Typically, they entailed the right to use or collect some portion of what
the land or other gift produced.[10]

Not infrequently the "gift" "returned" by superiors was the land or territory the
subordinate had previously ruled on his own or in relationship to some other superior king. Undoubtedly, such relationships were often established because the subordinate found this less objectionable than the alternatives the superior king threatened. Yet the subordinate's motivation for establishing such relationships was by no
means always military intimidation. Such relationships allowed kings to gain legitimacy that was partly independent of their association with Brahmans. Subordinate
kings gained legitimacy through their association with superiors; greater kings
gained legitimacy by the deference subordinate kings offered them. Sometimes
these relationships were primarily ritualistic; little kings offered grander kings ritualized deference, but not much else in the way of material resources or even assistance in war. Here too the Hindu puja served as a model and metaphor for the relationship between superiors and subordinates; gifts were offered to superiors, but
after being accepted, the bulk of the gift was returned to the giver as a symbol of the
sacred ties between the superior and the subordinate. This model seems to have
been especially important in South India during and after the Pallava dynasty, as a
means of extending solidarities beyond the royal family.[11]

In my theoretical terms, this exchange made possible status based on association
rather than simply on conformity. As pointed out earlier, staking one's legitimacy
solely on conformity to rajadharma was risky indeed. In addition to whatever military and economic support such alliances might provide, these linked hierarchies of
kings provided an additional source of status and legitimation, both for the superior
and the subordinate. The legitimizing effect of these linkages was strengthened by
developments in Puranic thinking that defined kings as incarnations of gods, usually
Visnu; there was now a legitimizing religious link from kings to the divinity not
solely dependent on the ritual actions of Brahmans. The association between kings
and divinity was further reinforced by a number of important rituals and festivals.
The celebration of the Navaratri (known in eastern India as Durga Puja), and the Ram
Lila (in Hindi-speaking North India) were especially important. The details of these
festivals were complex and variable, but the essential idea was that a sacrifice was
sponsored and sometimes even conducted by a king, commemorating and reenacting
the defeat of a mythical demon-king who threatened the dharmic order. A key thrust
of these festivals was to identify the king with the deity who defeats evil and reestablishes justice and prosperity, and thus associate the social order with the divine
cosmic order.[12] These festivals are still celebrated in contemporary India, though, of
course, kings no longer exercise political power.

These features of relationships between lesser and greater kings are seen in a relatively well-formulated indigenous paradigm of kingship. Rama, the hero of the *Ramayana*, is the famous example. This archetype seems to have had long-term and widespread significance in shaping the patterns of political and economic dominance at the macro level of organization. It was imported into Southeast Asia and modified in various ways. The basic features of the paradigm are seen in Tambiah's (1976) descriptions of Thailand and Geertz's (1980) descriptions of nineteenth-century Bali.

Relationships with Subordinates

The distinction between warriors, chieftains, and kings—at least lower-level kings—is rarely clear-cut. The successful warrior has often managed to transform himself into a king. Nonetheless, as my model of different types of legitimating associations suggests, an analytical distinction is useful between upward alliances (with those whom all would acknowledge as kings) and downward alliances (with those whom few would acknowledge as kings). The trick to successful downward alliances was to create solidarity and commitment and still be able to exercise authority and receive deference. Consequently, in some contexts the relationship is defined as a relationship between peers, while for other purposes, the emphasis is on inequality.

As I have suggested, the small Rajput kingdoms approximate the downward model. In this context the primary form of gift was a bride, or more specifically, the *kanyadana,* or gift of a virgin. Typically, multiple strata of the same caste are more or less formally differentiated. The ideal is for a man to marry a woman of a slightly inferior status. This creates a series of kinship linkages between superior and inferior strata of the warrior caste. We will explore this phenomenon at some length in Chapter 11, which focuses on marriage alliances. Two key points are relevant for the argument here. First, associations between those unequal in status are a key form of political alliance. While such cross-strata alliances are motivated by a number of concerns and have a number of consequences, one important effect is to buttress the solidarity between such strata and consequently the political legitimacy of those at the top. Second, the primary mechanism for maintaining such alliances and associations is also a particular form of gift or dana. This is what the general theoretical argument would lead us to expect.

To focus on marriage alliances is not to suggest that the other types of alliances and exchanges are not present. Nonetheless, a striking feature of this type of kingdom is the political importance of marriage alliances, not only by the royal family, but throughout the warrior castes.

Diverse Gifts, Similar Effects

In all three types of alliances—Brahmans and kings, kings and kings, kings and subordinates—gifts were the primary mechanism of establishing the alliances and associations needed. Yet the specific nature of the gift varies. In the case of giving to Brahmans, the gift is given upward to a ritual superior and this is a form of dana.

The same is true of the relationship between superiors and subordinates in Rajput warrior clans. The gift of a virgin bride (kanyadana) is from the inferior to the superior. In contrast, in the relationship between kings, the emphasis is on the gift of the superior to the subordinate. Here the gift is analogous to the food offering (prasada) of the puja; most of what has been given by the inferior is returned after it has been "tasted" by the deity—and increased in religious value. I have been unable to find clear evidence of whether or not such gifts would be called "dana."[13] It is also unclear how carefully and explicitly the actors involved would draw explicit distinctions between these three types of gift giving. They are all, however, part of the overall responsibility of kings to give gifts, and with respect to political legitimacy they are aspects of a common process.

Up to this point, the discussion has focused primarily on relationships between different elites. Equally important is the process by which legitimacy is maintained at the lower levels of a society. Here the focus is more on economic legitimacy than political legitimacy in its narrow sense—though as I emphasized at the beginning of this chapter, the line between the political and the economic in agrarian societies is a thin and ambiguous one. More concretely, we now come to the crucial question of how elites went about organizing local production and distribution—and this question brings us to the jajmani system.

The Jajmani System

When nineteenth-century Westerners looked at the mode of organizing labor in rural India, they implicitly compared it to two other more familiar modes. One was the "free" labor market of laissez-faire capitalism; the other was slavery. Against this backdrop, the organization of labor in agrarian India seemed relatively idyllic. Force and coercion were apparently less frequent and harsh than under slavery (or even Western medieval feudalism), and levels of social solidarity seemed high compared with the industrializing West. Undoubtedly these observers romanticized what they saw, yet perhaps their characterization contained a significant element of truth. Virtually all agrarian societies depended on considerable amounts of force, not to speak of less violent forms of coercion, to organize production and carry out distribution. This was certainly true of India. Compared to other agrarian societies, labor discipline was probably less dependent on the direct exercise of force, and local elites had relatively high levels of legitimacy. This is not to ignore the fact that peasants more or less continually resisted domination and at times engaged in open rebellion.

The social institution known as the jajmani system was one factor contributing to a relatively low level of open conflict. "Jajman" is a term with origins in the earliest periods of Vedic religion. The antecedent cognates referred to those who paid for elaborate Vedic sacrifices. In recent centuries, the core meaning of the term has referred to householders for whom Brahmans carry out religious rituals in exchange for gifts and fees (Dumont 1980:98); they are at the center of the jajmani system, which involves exchanges of a wide array of practical and ritual services. Kolenda gives a succinct description of the system:

Briefly, the *jajmani* system is a system of distribution in Indian villages whereby high-caste landowning families called *jajmans* are provided services and products by various lower castes such as carpenters, potters, blacksmiths, water carriers, sweepers, and laundrymen. Purely ritual services may be provided by Brahman priests and various sectarian castes, and almost all serving castes have ceremonial and ritual duties at their *jajman's* births, marriages, funerals, and at some of the religious festivals. Important in the latter duties is the lower castes' capacity to absorb pollution by handling clothing and other things defiled by birth or death pollution, gathering up banquet dishes after the feasts, and administering various bodily attentions to new mother, bride or groom.

    The landowning *jajmans* pay the serving castes in kind, with grain, clothing, sugar, fodder, and animal products like butter and milk. Payment may amount to a little of everything produced on the land, in the pastures, and in the kitchen. Sometimes land is granted to servants, especially as charity to Brahman priests. In this system, the middle and lower castes either subscribe to each other's services in return for compensations and payments, or exchange services with one another. (1981:12)

Several other features should be mentioned. The jajmani relationship is usually between families. A particular patron (jajman) family is linked to a particular serving family (*kaman*) of barbers, washermen, and so forth. These links between families tend to persist over time and, in principle, are inherited from one generation to the next. Some types of services and goods—normally expensive items needed only irregularly, for example jewelry for a wedding, or a new wagon—are not covered by the basic payments. These are negotiated on a case-by-case or piece work basis.

Analytically Decomposing the System

A number of scholars have focused their analyses specifically on the jajmani system (Wiser 1958; Gould 1958, 1967; Beidelman 1959; Harper 1959; Kolenda 1981; Raheja 1988; Fuller 1989) and a number of others have discussed jajmani relations as part of village studies (for example, Dube 1955; Lewis 1958; Mayer 1960). David Pocock (1962) has made two insightful suggestions about how best to proceed in the analysis of this phenomenon. First, he raises the question of whether jajmani relations should be considered a system at all. Second, he stresses the importance of distinguishing between "two categories in the complex of relationships known as the 'jajmani system'" (1962:91). The first category is "religious specialists"—Brahmans, barbers, sweepers—whose services are essential to the purity and status of their jajmans. The second are castes whose function is primarily "mere economic activity" and to which a ritual status is ascribed only by extension of the ideology of caste. Fuller (1989) extends the process of decomposition, pointing to another distinct "system" that in western India is referred to as the *baluta* system. In this system, services are not provided primarily to individual land controllers but to the village as a whole. The grain they are given at harvest time is made on behalf of the village as a whole. The providers of services are frequently quasi officials, such as village watchmen.

    In addition to there being more than one "system," Fuller points out, trade, money, and private property were important from very early periods in India, and laborers were often paid in money rather than in kind. His more general point is that the view of the isolated village sustained by barter and premarket "traditional" personal relationships greatly exaggerates the *Gemeinschaft* features of premodern Indian society and underestimates the variations over time and space. (He is not suggesting, however, that nonmarket relationships, such as those referred to as "jajmani" and "batula," are not an important feature of Indian village life.)

To understand the articulation of status and material resources, the process of decomposition needs to be taken even further. Four distinct sets of interests and social processes can be distinguished. First, jajmans (and land controllers in most agrarian societies) are concerned about securing reliable servants. Servants relieve elites of arduous and demeaning work and give ritualistic deference. Such services are highly valued, even when they involve a clear economic cost rather than a gain in total material resources. This occurs even in societies where concerns about pollution or inauspiciousness are marginal or nonexistent. Second, there are the specific concerns about ritual pollution; here the key actors are what Gould (1967) calls "contrapriests," who remove and absorb impurities. Upper castes must have these services to maintain their purity and ritual status. Barbers, washermen, and night soil collectors are examples of such contrapriests. Third, specialized artisans often create guilds in order to limit competition and improve their bargaining power. Fourth, land controllers in a number of societies attempt to secure an adequate supply of low-cost agricultural laborers by creating stigmatized, outcast groups.

Nearly all elites try to secure for themselves personal services that have little or nothing to do with technical efficiency or production; they are primarily matters of privilege, ego gratification, and status enhancement. In Western feudal societies, the significance of cupbearers, footmen, pages, falconers, maids-in-waiting, and the like had as much to do with increasing the status and dignity of the ruling classes as with functional services. Such servants and assistants were typically retainers rather than employees, which reduced their autonomy. Those of high status are reluctant to haggle over small transactions, for this lowers their dignity; if one has to bargain or explicitly threaten, one's status is implicitly called into question. We see the same tendency in the jajmani system in the preference for annual or seasonal payments, gifts, and concessions rather than direct payment for explicit services. Moreover, when retainers are dependent on patrons on a long-term basis, they are more likely to show ritualistic deference. As Kolenda says about the *hali* system, a form of indentured servitude in Gujarat studied by Breman, "having *halis* was a matter of status and prestige, more than a matter of economic need. A man was judged by the number of servants he could provide for, not by the number he needed; they were retainers giving a man power in the village" (1984:59). Such status and authority is not free. Patrons must take responsibility for meeting the minimum needs of their servants, even when it is not in their immediate interests to do so. "The *hali's* [plowman/servant] position was not considered to be one of degradation, but rather one of considerable security, since his master was obliged to provide for all the needs of the hali and his family" (Kolenda 1984:58). So what often emerges in such situations is a system of exchange relationships: there are high levels of status and material inequality, high levels of interdependence (usually resulting in minimal economic security for the subordinate), and at least certain types of social solidarity.

In short, there is both inequality and symbiosis. These relationships can be usefully described as symbiotic inequality.[14]

The second process involves "contrapriests," who specialize in the removal of pollution. This is the aspect most unique to India and the one Dumont sees as central. Since the concept and symbolism of pollution is taken up at some length in Chapter 9, we need only reiterate the point made by Dumont (1980:42–56): the purity of the upper castes to a significant degree depends on others removing and isolating them from impurities. Conversely, the impurities attributed to the lower caste contrapriests such as barbers, washermen, and night-soil collectors are due to their regular handling of impurities for others. The activities of these contrapriests and, conversely, the ritual services of the Brahmans are the aspects of the jajmani system most clearly connected to the religious ideas characteristic of Hinduism. Significantly, a relatively high percentage of these castes actually work at the occupation traditionally attributed to them. Given the importance of notions of pollution, it is not surprising to find a set of relationships that ensure the availability of purifying services to the upper castes and minimal subsistence to the lower castes who provide them. These services seem to be the last to be shifted from jajmani relations to pure market relations— probably an indication of their religious significance and centrality to the system as a whole.

The third set of processes are typical of skilled craft groups in many societies: the attempt to restrict competition by monopolizing specialized knowledge. This was characteristic of the guild system in Europe (Thrupp 1972; Black 1984) and the profession of medicine in the United States (Friedson 1971; Collins 1979; Starr 1982).[15] The monopoly of knowledge tends to be maintained by carefully restricting entry into the profession. Sometimes this takes the form of transmission by kinship, as in the caste system, by apprenticeship, as in guilds, or by carefully restricting admission to professional schools, as in modern U.S. medicine. The group's power is reinforced by boycotting clients who hire those who are not accepted members of the guild, or by having laws passed that forbid nonmembers to practice their profession.

As already suggested in the earlier section on Untouchables, creating stigmatized outcast groups is often a strategy to maintain labor discipline in an agrarian society. The process seems especially likely where neither markets nor slavery (or other systems based directly upon force) are considered desirable or practical by the land controllers. For example, in the American South, extreme racism and rigid segregation did not develop until after slavery was abolished, and legalized force was no longer available as a method of labor control (see, for example, Woodward 1974). This is undoubtedly one of the factors contributing to the large number of Untouchables in India. When the actual work of these groups is examined, one finds that the majority of their time is spent as agricultural laborers. Of course, many have additional duties that pollute, such as the Chamar's responsibility for removing the dead carcasses of hoofed animals and tanning the hides. Often the ritual activities have a seemingly tenuous connection with actual impurity. For example, many drummer castes in South India are Untouchables—supposedly because the skins of the drumhead are of leather (a polluting substance). Most spend the bulk of their time as agricultural laborers. Yet other drummers who participate in different ceremonies are not Untouchables. Similarly, indigenous

informants are hard-pressed to give a coherent explanation of why many basket
and mat weaving castes are Untouchables. Habib (1982) has suggested that
Untouchables emerged out of conflict between peasants and hunting-gathering
tribes, and the eventual subjugation of the latter. "It is of some significance that in
all early texts the ancestors of the later 'Untouchables' are extensively connected
with hunting, fishing, working with animal skins and dealing in bamboo. In other
words, their origins lay mainly amidst the food-gathering forest folk" (Habib
1982:15). Predictably, the characteristic activities of these groups, whatever they
were, became defined as impure. Then some rationale was developed about why
the activity was impure; for example, fishing involves killing. Moreover, dominant
groups probably made sure that low status groups were assigned some specific ritual activity that could be defined as impure. In other words, as Dumont and
Pocock argue, notions of purity and impurity were extended to marginal groups at
the convenience of dominant groups. Stated in Weber's terms, there was an
"elective affinity" between the logic of pollution and the interest of land controllers. When these two social forces were linked, the result was a stigmatized,
outcast laboring class, and therefore, relatively large numbers of Untouchables.
Moreover, this outcasting took a relatively unique form: even the outcast class was
fragmented by the logic of pollution. There are many different Untouchable castes,
and even within the same caste category in the same region, several different endogamous subcastes may exist. Often Untouchable castes are very concerned about
their relative status. For example, Chamars (leather workers) often adamantly
claim a higher status than Bhangis (night-soil collectors). In short, the logic of
pollution both separated the Untouchables from other laborers, and fragmented the
Untouchable class itself.[16]

Decomposing the Religious and Ritual Features

So far we have focused on differentiating fairly common concerns about economic
and status privileges, present in many societies, from the more specifically religious
and ritual features of the jajmani system. Now these ritual features themselves need
to be further decomposed.

The discussion of ritual activities has focused on the role of priest and
contrapriest in disposing of pollution. According to Raheja (1988), concerns about
pollution are a secondary feature of jajmani relations; the primary concern is the
manipulation of auspiciousness and inauspiciousness. Paralleling Hocart's (1950)
and Dirks's (1987) arguments that the king is the center of the system rather than
the Brahman, Raheja sees the dominant, land-controlling caste as the center of the
jajmani system at the local level. Its "ritual centrality," rather than the superior
purity of the Brahmans, makes the system operate. From this perspective, the primary task of both Brahman priests and lower caste contrapriests is the handling of
auspiciousness and inauspiciousness. As she notes, the data on which much of the
discussion of the jajmani system has hinged has been based on villages in which
Brahmans were the dominant land-controlling caste. This is not typical of Indian
villages. Consequently, the focus on the manipulation of purity and pollution is a result of the data from these unrepresentative cases. Her own analysis focuses on a

village in which Gujars are the dominant caste, and here the primary focus of inter-caste relations is the manipulation of inauspiciousness. The giving of dana by the Gujars is primarily a way of passing inauspiciousness on to others. This is also the preoccupation of transactions between kinship members of the same caste.

We will deal with inauspiciousness at some length in Chapter 9. One point is sufficient here: this notion focuses on relatively worldly and practical concerns, while purity is more related to concerns about salvation and ritual status. Both con-cerns, are present in most local Hindu communities. However, Brahmans and left caste groups are likely to be more attentive to matters of purity, while dominant land-controlling castes and their allies will be more attentive to matters of auspi-ciousness and inauspiciousness. The relative emphasis will vary from locality to locality depending on how strong and orthodox the Brahmanical and left caste tradi-tions are. These two alternative concerns are correlated, though not identical, with the classic tensions in religious life between magic on the one hand, and morality and worship, on the other—matters that are a concern of Chapter 12. In short, it is a mistake to reduce the jajmani system to either economic or ritual considerations, or to reduce the ritualistic aspects to either purity or auspiciousness.

The Jajmani System and Legitimacy

By the process of analytical decomposition, the jajmani system has been shown to be composed of a number of different elements. Some of these are mainly economic and political, others largely religious. Within these two broad categories, there are additional subelements. In short, the jajmani system contains an array of apparently disparate elements that are conflated, mingled, or fused in this cultural setting. Why does this conflation or confusion occur? This question brings us back to the main focus of the chapter: political legitimacy. The conflation is not accidental, but is an-other example of improving the status and legitimacy of one thing by associating it with something of higher value. One key way to legitimize systems of domination is to interweave them with elements of assistance, benevolence, worship, and practi-cal efficiency. If conflation has occurred, then attempts to protest one element are seen as attacks on all of the elements. This means that protesting exploitation in-volves attacking fundamental cultural assumptions often valued or taken for granted by even the disadvantaged. Conflation provides legitimacy to particular patterns (in-cluding forms of domination and exploitation) by associating them with patterns of benevolence and sacredness. Such blending raises the status of the patterns of domi-nation by linking them with more communal and transcendent features of the culture. This is not necessarily a self-conscious and manipulative strategy, although dominant groups at times deliberately attempt to disguise and protect their privi-leges by ideological obfuscation. More typically, however, the conflation of these various elements involves a taking for granted of fundamental cultural assumptions. Systems of domination are most effective when such acceptance is present.

This unquestioning attitude is most likely when relationships can be expressed in language, symbols, and concepts used in many other contexts. For example, moving out of your parent's home, competitive markets, constitutional civil liber-ties, riding a motorcycle without a protective helmet, spanking or even beating your

children, and commiting suicide can all be defined and defended in terms of a supposedly generalized concept of "freedom." The legitimacy of any one of these may
be justified by linking them, conflating one form of "freedom" with another.

Such conflation occurs with respect to gifts and dana in Hindu culture. Conflation
implies that local forms of dominance are part of the archetypical pattern of social relationships and exchange. As we have seen, the relationships between local land controllers and Brahmans are clearly an extension or example of the pattern seen at
higher levels of the system between kings and Brahmans. These in turn are modeled
on the puja. As various analyses of the system have pointed out, however, this
archetypical model does not seem to quite fit many of the gift relationships in Indian
culture. The payments that lower castes receive may not be called "dana"; if pressed,
local elites will probably deny that they are. As Trautmann (1981) has pointed out,
two distinguishable models of exchange are present in the Dharmasastras. Yet these
different kinds of distributions are carried out in a common cultural context, and for
some purposes they are defined as part of the same system.

This conflation is not, I think, due solely to inadequate ethnography or historical analysis—though this may play a role. The ambiguity and partial fusion of disparate elements is a mechanism for legitimation by association. The relationship
between the jajman and the laborer is culturally defined as, in some respects, parallel to the relationship between the jajman and the Brahman, or even the deity and
the devotee. The Brahman would, of course, insist on a conceptual differentiation.
While the land controller might acknowledge this, he is typically indifferent about
such matters. The lower caste laborers may or may not be conscious of such differences, but for them too the issue probably has little saliency. The net effect is that
those who are utterly different in one context are in some respects the same in
other contexts. What must be separated for one purpose can be combined for other
purposes. This is the core dynamic behind all forms of legitimation by means of
association.

For analytical purposes, I have discussed the acquisition of kingly legitimacy and
legitimacy of local land controllers via the jajmani system separately. No clear-cut
line exists between these two levels. At points, one level seems to serve as a paradigm for the other, and vice versa. This idea was central to Hocart's (1950) understanding of the caste system. In a similar vein, Dirks has commented:

> The kingdom was, in a sense, the jajmani system writ large, if by jajmani we mean
> nothing more than the exchange and redistribution of goods and services in the con-
> text of a hierarchical system of social relations. The king and his intermediaries (i.e.,
> those sanctioned and given gifts by the king), like high-caste landowning families in
> modern Indian villages, were provided goods and services by the various lower caste
> such as carpenters, potters, blacksmiths, watercarriers, sweepers, and laundrymen.
> This system also included relations of protection and worship. (1987:31)

Dumont has also argued that the village is a "reduced version" of the kingdom
(1980:160–63).[17] This may overstate the identity of the two levels for many areas
and periods, but it does make clear the centrality of a common cultural logic.[18]

Conclusion and Caveat

The purpose of this chapter has been to indicate how a theory of status relationships might be relevant to understanding the articulation of the status order and the realms of economic and political power. The focus has been on the ways political elites in India legitimize their dominance. The argument is that legitimation is the acquisition of a certain type of status. Accordingly, the means of attaining legitimacy will be various forms of conformity and association. The analysis has emphasized forms of association. The analysis of kings considered three types of associations: those with Brahmans, those with greater kings, and those with subordinate warriors. In each of these, approval (and the legitimacy this implied) was implicitly exchanged for gifts. This was the primary means of establishing and maintaining such relationships. At the village level, where land and labor are actually utilized for production, we find parallel processes in what is often referred to as the "jajmani system." As other analysts have argued, this phrase conflates a number of different activities and relationships, many of which vary considerably from the paradigmatic relationship of the Brahman and the king or the puja. I suspect this conflation and ambiguity is not entirely a matter of faulty data and analysis, but rather another form of creating legitimacy by association.

In addition to conceptualizing legitimacy as a form of status, and conformity and association as the sources of legitimacy, two additional theoretical points emerge from the analysis. First, as indicated at the beginning of the chapter, most discussions focus on power being limited or guided by norms and laws—in my terms, legitimacy by conformity. I certainly do not wish to deny the significance of this process. On the other hand, association seems to be an equally important mechanism of legitimacy. Many regimes not noted for integrity or meticulous commitment to legalities have held power for long periods, and have even been quite popular. Various urban political machines in the United States are an obvious example. Frequently, political elites identify themselves with actors, institutions, and symbols that have high status and legitimacy among those who are ruled. Symbols of ethnic and national solidarity seem to be especially important in this regard. In short, for both theoretical and empirical reasons, analyses of legitimacy should pay careful attention to processes of association.

Perhaps conformity to norms and laws has become more central to political legitimacy than in premodern societies. This is certainly one implication of Weber's typology of types of legitimate authority, which sees contemporary societies as increasingly dependent on rational-legal authority (1968:chap. 3). The recognition of this trend, however, should not cause us to overlook the continuing importance of association as a means of legitimacy; to do so would be a serious analytical mistake. Examples like those offered at the beginning of the chapter—high status consultants for research proposals, college presidents on corporation boards, and movie stars as spokespersons for charitable campaigns—are only a few of many examples of a process that is pervasive in even the most "rationalized" sectors of contemporary society.

The second point is a related one: we should look closely for implicit forms of exchange where such associations are important. In contemporary societies such exchanges will not usually take the form of gifts, but parallel mechanisms are likely to

be present. Moreover, if we look carefully, we may find analogues for the two different types of implicit exchange that have been identified. Contemporary political candidates create alliances with intellectuals, who provide both legitimacy and technical
advice, but such coalitions are harder to form if the politician is always opposed to
appropriations for universities, research institutes, and the like. Candidates also form
alliances with more renowned politicians, who serve as channels to the resources
needed to get nominated and to conduct campaigns; such sponsors expect loyalty and
unspecified favors in return. In research I conducted on metropolitan hospitals in the
United States (Milner 1980), I discovered links of cooperation between high status
and low status hospitals that were at first puzzling; while such associations were crucial to the functioning and legitimacy of the low status institutions, the superior institutions appeared to have little to gain and much to lose from such associations.
Closer examination uncovered elaborate forms of implicit exchange that contributed
to both the material needs of each institution and to their legitimacy. These examples are not meant to suggest that the precise patterns identified in India are relevant
in all societies. Implicit exchange is, however, likely to be a component of forms of
political legitimation. The nature of the exchange and what is kept implicit are also
likely to vary, depending on the relative status and function of the parties involved.

In ending this chapter, a crucial caveat is required; I want to stress how selective
this part of the analysis has been. The purpose has been to show how the general
theoretical arguments are relevant to a particular aspect of political and economic
dominance. Many of the enormous complexities relating to political dominance
have been ignored. If the nature of the status order has an impact upon the political
and economic order, the reverse is even more true. As Dirks (1987), Inden (1990),
and others have argued, the intensity and form of caste relations has certainly varied, historically and geographically. To a significant degree, this has been due to
variations in the forms of political dominance. Moreover, as Fuller (1989) has suggested, focusing on the jajmani system ignores the importance of markets and
money, and fails to capture the full complexity of agrarian relations in India. But to
acknowledge the selectivity of the analysis is not to admit to some form of mis-
guided Orientalism. More complex and adequate understandings are likely to come
about only by first limiting the focus of our analyses in ways allowing us to see
connections that would otherwise be overlooked.

8

A Theory of Status Relationships: Additional Elements

Now it is necessary to introduce some additional theoretical concepts and ideas.

Primary and Countervailing Patterns

Maps tend to point out the primary features of a region: the highest mountains, the biggest rivers, the busiest roads, the most famous or important buildings. This is also the tendency of sociological theories; they typically focus on the most prominent structural features of a social situation. One of the basic assumptions of this study, and of structural sociology in general, is that it is possible to meaningfully identify the primary patterns that help us to understand why people behave the way they do—at least much of the time. This has been the main thrust of the preceding chapters.

To identify primary patterns, though, is not to deny that secondary, subordinate, countervailing, and newly emerging patterns may also be present. Clearly secondary patterns, countertendencies, countertrends, counternorms, alternative structures, and deviant patterns are common. One familiar expression of these ideas are the concepts of thesis and antithesis made famous by Hegel and Marx. In a slightly different but related vein, every way of seeing something is, of course, a way of not seeing other things. As Parsons claimed, all theoretical perspectives illuminate some parts of reality at the expense of relegating others to areas of darkness. Parsons refers to these ignored features as residual categories (1937:16–20; also see Alexander 1983b:14–15). In a similar spirit Heesterman (1985) has attempted to grasp some of the complexities of India by using the notion of "the inner conflict of tradition."

I make no attempt to deal with all the "facts" that my analysis ignores or downplays by systematically fitting them into such notions as inner conflicts, countertendencies, antitheses, and residual categories. I do, however, try to indicate at least a few of these complexities by identifying some of the countervailing patterns in values, ideologies, and social structures.

Two things further complicate such an effort. First, it is not always clear what is the primary and what is the countervailing or deviant pattern. For example, compared to most other societies, it is accurate to say that the notion of equality of opportunity is a primary ideological notion in the contemporary United States. Virtually no politician or public figure would openly reject the legitimacy of equality of opportunity—however much they might disagree over what this means concretely. On the other hand, the right to inherit private property is an even more unquestioned ideological premise of U.S. society; public figures are certainly reluctant to question the legitimacy of such inheritance. This is so even though by almost any reasonable definition the inheritance of private property significantly qualifies and contradicts the notion of equality of opportunity. On the other hand, it would probably be a mistake for the analyst to declare that in the United States inheritance of private property is clearly a more primary ideological principle than equality of opportunity. Few politicians would make this a key point in their campaigns for office; to do so would identify one as a candidate of the wealthy. Consequently, it is quite difficult to say which is the primary and which is the countervailing ideological principle.

Second, there are often countervailing patterns within countervailing patterns: a primary pattern is relaxed or qualified, and then the qualification is qualified. For example, in the early stages of the U.S. civil rights movement, attempts were made to forbid employers, schools, and the like from seeking information about a person's religious, ethnic, or racial background. Similarly, quotas for minorities were seen as clearly unjust. Later, however, as it became apparent how recalcitrant such inequalities are, information about such characteristics was systematically collected, and in effect quotas were used to decrease inequalities. These in turn have sparked debates about "reverse discrimination" and have prompted laws and regulations against quotas. In short, for social behavior there are not just primary and countervailing patterns, but often "wheels within wheels within wheels." Sometimes these are historical patterns that occur over time, but in other cases the contradictions are concurrent and may coexist for indefinite periods.

The analysis in the next two chapters will look at relatively primary patterns, but it will also attempt to highlight countervailing patterns. To follow the analogy used above, I will fill in additional details on the map, and construct alternative maps that draw attention to features different from those that were the initial focus. This attempt to identify both primary and countervailing patterns will be sustained throughout much of the rest of the book. Even with this effort, however, the analysis will deal primarily with general tendencies and ignore many complexities.

The Objectification of Conformity and Associations

The precondition for a well-developed status order is the insulation of status from the mere possession of wealth or political power. More concretely, status should be based upon the quality of one's actions with respect to conformity and association, not the objects one possesses or controls. This is the feature of society to which this particular theoretical scheme draws attention. Under such conditions you cannot lose status by others appropriating it. But the opposite is also true; you cannot gain more by appropriating it from someone else.

Of course, people usually prefer to have it both ways: they want their status to be protected by inalienability, but they do not want to be dependent upon the opinions of others. In terms of the agency–contingency distinction, people want the freedom to raise their status, but security against any contingency that might decrease it, including the contingent nature of their own subsequent performances. They want opportunities for upward mobility, but protection against downward mobility. Accordingly, they often create social mechanisms intended to produce this result.[1]

This usually involves qualifying the major prerequisite for status groups by relaxing the strict separation of status from other forms of power. That is, a strong cultural emphasis on such separation creates countertendencies that were initially ignored by this analysis. Now it is time to draw attention to these counter tendencies. These qualify and relax the extent to which status is insulated from economic and political power. While wealth and political power per se are disqualified as direct sources of status, other objectlike sources of status are created. This brings us to the concepts of "objectivation," "reification," and "objectification."

Berger and Luckmann (1967:60, 197) use the word "objectivation" to translate the Hegelian-Marxian concept of *Versachlichung*. This concept was discussed in Chapter 3 in relationship to the terms "externalization" and "internalization." *Objectivation* means human action has been embodied in such a way that it is available to both the producer and others in a common social world. Writing is an obvious example. The ideas that were initially available only to the actor or to those with whom she talked become embodied in a text and can be read by innumerable people even centuries after her death. *Reification* refers to those objectivations that are treated as if they are something other than the products of human activity. Often they are seen as natural or inevitable features of the cosmos. This concept has a long and important genealogy and has been especially important within the Marxist tradition (see, e.g., Marx 1844; Lukács 1968; Israel 1971: chap. 9). A general discussion of the concept is not appropriate, but there is a subtype of reification that is of special interest to this analysis: that which occurs when social and moral processes and entities come to be defined as quasi-physical. I will refer to this type of reification as *objectification*. That is, human subjects and their activities are considered objectlike. Note the difference in spelling between Berger and Luckmann's usage and mine; it is intended to indicate that objectification is a special subtype of objectivation that involves reification of social processes into near physical or mechanical processes.

Some examples are in order. Status can be objectivated without being reified and objectified. Creating a "best book of the year award" and giving its author a certificate of merit is a form of objectivation; the giving of praise becomes public and is recorded and embodied in an object. Therefore people not directly involved in the process—even hundreds of years later—may know about this judgment. Their own judgments of the book and its author may be influenced by these earlier judgments. There is objectivation, but not necessarily objectification. Other examples of the objectivation of status include ribbons, trophies, diplomas, social registers, heraldry, genealogy, honor rolls, halls of fame, insignias, *Who's Who*, awards banquets, and honorary fraternities.

Objectification occurs when people think that mere possession of the certificate of merit (or any of the other examples of status symbols) would give one the status implied by the original award; a social and moral process is transformed into a quasi-physical process that involves the manipulation of objects. In status systems, objectification takes two primary forms, which I will refer to as "external objectification" and "internal objectification."

External objectification means status becomes embodied in substances or objects external to one's human identity and is then acquired by obtaining these or given by dispensing them. Often a continuum exists from status based on moral judgments to status based on mechanical causation. A particularly clear example of this comes from, of all places, Mao's China:

> On May l, Liang Heng goes with his group to the Summer Palace. "All that remained of him [Mao] was the touch of his hand on the hands of a few who had been lucky enough to get close to him. . . . Those Chairman Mao had touched now become the focus of our fervor. Everyone surged toward them with out-stretched arms in hopes of transferring the sacred touch to their own hands . . . shaking the hand of someone who had shaken hands with our Great Saving Star . . . until sometimes handshakes were removed as much as one hundred times from the original one." (Fairbank 1983:21)

This quote illustrates the continuum between the transfer of status through interpersonal association, and transfer by mechanical means. Mao's status had become objectified; instead of the implicit transfer of approval, status, and moral power through interpersonal interaction, we now have the transfer of the sacred by almost physical means. This process of affecting one's own condition by contact with sacred persons, objects, or places is common to many religions: the laying on of hands during ordination of Christian clergy; and the touching of sacred relics, and pilgrimages—whether to Jerusalem, Mecca, or Benares. But it is not limited to strictly religious behavior. Visits to Washington's Mount Vernon, Jefferson's Monticello, Lenin's tomb, Gandhi's Raj Ghat cremation site, Nehru's Shanti Bana memorial, the Baseball Hall of Fame, and even Elvis Presley's Graceland are in some respects strikingly similar to each other and to religious pilgrimages. More to the point, such visits create a connection or association to an honored person. This is even more the case for the owner of the eighteenth-century home who can claim, "George Washington slept here." The collecting of autographs and memorabilia of famous persons also has many similarities to the collecting of sacred relics.

The acquisition of objects can symbolize not only association with those of high status or sacredness, but also conformity to valued norms. The expensive art books displayed on the coffee table can be a partial substitute for knowing or caring about "high culture." Buying encyclopedias from the door-to-door salesperson can be, in part, an attempt to compensate for the education one does not have. Perhaps most striking is the popularity of "collectables" among the middle classes in contemporary U.S. society. This usually involves the systematic collection of often inconsequential objects—from beer cans to dolls—with low to modest economic value. Many of these are manufactured and marketed specifically to be collected. American society highly values the systematic accumulation of capital and the display of this wealth by the systematic collection of objects of "high culture." Unsurprisingly, those unable to compete in this arena seek status in the systematic collection of less valuable objects. This is, of course, the well-known phenomenon of acquiring commodities that have become status symbols. When status symbols take the form of easily purchased commodities, fashion becomes especially important, for as the number of persons who purchase such symbols expands, their status value declines and new symbols are sought. In a complex consumer society the causal direction may become reversed; instead of the consumer seeking new symbols, the producer of such symbols deliberately introduces new styles to make old symbols obsolete—in order to use peoples' concerns about status as a means to expand sales. The women's clothing industry is an especially clear example of this form of objectification and commodification of status.

As I mentioned, when it comes to human behavior there are "wheels within wheels." The manipulation of status symbols can be transformed back into a type of social process. The "original" reason for collecting status symbols may be eroded and "forgotten," and it may become an end in itself. People become admired or held in disdain not only or even primarily for the status associated with the objects they have accumulated, but for the skill and determination with which they "play the game." The collector is admired not simply for the content of his collection, but for the skill and sophistication that has gone into accumulating it. In other words, the acquisition of certain objects or conditions becomes the actual criterion of status.

Just as there is a continuum between status acquired through close personal association and the mechanical "touching the hand that touched the hand," there is a continuum between conforming to the appropriate lifestyle by learning elaborate norms and the skills necessary to conform to them, and the simple acquisition of objects that serve as status symbols. The more behavior approaches the latter end of these two continua, the greater is the degree of external objectification.

One motivation behind such tendencies toward objectification is that objects are more expansible and more alienable than the moral evaluations that constitute status. Consequently, they are more easily reproduced and transferred. The acquisition of status symbols then becomes not only a means of displaying one's status, but of purchasing objectified status. One obvious reason for sumptuary laws is to restrict such counterfeiting. When it cannot be restricted, status symbols are highly discounted. Classes seeking upward mobility are most likely to engage in external objectification; established classes are most likely to resist it—or acquire items that supposedly require high levels of sophisticated knowledge and judgment, such as "fine art."

Conversely, negative objectified status symbols can be imposed on people to degrade them. The shaven heads of military training camps and the emblems Jews were forced to wear by the Nazis are two obvious examples. When people have the option, negative objectivated status symbols—whether or not they are reified and objectified—are hidden, avoided, and discarded. The prisoner who escapes changes out of his prison clothes as soon as possible. Letters of reprimand are seldom displayed. The clerk who is promoted to an executive stops wearing uniforms. Material defined as pornographic comes in a "plain brown wrapper."

Internal objectification is motivated by the concern to eliminate another form of contingency: dependency upon the whim of what modern societies would call "public opinion." This is usually accomplished by making status objectlike in a somewhat different sense: status is identified with the biological characteristics of particular individuals and groups, for example, skin color, gender, age, the supposed purity of one's bodily substances, or "blood" lines. In a sense, status is objectified by being internalized in the object most closely identified with one's individual identity, that is, one's body—or more accurately, one or more biological features of the body. Consequently, status is no longer acquired through social interaction, but is inherited. Of course, the actors' understanding of such physical inheritance processes are culturally defined and may or may not match modern biology's notions of genetic inheritance. Like external objectification, status becomes identified with an object; in this case it is the body, which is thought to be relatively inalienable from individual identities. Here is probably where the term substantialization is useful: moral qualities like virtue are transformed into bodily substances, and conversely, one's moral qualities are limited or shaped by the nature of one's bodily substances.[2] (The term, however, has several other meanings in intellectual discourse and I have used it sparingly to avoid confusion.)

A crucial caveat: The line between what is internal and external is culturally determined, hence the clearness and rigidity of this distinction may vary considerably from one culture to another. Contemporary bourgeois culture, and the United States in particular, are probably the extreme cases of drawing a sharp line between the individual and his or her environment. As we shall see this is not true of all cultures; external and internal objectification may blend into one another. For example, eating "impure" food may be thought to produce "bad blood"; an objectified external corruption produces an objectified internal corruption.[3]

In sum, while the essence of status creation and distribution is a social and moral process, the very stress on these factors tends to create counter-processes that lead to various forms of objectification. External and internal objectification are similar in that they both transform a moral process into more mechanical-like processes in which the attributes that are both cause and effect are more objectlike. But these processes have opposite aims. External objectification increases the scope of a given actor's agency; status can be acquired not only by conformity to norms or acceptance by higher status people, but also by exchanging and manipulating objects.[4] Internal objectification intends to reduce human agency; the incompetent or deviant son of the king is of more value than the most brilliant or virtuous son of a serf; supposedly nothing that either one does can transform them into the other.

Agency, Contingency, and the Manipulation of Language

The next step in our argument focuses on additional processes that culturally define the boundaries of agency and contingency.[5] We have just seen how agency was manipulated by two forms of objectification. Now I want to look at a different way in which the boundaries of agency are "manipulated." No society considers the good and bad that people experience as due solely to either their conformity to social norms or to the associations they have had with others. Neither pure achievement nor pure ascription—or even some combination of the two—can convincingly account for the outcomes that people experience. In addition, human lives are affected by elements of contingency, luck, chance, destiny, fortune, fate, kismet, providence, and so forth. Most societies have vocabularies with which they can deemphasize human agency and, in a sense, de-moralize the outcomes of human experience. "Better luck next time," "condolences," "you win some, you lose some," "that's the way the cookie crumbles," "how lucky can you get," "it was manna from heaven," "it was dumb luck," "beginner's luck," "it was providential" and "it's God's will" are only a few of the phrases used in contemporary U.S. society to indicate that outcomes are sometimes beyond human control or have little to do with human agency and effort.

Ironically, the very vocabularies used to deemphasize human agency are often subtly redefined to allow human agency to be applied to them. People attempt to predict and even manipulate the categories created to recognize the elements of human existence that are beyond prediction and manipulation. For example, people attempt to identify lucky (and unlucky) days, places, and objects. Some instances are idiosyncratic: the day of the month one had a winning lottery ticket. Others are culturally standardized. In U.S. society, these include Friday the thirteenth, horse shoes, four-leaf clovers, rabbits' feet, black cats, spilling salt, breaking mirrors, and walking under ladders. Attempts are made to affect outcomes by associating (or disassociating) one's activities with these lucky (or unlucky) times, objects, and events.

Moreover, concepts such as luck, which are initially intended to indicate that humans are not responsible for what happens to them, are reinterpreted in moral terms. A person whose spouse is killed by lightning is seen as being punished for an earlier sexual infidelity. A person who wins the lottery is seen to be rewarded for pious religious devotion. In other words, people are often highly ambivalent about how they draw the boundary between agency and responsibility, on the one hand, and powerlessness and contingency, on the other. Hence their language about such matters is often highly dependent upon the context.

Not only are they frequently ambivalent about which concept they want to invoke, but they often disagree with others over whether to stress agency or contingency in explaining the desirable and undesirable outcomes they experience. Unsurprisingly, people are often moralistic about their own successes but see their own failures as due to factors beyond their control—and vice versa where it concerns others. The successful emphasize their diligence and fine breeding and attribute the inferior position of others to a lack of these. While occasionally people may credit their good fortune to the advice or action of others, they much more frequently blame others for their bad luck. Witchcraft, sorcery, and the evileye are common examples of this tendency in premodern societies, and modern societies have various conspiracy theories.[6] Of course, as already noted, this involves a certain contradiction in terms; outcomes are no longer seen as simply due to random chance, but to the evil intent and action of others. In short, the degree to which people attribute outcomes to human agency or contingency is a continuum. Moreover, the language they use to express variations along this continuum tends to be self-qualifying and even contradictory: the categories initially used to express contingency are often used to express agency over this contingency.

Such variations in conceptualization and language occur not only across events and individuals, but between social categories. When worldly rewards are unevenly distributed, the attribution of agency and contingency are often correlated with one's position in the social structure; strata often disagree over the extent to which unequal fortunes are due to the characteristics of the individuals or groups involved or circumstances outside of their control. In the contemporary United States, upper and middle strata are often moralistic about unemployment, drug use, welfare payments, and petty theft, and much less so about alcoholism, the inheritance of property, tax subsidies (e.g., the deduction of interest payments), and even tax evasion. Lower strata are frequently skeptical of such interpretations and stress their own bad luck, the use of coercion and manipulation by upper strata, or a past history of exploitation.[7]

Not only do social categories differ in their interpretations of the significance of human agency and luck, they often try to redistribute the risk and uncertainty associated with factors that are beyond human agency. Usually people attempt to pass bad luck on to others, and to appropriate the good luck of others. This occurs objectively to the degree that we know which locations and activities are more dangerous and assign people accordingly.[8] Of course, many risks cannot be predicted even on an aggregate actuarial basis, much less manipulated by social redistribution. These must be handled by affecting the subjectivity of individuals and groups rather than their objective circumstances. In these cases, what is usually redistributed is confidence and self-assurance. On this level, too, the upper strata are usually more successful in defining an ideological system that favors them. For example, they can exclude those defined as unlucky and pay to associate with those who are lucky, or at least those who will tell them they are lucky. Upper strata in premodern societies have seldom tolerated diviners, priest, magicians, or prophets who always predict bad news. Jeremiah of the Hebrew Bible is the ideal-typical example of the persecuted prophet of doom, but there are many others. Contemporary upper strata are unlikely to tolerate nannies or schoolteachers who use primarily negative sanctions, or administrative assistants who are both pessimistic and candid. Modern political leaders seldom retain economists whose forecasts are consistently gloomy.

The Social Sources of Contingency

All societies face the contingencies rooted in natural powers beyond their control: earthquakes, hurricanes, changes in climate, eclipses.[9] Of primary interest, however, are the social sources of contingency: How do societies, and social locations and positions within them, vary in their perception of agency and contingency?

Highly stratified societies are likely to have two types of activity that are associated with contingency. First, if there is significant inequality of power and privilege, inferiors are likely to perceive considerable contingency when they must interact with their superiors. By definition, the powerful have agency over their subordinates; the more absolute and capricious the power and agency of the superior, the greater the contingency experienced by the subordinate. Thus we can predict that the outcome of dealing with superiors who have high levels of near absolute power will be seen as problematic and perhaps unpredictable. Accordingly, subordinates are likely to attempt to use various kinds of devices—prayer, astrology, divination—to choose a propitious time for initiating such interaction.[10]

Second, boundaries may be elaborated not only between broad social categories such as classes and caste, but also within such groupings. Age stratification is especially common, and transitions from one stage of the life cycle to another are likely to be seen as highly significant. If these types of social boundaries have been well defined and highly elaborated, crossing them may be seen as fraught with danger and uncertainty. Therefore, high levels of contingency are also associated with life-cycle transitions such as birth, marriage, and death. Such events mean that the structures that contain and channel power must be momentarily relaxed; hence, as in the case of facing superiors, the outcome is seen as contingent. Accordingly, such events are likely to be associated with the language of contingency and with attempts to determine the most propitious time to conduct such events. Undoubtedly many other social sources of contingency exist, but these are the two that concern this analysis.

Let me summarize the point of this discussion of agency and contingency and relate it to the notion of objectification. Status groups tend to elaborate their norms and rituals. This is especially the case when membership is ascribed. These complex norms provide arenas in which agency, responsibility, and virtue can be displayed; virtue and morality nearly always assume some notion of agency or freewill. This is taken for granted in most modern societies that emphasize achievement. Yet even the most ascribed status system will have arenas of behavior in which the dominant ideology will define individuals as having considerable autonomy and agency; accordingly, they will be seen as responsible for conformity and deviance to valued norms and for choosing their associates.[11] Given this emphasis on agency and morality in some arenas, we should expect to find a countertendency: something that qualifies human agency and responsibility, some concepts and language that acknowledge contingency in human affairs. But—as we shall see repeatedly—there are often countertrends within countertrends: the language of contingency is subsumed under new forms of agency, so that luck and providence can be predicted and manipulated, usually by various forms of ritual. Hence, within status systems we should expect to find ideologies and practices that display a complicated dialectic between agency and contingency. In well-developed status systems that have significant inequalities and relatively strong and fixed boundaries between social groups, relationships with superiors and movements across social boundaries will be seen as involving significant levels of contingency. These perceived contingencies, in turn, are likely to lead to extensive rituals aimed at predicting or manipulating the factors that were initially defined as beyond human agency. Such rituals often involve the objectification of agency and contingency; luck, fortune, and destiny are likely to be associated with physical objects and substances, which can then be manipulated to affect the outcomes experienced by humans.

In the next two chapters we will see how objectification is used and related to notions of agency and contingency. In turn, these abstract theoretical concepts will be used to analyze Indian notions of (1) purity and pollution, (2) sexual asceticism, and (3) auspiciousness and inauspiciousness.

9

Cultural Codes and Rituals: I

Chapter 3 introduced the concept of secondary elaboration and ritualization. Status groups tend to elaborate and ritualize their norms in order to make it more difficult for outsiders to conform. This process is especially characteristic of upper status groups that wish to exclude those of lower status, but excluded groups also elaborate and ritualize to create counter norms and values. Elaboration is a means not only of excluding outsiders, but also of social control for group members. If ritualistic conformity to a multitude of petty rules is obtained, more crucial rules and orders are likely to be followed. Perhaps even more importantly, such obedience and the very existence of elaborate sets of cultural categories increase the taken-for-grantedness of the system as a whole. That is, they contribute to the institutionalization of the core norms of the group.

In Chapter 5, I discussed how much of the textual tradition of Hinduism, from the Vedas to the present, could be seen in part as an attempt to elaborate norms and rituals. This is especially true of the Dharmasastric tradition, which is looked upon as an explicit set of laws or rules intended to guide the twice-born householder in his attempt to conform to dharma. In Chapter 6, the tendency to elaborate social categories was discussed. Even if the textual tradition is ignored, an observer of the caste system and Hinduism cannot help but be struck by the elaborateness of the rules and rituals that govern the day-to-day conduct of Hindus, especially members of the upper castes. The elaborate and quite specific rules concerning purification, eating, and the arrangement of marriages are particularly noticeable.

Codes

In this and the next chapter we will focus in more depth on the elaboration and ritualization processes. In addition to the explicit elaboration of rules, we shall focus on the more indirect and unconscious ways in which cultural categories, symbols, and rituals are elaborated in support of basic cultural commitments. I will refer to these more indirect forms of elaboration as *codes*. The term is intended as a metaphor that draws on the language of cryptography. Cryptography means both secret writing and cryptic symbolization. With respect to the first meaning, the aim is to keep the message a secret from outsiders; to some degree I mean to imply this. Even more important, though, is the idea that codes can also keep things a secret from those who use them; they can be a means of simultaneously communicating information and repressing it. A famous example of such repressed codes are Freud's various analyses of the meaning of compulsive behavior and dreams; by means other than explicit communication we "say things" surreptitiously that are too threatening or painful to express openly—even to ourselves. This notion has some similarities to Bourdieu's (1977) concept of misrecognition, but I reject his contention that people's concern about symbolic resources is ultimately a concern about material interests. Leach also uses the notions of code and decoding in a manner similar to the meaning I have in mind (1983:2).

In addition to the notion of secret communication, cryptography implies cryptic symbolization, what Freud referred to as "compression." The relevant point for our purposes is that what I have called "elaboration" makes possible cryptic symbolization. A limited number of symbols at the end of a long elaborated chain of symbolization may be capable of implicitly communicating the whole set of related ideas. The obvious example of this is the metonym; a part serves as the symbol for the whole. A famous example of a pair of metonyms is the line from the Hebrew prophet Isaiah (2:4): "They shall beat their swords into plowshares." Obviously "swords" and "plowshares" each stand for a whole complex of human behaviors that lead to and make up war and peace respectively. Similarly the concrete and specific verb "beat" stands for much more general notions of transformation and change. By compression, three cryptic symbols communicate an elaborate set of meanings and values. Here the connection between the symbols and the broader meaning is self-evident and is intended to be explicit. I am, however, primarily interested in such symbols where the connection is less explicit or even denied—hence the use of codes.

An example from contemporary American politics illustrates what I mean by cultural codes and compressed communication. In the 1988 U.S. presidential election, George Bush emphasized that he was in favor of requiring schoolteachers to lead their students in the pledge to the national flag, even if such pledges were against their religious convictions.[1] Even though this requirement was almost certain to be ruled unconstitutional, this stand is credited with being a significant factor in Bush's ability to win the election. Obviously this issue was a cryptic symbol for commitment to a much more elaborate set of norms and values—patriotism, national solidarity, deference to authority, the responsibility of teachers to pass on core values of a tradition. Bush's position implied that those who were opposed to such a requirement did not support these values. To explicitly accuse his opponent of not being patriotic would have been considered beyond the bounds of legitimate criticism and might have lost him votes, but the accusation could be made in coded form by taking a stand in favor of the pledge.

My argument is that some of the behaviors defined as abhorrent in India have a similar—but often much more indirect—relationship to the more fundamental features of Hindu culture. This is certainly not a new idea; it has many features in common with Durkheim's (1965) discussion of totems and his observation that the emblem of the totem was often more sacred than the totem itself. What I hope to add to this observation is an explanation of how the elaboration of norms and rituals and the sacralization of related symbols operate as mechanisms for protecting less clearly articulated fundamental values and structures. I will attempt to show this by a process of decoding.

Like all metaphors, the notion of decoding has its limits. For coded governmental national security communications there is only one correct decoding of a given message. I do not mean to imply that this is the case with respect to cultural interpretation; cultural symbols often communicate multiple messages. On the other hand, deconstructionism and postmodernism notwithstanding, there are a finite number of accurate and appropriate interpretations—at least at the level of analysis that concerns us here.

Methodological and Theoretical Considerations

The main intent of Chapters 9 and 10 is to increase our understanding of India and the operation of status systems. But these chapters also have a broader methodological and theoretical point. One of the main debates in contemporary sociology concerns whether the discipline should strive to (1) develop causal propositions like those in the physical sciences, or (2) interpret cultural meanings more in the tradition of the humanities.[2] Two influential books published in the same year illustrate the two positions briefly. In *The Principles of Group Solidarity,* Hechter says:

> In contemporary sociology there is precious little consensus about the proper meaning of the terms *theory* and *explanation.* . . . Since it is not my intention to enter into the epistemological debates that are currently so fashionable in some sociological circles, I should clarify my position on these matters. I take theories to be *causal* explanations that provide *intelligible* answers to why-questions about *empirical* facts. (1987:1 [emphases in original])

In contrast, Wuthnow, in his *Meaning and the Moral Order,* says that

> the epistemological stance taken in this volume is that of *interpretive sociology.* The very business of sociology is assumed to be one of interpretation, not one of discovering objective facts from some Procrustean bed of empirical reality or of adducing lawful generalizations about the causal ordering of these facts. The hermeneutic circle, and all that it implies about the limitations of positivistic knowledge, is taken for granted. Cultural analysis, like any other branch of sociological inquiry not only *should* be but *inevitably is,* whether we like it or not, essentially an act of interpretation. (1987:17 [emphases in original])

The same debate occurs in anthropology, though the interpretive tradition is much more dominant and there are hotly disputed emphases within this tradition (see, e.g., Horton and Finnegan 1973; Clifford 1988).

My own position is that this is a false choice. There is no clear-cut line between causal and interpretive explanations. Causal explanations tend to focus on describing links between discernible identities;[3] how the behavior of one identity affects another identity.[4] Interpretive analysis tends to focus on discerning the boundaries and elements of such identities. But each of these is a matter of emphasis. The methodological purpose of this chapter is to show one way to link causal and interpretive analysis—and that they blend into each other.[5]

These two chapters are also intended to show the provisional nature of the resource structuralism I am advocating. They are primarily devoted to analyzing rather concrete practices. More specifically, they are concerned with the important role of what Giddens (1984) might call "routine" and what Bourdieu (1977) apparently means by "habitus." That is, we shall be considering how motivated, strategic, goal-oriented action is transformed into routine, taken-for-granted practices, thereby increasing the chances that the social structure will be reproduced. Actually I shall approach this issue from the opposite direction, by beginning with the routine practices, and attempting to decode their relationships to motivated strategic actions and rational choices. I do not claim that this analysis will satisfy all of the concerns of such theorists as Giddens and Bourdieu about overcoming the limits of objectivism and structuralism. It will, however, attempt to make a start toward linking thick descriptions (Geertz 1973:chap. 1) and hermeneutic interpretations with a structural analysis focusing on the nature of human resources.

What Is to Be Explained

We will focus on four sets of ideas that are at the core of Hindu culture: purity and impurity, sexual asceticism, Tantrism, and auspiciousness and inauspiciousness. Auspiciousness and inauspiciousness will be considered in Chapter 10. Some of the things that I will attempt to explain in this chapter include

1. Why the notions of purity, impurity, and pollution are so central to Hindu society, and more specifically:
   a. Some of the key aspects of the organization of physical and social space.
   b. The nature of dirt and filth and why keeping the pure and the impure separated is so important.
   c. The relationships between Hindu concerns about what enters and leaves the body (for example, food and feces) and the nature of the social organization.

2. Why sexual asceticism is important in Hindu society and more specifically:
   a. Why the retention of male semen is seen as a key source of power.
   b. Why in Hindu myths those who are great ascetics are repeatedly seduced.
   c. Why political power and more concretely kings are associated with female qualities.

3. How these and related features of Hindu symbolism are codes that play an important role in the maintenance of the status order.

4. Why Tantrism emerges as an important form of deviation from orthodox Brahmanism, and why it is ultimately reincorporated as an important aspect of the Hindu tradition.

Purity and Impurity

As noted earlier, Dumont argues that the basis of the caste system is the distinction between the pure and the impure.[6] Higher castes are purer than lower caste and must follow a lifestyle that conforms to the norms of purity if they are to maintain their superiority. According to Dumont (1980) the key to understanding the caste system is to see the centrality and distinctiveness of this concept in creating a *Homo hierarchicus* and a system of inequality that is fundamentally different from those found in the West. In contrast, I believe that it is more useful to see ideas of purity and impurity as one of a set of closely interrelated key symbols used to accentuate and reinforce status processes characteristic of many societies. The elaboration of these notions as crucial secondary norms and rituals has been of fundamental importance in stabilizing and maintaining a caste society. Let us now take up these arguments in more detail.

Space, Distance, and Status

A common metaphor for status is that of distance and spatial ordering. Spatial distance and ordering become a symbol for social distance and social order. Higher status people are literally raised up on thrones, stages, platforms, and penthouses. Moreover, the physical distance between people, and the social association it implies, is carefully regulated. How closely one is seated to the head table or chief guest is used to symbolize one's status. The size of an official's desk, and the distance it maintains between him or her and those who approach, is nearly always correlated with the official's rank. As Goffman has shown in his essay "Territories of the Self" (1971), distance and space is carefully regulated, and the amount available to a person is correlated with rank—even for very transient relations in public places.[7] Keep in mind that what Goffman analyzes is not property, per se, but interpersonal space in public places, for example, elevators, sidewalks, park benches, and public beaches. The metaphorical symbol of spatial distance for social status is such an obvious and common one that we need not belabor the point.

Certainly there are many instances of the use of this metaphor in the Indian caste system: the distance that South Indian Untouchables were once forced to keep between themselves and high caste persons; the fact that when villagers smoke together, higher caste persons will tend to sit on a bed, chair, or raised location, while lower caste members will squat down; the seating arrangements at public events; the layout of homes, with the kitchen being the most pure and restricted area, while bedrooms, courtyards, and latrine areas steadily increase in both impurity and accessibility to outsiders; the physical organization of villages, with the lowest status groups being relegated to the margins of the settlement area; the layout of temples, with the areas becoming increasingly sacred as one moves toward the inner sanctum.

Pollution and Association

If most social systems use distance to symbolize status differences, the metaphor of pollution—purity versus impurity—is also widely used (Douglas 1966). It is, however, especially characteristic of the Indian caste system.

To become polluted is to come in contact with something that is dirty or nasty. But what is dirt? Douglas argues that dirt can only be defined in relationship to a larger system of order; dirt is matter that is out of place, something that disturbs or threatens a system or order: "Uncleanness or dirt is that which must not be included if a pattern is to be maintained. To recognize this is the first step towards insight into pollution" (1966:40). The imagery of dirt can, of course, arise in any system of order. But it seems that it might be especially congenial where the metaphor of space and distance is used to represent status differences. The notion of "out of place" requires as a background assumption the notions of ordered space.

A second, subsidiary notion of dirt is noteworthy. As Douglas notes, drawing on the work of Sartre, things that are sticky and viscous are more typically defined as messy or dirty than are either solids or liquids (1966:38). There seem to be two reasons for this. First, viscous substances are somewhat of an anomaly: they are neither solids nor liquids, and hence present problems of classification. Probably more important, they are difficult to order. Molasses cannot be stacked or shelved; it must be kept in containers. Yet unlike liquids, it will not come out of the containers; it sticks to, and hence contaminates, everything it touches. Its idiosyncratic density makes it more likely to be disordered and anomalous with respect to spatial ordering. This is probably one of the reasons that feces are typically considered more filthy and contaminating than urine or most other bodily substances.

Perhaps even more important than the compatibility of the metaphors of pollution and distance is the suitability of ideas of dirt and pollution for expressing concerns about social interaction between those who are unequal in status. As we have seen, there is considerable structural pressure in status orders to interact with status equals, that is, for status homogeneity. Homogeneity is of course a central notion behind the concept of purity. For something to be pure means that it is composed of identical subcomponents uncontaminated by foreign matter—especially inferior foreign matter.[8] Therefore, we should not be surprised that the caste system, which emphasizes status homogeneity, has elaborately developed notions of pollution—though as we shall see, this varies by region and subgroup.

Pollution is, in part, a symbolic code that is a way of "talking about" and reinforcing status homogeneity. Not only is there the practical effect of having your status lowered when you extensively associate with inferiors—the consequence in any social system—but there are two additional negative consequences of such associations. First, to the degree that an abhorrence of dirt has been internalized, and to some degree it is in all cultures, one avoids contacts with inferiors because these produce psychological discomfort. Second, since such contacts violate the norms regarding purity, one must do ritual work in order to restore one's purity. This requires time, trouble, and, indirectly, wealth. This requirement in turn creates additional controls, for there is a tendency for rituals of purification to become magical. In terms of our theoretical discussion in Chapter 8, moral processes become objectified into physical processes. In such circumstances, simply avoiding deliberate associations with a lower caste person is insufficient. One becomes polluted even if there is inadvertent contact; a social and moral process is further reinforced by a mechanical and magical process. As Douglas notes (1966:113), a person who creates pollution, intentionally or not, is always in the wrong. Obviously, such demoralization tends to increase the energy people devote to avoiding pollution. Seeing pollution as a moral and magical mechanism for reinforcing status concerns is quite compatible with Weber: "As a status group, caste enhances and transposes the social closure into the sphere of religion or rather magic" (1958b:43).

Douglas places the connection between status groups and pollution in a more general context. She argues that concerns about pollution are likely to arise where there are concerns about maintaining boundaries:

> These are pollution powers which inhere in the structure of ideas itself and which punish a symbolic breaking of that which should be joined or joining that which should be separate. It follows from this that pollution is a type of danger which is not likely to occur except where the lines of structure, cosmic or social, are clearly defined. (1966:113)

The argument can be summarized in the following manner. Concerns with pollution are typically associated with boundary maintenance. Status groups, which are always to some degree concerned about their boundaries, and which typically use physical distance as a metaphor for social distance, often draw on notions of pollution. Where these ideas of pollution become highly elaborated, they significantly reinforce the already strong tendency toward restriction and regulation of cross-group associations and social mobility. In short, the norms, symbols, and rituals concerning pollution both express and reinforce structural pressures arising from a resource base in which status is an especially crucial feature. Connecting pollution to concerns about status boundaries is not, of course, to deny that Indians might also be concerned about other kinds of boundaries and might use notions of pollution to reinforce these. I am simply arguing that in India, status boundaries are unusually significant, and much of the preoccupation with pollution is related to this concern.[9]

Seeing pollution as a metaphor on status not only helps us to see why contact and associations are seen in relationship to their purifying or polluting effects, but also throws light on why outcast groups tend to emerge. Extremely low status strata are frequently characterized in terms of dirt and pollution: "stinking niggers," "poor white trash," "filthy beggar," "the squalid masses." Since status is relatively inexpansible, some must lose status if others are to gain status; similarly, if some are to be pure, others must be impure. One way to increase the status of even relatively powerless and underprivileged strata is to create an even less privileged polluted outcast group. Moreover, the stronger the attempts to give some strata very high status, the greater the pressure to create such outcast groups. As Dumont and others have suggested, the extraordinary purity of the Brahmans is not unrelated to the extraordinary impurity of the Untouchables. I do not mean to argue that pollution is an absolutely zero-sum concept, but I do mean to suggest that where pollution is a code or metaphor for status, there are strong tendencies in this direction.

The Human Body and the Social Body

Now let us consider a third symbol. According to Douglas, the human body is a relatively closed system with limited entrances and exits, and is often used to symbolize the social tensions that develop in closed groups:

[A]ll margins are dangerous. . . . We should expect the orifices of the body to symbolize its especially vulnerable points. Matter issuing from them is marginal stuff of the most obvious kind. Spittle, blood, milk, urine, feces or tears by simply issuing forth have traversed the boundary of the body. . . . The mistake is to treat bodily margins in isolation from all other margins. (1966:121)

Of course, all societies have some emotional connotations attached to things that enter and leave the body. But few societies have the enormous concern about the purity of what is taken into the body and the revulsion of bodily excrements that is characteristic of South Asia. This serves as another symbol, with its many related rituals, to reinforce the concern about the social boundary of castes and other status-based subgroups.[10] Just as the caste must be scrupulous about the status of those with whom its members engage in intimate expressive relationships, so must individuals be concerned about the purity of the substances with which they come in contact—especially those taken into the body.

Human Substance and Human Conduct

An ideology commonly associated with status groups concerns the inheritance of characteristics from one's parents. The frequency and power of this idea is undoubtedly, in part, based on the fact that children do biologically inherit many characteristics from their parents. Just as there has been a strong tendency to supplement or substitute magical processes for social processes of social control, there has been a strong tendency for status groups to emphasize biological rather than cultural transmission of characteristics. This objectification of both processes contributes to the same outcome: problematic and uncertain moral and social processes are transformed or supplemented with seemingly more reliable mechanical processes. The children of the elite no longer have to prove by their conduct that they too deserve to be elite; rather, they deserve to be elite because of the superior nature of their bodily substances. Their status is not dependent on the way they exercise their agency. Nor are they dependent on how others respond to their actions—something that is always contingent and uncertain. Rather, their status is supposedly based on the "objective" nature of their objectlike body. The most common examples in modern societies are theories of racial superiority. Obviously these kinds of arguments have been present in many societies throughout most of history, though they are by no means characteristic of all societies. Typically it is assumed, if not explicitly stated, that one's conduct is shaped and limited by the biologically inherited bodily substances. Hence those that did not inherit the appropriate bodily substances are excluded from certain social roles of power and privilege and consigned to social roles involving service and deference.

Quite commonly ideas about pollution are linked to those about the biological inheritance of bodily substances: hence we get notions of pure lineages. For reasons we need not explore here, these are often symbolized by the metaphor of "pure blood." (For discussions of the South Asian concept of "blood" and its relation to human reproduction, see Inden [1976] and McGilvray [1982].) This imagery is common in South Asia, and is one of the rationales used to justify caste differences, especially endogamy and the traditional division of labor.

Marriott and various colleagues have argued that the Hindu understanding of this process is significantly different from typical Western notions (see Marriott and Inden 1974; Inden 1976, 1985, 1986; Marriott 1976, 1989). Based on their study of South Asian texts and ethnographic literature, they introduce a critique of Dumont's work. They argue that despite Dumont's stated intention of rejecting Western ideologies and ideas about concepts of "stratification," his work is too dependent on Western dualistic concepts—especially on dualistic notions of the relationship between bodily substances and human conduct. As an alternative, they propose an "ethnosociology" that recognizes the monistic approach of Indic categories to the relationship between—what the West would call—moral and biological processes. The details of their analysis are complicated and subtle, but the essence of their argument concerns Hindu notions about the relationship between bodily substance and human conduct. While an individual's bodily substance is determined within broad limits at procreation, that substance continues to be shaped and modified by subsequent events (e.g., marriage) and personal conduct. In turn, a person's bodily substance shapes his or her subsequent moral behavior. Moreover, substances that are taken into the body—such as food—affect one's core substances, and in turn one's future actions. Thus morality and biology are understood monistically rather than dualistically—that is, as inextricably intertwined rather than as two separate realms.[11] The analytical implication of these observations is that the behavior of South Asians with respect to marriage, commensuality, associations, occupational activity, and so on should be analyzed in relationship to these notions that supposedly play a crucial role in guiding people's behavior in South Asia.[12] Stated negatively, sociologists will not be able to understand the key features of the caste system if they rely on their Western notions of stratification or Dumont's dualistic distinctions.

From my perspective, the South Asian categories Marriott and Inden have identified are, in part, a cultural code used to "talk about" and reinforce rules governing bodily pollution. Thus we have multiple layers of symbolic codes and rituals. (Here I am using the word "code" in the general sense indicated earlier, rather than in the restricted sense used by Marriott.) The Indic categories that Inden and Marriott have analyzed—for example *guna* and *purusa*—provide an indigenous rationale for concerns about bodily purity. In turn, the imagery and rituals surrounding the body—for example bathing and other forms of purification—symbolize more general notions of pollution. Finally, the metaphors of pollution, and socially ordered space and distance, symbolize concerns about interpersonal associations and the effect these have on individual and group social status. Each layer of symbolic material serves as a metaphor or code for the prior level; in a sense we can say that there is a code, on a code, on a code. I mean to suggest not that absolute differentiation and logical consistency reigns in the use of these various levels of symbols, only that it is useful to look at these cultural ideas as multiple layers of symbolism and ritual that, among other things, are indirect mechanisms of social control. They are, in some respects, analogous to the relationships that exist in the military between the (1) elaborate rituals about shining shoes, (2) bodily appearance, (3) drills and parades, and (4) a disciplined fighting unit; each prior set of ideas and rituals is used to symbolize the subsequent, more fundamental concern. In a sense each more specific level is a metonym for the next more general level.

For the actors involved, these ideas are not merely codes, metaphors, and metonyms. For many, the idea that pollution can be transmitted from those who are physically too close is real and literal. One way of thinking about the distinction is to ask to what degree something is a symbol of status versus a criterion of status. Is having gold stars on your uniform a sign that you are a general or does it actually make you a general? In the Hindu context, does donning a sacred thread actually make you a member of a twice-born caste? It is obvious that gold stars are a symbol. In the second case the answer is much more ambiguous. Simply donning a thread may bring outrage from members of the local upper castes, and in earlier times could get you a beating if not worse. However, getting reputable Brahmans to conduct a sacred thread ceremony for you may well get many people to acknowledge your twice-born status, even when your ancestry is suspect. Similarly, does eating the proper food symbolize your religious purity or does it actually make you pure? Here we move much closer to a situation in which the object or substance—in this case, the food— becomes the actual means to purity rather than simply its symbol. I will argue that in Hindu society the relationship between status and purity is variable. Often it will approximate the last case, and ritual status and purity will be a near identity. It is, however, I believe, a mistake to assume that this is always so. In the social realm, for example, the symbols of kingship rather than the symbols of purity are sometimes used to express high status. Knowledge is another important component and symbol of high status and sacredness, and is seen as partly independent of purity and pollution per se (see Babb 1975:181–83). Conversely, as Fuller (1979:473–74) points out, purity and pollution may symbolize things other than social status, for example, morality and goodness versus sin and evil. Consequently, an adequate analysis of both social and sacral relationships requires that we analyze purity and pollution without making this the fundamental analytical category. Rather, it must be seen as one—admittedly central—component and symbol of social and sacral status.

Sexuality and Asceticism

One of the central arguments of Chapter 6 was that the basis of Brahmanical power has been to steer a middle course between otherworldly renunciation and open pursuit of economic and political power. Stated more concretely, they have rejected becoming either ascetic renouncers or ruling kings. The core of their strategy has been to give up the right to political power voluntarily but to continue to participate actively in the local agrarian infrastructure as householders, and to adopt many of the rituals and disciplines of otherworldly renouncers. As we have seen, such a strategy has been subject to a variety of cross-pressures and contradictions. Success in balancing these countervailing demands has required high levels of self-discipline by individual Brahmans, local jatis, and the Brahmanic subculture as a whole. As Das's (1982) analysis of myths about King Aama shows, Brahmans have been repeatedly concerned about the temptations to stray from this difficult path.[13]

Now we will explore some of the metaphors that both express these psychological and social tensions and serve as mechanisms to help guide persons through them. In Geertz's (1966) terminology, they are "models of" the social structure and "models for" reproducing that structure.

Sex as a Symbol

A common symbol for restraint and discipline in many cultures is the notion of sexual abstinence. Many societies have ascetic and monastic traditions that emphasize the importance of limiting or avoiding sexual activity. Such sexual activity is typically identified with sensuousness, worldliness, aggression, and even chaos and disorder. In contrast, the ascetic is the epitome of virtuous self-control and spiritual otherworldliness.

If the ascetic motif is common to many cultures, it has special significance and unusual forms in India. Particularly striking is the Indian preoccupation with the loss of male semen. It is not just sexuality or even thoughts of sexuality that are to be avoided, but the loss of semen by whatever means. Semen is a highly distilled essence that contains highly concentrated power, and to discharge it is to lose this power. This is another example of what I have termed "objectification"; a moral and social concern is elaborated and represented by a more material set of processes. Accordingly, the actors' problem is no longer simply to regulate and discipline sexuality, but to physically control a material substance.

This idea comes out of the yogi tradition. As O'Flaherty notes, "the Upanisads regard the loss of seed as a kind of death" (1980:31). In part, this is so because losing semen is to abandon the powers that are available to the yogi: "The yogi, by drawing his semen to this special point, the site of the third eye [between his eyebrows], reverses the flow of normal sexuality and hence the flow of normal time; thus he transmutes seed into Soma, converting the fatal act of intercourse into an internal act that will assure immortality" (O'Flaherty, 1980:46; see also Eliade, 1969:267–68).

What is the relevance of this to the typical Hindu? According to O'Flaherty, "Although the yogi aspiration to transmute semen into Soma is taken literally, and acted upon, by only a small and esoteric section of Indian society, it is known and subscribed to on a theoretical level by most Indians, even nonliterate villagers" (1980:47). In his vast summary of the anthropological literature on India, Mandelbaum notes that a there is a common fear that a man is weakened through intercourse: "a wife is readily seen by her husband's family as an active temptress. A man is supposed to have only a limited amount of life-giving fluids and rapid loss is believed to weaken a man drastically. Women are not so debilitated by frequent intercourse" (1970:77). Daniel reports a similar finding:

> [I]n contemporary Tamilnadu it is said that a man's power, *sakti*, enters him in food and is stored in semen: "to increase and maintain this *sakti*, males must retain their semen and hence lead an ascetic life. Females, while having greater *sakti* of their own, also acquire, in intercourse, the *sakti* stored in the semen, thus further increasing their supply." (O'Flaherty 1980:45, quoting Daniel 1978:6)

So while the notion has its roots in the relatively esoteric yogi tradition, it has been widely dispersed throughout India over a long period of time.

The householder is not supposed to abstain from sex completely; one of his central obligations is to have children, especially sons. According to Dimmit and van Buitenen:

> The tension that exists between family and ascetic life in Hindu society is made abundantly clear. . . . Ascetic life is highly prized, but only for some. For if everyone renounced the world, society would cease and mendicant ascetics would have no means of support. So asceticism and the mendicant life, however highly respected in Indian culture, always depend on the existence of householders for their basic support. (1983:249)

To the degree that it is necessary for biological and social reproduction, sexuality is necessary. But the cultural ideal is to restrain one's sexual activity, for by doing so, one's power is created and maintained. This ideal is represented in the behavior of the seers and sages of the Puranas:

> For the most part seers or sages are wise and holy brahmins who are deserving of respect; they are usually married, but still live austere lives, often in hermitages, practicing tapas, or self-restraint. This practice for them as for the celibate yogin, gains the doer enormous powers; hence the awe in which they tend to be held by their associates. (Dimmit and van Buitenen 1983:245)

Or as Kane says: "The Manusmriti (V. 56) declares that eating flesh, drinking intoxicants and sexual intercourse are not sinful in themselves; all beings are naturally inclined to these; but abstention (from these) leads to great rewards (and therefore Sastra [*sic*] emphasizes abstention)" (1977:1628).

I want to suggest that, in Weber's terms, there is an "elective affinity" between these notions about sexuality and the Brahman's situation with respect to religious and worldly power. As I argued earlier, the Brahman's fundamental identity and basis of power is in a relatively inalienable religious status, and to maintain this status, the Brahmans abdicate political power. On the other hand, it is legitimate and necessary that they participate in the material basis of the agrarian economy. Both with respect to sexuality and worldly power the exhortation is not complete abstinence, but restraint. Sex and material power are necessary for certain purposes, but they must be carefully limited and always kept secondary. These attitudes toward sexuality can be seen, in part, as a set of secondary norms and as a metaphor that expresses the tensions of the Brahman's position of power in the social structure. This is not to argue that the Brahman's location in the social structure causes their attitudes about sexuality, in any simple unilinear sense. But there is a psychological and symbolic compatibility between the social structure and attitudes about sexuality that is mutually reinforcing. In many cultures sex is seen as involving, in part, aggressive power and domination. These same characteristics are often associated with political power. It should not be surprising, then, that when a group's primary strategy for gaining broad societal power is to forego any open contest for political power, per se, such restraint might also become expressed in the realm of sexuality.

The Danger of Seduction

The relevant symbolism does not stop with sexual restraint as a metaphor on political and economic self-restraint. A key threat to any attempt at sexual restraint by males is the danger—in fantasy, if not reality—of aggressive females. This theme is frequent in Hindu mythology. As O'Flaherty notes, "The dominant woman is dangerous in Hindu mythology, and the dominant goddess expresses this danger" (1980:77).

At times the myths emphasize the threat of seduction. The story of Kandu in the *Brahma Purana* is one example. A great seer gains so much power through practicing austerities that the gods come to fear him. They send an Apsaras, who is "fine-waisted, with beautiful teeth, full hips, and ample breast, and endowed with all the fine marks of beauty." They say to her, " 'go quickly where the hermit is doing *tapas* and seduce him, my pretty, to deplete his power of *tapas*' " (Dimmit and van Buitenen 1983:259). This theme is not restricted to obscure sacred texts. Marglin (1982:167, 1985) describes how the same motif is used in contemporary ritual at the Jagannatha temple at Puri. But here, as in many of the texts from the epics onward, the story is carried a step further. The heat generated by the sage's tapas is seen as the cause of a drought. He must be seduced in order for it to rain and end the threat of famine. The moral seems to be that a commitment to self-restraint and control is not enough; the power this generates may threaten the interests and power of others. The ascetic must therefore be wary of those who would, by seduction, deliberately weaken the power he has acquired. On the other hand, these other more worldly interests are seen as legitimate, and so seduction always works.

The threat of aggressive females may take a much more ominous form, the image of the devouring goddess. This is especially characteristic of the goddesses Durga and Kali:

> She appears as the killer of her demon lover; beheading him in a symbolic castration; she dances on the corpse of her consort, impaling herself upon his still animate phallus. This is the nonmaternal goddess, with whom the worshipper does not dare seek erotic contact for fear of losing his powers. But the dominant woman also appears as the mother goddess, with whom the worshipper does not dare seek erotic contact for fear of incest. (O'Flaherty 1980:77)

This theme of the danger of female power is an important theme in Hinduism in general and the tradition of Tantrism in particular (Brooks 1990:65).

Beneficence and Danger

There is, however, a third and more positive image of women in the myths: the image of the giving mother. The physical representation of this is the breast of milk and the central theme is generosity and beneficence. This is the image of what Kakar (1981) calls the "good mother," in contrast to the "bad mother." This image of the female is less threatening to the notion of male asceticism. Yet even here there is danger that beneficence can lapse into seduction and hence incest.

The second key point in my argument is that if male sexual restraint is a key metaphor for the Brahman's strategy for obtaining religious power, fear of dominant women stands for the threat of the king's worldly power. It is a way of expressing the tension that always exists between legitimate power in the form of authority and the illegitimate power of unrestrained self-interest, especially in the form of force. O'Flaherty has recognized that the male–female dichotomy frequently represents this tension: "The dichotomy between male authority and female power on the human level provides new conflicts when it sets a pattern on which divine hierogamies are modelled: any woman, especially a goddess, has power, but this power is tamed by making it subservient to her husband" (1980:77).

Marglin has specifically suggested that the power of the king is represented by the power of femaleness:

> It will be argued that royal power is essentially female power (*sakti*), a power which stands outside the realm of the pure and the impure. Furthermore, it will be shown that the king's relationship to purity and impurity is homologous to that of women. The king's link to hierarchy is through his Brahman preceptor (*rajaguru*) just as the woman's link to hierarchy is through her husband. This parallelism between the positions of king and wife is found not only in their respective relationships to purity and impurity but also in their roles and the kinds of power inherent in them. (1982:156)

> My suggestion is that in such a relationship the king stands for the wife and the Brahman stands for the husband. (1982:171)

Marglin is not the only one to draw a connection between Hindu notions of sexual relations and political relations. O'Flaherty (1980:118) and Nandy (1983:10) make similar arguments.

One final parallel can be drawn. As noted above, there is a positive female image in Hindu thought, the giving beneficent mother. It is not accidental, I think, that this is also a key function of the good king. Just as the power of the dominant female and the unrestrained and unguided king are threatening and frightening, such power used for beneficence and providing for the need of others is the essential characteristic of the good mother and the good king. Even more specifically, the female is responsible for fertility with respect to reproduction, whether it be at the human or divine level. It is Parvati who must seduce Siva to insure that there are children. In a similar manner it is the king who was responsible, at least in some parts of India, for the fertility of the land—and more specifically, for the coming of the rains (see Marglin 1982, 1985a). So in both its malevolent and beneficent aspects, female sexuality parallels the attributes of the king. We will take up this matter in more detail in the discussion of auspiciousness and inauspiciousness in the next chapter.

Caveats and Conclusions

The discussion has illustrated how various symbolic and ritual elements of Hindu culture are metaphors for the tensions that arise from the nature of India's social structure. The preoccupations with control of semen, on the one hand, and the production of sons to maintain the lineage, on the other, symbolize the cross pressures inherent in the Brahmanical strategy for maintaining cultural dominance and considerable wealth by, in principle, forgoing political power. The negative characterization of female sexuality represents the ever present threat of the unrestrained power and force of the king. Finally the notion of the female as the good mother represents the king when he is subordinate to and guided by Brahmans.

An important caveat is required: the argument that has been sketched out is certainly not all that the sexual conflicts in Hindu myths are about. Kakar (1981) and O'Flaherty (1980) have both analyzed in some detail the connections between these myths and the tensions and conflicts that arise between husbands and wives and in childrearing. But mythology and ritual are often multivocal, that is, many things may be said by the same set of symbols. Even if the sexual conflicts of Hindu mythology primarily represent the tensions of family life, the question remains why Hindu culture expresses these conflicts so much more frequently and vividly than most complex civilizations. One hypothesis worthy of exploration is that the conflicts of power within the family are not unrelated to the conflicts of power at the macro level of society, and that these both affect notions of legitimate and illegitimate sexuality. (This theme has been developed by Marcuse [1962], Laing [1971], and others with respect to Western society.) But whatever the causal connection may be between conflicts of power between elites and conflicts of power within the family, my argument is that the rich sexual symbolism of Hinduism is, in part, an expression and representation of the unusual distribution of power characteristic of traditional India.

Second, a theoretical and methodological note is required. In the analysis of social distance, pollution and bodily substances, I argued that each subsequent level in a sense parallels the previous level; that there is a code, on a code, on a code. Stated in the concepts of semiology, the relationship between the various codes is paradigmatic, with each subsequent level being a partial substitute for, as well as supplement to, the prior levels. This is not, however, the primary structure of the material concerning asceticism and sexuality. Rather, the material seems to be structured more syntagmatically. One set of ideas and symbols suggests and leads to the next set, which is typically the antithesis of the first. The symbols become elaborated as the problems and tensions that are explored become more elaborate. A story is being told, and each subsequent element adds an additional part of the story rather than simply repeating the basic message in a new form.

Finally, a methodological note is required. The material analyzed in connection with pollution and bodily substances involved primarily what I have called secondary norms and rituals. The analysis of sexual symbolism includes yet a third layer, the level of myths, which are often offered as a rationale for these norms and rituals. I have not tried to demarcate carefully these various layers. A more complete and systematic analysis would require attention to such matters. But our interest in this symbolic material is fundamentally substantive, not aimed primarily at elaborating the theory or methods of symbolic analysis per se. Whatever the formal structure of the symbols, the key point is that this striking and vivid material both expresses and reinforces crucial features of the social structure.

Purity, Asceticism, and Agency

The relationship between contingency and agency is a theme that runs through many parts of this book. A few words are needed about the relevance of this theme for the notions of purity and asceticism.

It is assumed that individuals have the power to reduce their level of impurity. The same is true of asceticism. Control of semen, for example, is a matter of systematic discipline, a matter of self-control by the individual involved; it is not primarily either a gift of grace or the outcome of fickle fate. That is, with respect to matters of pollution and purity, humans are assumed to have agency. Of course, the objection can be raised that with respect to the critical determinant of purity—one's varna, jati, or gender (at birth)—individuals have little or no agency. But as we shall see, the famous doctrine of karma is precisely about this issue. In its unqualified form, the doctrine claims that one's ascribed statuses are the result of one's own actions in previous incarnations. We will consider this matter in some detail in Chapter 14, but two provisional points are relevant here: (1) the level of purity incorporated in one's bodily substances at birth is determined by the sum of one's actions (karma) in past incarnations, and (2) the level of purity in the short run is affected by conformity to lifestyle norms, and the purity of one's associates. Therefore, with regard to matters of purity and asceticism, humans are seen to have high levels of agency. In the next chapter we will focus on symbols and rituals that are primarily concerned with the contingencies of human existence.

The Structural Sources of Tantrism: A Postscript

Building on the preceding analysis, I now want to suggest an explanation of how Tantrism—which is often seen as a rejection of concerns with purity and asceticism—found an important niche within the broader Hindu tradition. A theory that explains the key structural features of a highly ordered social unit should also be useful in predicting the forms of deviance and innovation likely to occur in it. A simple example illustrates the point. Where people are segregated by sex for extended periods, rates of masturbation, prostitution, and homosexual behavior are likely to increase, and/or sex will be defined as something that is inappropriate, dangerous, or even evil. On the other hand, those subject to sexual segregation—prisoners, monastics, soldiers, residents of frontiers, students in single sex schools—rarely react to their situation by advocating communities of promiscuous heterosexual free love or universal homosexuality. In other words, the pressures for deviance and innovation are more likely to draw upon and transform existing social patterns selectively.

Taking this rather self-evident idea, what can be predicted about forms of deviance and innovation within Hinduism, given the patterns we have already examined? Considering the strong emphasis on purity and control of sexuality in Indian culture, it would not be surprising to find deviant groups that wanted to emphasize the opposite values. Given the strong emphasis on avoiding and renouncing worldly power, we could predict that the exercise of power in this world might become a value for some; agency through the manipulation of purity may be rejected as inadequate, and supernatural power over this world may be sought. Given the tendency to define the present world as only a place of suffering (duhkha), some might seek to redefine it as a place of potential bliss (*ananda*). Given the tendency to define this world's reality as illusion (*maya*), an alternative view might emphasize the unity of the ultimate form of the divine (*brahman*) and the cosmos that has emanated from it. Given orthodox notions that union with the divine means the irrelevance of individual identity, agency, and power, an alternative might be to conceive of unity and closeness with the deity as a source of individual agency and power. Given the fear of the female as a threat to one's purity and power, others might emphasize symbols of the female as a source of power, thus goddesses might become prominent or even dominant deities. Given the strong emphasis on caste and kinship, it would not be surprising for some to advocate the irrelevance of these caste barriers.

Because of the highly structured social context of the caste system and orthodox Brahmanism, such deviance and innovation could easily result in people being outcaste. This would be especially likely for upper caste individuals. If such deviance emerged among lower caste groups, it would be defined by upper caste groups as proof of the inferiority that had already been assumed. This is why these ideas and practices are likely to be expressed in secret. But if unorthodox attitudes and practices are to be anything other than individualized social deviance, a group that can be trusted to keep such secrets is needed. This requires rigorous screening, selectivity, and discipline. If the authority of the family and caste is to be rejected (in spiritual matters), it must be replaced with some substitute authority, such as a guru. If the boundaries of such groups are to be maintained, it is likely that the same mechanisms used to maintain the boundaries of castes will be employed, that is, the elaboration of norms and categories, and coded symbols and rituals. Not only are implicit codes likely to be used to reinforce the social structure, but even more esoteric codes are likely to be developed for secret forms of communication. Complex and esoteric forms of knowledge and ritual practices are developed. It then becomes necessary to decide who is both competent and trustworthy to be admitted to the group. Consequently, rites of initiation become central. The formal criteria for initiation and membership are not birth and kinship, but obedience to one's guru and the acquisition of the special knowledge of the group. While such groups may be in principle open to all, it is primarily the more privileged who have the time and energy to acquire the necessary knowledge. If relatively secret societies do develop among privileged groups, it would be surprising if they did not begin to reinterpret their conventional public lives, so that their usual activities are redefined in terms of their alternative religious categories. Moreover, their unorthodox values and practices are likely to be surreptitiously inserted into more orthodox and public activities. But even then the more radical and esoteric forms of knowledge and behavior are likely to remain the province of the elite members of the group.[14] In short, what develops is an alternative form of highly structured status group that reverses the content of many of the orthodox values, but in most respects becomes an addendum to the dominant structures.

What I have been describing is a logic for the development of Tantrism within Hinduism. I do not mean to argue that it literally developed in this precise manner.

In all likelihood, many practices and ideas were borrowed from non-Aryan and non-Hindu sources. Rather, what I am suggesting is a structural logic about how Tantrism found an important place within the broader Hindu tradition. My claim is that this analysis adds something to the usual explanations of Tantrism, which say that it is the reversal of Vedic values, or, in the more complex version, that it combines elements of reversal and orthodoxy. The logic I have suggested gives some insights into why so many of the social forms—rigid boundaries, initiation rituals, strong authority, the importance of knowledge, the elaboration of norms and categories, the authority of the guru—were carried over from orthodox Brahmanism. But it also helps us see how values that seem so antithetical to orthodoxy come to overlap with that orthodoxy.[15]

Purity and asceticism have been defined as key areas of human agency for orthodox Hindus. Tantrism is primarily an alternative form of seeking more expanded forms of agency. The next chapter considers a set of cultural concepts that emphasizes the limits of such agency—and then attempts to mitigate these limits.

10

Cultural Codes and Rituals: II

As we have seen, the realms of purity and impurity strongly emphasize human agency and responsibility. Indian village culture seems to also be engrossed with notions of auspiciousness and inauspiciousness; it is analytically useful to view this preoccupation as a way of objectifying concerns about contingency. While such objectification does not eliminate forces that are beyond people's control, it is a means of both expanding the sense of human agency and of providing social and psychological mechanisms for coping with contingent forces.

I have argued that the concepts of purity and impurity are part of a complex set of secondary norms and rituals used to buttress status as a form of power against power rooted in wealth and force. Auspiciousness and inauspiciousness, on the other hand, typically concern mundane worldly well-being and, more abstractly, economic and political power. Purity and impurity are the special concerns of the Brahman, while auspiciousness and inauspiciousness are the special concern of the king and local dominant caste—though virtually all village Hindus are conscious of and affected by both.

Auspiciousness and Inauspiciousness

History of the Concept

The notions of purity and pollution have long been discussed in the scholarly literature describing Indian society (e.g., Dubois 1983). With the publication of Dumont's *Homo Hierarchicus* (1980), purity–impurity became the central interpretive concept used to understand Hindu society. While auspiciousness and inauspiciousness were discussed in the nineteenth-century descriptions of Indian customs (see Raheja 1988:34), only occasional references to these concepts appeared in the post–World War II ethnographic literature.[1] Not until the publication of the symposium edited by

Carman and Marglin (1985), and Marglin's (1985a) study of the *devadasis* (female temple dancers) in Puri, did the concept receive major attention from the scholarly community. With the publication of Raheja's *The Poison in the Gift* (1988), inauspiciousness became an important point of discussion. According to Raheja, the notion of inauspiciousness, and the various rituals intended to remove or disperse it, were so central to the life of the villagers she studied—and in many respects much more so than purity and pollution—she first thought she had stumbled across some strange deviant subculture. "That the dispersal of inauspiciousness structured and gave meaning to so much of Pahansu social and ritual life struck me so forcibly that it seemed inconceivable that other ethnographers had not placed it at the center of their interpretations of village life in India" (1988:31). Since the publication of Raheja's book, South Asianists increasingly suspect that the notion of inauspiciousness may be much more central than had previously been imagined. There is, however, no clear consensus about this.

My discussion of the history of the concept has been limited to the literature on India. Similar notions are common to many if not most agrarian societies, including other Asian societies (see, e.g., Tubielewicz 1980) and premodern Western civilization (see, e.g., Thomas 1971). Thus the concern of Indic civilization with auspiciousness is not as atypical as is their preoccupation with caste and pollution. There is not yet sufficient comparative material to determine which features of the auspiciousness-inauspiciousness complex are unique to India, though I will offer some theoretical speculations about this.

What Is to Be Explained

Detailed data about auspiciousness and inauspiciousness and how these shape behavior in India remains quite sparse. Nonetheless, several key facts seem apparent. Auspiciousness (*subha, mangala*) and inauspiciousness (*asubha, amangala*) are concerned with well-being and injury—those things producing benefit and harm.[2] Often the focus is on worldly well-being, as contrasted to salvation, though there are exceptions. Auspiciousness or inauspiciousness tend to be associated with

1. *Moments or times of transition, movement and change* such as births, marriages, deaths, puberty ceremonies, coronations, journeys, the conjunction of planets, building new houses, undertaking new business ventures, wearing new clothes, and so forth.
2. *A strong sense of contingency and uncertainty* about whether the outcome will bring well-being or harm, though some events are primarily associated with one or the other outcome, for example, marriage is primarily associated with auspiciousness while death is primarily associated with inauspiciousness.
3. *The giving of gifts (dana),* which can be organized into extremely complex patterns and is a means of transferring inauspicious substances from one person or group to another.
4. *Women and female qualities*, especially fertility.
5. *Notions of kingship,* both in terms of what will be auspicious for a ruler and the beneficence of the ruler toward his subjects.
6. *Signs and omens*, especially astrology, in order to determine the times, circumstances, and conditions most likely to be auspicious rather than inauspicious.

How and why are these things associated, and in what way are they related to other features of the social structure and culture? Since the ethnographic literature on which these "facts" are based is still very limited, the interpretation I suggest is necessarily quite tentative; the arguments that follow are a series of exploratory hypotheses.

Social Sources of Contingency in India

I have interpreted purity and pollution as a set of coded metaphors that reinforce the key structural features characteristic of status groups in general and caste in particular: the tendencies toward status homogeneity and boundary maintenance. That is to say, a concern with purity and impurity is rooted in social sources derived from certain features of the social structure. Similarly, I want to argue that the concern with auspiciousness and inauspiciousness is due to social sources, some of which are the centrality of status in Indian society and the structural features that this produces.

Movement and Change

I have suggested that human existence is characterized by both agency and contingency. Humans have some understanding of and power over their environment, but many things are beyond understanding or control. As I suggested in Chapter 2, the crucial collective means for coping with contingency is the creation of social structures. While their overall effect is to reduce contingency, the specific consequences can be mixed. Structures increase some forms and aspects of agency and simultaneously reduce others. Conversely, structures reduce some forms of contingency and create others. For example, I pointed out that well-defined ascribed social statuses reduce uncertainties about short-term social interactions—how others may respond to a particular action. At the same time, they reduce human choice and agency, and hence make social destinies seem more arbitrary and contingent.

A key characteristic of status groups and castes is their tendency to be preoccupied with stability and proper order. This is especially so with respect to their boundaries and key positions and roles within such groups. I have tried to show how concerns about pollution result in layers of secondary norms and rituals that reinforce and buttress social boundaries. Inappropriate relations or movements across social boundaries are "automatically" sanctioned because they result in pollution and impurity. This occurs even if others do not detect such deviance, and whether or not it is punished by social sanctions.

But no society is completely static. Nor are the social boundaries of groups and their social positions completely rigid and impermeable. If nothing else, all societies have to allow mobility through the various positions of the life cycle. Children become adults, the unmarried marry, adults become parents, and everyone grows old and dies.

Such points of transition produce anxiety in virtually all societies. Quite aside from the individual psychological anxieties, such transitions call into question the boundaries and structures that have been so carefully maintained. Most societies use various forms of ritual to transform the identity of those making these transitions, and to relax and repair the social boundaries that are being crossed. Van Gennep (1960) and Victor Turner (1967, 1969, 1974) have analyzed these liminal moments of transition in considerable detail.

My hypothesis is that the more time and energy people have invested in creating and maintaining social boundaries, the more the crossing of such boundaries will be defined as problematic. Further, upper caste and high status groups will be more concerned than lower status groups. By the same logic, crossing gender boundaries, for example, homosexuality and transvestism, is more problematic than life-cycle transitions.[3] In short, the level of perceived danger will be related to the strength and importance of the boundaries involved. The level of danger can also be affected by whether the changes are expected or unexpected, permanent or temporary.

Such transitions are not inherently bad or evil. Nonetheless, because things are fluid, they have the potential for either good or evil—or perhaps some combination of the two. Momentary relaxations of the structures are dangerous, but they can also release great power that has been "bottled up" in structures. Turner (1969) has emphasized the positive possibilities of such transitional moments in his concept of "communitas": the possibilities for fellowship, solidarity, transcendence, and emotional release in the liminal periods when the usual structures are suspended. Of course, the release of such power also can result in anarchy, disorder, and disaster. The concepts of auspiciousness and inauspiciousness in part focus upon the contingency inherent in the suspension of structure, "anti-structure" in Turner's terms, and the agency and power it releases. Thus, as Marglin (1985a) has emphasized, auspiciousness and inauspiciousness are not mutually exclusive conditions.[4]

Other forms of movement are also associated with auspiciousness and inauspiciousness—both because there are real parallels and by metaphorical extension. Travel and the initiation of new projects such as building houses, digging wells, or important business transactions are activities subject to auspiciousness and inauspiciousness. In all these there are both risk and possibility. The auspiciousness and inauspiciousness associated with wearing new clothes for the first time have a parallel source; this step involves a literal and figurative change in the boundary markers of the body and the self.

Nor is it accidental that auspiciousness and inauspiciousness are associated with women and goddesses. There seem to be two reasons for this. First, most of India is patrilocal and patrilineal, and women are the movers; they leave their natal homes and become members of a new family. This move is seen as such a radical transformation that it is culturally defined as involving a metamorphosis of bodily substances; the married woman becomes both morally and "biologically" part of the conjugal family. (We will take up this matter in more detail in Chapter 11.) Second, as in many societies, womens' virginity and monogamy are powerful symbols of the group's boundaries. Sexual relations with inappropriate partners are enormously threatening to the group's honor. Children out of wedlock are evidence and are symbols of this dishonor as long as they are living, and the memory of them may last for generations. Because women are both a key symbol of the group's purity and its social boundaries and because they are the transitional and linking beings who tie family groups together, they have great potential for auspiciousness and inauspiciousness.

Superior Power

So far I have focused on movement across social boundaries as a source of auspiciousness and inauspiciousness. Movement is dangerous because it relaxes the structures that contain and control power. My hypothesis, though, is that the ultimate fear is not of movement but of the contingency and danger of uncontained power. Hence we should not be surprised that auspiciousness and inauspiciousness are also associated with being in the presence of great power. Those who must approach the very powerful face high levels of contingency. By definition, the less powerful have less agency; a lowly person has difficulty preventing the person of great power from doing them harm. On the other hand, associating with the powerful can bring great good. Since the outcome of interaction with those of great power is contingent upon factors beyond the control of the weaker party, such encounters contain the possibility for both auspiciousness and inauspiciousness.

Unsurprisingly, Hindu kings are associated with auspiciousness. With considerable oversimplification, it can be said that there were two key kingly functions. *Danda*, the exercise of force (literally, "the rod"), was the essence of kingship, both theoretically and practically. By this means, kings were responsible for avoiding chaos and disorder (*adharma*). It is hardly surprising that the figure who wielded such power would be seen as both potentially beneficent and dangerous. The sense of danger is undoubtedly accentuated because according to the Dharmasastras the king's powers of command (*ksatra*) are nearly absolute. As Lingat notes, "*Ksatra* confers on the king independence, the right to act to suit himself without depending upon anyone else. The king is independent of subjects, as is the spiritual preceptor of his pupils and the head of the family of the members of his household" (1973:211).

The second key function is to ensure the prosperity of the realm, more literally to provide food (*annadata*). The king is responsible for the fertility of the soil and, more specifically, for the rains, the key to agrarian productivity and prosperity. As Inden says, "Kings were . . . those manifestations of Visnu (or devotees of Siva) who were supposed to bring about the well-being of the countries they ruled; they were, toward that end, enjoined to engage in daily conduct and in the execution of rituals that were designated as *mangala* [auspicious]" (1985:31). In some periods, kings were not conceptualized as independent rulers, but were part of a hierarchy of kings ruled over by a king of kings (Inden 1982). Kings were potent agents who exercised power over others and thus were a source of auspiciousness and inauspiciousness, but they were also subordinates who were subject to the power and agency of superior kings. Stated in our theoretical terms, kings were both subject to and the source of contingency because they were both liege and vassal.[5] Even in periods when this hierarchy of rulers may not have had salience, kings always faced high levels of contingency; as I have argued earlier, political position and wealth can always be appropriated by the outside conqueror or the rebellious upstart. Moreover, the scope of their responsibilities and their close identification with their kingdoms meant that all contingencies were relevant. As Inden notes:

[B]ecause the king includes the people and country of his kingdom within his persona, every portent that appears in his kingdom, no matter where, is also a warning to him.

And every calamity that occurs in it, no matter who is directly affected, is also a cata-
strophe for the king. This is why the king, above all others was concerned with omens
in ancient and medieval India. (1985:35)

In sum, I am arguing that auspiciousness and inauspiciousness is largely concerned with contingency and especially the contingencies that are involved when
people face great or unknown power. Hence we should expect these concepts to be
of special relevance during periods when well established structures are relaxed to
allow change and movement, and when actors must face others who have great
power, especially power that could fundamentally change one's structural position.

Factors and Omens

When agency seems limited and contingency seems great, humans have an intense
concern to predict the time and place when powerful external forces will impinge
upon them. If the forces that confront them cannot be controlled, perhaps the conditions under which these powerful forces must be faced can be manipulated to be
more or less favorable. If you can avoid it, you do not set sail on a long ocean
journey in a small boat during the stormy season. Nor do you ask a powerful person
for a favor when he is angry and upset. Much of astrology is concerned with identifying the times that will be propitious for particular undertakings. Raheja reports:

> Most villagers are aware of, and constantly discuss, the solar and lunar days, and
> lunar months that are auspicious or inauspicious in relation to specific activities.
> Nearly all villagers can list the days that are inauspicious for smearing floors with
> cow-dung (Tuesday, Thursday, and Saturday), auspicious for beginning the wheat
> harvest (Sunday or Tuesday), inauspicious for wearing new bangles (*parva*, the first
> day of a lunar fortnight; *amavas*, new moon day; and Wednesday), auspicious for
> traveling in any direction (Tuesday), inauspicious for setting out on a journey
> (Saturday), or inauspicious for putting on new clothes for the first time (the first or
> eleventh days of a lunar fortnight, a new moon day, and Tuesday). (1988:38–39)

Whether a time is auspicious or inauspicious is related to the particular activity
and the social position of the people involved. Saturday is generally inauspicious for
beginning a journey, but a married daughter may safely be sent to her conjugal
home on that day; yet a bride cannot be sent to her natal village.

In addition to taking into account uncontrollable factors that may influence the
outcome of an action, people look to signs and omens. Not only do you avoid long
boat trips in the stormy season, and avoid the king when he is in a bad mood, you also
consult those who can predict the weather, and you look for clues about the king's
mood. By looking for signs and omens you fine-tune the cultural knowledge about
the usual auspicious and inauspicious times and locations. This seems to be one of the
key motivations behind divination. Divination is found in many societies and takes a
wide variety of forms, including astrology, fortunetelling, possession and seances,
dice and other mechanical techniques, and "reading" tea leaves, palms, and the
entrails of sacrificed animals.

Inden (1985) reports that medieval texts focused on irregularities and unusual oc-currences. These include eclipses, a double sun or moon, rain that is colored, fires with no apparent fuel, animals of the forest that enter a village, animals of the water crawling on land, and so on. Such irregularities are considered portents of things to come. As we might expect, many signs and omens are things or events outside of the usual categories and boundaries—since one key source of auspiciousness and inaus-piciousness is the transgression of social boundaries. But the rules governing signs often become highly complex and context-specific. For example, seeing a pregnant woman inside the house is auspicious, but seeing one outside is inauspicious; when starting a journey seeing someone sneeze is inauspicious, but it is auspicious to see someone sneeze after dinner (Raheja 1988:38). An extremely important source of inauspiciousness is the position of the planets at the time of one's birth as analyzed in horoscopes. These deal not so much with irregularities as with relatively rare conjunctions within a highly ordered system of celestial events. So while generally signs tend to be some form of irregularity, the logic behind what is defined as an ir-regularity is by no means always obvious, even to the actors involved. My guess is that systems of signs and omens become elaborated with secondary and tertiary layers of norms and codes analogous to those described for purity and pollution. If parts and layers of the system fall into disuse, the logic of the remaining system is ex-tremely difficult to decode, at least in detail. Moreover, most, if not all, meaning systems have lacuna and inconsistencies and are an infinite regress because of what Garfinkel calls indexicality.[6] Consequently translation, decoding, or interpretation leaves loose ends. As Bourdieu notes:

> [W]hen one tries to push the superimposition of the various series beyond a certain de-gree of refinement, behind the fundamental homologies . . . , difficulties begin to multi-ply systematically, demonstrating that true rigour does not lie in an analysis which tries to push the system beyond its limits, by abusing the powers of the discourse which gives voices to the silences of practice. (1977:155)[7]

Nonetheless, it seems useful to see a large percentage of signs and omens as taking the form of irregularities, even if the precise nature of the irregularity cannot be specified.

Not surprisingly, the line between the forces and the predictor of these forces can become blurred. This seems to be especially the case with respect to astrology, where sometimes the planets are seen primarily as predictors, other times they are seen as causal factors, and still other times they seem to represent gods who deliber-ately affect one's fortunes. Yet, Raheja reports, there is a distinction between signs (*sakun*) or omens (*apsakun*) and a "factor that is itself either facilitating (*labh-karak*) and appropriate or detrimental (*hani-karak*) and inappropriate to the pro-posed activity" (1988:38). She continues:

> [T]here is a fundamental difference between these two usages. In the case of "signs" and "omens," *sakun* and *apsakun* appear as more or less arbitrary, noncausal portents (*sucak*); in notions of *labh-karak* and *hani-karak*, the occurrence of the terms *subha* and *asubh* is related, not to signs that convey information (*sucna dena*), but to factors

(conceived in terms of substances) that are themselves facilitating or detrimental to the undertaking or the event. (1988:42)

We will return to the significance of such substances shortly.

The Dialectic of Agency and Contingency

In Chapters 2 and 8, I argued that in highly developed status systems we should expect to find a complex dialectic between agency and contingency. Here my thesis is that the concepts of auspiciousness and inauspiciousness are elaborated when humans feel they possess limited agency and face high levels of contingency. These notions are an idiom for "talking about" the contingency that is experienced when boundaries must be crossed and the powerful must be faced. Such conditions are, of course, especially likely in societies that emphasize hierarchial differences and maintain relatively rigid social boundaries. But humans are seldom content simply to "talk about" their lack of agency; typically they search for ways to augment and expand it. The very idiom used to recognize contingency is also used as a means of extending human agency. Stated in slightly different terms, the concern with inauspiciousness is, in part, a way of objectifying concerns about contingency. The objectification of forces beyond human control does not erase such forces. It can, however, expand the perceived realms of human agency and provide social and psychological mechanisms for dealing with the uncertainty involved.

This objectification happens in at least two ways. First, gods and other active agents can be defined as the source of these forces beyond human control; then attempts can be made to appease and propitiate these agents.[8] This is the strategy typically taken when the concern is about the power of superiors. According to Inden:

> [P]rodigies are signs emitted by the gods in response to the immoral acts of men, . . . they are warnings of disastrous events to follow. . . . How was a king supposed to respond to a portent? Each and every marvel or prodigy was a rupture or reversal of order in the visible domain of an invisible, divine lord. In order to prevent the disaster it portended, the king was supposed to determine which [divine] lord was responsible for the omen and perform an auspicious ritual. (1985:34–36)

Such behavior is not, of course, limited to kings. Traditionally villagers confronted with a disaster such as a smallpox epidemic follow a parallel procedure by directing rituals to the appropriate deity. According to the texts analyzed by Inden, contingency becomes completely transformed into agency:

> Human and natural events were, moreover, never in an accidental or chance relationship to one another. They were part of a complex dialogue between men and gods in which unwanted natural events—floods, plagues, infestations, fires, and the like were always responses by gods to human acts of disobedience. A man ignorant of the science of signs might not know the reasons for his affliction or what to do about it, but the reason was there nonetheless. (1985:39)

Not all inauspiciousness was so clearly defined as the result of active agents (such as spirits and gods) per se. In Raheja's analysis of inauspiciousness in the Uttar Pradesh village of Pahansu, the emphasis is much more on qualities and substances that invade or infect people during liminal periods. Both structure and transitions are conceived of in the quasi-physical terms of bodily connections: "Inauspiciousness flows, as we have seen, through the 'connections of the body' (*sarir ka sambandh*) between persons, and when these connections are transformed (at birth) or attenuated and created anew (at marriage), inauspiciousness flows over, as it were, and must be channeled and removed" (Raheja 1988:147). What "flows over" is seen in near physical terms: "*Nasubh* and *kusubh* . . . both may be translated as 'inauspiciousness' . . . [and] denote qualities and substances that themselves are the causes, or more precisely, the embodiments of ill-being" (1988:42).

In terms of our earlier theoretical concepts, the factors that affect human behavior are objectified into substances that become the immediate source of inauspiciousness. These substances are seen as the embodiment of alien and foreign forces. At times these forces are thought to originate from the hostile actions of otherworldly beings such as ghosts (*bhuta*), and the souls of the dead (*preta*) who have not been ritually transformed into ancestors (pitr); they are liminal beings who haunt the boundaries between this world and the next.[9] Humans who are themselves in some liminal, transitional state are seen as especially vulnerable to the evil substances created by the hostile actions of such otherworldly beings. At other times these harmful substances are seen as coming from the gods. According to the mythology this can be punishment for sins, but in other instances the gods are simply passing on harmful substances to others. But in all of these cases the more immediate concern is with a near physical substance that must be disposed of if it is not to cause harm.

Just as movement across boundaries is a primary source of auspiciousness and inauspiciousness, movement is the mechanism for disposing of inauspicious substances; they must be given away. Inauspiciousness is transferred to others by giving them gifts (Sanskrit: dana; Hindi: *dan*).[10] Raheja reports, "virtually all of my interpretations hinged on one crucial fact—that the significance of *dan*, and thus much of the giving and receiving that constitutes intercaste and kinship relations in Pahansu, was focused on the transfer of inauspiciousness from donor to recipient" (1988:31). Dana are ritual prestations that are given to those who have an "obligation" (*pharmaya*) to receive them.[11] This is in contrast to prestations such as *daksina*, *lag*, and *neg*, which are the recipient's "right" (*hak*) and are, roughly speaking, "payments" for services rendered.

Raheja (1988:69) notes that next to prasada, the most important kind of prestation in Pahansu is a particular type of dana known as *carhapa* or *pujapa*. In contrast to the prasada, of which all can partake, the carhapa must be given to a particular relative or ritual specialist. Less commonly, it must be deposited in certain places—usually those that symbolize a boundary or transitional area, such as a crossroads or the edge of the village. The giving of carhapa typically involves three logical steps. The first is the disarticulation or loosening of the sin, evil, sickness, danger, and the like from the giver. Typically this is conceptualized as being brought about by heat, especially the heat generated by various kinds of ascetic austerities (tapas). Second, these various forms of inauspiciousness must be passed on in the form of dana to an appropriate recipient, who is thought of as a receptacle or vessel (*patra*). The patra is a ritual specialist such as a Brahman family priest (purohit), a Barber, a Bhangi Sweeper, an in-law (or more accurately, a wife-taking affine), or sometimes a physical place. Often an intermediary step is involved, in which the dana is first offered to a god or ghost before it is passed on to the appropriate patra. Third, the recipient patra must then "digest" the harmful substances incorporated in the dana. Brahmans are supposedly able to do this because of the austerities they regularly practice. Other castes supposedly generate the necessary heat for digestion by various routine activities such as husking, churning, grinding, and sexual intercourse, that is, by an exercise of agency appropriate to their social position. But this is problematic and dangerous work; the transferred inauspiciousness may harm those who undertake to digest it. Consequently, dana usually involves a gift of some value; that is, something of value must accompany the inauspiciousness that is being transferred. This is not simple exchange, since bargaining is, in principle, verboten, though in practice quibbling is not unknown.

Raheja's account stresses the "centrality" of the dominant Gujar caste. The Gujars control most of the land in Pahansu and are the patron-employers (jajmans) of most others in the village. Equally important, the Gujars are the main sponsors of ritual activity in the village; more concretely, they are the main givers of dana. Raheja claims that in addition to a hierarchy of purity and status, there is a nonhierarchial differentiation based on ritual centrality. Here the dominant Gujar jajmans, rather than the Brahmans, are seen as the core of the system. Others also give dana but the Gujars play the dominant role.[12]

This highly condensed summary does not do justice to the richness of Raheja's ethnography; it does, however, focus our attention on the main points relevant to this analysis. How do such findings relate to my general theoretical argument? As I have suggested earlier, human existence is always some mixture of agency and contingency. Organized societies create enclaves of moral order and agency in an ocean of contingent and deterministic processes. Only some of these are understood, and even fewer are controlled. The boundaries between the areas over which we have some degree of agency and responsibility, and the contingent world over which we have little control, are always ambiguous. Thus, in most complex cultures, people ponder whether the apparently contingent and uncontrollable are in some way due to their own actions. Was there anything we could have done? Is there anything we can do, to avoid such disasters in the future? Paradoxically, such questions are most acute for those who exercise power and authority; they have the most agency and thus the most responsibility. Furthermore, those who exercise domination are inevitably involved in moral ambiguities if not immorality and amorality (Biardeau 1989:53–58). Moreover, they have the most to lose from contingencies that might harm the system as a whole. Of course, they are also the ones best able to redistribute risk and deflect blame. It is hardly surprising that kings and dominant castes are central actors in matters of auspiciousness and inauspiciousness.

Predictably, the core of the ritual activity involves the transfer of inauspiciousness from these wielders of power to either those who specialize in acquiring the merit needed to digest such negativity, for example, Brahmans, or those who are relatively powerless to resist such transfers—for example, Untouchable Sweepers.[13]

In both cases they must be compensated for accepting such transfers. All recipients, but especially those who claim moral and religious superiority, recognize they are negatively affected by the acceptance of such "gifts." Religious functionaries frequently have an ambivalent relationship with the ruling class, and Brahmans have been, in theory if not always in practice, traditionally reluctant to receive gifts.

The source of their discomfort is that such gifts are likely to contain potentially harmful inauspiciousness. Without denying the reality of this perception for the actors involved, it seems likely that this reluctance is also implicitly related to two latent considerations. First, the acceptance of such gifts, especially when such acceptance is coerced, symbolizes and ritually enacts dependency and subservience. Second, and perhaps more important, it implicates the recipients in the moral ambiguities of power. As I indicated in the discussion of the inalienability of status in Chapter 3, the means by which material resources are gained influence the legitimacy of accepting these resources as gifts. Obviously it would be considered illegitimate for a university to accept money illegally stolen from others. But during the Vietnam War many thought accepting money from the U.S. government, especially money for defense-related activities, seriously compromised the integrity of higher education. The distinction between dana and the other prestations (daksina, lag, and neg), which are for services rendered and do not involve accepting negative substances, seems to support this interpretation. I do not want to overstress such considerations; clearly the primary concern for Indian villagers is the more concrete benefit or harm that might result from accepting dana. Nonetheless, I believe that a latent and implicit apprehension is the danger of sharing in immoral and ill-gotten gain derived from dominant worldly power. This is, according to my earlier interpretation, one of the Brahman's classical dilemmas. Their ardent ritual conformity gives them the high levels of purity that enable them to "digest" inauspiciousness, but this very superiority means that they have more to lose by contact with worldly evil.

Finally, because agency and contingency frequently blend into one another in human experience, we should not expect the notions of auspiciousness–inauspiciousness and purity–impurity to be completely distinct. As Parry (1991) has complained, the recent emphasis on auspiciousness and inauspiciousness has either subsumed these concepts under notions of purity and impurity or attempted to draw a clear-cut distinction between the two sets of notions. He provides a number of examples from death rituals that make either alternative highly questionable. When a key underlying concern is to express the human experiences of both agency and contingency, we should expect some ambiguity in the terminology used. Sometimes we feel sure we are in control and therefore responsible; sometimes we are sure we are not; much of the time we sense some mixture of the two. We should expect a similar variability with respect to the distinction between purity–impurity, and auspiciousness–inauspiciousness on the other.

The idiom of contingency, then, is dialectically transformed into a medium of agency. As in the case of purity and pollution, this process sometimes involves significant elements of reification and objectification. Contingent processes are attributed to the actions of higher beings, and/or to substances that intrude in moments of liminality. One of the major preoccupations of traditional Indian culture has been the handling of these dangerous beings and substances. This preoccupation is not primarily a concern with spiritual matters, but with the potential effects on worldly well-being.

Now we must turn to the relationship between such worldly considerations and the otherworldly concerns supposedly so central to Indian culture. Stated more abstractly, we need to explore the relationship between power and legitimacy. This will lead us again to a further analysis of the relationship between the concepts of auspiciousness–inauspiciousness and purity–impurity.

Power, Legitimacy, Auspiciousness, and Purity

In Chapter 7, the processes associated with political legitimacy were analyzed. Now I want to point out a tie between those processes and the ones we have been discussing here. As noted earlier things are auspicious and inauspicious mainly in terms of how they affect one's worldly well-being. Carman (Carman and Marglin 1985:114) has proposed that auspiciousness can be understood in relationship to the purusarthas, the four traditional goals of the Hindu life: kama, desire for pleasure; artha, pursuit of material interests; dharma, the seeking of righteousness and virtue, and moksa, release or salvation. Carman suggests that it is useful to see kama and artha as being subservient to and encompassed by dharma, which in turn is secondary to and encompassed by moksa. In some respects the more mundane goals contribute to the next higher goal, but they are also in tension and contradiction with it. When the order of the concepts is reversed, the matter might be conceptualized in the following way:

moksa vs. [dharma vs. artha/kama]

Moksa is beyond concerns with virtue or purity, and dharma is preoccupied with these, whereas artha and kama are concerned with worldly well-being. The concepts of auspiciousness and inauspiciousness typically refer to concerns related to artha and kama. While the primary referent of artha is material wealth, in an agrarian society this implies control of land and hence political power broadly conceived. Kama refers not only to pleasure, including sexual pleasure, but also implies fertility; both fertility needed to reproduce children, particularly sons, but also the fertility of the land necessary for food and sustenance. Hence artha and kama can be understood as the means and bases of material power. These closely parallel the categories of goods/services and force in my initial typology of power. Dharma, on the other hand, is analogous to status as a form of power. To pursue duty and virtue is to conform to the norms appropriate to one's station (svadharma). Such conformity is a key source of status. The Brahman way of life is the epitomy of conformity to dharma. The point is not simply to establish some facile analogue between the categories of my typology and the categories of the classic typology of goals for the Hindu life (purusarthas). Rather the point is that this parallel can help us to understand some of the the key characteristics of auspiciousness. Let us see how this is so.

Marglin (1985a:282–98) has pointed to a significant difference in the way auspiciousness is related to inauspiciousness compared to the way purity is related to impurity. Purity and impurity tend to be mutually exclusive concepts: if something becomes purer, by definition it becomes less impure. In contrast, something can become both more auspicious and more inauspicious simultaneously. Or perhaps more accurately, its potential for either auspiciousness or inauspiciousness can increase. As Marglin says: "When these two opposites are found together . . . , they signify a potent moment, full of possibilities. The moment is a dangerous one precisely because of its potentiality which can resolve itself in either of the two directions, towards auspiciousness and renewal or towards inauspiciousness and decay" (1985a:298).[14]

As Marglin indicates, and as we shall see in more detail later, auspiciousness is associated with *sakti*, which is normally described as "female power." This is the power necessary for worldly well-being and especially implies fertility and bountifulness. It is the source of both auspiciousness and inauspiciousness. According to Marglin:

> Female power, *sakti*, signifies the potency of the joining of both auspiciousness and inauspiciousness. In union with a male, the potentiality has resolved itself in a positive direction. This explains why goddesses represented along with their [male] consorts are benevolent, whereas goddesses represented alone are sometimes benevolent and sometimes malevolent. (1985a:299)

The "raw" potential of the sakti must be channeled and controlled by responsible authority. In the concepts of the purusarthas, kama and artha must be guided and directed by dharma. In Weberian terms, power must be made legitimate. In the concepts of Chapter 7, this is legitimation by conformity to norms. In the concepts of my initial typology of power, force and goods/services must be directed and guided by the norms that are the bases of status, that is, material forms of power must be exercised in such a way that they receive social approval. In most societies, great force and great wealth are seen as power that can be used for either good or evil, for either legitimate or illegitimate purposes. In sum, the concepts of auspiciousness and inauspiciousness recognize the potential of worldly material power to have great consequences on those over whom it is exercised. Whether it is perceived as auspicious or inauspicious depends, in part, on whether it is exercised legitimately.

Whether the power of sakti has an auspicious or inauspicious outcome is not itself solely a matter of chance or contingency. Human agents play a role in determining whether sakti is guided by dharma. And this role too seems to be expressed in the indigenous symbolism. The material form of sakti is menstrual blood, which is usually but not always polluting, depending on how it is used. Sakti therefore is related not only to auspiciousness and inauspiciousness, but also to purity and pollution. As with the relationship with agency and contingency, and power and legitimate authority, it is not always clear where one begins and the other ends. Accordingly, as Parry (1991) has argued, it is probably a mistake to try and draw too rigid a conceptual distinction between purity–impurity and auspiciousness–inauspiciouness.

Conclusions

Summary

The last two chapters have been long and complex. It is appropriate to try to briefly summarize the key points. First, let us consider the concepts of secondary norms and rituals. My argument is that when status is a key resource there will be a tendency to elaborate norms and rituals in order to exclude outsiders and, to a lesser degree, to differentiate insiders and to reinforce social control. These norms and rituals frequently take the form of "codes" which implicitly symbolize and communicate the group's concerns. I have analyzed three examples of such codes:

1. The norms, symbols, and rituals concerning purity and pollution illustrate elaborations designed to maintain status homogeneity and reinforce status group boundaries.
2. Notions about the importance of sexual reproduction of the lineage, on the one hand, and semen retention and asceticism, on the other, symbolize the cross-pressures typically experienced by Brahmans.[15]
3. Anxieties about uncontrolled power are symbolized by the notions of auspiciousness and inauspiciousness.

These various concerns about social and political processes are commonly objectified and expressed as a concern over the manipulation of quasi-physical substances: the handling of the dirt and filth that creates pollution, the retention of semen, and the transfer of inauspicious substances by the giving of gifts (dana). While these concerns are most central to Brahmans and dominant landed elites, including kings, they are shared in varying degrees by many segments of the society.

Two other recurring themes are evident. First is the tension between (1) the need for material resources (and dependency on those who control these) and (2) the rejection of such resources as the bases of status and legitimacy. In India this takes the form of the tension between kings and land-controlling castes, on the one hand, and Brahmans, on the other hand. Second is the recurring emphasis on both human agency and contingency. The two themes are represented by the culture's preoccupation with both purity and auspiciousness, where purity is identified with agency and nonmaterial bases of status, and auspiciousness is associated with contingency and material well-being. Finally, there is a dialectic between agency and contingency; when one of these is strongly stressed in a particular set of concepts, those same concepts may be redefined to allow room for the opposite notion. Auspiciousness, which fundamentally expresses a concern about contingency, is related to rituals for transferring dana, which produce a kind of agency over precisely those factors initially defined as contingent. Consequently, in many contexts the notions of purity–impurity and auspiciousness–inauspiciousness blend into one another.

Scope of the Generalizations

Are such codes a peculiarity of Indian culture, or does the argument have relevance to other societies? I have, of course, already discussed how the concept of secondary norms and rituals can be useful in understanding the modern military. As already pointed out, notions of purity and pollution are extremely common across an array of societies and are usually related to maintaining status-group boundaries. Ancient Greece is considered the seminal source of Western civilization, which is supposedly so different from hierarchical India. Yet Parker, commenting on Pythagoras (who may be quoting Hesiod from the eighth century B.C.E.) says, "These rules find parallels in sacred books of the East, the *Laws of Manu*, for instance, and the areas of concern that they reveal—sexuality, washing, bodily functions, purity of kitchen utensils—are commonplace in many anthropological discussions of pollution" (1983:292). On the other hand, it seems that ancient Greece did not, according to Parker, make purity and pollution as central as Hinduism did:

> Two claims that are most relevant to our theme have been made about Greek asceticism, and the age in which it emerged. One is that Greek religion was now on the road to becoming, like Hinduism or Zoroastrianism, a religion of lustrations and ceremonial purity. The other, closely connected, is that purity rather than justice was the means to salvation. It should be remembered, however, that Greek religion had always been a religion of lustrations; the author in whom the act of washing is most charged with meaning is Homer. New applications the idea of purity certainly received, but it is not clear that physical lustration gained greatly in importance in these movements, except in the cults that substituted instantaneous purification for a way of life; and there is certainly no sign that purity was becoming a dominant idiom to which all other forms of evaluation were subordinated. As for justice, it was as Plato knew, always possible to interpret even orthodox Greek religion as if the gods were swayed by ritual more than righteousness. (1983:305–6)

In short, there were similarities and differences between India and ancient Greece.

Nor are the parallels restricted to purity and impurity per se; there are also notions that strongly resemble Indian notions of auspiciousness and inauspiciousness:

> In Greek popular belief, there seem to be two kinds of contagious condition, neither closely related to modern infections. On the one hand, there are pollutions such as those of birth, death, and blood-guilt that are communicable according to specified principles and demand the formal seclusion of affected persons. On the other, there are a series of undesirable qualities and conditions that can be "wiped off" on people and with which one may be "filled"—folly, immorality, bad luck, and the like. The contagiousness of bad luck often appears in comedy. "Who goes there?" "An unlucky man." "Keep to yourself then." (Parker 1983:218–19)

Parker goes on to note that people responded to bad luck and bad news by spitting, probably a simple ritual for expelling such evil influences. He continues:

> It would be wrong to see the threat of contagion in all these cases as a mere metaphor. We hear, for instance, of unconquered troops who were unwilling to be joined in one division with their defeated comrades, and a Euripidean Theseus warns of the danger of marrying into an unfortunate household. (1983:219)

In ancient Greece, honor and status were extremely central to social organization—though of course this varied by region and period. While there was never anything approaching a full-fledged caste system, status groups were a central feature of the social organization. Predictably, we find notions that closely parallel Indian notions of purity–pollution and auspiciousness–inauspiciousness. Obviously, my analysis does not demonstrate the utility of my theoretical arguments for ancient Greece—my point is a more modest one. There is considerable evidence of parallel structures and cultural codes. Therefore, it seems more analytically fruitful to look for both similarities and differences rather than to adopt a cultural essentialism that makes the concepts and propositions relevant for the analysis of one of these civilizations irrelevant for an analysis of the other.

The case with which India is often compared is the segregated American South between the end of the Civil War in 1865 and the rejection of legalized segregation of schools in 1954. The classic sociological essays emphasizing the differences and similarities in the two systems are by Cox (1948) and Berreman (1960). Many parallels between India and the segregated American South are obvious: blacks were in largely subservient and dependent economic positions, though they often worked closely with whites in actual production activities; dominant groups could use intimidation and even violence against blacks with near impunity; most consumption and expressive activities were separate, including schools, neighborhoods, places of worship, and theatres; this domination was reinforced by a clearly articulated notion that blacks were dirty, immoral, and impure, and this ideology was implemented in laws that segregated hotels, public transportation, drinking fountains, restaurants and toilets; eating together was "not done"; and above all, intermarriage was illegal and verboten. Cox argued that despite these structural parallels between the India and the American South, two fundamental differences existed. First, according to Cox, lower caste Hindus accepted the basic legitimacy of the system, while blacks in the United States did not. Subsequent research (e.g., Gough 1960; Lynch 1969; Moffatt 1979; Khare 1984) shows that this is a matter of degree rather than kind. Lower caste groups often resisted domination and exploitation; the extent to which they have rejected the caste system as a whole and the associated ideology is more mixed and ambiguous. This leads to Cox's second point: the Indian caste system is rooted in the religious ideas of Hinduism, and there is not a parallel religious legitimacy for the treatment of blacks in the South.[16] This is another version of Dumont's main point: there may be structural similarities between Indian caste and other forms of stratification, but these are superficial when they are disconnected from the ideology that supplies the logic of the system. According to Dumont, the logic of hierarchy is rooted in the distinction between purity and impurity. In short, one perspective emphasizes the structural similarities and the other emphasizes the ideological and cultural differences.

I have argued that both the structural features of caste and its ideology are rooted in a more fundamental logic that is derived from the nature of status as a resource. In Chapters 3 and 5, I tried to show how the structural features of caste were an extreme form of the characteristics of status groups in general. This is an old theme taken from Weber. What is new is to show how the key structural features of status groups and castes—restricted mobility, endogamy, commensuality, elaborate lifestyle norms—can be explained and predicted from the characteristics of status as a resource—its relative inexpansibility and inalienability—and the sources of

status—conformity to norms and association. In Chapter 9 I showed that the ideology that gives the Indian system its special character is not *simply* some contingent act of Indian history, but is rooted in the logic of status groups per se. That is,
there is a strong "elective affinity," to use Weber's term, between status systems
and ideologies of purity and impurity. Similar elective affinities lie behind notions
of semen retention, worldly power as feminine, and auspiciousness.

The strongest claim is that the theoretical perspective that I have proposed will
help us to explain both the similarities and differences between various cultural settings in general theoretical terms. Let me cite two examples to illustrate my point.
The first concerns the time in which an emphasis on purity and impurity emerged in
the American South. In his now classic book *The Strange Career of Jim Crow*
(1974), Woodward makes it clear that the most rigorous forms of segregation and abhorrence of contact with blacks did not develop during the period of slavery. Rather,
they developed toward the end of the nineteenth century, after the South's ability to
dominate blacks by political means had been significantly reduced (though, of
course, not eliminated) and after the region's economic power had been considerably
eroded as well. Because of this, status (based on race rather than economic or political power) was made increasingly central to Southern culture; it was white
Southerners' most available inalienable resource. Accordingly, social contact with
blacks was increasingly regulated, and the secondary norms and rituals that degraded
blacks and set them apart were elaborated. This process was buttressed by various
forms of objectification, in which even casual physical contact with blacks—unless
it clearly expressed white dominance—came to be defined as offensive and threatening. The key theoretical point is that the differences between India and the old South
were not primarily due to the absence of hierarchy and the ideology of purity and impurity in the United States. For when status not based primarily on economic or
political resources became more central to the patterns of domination and stratification, an ideology of purity and separation was elaborated, and ritualized conformity was demanded.

Even in this period, significant differences remained between the American
South and India. One striking example is the norms concerning food preparation. In
both places, the norms of commensuality were emphasized; in India one normally
dines with members of one's own caste, and in the South whites would not eat with
blacks. But in the South blacks prepared, cooked, and served the food eaten by
whites. The parallel was unthinkable in traditional India; the status of the person
preparing the food was crucial to its purity.

How are we to understand this difference? My interpretation is that objectification was less elaborated in the United States. While blacks were impure, the
notion was still largely moral *or* biological; the two were not conflated.[17] In
Marriott's (1976) terms, a Western dualistic concept was operative; humans were
not believed to be composed of monistic substances that were inextricably both biological and moral. Even though notions of white purity and the polluting effect of
contact with blacks were common, this concept was mitigated by Western dualistic
notions of the relationship between biology and morality. One might be made sick
by food prepared in unclean conditions—by blacks or whites—but one's moral
status was not affected by the status of those who prepared the food. Physical inti-

macy with what was taken into the body did not have the strong implications of social intimacy that it did in India, and so was irrelevant to concerns about purity and status.

These types of cultural ideas must be taken into account if we are to understand the details of the social structure. It would be a serious analytical mistake, though, to use these cultural notions as our central analytical framework. To do so would eliminate the possibilities of explaining the similarities that do exist between South Asia and social structures elsewhere. To repeat the general theme, what is required is attention both to more abstract sociological concepts and propositions, and to the more particularistic cultural ideas of India and South Asia. Often these ideas will be institutionalized in implicit "codes" that require interpretive analysis. But just as cultural analysis—the analysis of specific indigenous cultural concepts—is not a substitute for more general concepts and propositions, interpretive analysis is not a substitute for causal analysis. Both are required.

A Provisional Resource Structuralism and Reductionism

This identification of elective affinities is an additional virtue of a provisional structuralism that focuses on resources: it suggests how ideologies are linked to structural features. That is, ideologies tend to reflect the features of the dominant resources around which structures are built. As we have seen, inexpansible status tends to be linked to ideologies that stress boundary maintenance, such as purity and impurity. There also seems to be an elective affinity between societies in which highly alienable, socially produced goods and services are central, and ideologies stressing the inalienable rights of private property. When knowledge—which is highly expansible, inalienable, and easily transported from one location to another—becomes more central, ideologies tend to stress mobility, equality of opportunity, and achievement. In short, the nature of resources suggests not only structural features, but the content of ideologies.

I am not, however, suggesting an unqualified reductionism or determinism. Each level is not a simple function of the preceding levels, but to some degree each has its own history and pattern of development. Just as it is a mistake to treat intellectual history as a self-contained entity detached from economic and social developments, it is also a mistake to treat intellectual ideas as if they were simply a reflection of the social and economic. The same is true for the different levels of cultural codes upon which we have focused. In principle any of these levels can have an independent effect on behavior and the other levels of symbolism.

If no reductionism is implied, there is the implication that some things are more fundamental or primary than others. The centrality of status as a resource and the resulting structural features of status groups are, in combination, more likely to produce the kinds of cultural and ideological constructs we have discussed than a situation where these features are not present. But even this assertion must be highly qualified. Causation is by no means unidirectional, and there are situations (some of which will be considered later) where cultural constructs and ideologies seem to play a key role in transforming the structural features of a civilization. No simple distinction between economic base and ideological superstructure will provide adequate social analyses. Nonetheless, some things tend to be more fundamental than others—fundamental in that they are likely to set the parameters within which the other factors will vary. Industrial societies will have some characteristics that are not found in agrarian societies, and vice versa. Those agrarian societies in which status is a central resource (and is not based on wealth or political power) will have some structural characteristics and cultural codes that are unlikely to be found in those that conflate status, wealth and power. Not to recognize this in order to supposedly avoid all hints of reductionism or determinism is to greatly handicap any attempt at analysis and explanation.[18]

11

Status Relations in Marriage Alliances

How the caste system emerged, and which aspect of it came first, is shrouded in uncertainty.[1] But there is little doubt about what serves as the core of this system in the modern period; it is the maintenance of some degree of endogamy through marriage alliances. If most Indians ever carried out their "traditional" caste occupations, this time has long past. While some continue to participate in the traditional division of labor, the modern economy has severely eroded this part of the caste system; this trend is almost certain to continue. Radical changes have also occurred with respect to the norms of commensuality. In urban areas intercaste dining is common. Even in rural areas, the rigor of these norms has been greatly relaxed.

In contrast, the overwhelming percentage of Indians still have arranged marriages that carefully take into account the status of the marriage partner's family. At the core of the caste system is the arrangement of marriage alliances based on religious or ritual status. When marriages between Brahmans and Untouchables become common, or marriages take into account only the socioeconomic position of the families, the caste system will have ceased to exist.

Hence at the core of any analysis of the caste system must be an explanation of what governs the status relationships in marriage alliances. This is the focus of this chapter.

The Phenomena to Be Explained

In status groups in general and castes in particular, there is a strong tendency toward endogamy and the marriage of equals. Dumont summarizes this as follows: "A man of caste X marries a woman of caste X and the children belong to caste X" (1980:112). An explanation for this tendency was offered in Chapters 3 and 5. But as Dumont notes, while this is "roughly true . . . it is, of course, a little too simple" (1980:113). Not only do marriage partners frequently differ in status, sometimes the partners are from different castes.

These departures from endogamy and status homogeneity are not simply a matter of deviance on the part of particular individuals or families. Rather, the legitimate and institutionalized definitions of what constitutes an ideal marriage alliance varies for different regions and castes (Kolenda 1987b). The purpose of this chapter is to attempt to explain some of the most common and striking of these manifold variations. Let me repeat, the phenomenon to be explained is not the actual statistical distribution of different types of marriages, but rather variations in cultural ideals of what constitutes an appropriate marriage alliance. Of course, the normative ideals and the actual behavioral patterns are significantly correlated.

Before we proceed, some terminology is required. Anthropologists refer to marriage alliances in which the status of the two families are roughly equal as *isogamy*. When the bride's family is superior, the term *hypogamy* is used. Such marriages are prohibited or frowned upon throughout most of India, as indicated by the Sanskrit term used to describe them, *pratiloma*, meaning hair "brushed the wrong way" or "against the grain." If the groom's family is of superior status, the pattern is called *hypergamy*. Hypergamy is often the ideal; such marriages are referred to by the Sanskrit term *anuloma,* meaning "with the grain" or "following the hair." When people explicitly recognize different strata within their own caste, and men marry women of their own stratum or one of lower status, I will refer to this as fully developed or *institutionalized hypergamy*. Now let us list some of the specifics that require explanation.

1. Why are the predominant patterns of marriage alliances different for the North and the South—or more accurately, between the Dravidian South and the rest of India? The dominant pattern in the South is isogamy, while in North India both isogamous and hypergamous marriages are permitted.
2. Why, however, are there groups in the North, such as many Punjabi and Bengali castes, that one would expect to be hypergamous, but in fact are isogamous?
3. Why do systems of institutionalized hypergamy emerge, why in such systems do the size of caste groups tend to be large and widely dispersed, and why is there a tendency for such systems to move through cycles of stability and instability?
4. Why, in most areas, are upper caste groups more likely to be hypergamous than lower caste groups?
5. Why, in most areas, are lower castes more likely than upper castes to be isogamous, but also have greater rates of individual deviation from the caste ideal or dominant pattern?
6. Why, in virtually all castes and all areas, is hypogamy looked down upon, if not forbidden?
7. Why, among upper castes, do bridegrooms tend to be treated as near deities, and why in many respects are both the marriage ceremony and subsequent relationships between wife-receivers and wife-givers similar to patterns of worship?

The complex "matriarchal" patterns characteristic of some South Indian and Sri Lankan groups, such as the Nayar, will not be analyzed here. Such an analysis would require the introduction of complex material of interest primarily to specialists. These patterns can, however, be explained in terms of the arguments offered here. An analysis of this material has been published elsewhere (Milner 1988).

Theoretical and Methodological Considerations

The Connection with the General Argument

The two sources of status are conformity to norms and the manipulation of social associations. An implication of the first source is that status groups tend to elaborate and complicate their norms. The last two chapters have looked at key aspects of this elaboration process:

This chapter considers some of the implications of the second source of status, social associations, for marriage alliances. The explanations of the general tendencies toward endogamy and status homogeneity, and hence isogamy, have already been suggested in Chapters 3 and 5. But as we have tentatively seen in the list of phenomena to be explained, the system of marriage alliances in India is highly complex; it is not simply the case that people must marry within their own caste. Hence, the bulk of this chapter is devoted to explaining the complexities and "exceptions" to simple caste endogamy.

The Explanatory Strategy: Ad Hoc Exogenous Variables

A major purpose of this endeavor is methodological—not in the sense of how data should be collected, but with respect to the appropriate explanatory strategy. Any general theory is necessarily abstract and focuses on a few key variables. Yet in a given concrete social situation, the actual patterns of behavior are influenced by more factors than those included in any general theory. Thus an adequate explanation requires the consideration of factors that are not part of the general theory as such, but are important to understanding the phenomenon under analysis. What is required is to show how these other factors qualify and deflect the general tendencies predicted by the theory. The classic example of this is the application of Newton's laws of falling bodies to contexts in which the phenomena being observed do not occur in a vacuum. It is not that the relationships specified in Newton's theory do not operate in the atmosphere; rather, the general tendencies which Newton's theory identifies must be qualified to take into account the effect of the resistance of air. This does not mean that the theory is wrong, but rather that it is not complete in and of itself. An analogous situation exists with respect to the principles of status associations and Hindu marriage alliances. One purpose of this chapter will be to identify various exogenous variables and to show how they qualify the general tendencies of status associations. The point of the exercise is to show how a general theory can be integrated with particular historical considerations. The claim is that such an approach can provide a more systematic and parsimonious explanation than either approach taken by itself. The same procedure was used in Chapter 6; a general model of elites was developed and then modified by additional information about the specific characteristics of India. More generally, this is the procedure that has been used in approaching the analysis of Indian castes as a special case of status groups.

Using Rational Choice Theory

This chapter is intended to make another key theoretical and methodological point. The provisional resource structuralism advocated in Chapter 1 does not exclude the possibility of using more micro perspectives. Earlier I suggested that the analyses provided in Chapters 9 and 10 were not only more interpretive and hermeneutical in style, but approximated the concerns of theories of practice to elucidate the important role of such notions as routine (Giddens) and habitus (Bourdieu) in the reproduction of social structure. Here too I want to reemphasize the provisional nature of the resource structuralism I am advocating by drawing on a rational choice perspective to analyze patterns of marriage alliances. In this chapter I am attempting to explain variations in relatively macro patterns: why in some areas (or among some castes) the ideal or normative pattern for marriage alliances is different from that in other areas. I will attempt to explain these variations by making two assumptions. First, in general, families pursue their self-interests by attempting to arrange alliances that over the long run maximize their status in the community. Second, on the whole they make rational choices among the opportunities available to them.

Such choices, though, are shaped by two types of constraints. The first type of constraint is what might be called *emergent properties*: the processes and structural features that develop precisely because families are attempting to improve their ritual status. For example, as we have seen, the attempt of people to improve their status by increasing upward associations and minimizing downward associations leads to a macro pattern in which the predominant forms of associations are between equals. But the consequences of rational strategies and choices are multilayered. The first macro outcome produces constraints, or reorders motivations, that in turn change the nature of subsequent macro outcomes. To attempt to capture some of these complexities I will refer to these various levels as first, second, third, and fourth order tendencies.[2] The second type of constraint is what I have already referred to as ad hoc *exogenous variables*: factors that shape the choices people make, but which cannot be explained by reference to the concepts and propositions of the theory under consideration. An example in the following analysis is the importance of cross-cousin marriage in South India; it is crucial to understanding the patterns of marriage alliance, but it is not itself explained by, nor a variable in, the more general model. Of course, the distinction between these two types of constraints is strictly formal. Presumably the ad hoc exogenous variables are also emergent properties; they simply happen to be those for which the current perspective has no explanation.

A General Theory of Status Alliances

In both Chapters 3 and 5 the key arguments about the significance of marriages for status relationships were sketched out. Now they must be elaborated.[3]

The Insulation of Status from Other Forms of Power

The *first order* or fundamental prerequisite for status groups is that status must not be directly based on economic and political power; there must be criteria of status other than wealth and force. Under these conditions, several tendencies are likely to emerge.

Pressures Toward Status Homogeneity

Lower status people will try to associate with those of higher status, while those of higher status tend to carefully limit and regulate their associations with those of lower status. These countervailing interests tend to result in a pattern of social associations between those who are roughly equal in status, that is, in a strong tendency toward status homogeneity. This strong tendency toward status homogeneity can usefully be identified as a *second order* process. This tendency toward homogeneity is especially characteristic of intimate expressive relationships such as marriage. Thus the fundamental dynamic in a status system is a strong tendency toward status homogeneity, especially for publicly visible intimate expressive relationships. This is, of course, the key source of isogamy.

Pressures Toward Status Heterogeneity

The insulation of status from wealth and political power and the tendency toward status homogeneity are not all-powerful. The first process has made status more valuable, and hence increases motivations to try and translate other resources into status. Conversely, since the preoccupation with status and lifestyle limits and handicaps the acquisition of wealth and political power, the motivation increases to exchange status for these resources. Accordingly, there are constant attempts to translate economic and political resources into status, and vice versa. Likewise, lower status actors frequently attempt to increase their associations with those of higher status. Remember that the very pattern of status homogeneity arose out of motivations to associate with superiors and avoid inferiors. That is, there are important *third order* tendencies toward status heterogeneity. To use an analogy from population genetics, these can be thought of as recessive tendencies that only become apparent in particular circumstances. The more obvious first and second order tendencies can be thought of as the dominant tendencies.

The most obvious source of status heterogeneity in marriage alliances derives from *the exchange of status for wealth or political power, and vice versa*. This exchange involves two separate but mutually reinforcing processes. The first is the economic burden of maintaining an esoteric style of life. This way of protecting the group from outsiders is also a handicap in maintaining the wealth needed to conform to a high status lifestyle. For example, Brahmans and Rajputs are prohibited from putting their hand to the plow—the quintessential productive activity in an agrarian society. The second process involves the conversion of status into other resources, and vice versa. High status families experiencing a shortage of wealth or power frequently resort to admitting into membership those from lower status backgrounds— if these new members can bring with them needed resources. Often the exchange of status for wealth takes the form of a dowry. As we have seen, such exchanges are problematic; the very act of "selling honor" is a contradiction in terms. Therefore, elaborate ideologies to justify or disguise the nature of such exchanges are likely.[4]

A second source of status heterogeneity in marriage alliances is the *problematic nature of directly exchanging praise or blame*. The most convincing praise or blame comes from those who are perceived to expect nothing in return. If, when you offer a compliment, it is apparent you are "fishing" for one in return, the initial praise and any praise that is returned is seriously discounted. One possible solution is to make the return of praise as implicit as possible. The exchange among equals of explicit praise, for implicit praise though, is seldom perceived as a fair trade. However, such exchanges between unequals may be considered beneficial to both parties: the lower status actor offers explicit invitations or gifts, while the mere acceptance of these by the higher status actor is a form of implicit praise. The acceptance of your invitation to attend your daughter's wedding by the president of your company is reward enough, even if he does not reciprocate when his daughter is married. The ideal-typical example of this form of exchange is worship—especially in religions where the deity is considered to be under no obligation to reciprocate in any direct way, but does so only because of its beneficence or grace.

A third source of heterogeneity is the *desire for inequality within an ongoing social relationship*. When one partner is expected to be highly subservient and deferential, it may be acceptable or even desirable that this partner come from a lower status background. Moreover, the more inequality anticipated within a relationship, the less initial levels of inequality will affect the status of either partner. To be invited to the home of a higher status person and be treated as an equal and an honored guest is one thing. To be invited in order to be treated condescendingly or to provide demeaning services is quite another. For the latter role, someone of relatively low status can be admitted to the inner sanctum of superiors without significantly changing anyone's status. Servants and prostitutes are obvious examples. Similarly, in marriage alliances, a low status woman can become a member of a large harem without lowering the status of her master; the effect would be much greater if she became his first and only wife and his equal. Accordingly, those of high status are more likely to accept low status marriage partners if it is expected that they will be subservient and deferential spouses. This association between *initial and subsequent inequality* is also relevant to the relationships between the two families. Lower status families are usually more willing to offer deference to those who are initially clearly their superiors. Conversely, higher status families are more inclined to make an alliance with a lower status family, if the latter are likely to be consistently deferential in subsequent relationships.

When these third order tendencies toward asymmetrical alliances do become prominent in worldly status systems, such as in systems of hypergamy, they may create fourth order countervailing processes. These will be taken up later.

Recapitulation

Up to this point I have been tracing out some implications of the premises of the general theory of status relations. Under *first order* conditions, where status is significantly insulated from economic and political power, the following processes have been identified. Most individuals and groups would prefer to increase their associations with those of higher status, and restrict their associations with those of lower status, especially with respect to intimate expressive relationships. This set of motivations produces countervailing interests resulting in equals associating with equals, and hence the *second order* tendency toward status homogeneity and a pattern of isogamous marriages. Third, three sets of processes potentially produce countervailing *third order* pressures toward asymmetrical associations and result in patterns of relationships between unequals. These three factors are the high cost of esoteric life-styles, the problems involved in equals exchanging praise and blame, and the desire of superiors for certain types of relationships with inferiors.

The Inferiority of Wife-Givers: An Ad Hoc Variable

What the theory does not predict is: (1) When will the countervailing processes produce a departure from homogeneity and isogamy? (2) Which party to the alliance—the groom's or the bride's—is likely to be the inferior one? Thus at this next step in the argument, the logic of the analysis shifts. Instead of tracing out the implications of the premises, an exogenous empirical fact will be introduced in order to extend the analysis: in much of South Asia, wife-givers are considered inferior to and must act deferentially toward wife-takers.

In many castes throughout much of India, the wife's family acts deferentially toward the husband's family (see, e.g. Madan 1975; Parry 1979:274, 289; Gray 1980; Hershman 1981; Fruzzetti 1982). Often the wife's family is expected not only to provide a substantial dowry, but to continue to make periodic gifts and prestations to the husband's family. In contrast, members of the wife's family will accept virtually nothing from the husband's family, or perhaps only the most minimal of hospitalities. Rarely, if ever, would they eat a meal or spend a night at the home of their married daughter, who, of course, lives in her husband's home village and in the early years of the marriage with her husband's parents. This pattern is very general—though several important caveats will be discussed later. What will concern us are the consequences of the inferiority of wife-givers; by analyzing this we can begin to explain the regional and caste variations in the incidence of hypergamy and isogamy and related features of marriage patterns.

Alternative Responses: Hypergamy and Exchange Marriages

Since differences in status are very important in India, public acknowledgement of one's inferiority is no small matter—especially if the role as an inferior is to be a long-term one. Since in many castes wife-givers must take on such a publicly inferior and deferential role, how do families respond? Obviously one response is to prefer to maximize the times one is a wife-receiver and minimize the times one is a wife-giver. Hence the strong preference for sons over daughters (though this is probably not its only source). Short of female infanticide, though, families have little control over the sex ratio of their children. Moreover, infanticide can be effective only for a limited number of families or subpopulations. If widely practiced by the whole population, the sex ratio would be seriously out of balance, producing wide-ranging consequences. Consequently, a preference for sons and female infanticide cannot be a widely adopted institutionalized response to the problems of being a wife-giver.[5]

There seem to be two primary institutionalized responses. One is to attempt to marry one's daughters to those who are unquestionably of higher status. If one must be deferential to wife-takers, then the cost can be offset by an alliance with a family that one's peers would acknowledge deserves deference, and who in the very act of accepting your deference, helps to increase your status. This is, of course, one of the third order processes that creates tendencies toward status heterogeneity. The other response is to reverse roles as quickly as possible in order not to let status differences accumulate. If two families or lineages exchange wives in a time span sufficiently short for these exchanges to be remembered, then the status differences and deference patterns created by a particular marriage are not likely to build up and produce a fundamental status difference between the two lineages. The equalizing effects of this turn-about-is-fair-play strategy are even greater if the process is continued over a number of generations.

The first of these strategies takes the form of a clear tendency toward hypergamy. This may or may not result in explicitly labelled and formally ranked strata within the caste, which I have referred to as *institutionalized hypergamy*. The second of these strategies results in various forms of exchange marriages, including the patterns of cross-cousin marriage in south India and Sri Lanka. We will now use the notion of these two ideal-typical responses to analyze some of the regional and caste variations in marriage patterns, beginning with hypergamy.[6]

Hypergamy

The task here is to explain both the source of hypergamy and the key structural characteristics and dynamics of this system of marriage alliances. Equally important, I want to provide an explanatory structure that will allow us to see hypergamy in relationship to other patterns of Indian marriage. While arguments will be deliberately stated in general terms, they were developed primarily with reference to Parry's (1979) discussion of hypergamy among the Rajputs of Kangra. The Kangra Rajputs are divided into four named strata called *biradaris,* which roughly means "brotherhoods." In principle, the members of a single biradari are equal and intermarry. Wives should come from within the biradari or from the biradari immediately below. Daughters are to be given to your own biradari or, preferably, to a higher status one. Now let us consider how such a system might emerge and some of its structural dynamics.

As noted earlier, for many castes throughout much of India, wife-givers are seen as inferior to wife-receivers. This in and of itself cannot account for tendencies toward hypergamy. For the inferiority of women or their families could just as logically lead to hypogamy. If the status of a family is lowered when it takes on the role of wife-giver, then wife-takers might well seek alliances with those who are, in other situations, their status superiors. So while the inferiority of wife-givers may be one precondition for the abandonment of isogamy, it is not an explanation of hypergamy.

Sources of Hypergamy

Several factors push things in the direction of hypergamy. Let us begin with patriarchy (i.e., male authority over the family), and patrilineal inheritance (i.e., the transmission of property and status via the male line). These patterns are not unique to India. Within India their intensity varies by region and caste. But where these patterns are normative, the recruitment of women from lines of superior status is potentially problematic. Such women are likely to be more resistant to the authority of their lower status husbands and in-laws. In contrast, women are likely to be more subservient to male authority if they come from families of lower status. Hence hypergamy tends to buttress male dominance, and reduce the likelihood of the wife's family interfering in the affairs of the husband's joint family.[7]

Probably the principle source of hypergamy among Hindus is the concept of *kanyadana*. The concept of dana, discussed in previous chapters, refers to a special kind of gift in which something of value is given and, at least in many instances, something inauspicious is simultaneously transferred to the recipient. In the marriage ceremony what is being given is a virgin, that is, a *kanya*. Hence kanyadana or "gift of a virgin." Dubois's description, probably the earliest Western ethnographic account of this part of the marriage service, is still worth quoting:

> Then follows the most important ceremony of all, . . . the gift of the virgin. This is what takes place. The bridegroom being seated facing the east, his father-in-law performs the *sam-kalpa* [preliminary mediation on the great gods], places himself in front of [the groom], and looks at him fixedly for some time without speaking. He is supposed to imagine that he sees in his son-in-law the great Vishnu; and with his mind he offers him a sacrifice. . . . A new copper vessel is brought. In this the young man places his feet, which his father-in-law washes first with water, then with milk, and then again for the third time with water, while reciting suitable *mantrams* [memorized prayers]. . . . Then holding betel in one hand and taking his daughter's hand in the other he says a prayer to Vishnu, begging him to look with a gracious eye on this gift that he is making of his virgin daughter. (1983:223)

Though the symbolism is complex and undoubtedly has multiple meanings the basic thrust is clear: the groom is seen as a god and he is given deference and worshipped by the father-in-law. Accordingly, the bride is a religious gift analogous to (or even the same as) those given to gods in worship; it is the supreme religious gift.[8]

The purest and most intense forms of worship involve adoration, not negotiation. Religious rituals conducted with the expectation of a direct quid pro quo more closely resemble economic exchange or magical manipulation rather than worship. The logic of worship pervades the kanyadana relationship, for the groom's family is neither expected nor allowed to give anything in return. The bride's family is rewarded by the honor of having their gift accepted. For them to accept something in return negates the value gained from making such a gift. This asymmetry of gift-giving is continued for years to come, with the bride's family being unable to accept even food from the groom's family, or, in some parts of India, to even enter the village of their son-in-law. In contrast, the bride's family continue a regular flow of gifts and prestations to their married daughter, the groom, and his family. A second more pragmatic logic also is present. Since dana typically involves passing on inauspiciousness to others, the purpose of such gifts is defeated if the inauspiciousness is returned.

This logic also operates in a more specifically religious context, when sin and evil are passed from the devotee to the deity or his mediator; the purpose of the transaction would be defeated if the sin and evil were returned—either immediately or at a later date. Such asymmetrical exchanges occurs in a wide variety of religious contexts. In many sacrifices, the sins of the devotees are placed upon the animal or other object to be sacrificed and then offered to the god. In Christianity, Jesus is "the Lamb of God which taketh away the sins of the world."[9] Similar logics are expressed in various forms of bhakti. But the direction cannot be reversed; for obvious reasons, what is given must be transformed, not simply returned.[10] The relevant point here is that the asymmetrical kanyadana, or gift of the virgin, is a special case of a very common type of sacral relationship—one we shall consider in more detail in the analysis of worship in Chapter 13.

This logic underlying kanyadana implies hypergamy. An important regional and caste variation is how rigorously the prohibition against counter-prestations is interpreted and followed. The crucial question is whether relatively direct exchange of women between lineages is prohibited. Where such exchanges are prohibited, the key means of preventing the disabilities of being a wife-giver from accumulating are eliminated; the inferiority of giving a wife cannot be erased by becoming a wife-taker to your wife-taker. Families are, then, more likely to attempt to reduce the negative cost of being a wife-giver by making an alliance with a family of higher status. If this becomes widespread, then identifiable strata and institutionalized hypergamy are likely to emerge.

In sum, the inferiority of wife-givers counteracts the tendencies toward isogamy, and makes asymmetrical relationships attractive: the "gift of a virgin" and related dowries are exchanged for acceptance by superiors. The logics of worship and inauspiciousness implied in the notion of kanyadana provide a rationale for such asymmetrical exchanges and forbid that they be qualified by exchange marriages. In addition, the patriarchal components of kanyadana, and Hindu society in general, eliminate the legitimacy of hypogamy. Hence, when wife-giving threatens one's status, the most culturally available alternative is hypergamy.

Institutionalized Hypergamy

Where institutionalized hypergamy does emerge as a dominant pattern, three corollary processes tend to occur. First, the number and geographical distribution of exogamous relationships (i.e., those within one's caste who are culturally ineligible as marriage partners) tend to increase.[11] This is in part the result of the prohibition against exchange marriages, which is often expanded to include those with whom alliances have been formed in the memorable past. Hence the circle of people one cannot marry is significantly expanded. Another possible source of the increased size of the exogamous group is the weaker impact of approval from those already closely associated with you. For example, households linked by ongoing marriage alliances, as those in South India or Bengal, are likely to have about the same status rather than a significantly higher status, and, as our general theory suggests, direct exchange of praise between equals tends to be discounted as "tit for tat." If they do have a higher status, the effect of their acceptance of your daughter is likely to be discounted, compared to a family considered to be more remote and thus objective in their evaluation of your status.

The second tendency is an increase in the size of the marriage circle and the endogamous group. If the proportion who are ineligible to marry one another (i.e., exogamous) is increased, this creates pressure to expand the size of the group. There is also a second pressure for expansion, because of the emergence of strata within the caste: if daughters cannot be given to lineages with lower status, then the number of eligible grooms is further decreased. The expansion of the size of the caste group does not, of course, fundamentally solve the problem, if the proportion of those who are appropriate partners does not increase. A larger size mitigates the problem, however, because the chances of finding the precisely appropriate match increase as the size of the "market" increases—even if the aggregate ratio of supply and demand stay unchanged. (These tendencies are for the most part rooted in the fourth order countervailing processes and will be discussed in greater detail when we consider the long-term dynamics of systems of hypergamy.)

The third process likely to occur is an increase in the explicitness and formalization of rankings within the endogamous caste. Families and lineages within the caste begin to be grouped into specific named subcategories such as the biradaris of the Rajputs (Parry 1979), the *kulas* of high caste medieval Bengalis (Inden 1976), and the *anks* of the Kanya-Kubja Brahmans (Khare 1970). In time, these are likely to be explicitly ranked. This development of explicit subcategories and ranks is probably a response to the difficulties that guardians have in determining the rank of potential marriage partners in a large, widely dispersed caste. Two additional sources of such segmentation and internal ranking seem likely on theoretical grounds. The more intense the competition for grooms, the more important small differences are likely to be, and the more likely they are to be labelled. Second, formal categories and rankings seem more likely if there is a formal authority to arbitrate and impose decisions. Such an authority may develop from within the caste itself, such as a jati or biradari council that standardizes categories, settles disputes, and disciplines or excommunicates deviants. On the other hand, the authority may be external—a role played by both traditional rajas and colonial authorities. This was probably one of the consequences of the British attempt to provide an official census ranking of caste groups.

The analysis implies a built-in progression. The increase in the proportion of those who are defined as exogamous leads to the expansion of the endogamous marriage circle. But the problems solved by larger marriage circles create problems of visibility and social control. These problems in turn lead to more formal categories and to formal structures of authority. But two sets of factors limit the tendencies described. First, the cultural factors initiating the process can be limited or contained. For example, the intensity of patriarchy or the kanyadana ideology may be less in some areas or among some castes. We will consider such circumstances in the analysis of nonhypergamous areas. Second, hypergamy has some internal dynamics that limit or even reverse the processes we have described.

The dynamics that limit the tendency toward institutionalized hypergamy can be usefully viewed as *fourth order* countervailing processes. These can roughly be divided into two types, the psychological and the demographic. With respect to the first type, hypergamy undermines the solidarity of a given strata, group or subgroup. To begin with, marrying up (unlike exchange marriages) cannot prevent the loss of status for all members of the marriage circle; some will gain at the expense of others. What is a perfectly rational strategy for a particular wife-giver cannot work for everyone. The essence of the process is to create inequalities, and this produces the potential for resentment, resistance, and rebellion by subgroups who feel unjustly deprived.

In addition, however, to resentments about inequalities per se, very concrete practical problems emerge because of what might be called the demographics of hierarchy. By definition, hierarchies are pyramidal or diamond-shaped: a small group at the top, and ever-larger groups toward the bottom, or toward the middle. The contradictions arise when attempts are made to maintain interpersonal relationships between the members of groups that are unequal in size. For example, it is difficult for all of the members of a group of one hundred to maintain close friendships with the members of a group of ten—there are not enough friends to go around no matter how friendly everyone is. In contrast, it is perfectly possible for most members of a group to have personal friends in another group of approximately equal size.[12] This same type of contradiction arises in creating and maintaining marriage alliances between caste strata of unequal size. The specific cultural feature that accentuates the demographic problem is the requirement that brides move only in an upward direction (or stay in their own strata). One crucial result is the inevitable tendency to create a surplus of brides at the top and a shortage at the bottom. Moreover, who is to marry the daughters of the highest strata?[13] The problems are mitigated by a sharper pyramid of inequality. For if each higher stratum is much smaller than the stratum below, then only a small proportion of the daughters of the lower stratum are required to satisfy the demand for wives in the higher stratum. But, of course, this lesser demand cuts both ways, because fewer of the lower stratum will have an opportunity to increase their status by marrying up. The strata under the greatest strain will be those with a relatively larger stratum above and a relatively smaller one below; this will produce a high demand for its daughters, but an inadequate supply of brides from the strata below. As mentioned, the strata at the top face the problem of a surplus of daughters. Among Rajput groups this was frequently reduced by high rates of female infanticide and polygyny (Plunkett 1973), though these remedies produce other social strains. At the lower end of the hierarchy the shortage of wives is often solved by taking wives from the caste below. This will, of course, tend to obscure the lowest boundary of the supposedly endogamous group (see Parry 1979:228–31; Shah 1982:11–16). This shortage of wives has some benefits for the lower strata; they can surreptitiously charge a bride price for their daughters (Parry 1979:228; Shah 1982:24), though this is clearly contrary to the ideology of kanyadana. This, however, creates another structural contradiction in the strata immediately above. These groups must give large dowries in order to get higher groups to accept their daughters as wives, and at the same time they may have to pay a high bride price to secure brides for their sons. Obviously this puts middle level strata under great economic strain. Sometimes these strains are alleviated by men postponing the age of marriage. This is commonly associated with labor away from the village, typically military service. While these various remedies may reduce the contradictions, they cannot eliminate them. According to Parry, systems of hypergamy are inherently unstable or, more accurately, tend to be in what he calls oscillating equilibrium. That is, "reform movements" develop at regular periods advocating isogamy and equal exchange either for a particular stratum, such as a biradari, or even for the whole caste. Such reforms last for a while, but some members are inevitably tempted to gain advantage by marrying their daughters up. Eventually the reforms erode and the features of hypergamy re-emerge—until the pressures it creates produce another reform movement.[14] In theoretical terms, this can be conceived as an oscillation between the third order pressures for status heterogeneity (and the creation of social mechanisms to stabilize and elaborate such tendencies), and the fourth order countervailing pressures. The latter develop to some degree in any hierarchy—that is, in any ranked, skewed distribution—that allows cross-strata associations and mobility. They become even more acute given the specific characteristics of institutionalized hypergamy.[15]

Upper Castes in the South

I have argued that two factors produce hypergamous marriage patterns in North India. First, the inferiority of wife-givers creates pressures to depart from isogamy. Second, patriarchal institutions and the ideology of kanyadana block the possibility of either hypogamy or exchange marriages. This leaves hypergamy as the most attractive alternative.

The relatively isogamous marriage patterns of the ritually high caste groups in South India are not due simply to an absence of the two features that produce hypergamy in the North. Both these features—the inferiority of wife-givers and the ideology of kanyadana—are also characteristic of many of these castes.[16] The explanation of upper caste isogamy in the South lies in identifying a third factor that contains and modifies the effects of the first two factors. This third factor is the Dravidian kinship system and, more specifically, the institution of cross-cousin marriage. "Cousin" means approximately what it means in Western societies: the children of one's parent's siblings. "Cross" refers to parental siblings of the opposite sex: your mother's brother, but not your father's brother; your father's sister, but not your mother's sister. Accordingly, cross-cousin marriage means that a specified male is supposed to marry the daughter of a parent's siblings who are of the opposite sex of his parent. That is, he is supposed to marry his mother's brother's daughter or his father's sister's daughter—but not his father's brother's daughter or his mother's sister's daughter. There are several different types of cross-cousin marriage. Bilateral cross-cousin marriage involves the direct exchange of daughters between two families or lines: the son of the first family marries his mother's brother's daughter and the son of the second family marries his father's sister's daughter. Patrilateral exchanges involve the son marrying the father's sister's daughter and result in the exchange of brides in alternative generations. Matrilateral patterns involve the son marrying the mother's brother's daughter and result in indirect exchange between three or more lines: A gives to B, B gives to C, C gives to A.[17] Over the long run, they all produce the exchange of daughters between families and lineages.[18] Of course, these patterns, like all marriage alliance norms, are limited by the demographic possibilities. When the most appropriate type of cousin is not available, compromises are made—similar to the compromises that are made in most societies when war depletes the number of men, and women have to marry those who in normal circumstances are considered too old or too young.

Most of the languages of South India are classified as Dravidian rather than Indo-European. Closely associated with this language group is a type of kinship structure and terminology. A variety of Dravidian-type kinship systems are found in contemporary South India, but these derive from a common proto-Dravidian system.[19] The key structural feature is the institution of cross-cousin marriage. As Trautmann says, "In order to specify the broad features of the Dravidian . . . we begin with a concept basic to the understanding of the Dravidian, that of cross cousins" (1981:22). Dumont agrees: "To put it in a nutshell what distinguishes South India from North India is cross-cousin marriage" (1983:160).[20] The source of this core feature need not concern us. The consequences are significant: cross-cousin marriage results in at least a rough equality between lineages that exchange brides. As Dumont says, "South Indian kinship presents us with a contrast . . . something like an island of equality in an ocean of caste" (1983:167). Trautmann notes that even where demographic or other local influences in some respects limit or restrict cross-cousin marriages, "Dravidian marriage always has the character of an exchange" (1981:24). Over time this results in the perpetuation of alliances between two lineages: my sister marries you and I marry your sister; my daughter marries your son and your son marries my daughter, and so on. This pattern of exchange marriages—switching roles as wife-givers and wife-takers—prevents the inequalities in any one marriage alliance from accumulating, and thus averts institutionalized hypergamy; the result is inequality in the context of a specific marriage ceremony, but the macro pattern is one of isogamy.[21]

But how is the practice of cross-cousin marriage, with its implications of equality and quid pro quo exchange, reconciled with the notion of kanyadana? The writers of the Dharmasastra texts struggled with this contradiction off and on over the centuries. Numerous texts authorize cross-cousin marriage, provided the practice is restricted to the South. While more elaborate rationales were developed, all contain contradictions (see Trautmann 1981:238–315), and the tensions within the tradition are never completely resolved. In the Dravidian South, both cross-cousin marriage (and hence exchange marriages) and the ideology of kanyadana are widely embraced. We will examine some of the mechanisms that help to alleviate these contradictions later.

Intermediate Patterns: Handling Contradictions

Fully developed hypergamy and the exchange of brides based on cross-cousin marriages are alternative polar responses for dealing with the cost of being a wife-giver. In addition, intermediate patterns exist that embody only some of the elements previously described. We will consider the Punjabis and the Bengalis. The Punjabis maintain a strong commitment to asymmetrical marriage relationships—that is, no exchange marriages—but this does not result in institutionalized hypergamy. The Bengalis regularly engage in exchange marriages, but this is not based on cross-cousin marriages. Hence, these two cases represent important variations on the patterns previously discussed. In each case the pattern involves contradictions, and in each case these are handled by what I will call encapsulation—the restricting of contradictory elements of ideology or role expectations to their own limited spheres. As we shall see, there are two primary types of encapsulation. These can be seen as the supplementary institutionalized responses to the "problem" of being a wife-giver where kanyadana is institutionalized.

Punjabis and Structural Encapsulation

The most extended discussion of Punjabi marriage patterns is by Hershman (1981), which focuses primarily upon the Jats, a caste of yeoman farmers. Hershman's own analysis parallels many of the arguments presented here:

> To give a woman in marriage is to place oneself in a position of inferiority to the taker; to take a woman is to assume a position of superiority to the giver; and to exchange women is to maintain a position of equality. Punjabis resolve the problem of having to give their sisters in marriage and yet at the same time of preserving their honor, in two quite distinct ways: Punjabi Muslims maintain and exchange their women within closed groups thus preserving their honor within the group by arranging the marriages of their sisters to one another; while Punjabi Hindus and Sikhs solve the problem by accepting the inferiority of the wife-giver role and by creating from this premise a system of exogamy based upon the principle of non-exchange. (1981:191)

Apparently, the strategy of the Muslims for preserving their status closely approximates one of the two major strategies discussed above—even though the legitimacy of exchange marriages may have quite different roots from Dravidian cross-cousin marriage. Punjabi Hindus and Sikhs are of even more interest, because they form an important intermediate case: wife-givers are clearly inferior and exchange marriages are unambiguously prohibited, yet the normative pattern is isogamy rather than hypergamy. If our basic argument is correct, how does this pattern persist? The answer lies in limiting the scope and effect of the inequalities created by marriage alliances.

Hershman identifies five processes that contribute to this outcome. First, the inequalities caused by wife-giving and wife-receiving are largely limited to specific ritual contexts, for example, at weddings and funerals (1981:199).[22] Second, only the husband himself acquires any real honor from being a wife-taker, and only the wife's immediate family shares the dishonor of being a wife-giver. The more remote kindred have their status affected in only nominal ways. Third, interaction with affines or in-laws is largely restricted to the relationship of a man to his wife's family. Except at weddings and funerals, other members of the husband's family would rarely come into contact with their wife-giving affines. Furthermore, the marriage alliances of any one family tend to be widely dispersed across different villages and families, and hence do not reinforce one another.[23] Fourth, the inequalities created by wife-giving are limited, because they are not significantly related to control of the means of production. While marriage alliances definitely affect the distribution of liquid forms of wealth in the Punjab, they rarely affect the distribution and control of land. Hence inequalities created in one sector seldom accumulate into generalized inequality. A fifth factor may retard the development of hypergamy and other forms of inequality: the influence of Sikhism. In principle, Sikhism is much more egalitarian than Hinduism, though the actual practices are more similar than their ideologies would suggest. Nonetheless, the influence of Sikhism has increased in this region since the partition of Pakistan and India, and the influence of Brahmans has declined. While this does not seem to have significantly affected the relative status of wife-givers and wife-receivers in either community, the Sikhs do seem less committed to strictly asymmetrical relationships between affines. For example, the Hindu tradition has strictly limited, if not forbidden, wedding gifts from ego's father's sister because this would be to accept something from one's wife-takers. But as Hershman notes, "the 'more' Sikh a caste is, the more likely its members are to accept gifts from "daughters" who are older female agnates. Therefore it is clear that the hierarchical Brahmanical ideology and egalitarian Sikh ideology have important implications for the nature of affinal relations in different castes" (1981:216). It is clear the influence of Sikh ideology has increased in recent years. The precise impact this has had in producing an absence of hypergamy is impossible to determine, but it is probably another contributing factor.

I will refer to this complex of processes which limits the consequences of being a wife-giver as structural encapsulation.

Bengalis and Ideological Encapsulation

Scholars have devoted considerable attention to Bengali marriage patterns (e.g., Klass 1966; Fruzzetti, Ostor, and Barnett 1976; Inden 1976; Inden and Nicholas 1977; Fruzzetti and Ostor 1983; Davis 1983). The ideology of kanyadana is well known and deeply rooted in Bengal; Fruzzetti entitles her monograph on Bengali marriage *The Gift of a Virgin* (1982). Nonetheless, marriages are essentially isogamous: "The status of the contracting lines and houses should be as close as possible. Marriage alliance in Bengal establishes the equivalence of different lines and houses" (1982:34). While the marriage ritual clearly contains hierarchical elements, this does not result in long-term inequalities. This is in part due to structural encapsulation, for, as Fruzzetti notes, "The inferior/superior relationship is limited to the giving and receiving of the gift of the virgin" (1982:111).

But even more important, among many castes exchange marriages are common: "the Bengali system does not follow the classical pattern of hypergamy. The reversal of the direction of marriage is quite common in Bengal. Such unions are known as *badal biye* (exchange marriage), and these are as common as marriages in entirely new directions" (Fruzzetti 1982:34). This not only involves exchanges between different lines (*bangsa*), but also between specific pairs of households (*ghars*): a brother and a sister of one household have spouses who are brother and sister of another household. Such exchanges are not simply tolerated as deviant patterns. Fruzzetti reports, "Exchange marriages are encouraged, and this reversal in direction works contrary to the notion of hypergamy, where women—as goods—are supposed to flow in only one direction" (1982:112). Fruzzetti's data are based on upper and lower castes in a subdivisional town and related rural areas.

But this acceptance of exchange marriages cannot be attributed to the influences of cross-cousin marriage. The practice is usually proscribed in Bengal. The kinship terminology is certainly not of the Dravidian type. While some preference exists for repeated marriages between two lines (bangsa), new alliances are as common as repeated ones. Hence marriages do not necessarily result in any permanent alliances with affines or for that matter in any other "groups" (Fruzzetti and Ostor 1976:93).[24] This absence of Dravidian kinship patterns is evidence that the crucial factors in cross-cousin marriages producing isogamy are not necessarily linked to special features of Dravidian culture (e.g., the kinship terminology), but rather, lie in exchange marriages per se.[25] In sum, Bengalis both affirm the ideology of kanyadana and regularly engage in exchange marriages. The latter is a clear contradiction of the former.

How does Bengali culture handle such contradictions? One characteristic of Bengal seems to be its long tradition of heterodoxy and syncretism; the ability to encapsulate contradictory elements of culture seems to be a common phenomenon there. While Bengal has deep traditions of Brahmanical orthodoxy, the Tantric traditions have long been popular. Somehow the Bengalis have for centuries managed to hold what are in many respects antithetical traditions in a close alliance. This is not just a matter of tolerating unorthodox sects, but rather, of making the heretical a central part of conventional orthodoxy. This situation provides a broader cultural context for understanding the Bengali's adherence to and deviation from the doctrine of kanyadana.[26] I will refer to this process as ideological encapsulation.

Drawing primarily on Fruzzetti and Ostor's data, I have argued that in Bengal, exchange marriages are legitimate and a primary source of the basically isogamous pattern. This may require qualification when we consider the highest caste groups. We know, for example, that hypergamy was the ideal among upper caste Bengalis in previous centuries (see Inden 1976). Many of the upper class groups that came to be known as the *bhadralok* (respectable people) probably followed similar patterns. Thus, the analysis used here may not apply to the very highest castes in Bengal. Despite the strong presence of the kanyadana ideology, though, Bengal is much less preoccupied with hypergamous patterns than many areas in North India. Our theoretical arguments, supplemented by the notions of structural and ideological encapsulation, suggest an explanation for this social fact.

Obviously, the concept of ideological encapsulation is relevant to the South Indian contradictions between the kanyadana ideology and cross-cousin marriages. As noted earlier, the legitimacy of both sets of values and norms are strongly affirmed in the Dravidian South. But the mechanisms of legitimizing these contradictions may vary for the two regions. Exchange marriages are much more central and deeply institutionalized in the South than in Bengal. As we have seen, the very kin-ship terminology in Dravidian languages assumes cross-cousin marriage. To change this would require a fundamental reordering of Dravidian cultural categories. In Bengal, the cultural significance of exchange marriages seems much more limited. It is when patterns are tenuous that societies most need mechanisms to reduce the contradictions threatening such patterns. Hence the notion of encapsulation has been our primary focus in the case of Bengal.[27]

As we shall see, encapsulation can also be used to limit tendencies toward equal-ity, as when bhakti sects limit relations of equality to religious contexts and Tantra sects limit such relationships to contexts that are kept secret from the rest of society.

Alliances in Lower and Middle Castes

Most of the analysis has been devoted to explaining departures from what I have called the dominant tendencies of status groups. Thus, it is appropriate to conclude by focusing on cases where these dominant tendencies prevail. Almost by defi-nition, lower and middle castes are less influenced by Brahmanical ideology than upper castes. While the kanyadana ideology and the inferiority of wife-givers are common in South Asia, not surprisingly, most of the lower caste groups are not strongly influenced by these ideas, and their influence on middle caste groups is at best uneven (see, e.g., Dumont 1986a). Undoubtedly the greater economic contribu-tion of women's labor in these strata also plays a role, as a result of which mar-riages among these groups are usually isogamous. Perhaps more accurately, the same systematic tendencies toward hypergamy, common among more orthodox castes, are not present. This conclusion is reinforced by the fact that Brahmanical-type dowries are much less common among such castes and the use of bride price, especially among lower caste groups, has been widely documented (Beals 1962; Orenstein 1965; Ishwaran 1968; Beck 1972; Berreman 1972; van der Veen 1973; Kolenda 1978; Parry 1979). Of course, gifts (or more accurately, prestations) nor-mally flow in both directions (see, e.g., Tambiah 1973; Vatuk 1975; Srinivas 1984; Dumont 1986a; Kolenda 1987a). Moreover, as we have noted earlier, bride price may occur toward the bottom of a hypergamous system (Shah 1982). Classical hypergamy is antithetical to a bride price (van der Veen 1973). The lack of Brahmanical orthodoxy among these castes can also have a second effect: a relaxa-tion of the rules of endogamy (e.g., Berreman 1972:232). The result is likely to be more random deviations, even if the norm remains isogamy.

The theoretical interpretation of these patterns among middle and lower castes is quite straightforward. When neither kanyadana nor the inferiority of wife-givers is significant, the outcome—both normative and empirical—conforms to the dominant tendencies toward status homogeneity and thus, isogamy. On the other hand, since concerns about status and purity are to some degree the luxuries of the relatively well-to-do, there is more variation between caste groups and individuals in the de-gree to which they are concerned about these matters, and thus in the extent to which isogamy is enforced.[28]

Conclusion

Limitations and Accomplishments

First I must remind the reader not familiar with South Asia that only a few of the important variations have been considered (though several other variations have been analyzed in Milner 1988). The arguments are presented as tentative hypotheses for which there is some support, but which are by no means conclusive.

The purpose of this chapter has been to suggest a set of interrelated explanations of status relations in Hindu marriage alliances derived from a general theory of status relationships. The theory purports to explain the strong tendencies toward status homogeneity, and thus isogamy and endogamy, and the counter-pressures toward heterogeneity and thus hypergamy or hypogamy. In addition to the propositions of the general theory, there have been two important supplementary parts of the analysis. The first was the identification of the particular cultural and historical factors that in some situations tip the balance toward status heterogeneity, and more specifically, hypergamy; these are the inferiority of wife-givers, and the ideology of kanyadana. The second was the identification of social and cultural mechanisms used to contain and limit these pressures toward heterogeneity; these are exchange marriages, structural encapsulation, and ideological encapsulation.[29] Even within institutionalized hypergamy, demographic and cultural factors intervene to limit the tendency toward asymmetry.

The claim is that a general theory of status relations, supplemented by particular cultural and historical facts, can help us to systematically organize the data concerning status relations in marriage alliances. A variety of seemingly disparate patterns are seen as variations on a few common themes. The aim has been to suggest how we might develop social theory that (1) has significant utility across cultures, (2) takes seriously the categories of particular cultures, and (3) takes into account the subcultures present in any complex society. Neither general theory, cultural analysis, nor local ethnography will suffice; all three are necessary for adequate sociological analysis.

Rational Choice Theory

This chapter has also tried to make a more methodological point: a provisional resource structuralism does not preclude modes of analysis that begin from a more micro perspective. More specifically, I have tried to show that for the purposes of analyzing marriage alliances, it is useful to use a very simple form of rational choice theory: assume people make rational choices in pursuit of their interests, specify the nature of these interests in a particular cultural context, trace out the consequences of such individual level behavior for the construction of macro-level patterns.

Two points need to be made about the usefulness of this approach. First, it is likely to be most powerful in situations where individuals, or relatively integrated social units such as families or firms, are socially expected to make specific rational choices. Marriage "markets" meet this criterion. Conversely, the data in areas where goals are more implicit and ambiguous are likely to be more opaque to such an approach. For example, I doubt that the kind of "decoding" of pollution, asceticism, and auspiciousness carried out in Chapters 9 and 10 would have worked as well if I had begun with a rational choice perspective. In part, rational choice theory works well in this chapter precisely because various forms of structural analysis have helped to clarify the nature of the social context within which marriage alliances in India are formed.

12

On the Nature of Sacredness

Before the empirical analysis can be extended, additional theoretical concepts are required; more specifically, the nature of the sacred and its relationship to status must be considered. I have tried to keep this abstract level of discussion to a minimum; the enormous literature on the nature of the sacred is only touched upon. The purpose of the discussion is to connect this part of the analysis with the theoretical arguments that have guided the whole endeavor.

Status and Sacredness

If Weber laid the groundwork for scholarship on status and status groups, Durkheim was most seminal to a sociological understanding of the sacred. It is a great irony that little attempt has been made to systematically analyze the relationship between these two concepts, which obviously overlap. Perhaps this is because in *The Elementary Forms of Religious Life* Durkheim stresses the total otherness of the sacred and the profane (1965:55–56). Durkheim's claim that the two realms were always of a totally different order has not, however, gone unchallenged (see, e.g., Lukes 1973, 1979:26–27; Pickering 1984:143–48). In footnotes and asides, Durkheim himself acknowledged that the distinction between the sacred and the profane was ambiguous and relative.[1]

If, then, there is an overlap or a continuum between the sacred and the profane, what is the equivalent of the sacred in the profane world?[2] The answer is, in part, social status. Or to reverse the idea, the sacred is, in part, a special type of status: key aspects of sacredness are status in the "other world." In Chapter 2 I suggested that Durkheim's theory of social solidarity, which focused on sacredness, was in some respects the mirror image of the Parsons–Dahrendorf theory of the origins of social inequality as status differentiation. If this is the case, we should be able to detect clear parallels in the characteristics of social status and sacredness. A main purpose of the next several chapters will be to demonstrate these parallels. That parallels may exist between worldly and otherworldly relationships is of course an old idea that has played a central role in the sociology of religion at least since Marx.

I do not claim that the perspective I am offering will capture all of the richness and complexity of religious phenomena—even from the point of view of the empirical analyst, not to mention that of the religious devotee. As with the earlier parts of the analysis, I will simply try to show how it can help us see concatenations and relationships that might otherwise be overlooked.

Sacredness and Power

Otherness

The two seminal works on the nature of the sacred, both published in the first quarter of the twentieth century, are by Durkheim (1965) and Otto (1972). They were very different works—Otto was a theologian—but both in effect define the sacred in terms of "otherness." This has continued to shape most conceptualizations of the sacred. If sacredness is defined primarily in terms of otherness, the obvious question is: Other than what? That is, the content of the sacred will depend on the referent to which it is compared. The broad answer is, of course, the profane. This is so general as to offer only minimal guidance. Implicitly the referent of comparison has frequently varied for different analysts. A full, systematic analysis of the different referents that have been used and the different meanings that have been attributed to the sacred would require a major digression that is not necessary for the task at hand.[3] Rather, I will simply try to be clear about the aspects of the profane world that serve as the counter-model for my notion of the sacred.

The Limits of Human Power

Why have human beings been so preoccupied with these realms of otherness? Why have religion and other forms of the supernatural been such universal phenomena, and why have they continued to shape human behavior and history? It is, at least in part, because these realms offer humans a crucial source of power. In his overview of popular Hinduism, Fuller notes, "Above all else, it is the vast and variously imagined power of the deities . . . that is taken for granted by the overwhelming majority of Hindus" (1992:29). In the context of analyzing Biblical materials, Leach says much the same thing: "impotent Man on Earth is polarized against omnipotent God in Heaven. Religion is concerned with mediation between the two spheres such that a channel is provided through which divine potency from Heaven is brought to bear upon the affairs of impotent Man on Earth" (1983:67).

In the terms used in earlier chapters, humans face many contingencies. Perhaps the only certainty is that we all must die. While collectivities may survive across generations, they too are historical creations that appear and disappear. Moreover, as Berger emphasizes, human social orders are, from some points of view, extremely fragile. Marginal situations such as dreams, fantasies, and especially death, call into question the assumptions of common-sense everyday life. As Berger says,

"Every socially constructed nomos must face the constant possibility of its collapse into anomy. Seen in the perspective of society, every nomos is an area of meaning carved out of a vast mass of meaninglessness" (1967:23).

But even if the "world as we know it" is not threatened with chaos and meaninglessness, our place within it—or at least the place we would like to have—may be. In addition to death, most humans face numerous frustrations beyond their power to change or accept. For the Indian peasant these may involve bad weather, disease, the inability to have a son or to arrange a good marriage for a daughter, a rapacious landlord. Those with worldly power suffer fewer of these frustrations than the weak, but even the mighty must face death. Perhaps even more significant, since the privileges and identity of elites are much more tied to the existing social order, threats to it are even more menacing to them than to others. When the Muslims and then the British conquered India, the Hindu raja was much more affected than the typical peasant.

The key point is that all human beings face contingency and moments of powerlessness, and they seek techniques and alliances that will make them less vulnerable. This may involve creating relationships with those who, at least potentially, have the power to help them overcome their frustrations and disappointments. Or it may mean that powerful actors who would cause them harm have to be propitiated. One such crucial form of alliance is that which humans make with deities or other supernatural powers. Now we must turn to the nature of these powers, so that we can then consider the nature of human relationships with them.

The Nature of Deities and Other Sacred Powers

Wadley in her study of the conceptual structure of religion in Karimpur, a north Indian village, defines deities as "power-filled" supernatural beings:

> The basic characteristic of any god, demon, or ghost is the powers which he/she controls and represents—the fact that he/she is, in essence, power. The only noun in Hindi which comes close to including all possible powerful beings is deva, which is defined to include both demons and "good" deities, but not the most evil beings—ghosts and other spirits of the dead. *deva* [*sic*] can be contrasted to *devata*, which definitely refers to only good or goodish supernatural beings. Fortunately, there is an adjectival phrase which refers to all gods, ghosts, demons, etc.—shakti-sanpann, "power-filled." Those beings filled with power are the supernatural beings; they make up the village pantheon. (1975:54–55)

Note that the central organizing concept of the pantheon is not purity, but power, sakti. Humans interact with gods and other supernatural beings in order to make use of or protect themselves from their power. Sakti is most commonly associated with the female energy of the goddess Sakti, but more generally it is considered to be "the energizing principle of the universe without which there would be no motion" (Wadley 1975:55).

The power of deities should not, however, be overstated, for one of the important characteristics of Hinduism is the absence of a clear dividing line between the sacred and the profane. In Hindu mythology gods often act like humans and in many contexts humans are considered divine. Gurus, for example, are often treated as near gods. Similarly, for certain purposes Brahmans are gods. On their wedding day the bride and the groom are considered to be divine and are worshipped. Hence while deities are sacred because they are powerful, their sacredness and power is primarily a matter of degree. Similarly, there are no clear lines between different aspects of sacredness. This is one reason why polytheism is not a problem from the Hindu's point of view. There are thousands of gods, but for some purposes all gods are one, and in some respects all of reality is sacred.

The relationship between sacredness and otherworldly power parallels the relationship between social status and worldly power. Social status can be solely rooted in physical resources like wealth or force, or it can be rooted in attributes that are quite distinct from physical resources, such as the purity of the Brahman or the virtue of a saint. Similarly, the sacredness of a god can be rooted solely in its assumed power to intervene in the natural world, or can be rooted in the spiritual virtues attributed to the god by devotees. The power of these spiritual virtues is exercised not by the god's direct intervention in the physical world, but rather by the effect on the devotees. This effect occurs through intimate communion with such a god. Worldly status can be raised by intimate association with someone of higher status—even if they fail to give you any wealth or political power. Similarly, the spiritual power of the deity becomes available to the devotee who stays in intimate relationship with his or her god. The primary effect of such power is to transform the identity of the devotee, rather than intervening in the cause-and-effect relationships of the physical world.[4] Of course, in most historical religions the power of the gods is conceived as some mixture of these two processes. The relationships devotees have with these power-filled beings is primarily determined by the types of power that are sought and exchanged; this is the topic to which we now turn.

Types of Relationships to the Supernatural

Early on, I made the unremarkable argument that rocks and humans are different; this was a way to contrast the realms of physical causation and social interaction. Within the realm of social interaction, I have claimed that there are three primary types of power rooted in different types of sanctions: force, goods and services, and expressions of approval and disapproval. Correlated with, but not identical to, the three types of sanctions are three orientations or attitudes toward the other person that tend to define the nature of the relationship. The intent behind force is usually *coercion*. The use of goods and services as a sanction is usually associated with some notion of *exchange*. Finally, expressions of approval usually suggest an attitude of admiration or even *worship*. Now I want to argue that the same typology is useful in distinguishing between the different types of otherworldly power and relationships. That is, people have tried to influence their other worlds by processes that are at least analogous to four types of relationships: physical causation, and the three types of social power and relationships.

In some cases, the relationship between humans and the supernatural are analogous to those of *physical cause and effect*. An ideal-typical model of magic is the

most obvious example; the appropriate secret techniques produce the desired results. Of course, in actual historical situations this idea is usually qualified or used
in conjunction with the other techniques to be discussed. In nontheistic religious
systems, activities are often conceptualized as causation rather than interaction,
since there are no deities or other supernatural agents with whom to interact. The
focus tends to be on special knowledge and techniques. Some of these stress the
power that the actor can obtain over this world and the next; most forms of Hindu
Tantrism have such an emphasis (Brooks 1990). Others emphasize knowledge that
transforms the actors' perspective or world view. The goal is not so much to alter
the world or one's position in it, but to see the world in a new way. As we shall
see, the Samkhya-Yoga schools of Hinduism, as well as early Buddhism, closely
approximate this model.[5] In all of these perspectives, the primary responsibility lies
with the human actor, hence knowledge and discipline are central. The interest
or aim, however, is not primarily moral conformity to some divine law, but self-
empowerment or transcendence.

In other cases the social world, rather than the physical world, is the implicit
model for sacral relationships. Here humans must influence the gods or other sacred
entities by interpersonal interaction. The form and content of the interaction can
vary considerably. Sometimes it approximates *coercion*.[6] It could be analogous to
the legitimate force of the police or the opportunistic force of the robber. That is,
the connection between the human actor and the sacred may or may not involve any
sense of a moral relationship. Voodoo is probably the most famous system that
emphasizes coercive magical interaction between humans and the supernatural.
Vedic sacrifices seem to contain elements that range from pure physical causation,
to interaction by means of coercive magic, to the dutiful performance of divinely assigned responsibilities.

Fully social relationships, however, involve significant elements of morality.
Neither side has the power to cause the behavior of the other, but they have the
power to react to it in positive and negative ways. The gods can punish and reward
humans for their behavior; humans can give services and devotion or withhold
these. The relationship between humans and gods is based on some form of covenant in which the expectations of the gods are made known through divine revela-
tion, which is often embodied in laws.[7] Humans also have their expectations; if gods
are perceived not to keep their promises—at least in the long run—they lose their
followers. The content of such relationships is primarily *exchange*, though not necessarily or even usually explicit exchange. According to Wadley (1975), this is the
most common form of relationships between typical Hindu peasants and their gods.

The fourth type of relationship is based, not on quid pro quo, but rather on unqualified devotion. The primary content of such relationships is *worship* and adoration given without the expectation of anything in return. Here the gods receive devotion simply because they are supreme beings. The converse of this is that humans
receive boons and salvation, not because of anything that they have done to deserve
it, but simply because of the gods' love and grace. This concept is antithetical to the
previous notions. In this view, gods should be worshipped, not coerced or paid off.
Similarly, humans cannot demand or earn salvation, much less work out their own
salvation by knowledge and technique; they can only accept the grace of the gods.

These distinctions are, of course, analytical ideal-types. Actual patterns of religious behavior vary in the mix of these four types of relationships, and rarely is any one of them found in its pure form. In theory, unqualified devotion may be the appropriate attitude of the true bhakti devotee, but as Wadley notes, "In the world of the Hindu peasant, action without reward—love of god merely to love god—is without meaning and support" (1975:86). Similarly, theologies that offer absolutely unqualified grace are rarely viable for very long. The devotees lapse into various forms of antinomianism, and some form of specified morality is then reinstated. In short, there seems to be a constant interplay and dialectic between these four, as humans work out their relationships with their other worlds. To say there is usually a mixture of these four is not to deny that there are historical variations in the mix. Certainly Vedic sacrifices involved much more emphasis on causation than bhakti; the system of indulgences of medieval Catholicism involved much more quid pro quo exchange than the predestination of Calvinism. We will consider some of the historical variations later.[8]

Congruent and Incongruent Relationships

While in most historical religions a mixture of these types can be found, mixing is nearly always problematic; it creates relationships that are incongruent.[9]

As noted before, attempts to use one kind of sanction to gain another kind of sanction are often problematic. In human relationships, those who use force to gain goods and services are nearly always resented, whether they are contemporary muggers, feudal rulers, or tribal raiding parties. Those who attempt to gain praise by purchase or intimidation, or give praise for material reward, often find their status significantly discounted or even derided. While history is full of such behavior, it is usually hidden or disguised.

The precise analogue of this problem arises in humans' relationships to their gods. If gods or supernatural powers can be coerced by magic, they have rather low status—that is, they are not very sacred—though they may be seen as quite powerful in other respects. Similarly, a god whose favors can be bought, in exchange for either services or worship, has a reduced sacredness and transcendence, though not necessarily a reduced popularity—until such time as their powers to provide such blessings are perceived to fail. In contrast, the god who wants only authentic worship and returns only the transformation of the devotee's spiritual status does not face these contradictions, but may be irrelevant for those concerned about their immediate worldly problems. A god's sacredness is rooted in its otherness from the mundane and the profane, yet this limits a god's abilities to intervene in human affairs. This is, of course, the dilemma even of humans whose status is based on the rejection of force and wealth; spiritual leaders who become too implicated in politics or economic activity run the risk of destroying their religious status, which is the source of their spiritual power. Despite the omnipresence of this dilemma, people often attempt to influence the sacred through a mixture of these approaches; as in the case of human relationships, such mixtures set up contradictions that either limit a god's sacredness or worldly relevance.[10] Often sectarian disputes arise precisely over what mixtures are the appropriate and effective means of relating to the sacred. For example, this was expressly why Martin Luther initially criticized the papacy: the system of indulgences (contributions to the Church) to reduce the time souls spent in purgatory implied that humans could manipulate and bargain with God. As we shall see, the same issue divides various sectarian groups in Hinduism.

The Sacred as the Realm of Reversals and Compensation

Analyzing sacral relationships with the same concepts and propositions used to analyze profane status relations raises the issue of reductionism. Fuller (1979) claims that sacral relations cannot be satisfactorily explained as projections of human relationships. For example, he points out that for Hindus, eating the leftover food from humans is degrading, but eating the leftover food of the gods is the most sacred of sacraments. Fuller's point is that sacral relations are not simply modeled after human relations. But this does not mean that there is no connection between the patterns of relations among humans and the patterns of relations between humans and deities.

In fact, sacral relations tend to both copy and transform patterns of social relations. Where the supernatural and the sacred overlap, mundane relationships are often reversed. "Blessed are the poor in spirit: for theirs is the kingdom of heaven. . . . Blessed are the meek: for they shall inherit the earth." These opening sentences of The Beatitudes of Jesus' Sermon on the Mount (Matthew 5:3–5) express the notion that the resources and deprivations of the present world shall at some point in time be redistributed. Though the details vary, virtually all historic world religions hold some notion that the deprivations and injustices of the faithful will be compensated at some time in the future.[11] Associated with this idea is the notion of reversal: the darkness will become light, the mighty will be made low, the lowly will be raised up, the old kind of wisdom or knowledge will be seen as illusion, what was once seen as valuable will be seen as worthless. Thus if we are to analyze religious phenomena as projections, we should expect that aspects of these patterns will be reversals rather than copies of human structures. On the other hand, not even visions of heaven or planned utopias can be totally new; new ideas must be constructed with existing concepts. Accordingly, we should expect religious phenomena to be a mixture of patterns copied from the mundane world and reversals or transformations of those patterns. Using the terminology of the last chapter, the features of the world-to-come are second order processes that often compensate for and even reverse the first order processes of the profane world.

There are, of course, elements of this idea in many previous analyses, from Feuerbach to Lévi-Strauss. What I intend to show is how this idea, combined with the propositions that have been used to analyze status and caste systems, can provide insights into the connections between religion and social structure. More specifically the following hypotheses are suggested:

1. Because status is a relatively inexpansible resource, status in sacred other worlds will rarely be a completely plentiful resource. While status may be defined as more plentiful in the world to come, or the deity may be described as more gracious in dispensing status than worldly actors and structures, this will usually have significant limits in complex societies with "world religions."[12]

2. Because status is relatively inalienable in this world, we should expect that the alienability of status, and thus mobility, will be a common feature of the transition from this world to the other world. If it is not, and the other world simply reproduces the stratification of the present world, it will not be very "other," and is likely to be of little interest to anyone other than the privileged, and thus is unlikely to become a "world religion."

3. Because of the relative inexpansibility of status, much of the mobility that occurs will be circulation mobility: if someone moves up, someone else moves down. Since mobility is likely to occur during the transition from the profane world to the other world, many religions will have a notion that the status position of individuals will be reversed: "the first shall be last."

4. For status reversals to occur, the means of status and mobility will often have to be reversed. That is, systems that emphasize conformity to norms in this world will often emphasize associations as the source of status in the world to come, and vice versa. If the same criteria are used, the structures of this world would simply be reproduced in the other world.

5. In the terminology introduced in Chapter 11, the recessive tendencies often become the dominant tendencies, and vice versa. For example, in marriage relations the dominant pressures were toward status homogeneity and isogamy, but these activated recessive second order tendencies toward status heterogeneity and hypergamy. The dominant tendency in relations with deities is toward toward highly asymmetrical relationships—gods are greatly superior beings who must be worshipped—but there are counter-tendencies that emphasize intimacy, communion, and even identity between the deity and the devotee. The primacy of asymmetry is indicated by the fact that people would not seek communion with gods if they were not superior beings.

6. In routine contacts of devotion and worship with a deity or other sacred entity, interactions will tend to follow the *form* of status associations between low and high status actors. However, great sacral distance between the devotee and the deity may produce significant differences in the *content* of the interaction. For example, eating the leftover food of humans—even high status ones—is usually considered degrading, but eating the leftover food of the gods is spiritually elevating.

These rather abstract propositions will be given more concrete form in the next three chapters. They are intended not as ironclad laws, but as tendencies that will guide the analysis.

The Focus of What Follows

The following analysis of sacral phenomena is quite selective in two senses. First, it considers only a few features of Hinduism: worship, soteriology, and eschatology. Obviously, extensive chapters could be written on deities, sacrifice, pilgrimages, temples, and death and other life-stage rituals—to give only a partial list of what is ignored. The aim is not to be comprehensive, but to show the usefulness of a particular strategy and framework in showing the interconnections between the status order and the sacral order. Second, the analysis focuses primarily on one of the four types of sacred relationships that have been outlined: devotion and worship. The theory of status relationships is primarily about the operation of status under conditions in which it is insulated, to some degree, from material forms of power. Where wealth or political power are the sole criteria of status, it is not particularly useful to focus on or analyze the status order. But just as status is never completely insulated from material forms of power, rarely is it a simple function of wealth. Similarly, people's sacral activities are seldom completely indifferent about outcomes in the empirical world, but in the historic world religions it is rare for sacral power to be preoccupied solely with worldly gain. Accordingly, the theory of sacral relationships is primarily about forms of sacredness that contain significant elements of devotion and worship, rather than simply magical manipulation or quid pro quo ritual activity. This in no way suggests that these other forms of sacral relationships are unimportant to Hinduism—any more than the theory of status relations is intended to suggest that class relations are unimportant in Indian society. Rather, as with the whole analysis, the aim is to highlight the significance and the operation of non-material resources.

13

The Worship of Gods

Some of sociology's most insightful theory is built on Durkheim's (1965) analysis of worship of the sacred in *The Elementary Forms of Religious Life*. Goffman (1967, 1971) drew on Durkheim's notions to brilliantly analyze face-to-face interaction in contemporary society. Collins has formalized and extended Goffman's work to help us explain variations in the class subcultures and ritual styles of different types of societies (1975, 1982, 1988).[1] Goffman's seminal insight was that Durkheim's analysis of worship could serve as a paradigm for understanding the rituals of everyday life, and that many of these rituals were directed toward something analogous to the sacred. Yet despite the enormous fruitfulness of drawing on Durkheim's understanding of the worship of the sacred, virtually no attempt has been made to extend our understanding of these paradigmatic notions.[2] Both Goffman and Collins treat ritual and sacredness as largely undefined terms.

The purpose of this chapter will be to clarify and extend our understanding of worship (as the paradigm for many rituals) and sacredness.[3] The strategy for doing so will be the reverse of Goffman's. Instead of using our knowledge of religious processes to analyze everyday life, I will draw on the understanding of status process that earlier chapters have elaborated to illuminate the nature of worship and sacredness.[4]

The main focus of the analysis will be to explain the content of worship rather than its effects; that is, I will look at worship as a status process.

Worship as a Status Process

Perhaps the most common kind of sacral relationships are those that take place in the context of worship. Obviously, much of what happens in worship is modeled after relations between people of unequal status. For example, in some languages there is a direct semantic relationship between status deference and worship. In English the earliest known uses of the word "worship" refer to "the condition (in a person) of deserving, or being held in, esteem or repute; honor, distinction, renown; good name credit." According to the *Oxford English Dictionary*, this meaning was common into the sixteenth century. Even contemporary dictionaries, such as *Webster's New Collegiate*, still list one meaning of "worship" as "a person of importance—used as a title for various officials."

The task of this chapter is to show how we can develop a more systematic understanding of the patterns of behavior referred to as worship by drawing on the same ideas that have been used to explain the characteristics of status relationships and the caste system. Let us begin by briefly reviewing some of the key features of status relationships.

Since intimate associations affect the status of the actors, they usually try to increase their interaction with those of higher status and decrease interaction with those of lower status. There is an important corollary: when lower status actors want to approach and interact with those of higher status, they will attempt to highlight their high status attributes and downplay their low status attributes. To the degree possible, people will manipulate their actual characteristics and transform themselves into higher status actors—though there is seldom a clear line between transformation of the actual attributes and the manipulation of appearances. For example, when one goes for a job interview or is invited to the home of a high status person, one is likely to clean and groom oneself, to "dress up" (the term itself is instructive), to use more formal language, and to talk about one's accomplishments rather than one's failures. Furthermore, high status friends and acquaintances are more likely to be mentioned than low status ones. While this involves emphasizing the associations and attributes one supposedly already has, much of this behavior can also be conceived of as actually increasing one's conformity to the norms of those with whom one wishes to associate.

Attempts to raise oneself must be linked with appropriate deference; it is crucial to acknowledge the superiority of those who are clearly of higher status. This may involve highly elaborated public displays of deference and honor toward superiors. An important component of this activity is to listen attentively to the opinions and defer to the requests of the higher status actor. One effect of such attentiveness and deference, especially if they are sincere, is to further raise the status of the superior. Any petitions or requests to high status actors usually come after the processes already described, and they too must be stated deferentially.

The crucial question, however, is whether one is accepted by those of higher status. To become regularly intimate with those of significantly higher status raises and even transforms one's own status. One's specific petitions are also more likely to be granted. Moreover, the praise and deference that sustains and even raises the status of superiors can in turn have an indirect effect on one's own status: if one remains intimate with the now even higher status actor, one's own status is raised accordingly.[5] But acceptance is rarely a foregone conclusion; one can be rejected. Even worse, one may be publicly reprimanded or punished for presumption. Thus an attempt to become intimate with someone of higher status always involves risks and even danger.

In summary there are three basic processes. First, the separation of self from that which is lower and the maximization of one's conformity and association with superior behaviors, things, and actors. Second, the public acknowledgment of superiors through praise and deference (which may further increase their status). These two things are the precondition for the third, the intimate association with superiors which increases one's own status and increases the likelihood that one's specific petitions will be granted. The first two steps are, in part, necessary to reduce the dangers of rejection or even punishment for one's presumptuousness, which is not to suggest that such behaviors are necessarily calculating or insincere.

These social processes characteristic of status deference are the paradigm for worship. Worship consists primarily of three processes: (1) making oneself and one's immediate context worthy—or at least less unworthy—of the deity's presence; (2) praising and deferring to the deity; and (3) coming into intimate contact with the deity, which can lead to either rejection or communion. When the outcome is favorable, the devotee's self is transformed by this contact, and his or her welfare is more likely to be of concern to the deity—whether or not specific petitions are granted.[6]

Before this argument is elaborated and applied to Hinduism, we must clarify the relevance of purity and pollution for analyzing Hindu worship. To this preliminary consideration we now turn.

Purity, Pollution, and Sacral Status: A Preliminary

In Hinduism, the three processes just discussed are often carried out in the idiom of purity and pollution. That is, notions of purity and cleanliness are the key symbols and metaphors for high status, and pollution is the symbol of low status. As indicated in the analysis of Chapter 9, at least in part the idiom of purity and pollution involves objectification. To say this is not to suggest that they are "merely" symbols. In Hinduism, they often become the actual criteria of status and sacredness. Purity rituals are required not simply as a matter of respect to the sacred; rather sacredness becomes identified with purity. This identity between status and purity is characteristic of Dumont's (1980) as well as others' analyses of Hinduism, such as Harper's (1964) and Babb's (1975). However, as I have argued in earlier chapters, purity and social status are often too closely identified. I believe that too heavy a reliance has been placed upon notions of purity and pollution in both the social and religious spheres. Thus while worship in Hinduism sometimes is nearly identical with the manipulation of purity and impurity, there are many cases where the core notion is honoring, and purity is recognized primarily as a symbol of honor. I shall tend to stress this aspect of Hindu worship, for two reasons. First, this emphasis has tended to be neglected in the theoretical discussions of Hindu worship even though it is clearly present in empirical descriptions. Second, the perspective developed here focuses on symbolic resources, and is likely to be more powerful in explaining worship that is conceived of primarily as honoring rather than as the mechanical manipulation of quasi-material substances. Later I shall have a few words to say about other forms of worship and religious ritual.

With this important qualification, let us now return to the main line of our argument and an analysis of the three aspects of worship as they apply to Hinduism.

The Fundamental Elements of Puja

The puja can be either a public ceremony, as in a temple—roughly analogous to the Roman Catholic mass—or a private ritual performed in the home. In his influential discussion of puja, Babb (1975:chap. 2) examines a variety of forms, but identifies an elemental set of activities that are characteristic of all pujas.[7] He labels these (1) "Purity: Approaching the Deity," (2) "Pranam: The Feet of the Gods," and (3) "Prasad: The Food of the Gods" (1975:46–61). My claim is that these three categories are more concrete examples of the three basic processes of worship that I have outlined above.

Approaching the Deity

Purification is one way devotees maximize their sacral status so as to be worthy of approaching and coming into the presence of the deity. But the core idea is not simply to be physically clean, but rather making oneself fit—or at least less unworthy. In many religions, this is expressed in terms of both literal and figurative cleaning—the removal of those portions of the self that are unworthy. Hinduism is noted for having emphasized the idiom of purity and having taken this metaphor relatively literally—or perhaps more accurately, having merged or conflated the symbolic and the material. But most Hindus would acknowledge that the literal physical cleanliness is not the sole determinant of one's religious status or prospects of salvation. The preparation for contact with the deity is not restricted to the person of the worshipper. The injunction often applies to the physical place where contact is sought and to other items that will be used in the worship, especially offerings that are expected to come into contact with the deity. At least in many contexts, the crucial idea is not purity, but honor. As Fuller comments:

> [A]lthough a state of purity—in both temple and worshippers—is a precondition for worship, the basic aim of the ritual . . . is to honour powerful deities, not to purify them. It is, however, clear that worshippers must purify themselves before beginning *puja* in order to make themselves fit to honour the deities and benefit from the ritual, and not simply to avoid polluting the deities. (1992:76)

This is not to deny that for some Hindus the manipulation of purity and impurity is the core concern of most religious ritual.

If purity is in part an idiom of social and sacral status, then we should expect that the sources of purity will parallel the sources of social status in general—and this is the case. Status can be increased by associating or coming into contact with things and actors of higher rank, and by reducing associations with things and actors of lower rank. Babb's description of the means of purity is a clear analogy:

[T]here are essentially two ways to bring about a condition of purity. Certain substances or things seem to have the ability to ameliorate pollution directly. Cow dung
appears to have this property, and is widely used as an agent of purification. . . .
However, water is the most common method of purification, and here the principle involved seems to be somewhat different from direct amelioration. . . . While it is true
that some water, such as that of the Ganges, has special inherent powers of purification, the evidence suggests that the efficacy of water as an agent of purification lies
not in intrinsic purity, but rather in the capacity of water to absorb pollution and thus
carry it away. (1975:48)

In short, things are purified by bringing them into association with things that are
pure, and disassociating them from impurities. Ganga water is, in a sense, the exception that proves the rule: because of its special sacredness it increases the purity
of things with which it comes into contact and, like all water, it carries off polluting
elements.

This interpretation seems to contradict the common argument that purity is simply the absence of pollution:

[P]ollution has a substantive character while purity does not. In other words, pollution
is an existent; purity is its absence. To become pure is to rid oneself of pollution; it is
not to "add purity." A person in a state of purity is not purified by contact with someone in a state of purity. However a person in a state of purity will become polluted by
contact with a person who is polluted. Hence to remain pure is to remain free from
pollution; to become pure is to remove pollution. (Babb 1975:49)

Admittedly, there is this tendency in Hindu thought, but this description overstates the case. Babb's own data point to the fact that some items—for example,
cow dung, *darbha* grass, ghee, sandalwood paste, the tulsi plant—seem inherently
pure and purify things with which they come into contact. Of course, the purity of a
particular unit of these substances may be diluted by contact with what is impure
and thus may have to be renewed. The key point, however, is that some items do
seem to have positive purity that raise up other things. As we shall see in the next
chapter, whether one's sacral status is conceptualized simply as the absence of
pollution varies for different sectarian traditions within Hinduism. The key point to
be made now, however, is that purity, like status in general, can be acquired either
by increasing contact with things that are purer or decreasing contact with things
that are impure, though the latter is certainly the more common mechanism.

Hindu traditions disagree over whether gods suffer pollution, but it is clear that
in many if not most traditions they are not polluted daily by bodily functions
(Fuller 1992:76). Of course there is the danger that one may be rejected by the
deity if one is impure. But this is because the impurity is seen as a sign of disrespect, not because the deity's purity will be compromised (Fuller 1979, 1992:76) or
because the deity is incapable of transforming the impure; rather, the impure is rejected and punished when it is a sign of irreverence; the gods are angered, not polluted. The basic process is the same in the profane and the sacral realm, except the
high level of power and purity available in the sacral realm—at least to the high

gods—reverses the consequences of the impure coming into contact with the pure. In a sense, the raison d'être of the sacred realm is the presence of entities of sufficient status to raise up the lowly rather than to be degraded by them.

As with most matters, there is often a gap between the ideal and the actual. Thus despite the emphasis on purity in Hinduism, in relatively simple forms of puja, preparatory rituals of purification may in fact be neglected. It is, however, clearly recognized that in principle they should be conducted (Fuller 1992:64).

In sum, the first essential element of the puja, as in virtually all worship, is to show reverence and respect for the deity by disassociating from the low and the profane and presenting one's best self before attempting to approach that which is wholly other. In a similar fashion the worshipper attempts to choose and manipulate the physical context and the time so as to minimize any disrespect that is implied by human attempts to approach the deity. In Hinduism, the primary but not sole idiom for doing this is purity.

Praise and Deference

Babb identifies *pranam* as the second basic element of the puja. This is essentially a bowing motion that is elaborated in various degrees to show respect both to deities and to higher status people. The elaborateness of the motion is usually related to the status distance between the parties involved. Thus in social relationships where there is great social distance, or a desire to show great respect, the lower status persons may prostrate themselves and touch the feet of the high status person. In everyday greetings between those of roughly equal status, it may take the less elaborate form of the *namaste*—putting the palms of the hands together and bringing them up to the face as the head and shoulders are bowed slightly. These gradations further support the thesis of a continuum between status and sacredness. According to one of Babb's informants, the namaste "salutes 'that bit of god which is in every person'" (1975:52). When the recipient is a deity, "informants say that this is simply a way of 'greeting' the god or 'giving respect' to the god" (1975:51).

There is, however, danger in treating the pranam as the quintessential example of this element of the puja; a gesture of bowing may be taken to imply that subservience or servility is the primary element of worship in general, and the puja in particular. More important, however, is the notion of praise. This is clearly shown in Babb's description of the chanting of the *Shri Durga Saptashati*, an important Puranic religious text: "In so doing, one praises the goddess in the most extravagant terms" (1975:40). The theme of praise is also seen in his description of a meeting to sing *bhajans*, devotional hymns. "First the host sprinkled a few drops of water on the glass front of the framed picture of Krishna. He then sprinkled a small quantity of red powder on the picture. He explained later that in so doing he was honoring the god" (1975:38). Babb (whose ethnographic work is in the area that is culturally identified with North India) notes:

> Informants are quite clear about the purpose of all that follows. The deity, one is told, must be "honored." Honoring the deity may take any of a variety of forms. Garlands

may be offered, a *tilak* may be applied, clothing may be given, *mantras* may be chanted, devotional songs may be sung, *arti* may be performed; or less conventional procedures, such as having a herd of cattle circumambulate the god, may be employed. (1975:54)

Fuller (whose own ethnographic work on puja is in a Minakshi temple in the heart of South India) makes the same point. "*Puja*, at its heart, is the worshippers' reception and entertainment of a distinguished and adored quest. It is a ritual to honour powerful gods and goddesses, and often to express personal affection for them as well" (1992:57). After outlining the structure and meaning of the puja, he concludes:

> It should now be clear that *puja* is, in the first place, an act of respectful honouring and that this meaning is inherent in its structure. . . . That worship is an act of homage to powerful, superior deities is explicitly understood by priests in the Minaskshi temple and by many, if not most, Hindus throughout India. (1992:68)

I stress this point because it is so often overlooked because of the emphasis on purity and pollution.

It may seem that there is no significant difference between this second element and the first element that was discussed above—they both focus on offering respect. But praise and deference from those that are unworthy is valueless; the would-be worshippers must first make themselves and the context worthy, so that the praise they offer is valuable and glorifies the recipient.

Communion

If the sacred and profane must be kept separate, they must also be brought into contact. This usually involves descent by the superior and ascent by the inferior. As Fuller says, "In its form as an image, the deity, so to speak, has come 'down' towards the human level, but through the performance of worship, the worshipper goes 'up' towards the divine level to achieve, finally, identity with the deity" (1992:72).

The third fundamental element of worship is association, or at least interaction, with the deity. In many religious traditions, such activity involves the possibility of rejection and thus danger. But when the benevolence and grace of the deity is emphasized, the typical outcome is communion and the positive transformation of the devotee. As the famous medieval Hindu theologian-philosopher Ramanuja indicated, "the Lord is characterized both by his utter Supremacy (*paratva*) and his gracious Accessibility (*saulabhya*)" (Eck 1981:34). Intimate communion is possible, at least in the bhakti tradition, because of the voluntary descent of the supreme deity, who makes himself dependent upon human caretaking (Eck 1981:36). Just as intimate relationships are the symbol of acceptance within the social system, they are the essence of the deities' acceptance of the devotee. Not surprisingly, some of the same behaviors that symbolize social intimacy also express intimacy in the sacral realm.

Media of Communion

The most common idiom of expressing such intimacy and communion is eating food that has been offered to and blessed by the deity. In some religions this communion is unambiguously modeled after a meal shared by family or intimate friends; despite the enormous sacral distance between the deity and the devotees, they are treated as intimates entitled to share food with the god. In other traditions there is more emphasis on the presentation of the food as a sacrifice or offering to the deity, who then returns it to the devotee as a transforming blessing.

Whichever of these is emphasized, the devotee has come into significant contact with the deity and has been blessed by the event. The intimacy implied may go beyond being a blessing and even create an identity between the god and the devotee. According to at least one analysis, in Hinduism "the *naivedya*, food offering, has the meaning of 'realization of the identity of the worshipper with the worshiped'"(Wadley 1975:178, citing Varma 1956:462). Whatever the details, the key point is that the sharing of food implies a transforming intimacy.

As Babb notes, despite the enormous amount of variation in the details of the Hindu puja, "one requirement stands out as a constant: the deity must be fed. Food offerings were a central feature of each of the four rituals I have described. . . . Indeed, without a food offering of some kind the ritual would simply not be a *puja* in the conventional sense of the term" (1975:54). The type of food and the elaborateness of the ritual can vary enormously, but "the mode of giving seems always to be the same: food is given to the deity, it is taken back, and it is distributed to the worshipers as *prasad*. . . . [This is] in some ways the central and indispensable act, the core around which all else is elaboration and overlay" (1975:54).

If food is the most common idiom or means of intimate contact with the deity, it is certainly not the only one. As Fuller notes:

> In the literature on popular Hinduism, *prasada* is often just defined as sanctified food, but this is an error; *prasada*, despite the undoubted importance of food, comprises a wide range of sanctified substances.
>
> *Prasada* is the material symbol of the deities' power and grace. During *puja*, different substances—be they ash, water, flowers, food or other items—have been transferred to the deity, so that they have been in contact with the images or, as with food, have been symbolically consumed by the deity in its image form. As a result, these substances have been ritually transmuted to become *prasada* imbued with divine power and grace, which are absorbed or internalized when the *prasada* is placed on the devotee's body or swallowed. (1992:74)

An idiom of intimacy that is logically prior to prasad is that of *darsan*, the seeing and being seen by the deity. The eye is considered to be the last part of the body that begins to function after birth. Following this notion, the last thing an artisan does when making an image of a god is complete the eyes. In many contexts, special ceremonies and actors are required for the *chakshu-dana*, literally the "eye-giving" or "gift of the eyes." In some temples, Brahmans are required to complete this process.

As might be expected, since the eye is a special organ it is capable of more than neutral perception. When combined with the intent of the actor, the eye becomes an organ of communication and power. The most dramatic case of the latter is the "third eye" of Siva, which can project all consuming power. The notion of the evil eye is also widespread, and the use of ritual and symbolic defenses to ward off this danger is very common. The eye can also be an organ of communication and intimacy. Gonda concludes, "That a look was consciously regarded as a form of contact appears from the combination of 'looking and touching.' Casting one's eyes upon a person and touching him were related activities" (1969b:19, quoted in Eck 1981:7). Seeing is also a form of knowing, not only in the common and literal sense, but also in the mystical and supernatural sense.

While there are traditions in Hinduism that reject the use of images of the gods, or consider them only as aids to meditation, for the vast majority of Hindus, the god is present in the image. Thus, seeing and being seen by the images is a central element of Hindu worship. People go to temples both to see and be seen by the deity, to give and take darsan. This is also why people go on pilgrimages. The darsan of holymen (*saddhus*) is also valued, for the "mere" sight of the holy brings benefits. As Eck says, "Beholding the image is an act of worship, and through the eyes one gains the blessings of the divine" (1981:3).

Finally, the whole concept of puja is to treat the god as an honored guest. In temples there are as many as sixty-four forms of attending, or "approaches" (*upacara*), to the deity. The god is not only fed, but is awakened, bathed, clothed, sung to, fanned, and so forth. These various upacara in part symbolize the humility of the devotees and the superior status of the god. But as already noted they also imply intimacy and the god's willingness to be dependent upon humans. Thus, virtually every element of the puja implies a communion between the god and the worshipper.[8]

The Relationship Between the Three Elements

A caveat concerning the relationship between the three elements of worship is required. I have organized the discussion as if these elements were related in a linear fashion. To some degree this is true; there is a definite tendency for acts of confession and purification to precede deference and praise, and for these to precede communion. Yet this is only a tendency. These categories are analytic concepts; any actual act of worship may include various combinations of the three analytical elements. For example, a given prayer may combine all three. Nonetheless, these categories do help us to see the common features of most worship and to see the relationship between worship and other forms of status-oriented relationships. Moreover, there is at least some evidence that conceiving of worship as three elements is not solely a set of categories created by the analyst. Shulman notes:

> Color symbolism offers yet another analogy: Brenda Beck has shown that many South Indian rituals follow a sequence of three stages—an initial cool state symbolized by white gives way to a transitional "hot" red stage, which then leads to a final state of coolness, again white. The white border of coolness containing the heat released in the ritual is correlated with purity, while the heat indicates impure but vital

power. . . . the conjunction of purity with the impure forces of life seems based not so much upon opposition as upon interdependence, i.e., the white and the red joined in productive symbiosis. (1984:18–19)

In my terminology, the red or hot stage represents the attempt to approach the deity to engage in praise and adoration, and thus the danger of rejection or punishment instead of acceptance and communion. I do not claim that there is a precise analogue between the three processes I have identified and this color symbolism, but there does seem to be a parallel that merits more detailed analysis in future research.

The next question is whether these three elements are relevant to forms of worship other than the Hindu puja.

Christian Worship

These three processes are clearly central to Christian worship. First, prayers of preparation and confession focus on making the devotee fit for worship—for example: "Almighty God, unto whom all hearts are open, all desires known, and from whom no secrets are hid: Cleanse the thoughts of our hearts by the inspiration of thy Holy Spirit, that we may perfectly love thee and worthily magnify thy holy name" (*The Methodist Hymnal* 1964:715; *The* [Episcopal] *Book of Common Prayer* 1979:323).

Second, in most Protestant services hymns of praise and adoration are a central element. The first verse of the first hymn in a Presbyterian hymnal reads: "Praise ye the Lord, the Almighty, the King of creation! O my soul, praise him for He is thy health and salvation! All ye who hear, Now to his temple draw near; Join me in glad adoration!" (*The* [Presbyterian] *Hymnbook* 1955:1). Similarly, the first hymn in the *Pilgrim* [Congregational Church] *Hymnal* (1935:1) and the *Baptist Hymnal* (1975:1) begins, "Holy, holy, holy! Lord God, Almighty!" These words are, of course, a variation on the Sanctus of the Roman Catholic mass, which in turn is taken from the Hebrew Bible (e.g., Isaiah 6:3).

Third, it is well known that the Eucharist as "Holy Communion" is the climax of worship in the Roman Catholic and Anglican traditions. While some church traditions tend to celebrate the Eucharist less frequently, they create other forms of communion. For example, their prayers are notably less formal and imply easy intimacy with the deity: "Jesus, we just want to ask you to . . . " In other words, communion is not limited to the Eucharist. Even in the low-church tradition, the Eucharist is used to express this idea. While the term "Lord's Supper" is usually substituted for the term "Holy Communion," it is clear that even here the key idea is a transforming intimacy with the deity. For example, in the *Baptist Hymnal*, the first hymn in the section on the "Lord's Supper" begins:

> Where can we find thee, Lord, so near,
> So real, so gracious, so divine,
> As at the table set with love
> By those who know themselves as thine?
> (1975:245)

This communion is seen as transforming:

> Come thee, O holy Christ,
> Feed us, we pray;
> Touch with thy pierced hand
> Each common day,
> Making this earthly life
> Full of thy grace,
> Till in the home of heav'n
> We find our place
>
> (1975:246)

An analysis of the Roman Catholic mass would show that most of its elements are also oriented toward the same three processes.

A Note on Sacrifice, Prayer, and Preaching

Some elements of worship may seem not to fit into these three categories, for example, the preaching of sermons. Now let us consider the relationship between such features and the three analytical elements that have been identified.

Obviously, sacrifice and prayer are very common elements of religious ritual; their relationship to the three elements of worship needs clarification. As a preliminary matter, it must be noted that sacrifice and prayer can be aspects of magical coercion or quid pro quo exchange as well as worship per se. Weber claims, "Sacrifice, at first appearance, is a magical instrumentality that in part stands at the immediate service of the coercion of the gods" (1968:423). Similarly, prayers can be magical—for example, mantras which supposedly have the power to coerce the gods. According to Weber, prayer frequently takes the form of exchange: "in most cases such prayer has a purely business-like rationalized form that sets forth the achievements of the supplicant in behalf of the god and then claims adequate recompense therefor" (1968:423).

To the degree that religious ritual shifts toward worship per se, sacrifice and prayer can express any one or all three of the elements previously identified. First, the sins and impurity of the devotee can be "placed upon" the sacrificial victim. The victim's destruction then symbolizes the casting away of these undesirable characteristics, resulting in an improvement in the devotee's spiritual status. Second, sacrifice can take the form of an offering that symbolizes both the deference of the worshipper and praise of the deity. Finally, sacrifice can be the means of communication and communion with the sacred. The classic study of sacrifice by Hubert and Mauss notes:

> We noticed then how the sacrificer, by the laying on of hands, imparted to the victim something of his own personality. Now it is the victim or its remains which will pass on to the sacrificer the new qualities it has acquired by the action of sacrifice. This communication can be effected by a mere blessing. But in general recourse was had to more material rites: for example, the sprinkling of blood[,] the application of the skin of the victim, anointing with the fat, contact with the residue of the cremation.

> Sometimes the animal was cut into two parts and the sacrificer walked between them. But the most perfect way of effecting communication was to hand over to the sacrificer a portion of the victim, which he consumed. By eating a portion of it he assimilated to himself the characteristics of the whole. (1964:39–40)

In short, sacrifice is so common in religious ritual because of its capacity to powerfully symbolize all three of the elements of worship, as well as the elements of magic and exchange.[9] The same can be said for prayer. Stated another way, sacrifice and prayer are two important means of symbolic communication. Along with other such media, they can be used to symbolize or communicate all three of the elements of worship.

Preaching can also be used to express all three elements. Thus in certain religious traditions, such as Calvinism and Sikhism, "the word," and thus the reading and exposition of sacred texts, becomes the core of worship. Typically, however, listening to sermons is primarily a matter of deference, an aspect of the second element. The deferential listening to God's word is the equivalent of listening to the ideas and instructions of a high status person. To refuse to do so is to deny the validity of a person's status. Whether one actually follows such instructions later is a matter of obedience to authority and is not, in the narrow sense, a matter of honor via deference. Humans frequently obey people they do not honor, and honor people they do not obey. But it is rare that they refuse to listen deferentially to people they honor. The same can be true for sacral relationships. Thus, the refusal to deferentially listen to God's word is to dishonor the deity; it is the opposite of praise and adoration.

Again, there is an exception that proves the rule: traditions that deemphasize preaching and listening to "the word" attentively are precisely those traditions that have other elaborate forms to express praise and deference of the deity; conversely, the more "the word" and preaching are emphasized, the more simplified and informal forms of worship are likely to be.

Therefore, the specific activities of worship do not necessarily have a one-to-one relationship with the three elements we have identified—though sometimes they do. Rather, these three elements are analytical categories; they help us to see how worship can be usefully conceived of as status transformation and maintenance.

The Relationship Between Social and Sacred Models

While it is clear that some of the symbols of sacral relations are drawn from models of social relations, the precise connection between the social models and the sacral relations is open to question. We can clarify the nature of this connection by examining the parallels and differences in the norms governing the exchange of food between people and the exchange of food between people and high gods. Babb argues, "Food offerings in *puja* exemplify principles relating to food exchange that are operative in other areas of Chhattisgarhi life" (1975:54). He cites Marriott's (1968) well-known description of the relationship between exchange of food and caste rank as describing well the principles that are involved. According to Marriott, caste rank is indicated by, even determined by, the willingness of lower caste groups to accept food from their superiors, but the unwillingness of superiors to accept food from those whom they consider inferior. However, Babb notes, the willingness to accept food also depends on the type of food involved. For example, foods cooked in ghee are less subject to pollution, thus less relevant to status differences than foods cooked in water, like rice. The leftovers of another person, *jutha*, which have been contaminated by his saliva, are the most polluted type of food, and acceptance of these implies maximum deference and social distance; in most areas only a few Untouchable castes will accept jutha. Babb then identifies the acceptance of prasada by worshippers as the equivalent of accepting jutha, and interprets this as an act of "the most profound humility" (1975:55).

It is precisely this attempt to draw a close analog between social behavior and religious behavior that Fuller (1979) finds inadequate. For example, he points out that if the religious pattern is simply a projected model of the caste system, gods should not accept food offerings from humans. Moreover, it is only the temple priests who can offer cooked food to the gods; higher ranking ordinary Brahmans can offer only raw food. He concludes, "It is therefore impossible to explain the relationship between gods, priests and devotees by the logic of inter-caste food exchange" (1979:471).

In some respects Fuller is correct; the food transactions characteristic of puja are not a simple copy of those of local caste relationships. This does not, however, mean that religion is sui generis in an analytical sense. Rather, the appropriate strategy is to see both the transactions of the caste system and of puja as special cases of the principles that affect status relationships—taking into account the tendency of religious projections to reverse key features of the profane reality. Therefore, while the acceptance of the god's jutha as prasada does symbolize the devotee's humility, this is only one motif and probably not the most important one. In addition, the god or goddess is seen as so superior that anything received from him or her is of great purity, thus capable of positively transforming the devotee.[10] Relationships that would be degrading in the profane realm have precisely the opposite effect in sacral relationships—that is the raison d'être of such sacral relationships. This is not because the basic logic of the relationships is different; rather, it is because the status of the deity is so great compared to that of the devotee, that what would be demeaning in a profane setting is elevating in a sacral context. Similarly, while receiving something from inferiors may compromise Brahman superiority, it is irrelevant to the supreme superiority of the high gods and goddesses.

Another important example of the sacral value of things that are devalued in the profane world is the worship of the feet and sandals of those considered sacred. Normally feet are considered to be a very impure, and low status part of the body, and it is rude to let them come into contact with other people. The aversion to shoes and sandals is even greater; like jutha, sandals are normally considered very unclean and only those of the lowest status would willingly come into contact with someone else's sandals. The ultimate insult is to threaten to beat someone with your sandal. Yet it is not uncommon for feet or sandals or their image to become the focus of religious veneration. Perhaps the best-known example is the image of Rama's sandals, which are a common object of devotion in many parts of India. But even more common is the desire of devotees to touch the feet of gurus and holymen. Babb gives an especially vivid account of this behavior among the members of the Radhasoami movement based in Agra. "Displayed prominently at the central altar are the wooden sandals used by Soamiji Maharaj [the movement's founder] during his life-time. Devotees touch these with their hands and foreheads, and some informants re-port having spiritual experiences when they do so" (1986:62). Such devotion is not limited to the literal relics.

> When members of the Soami Bagh congregation living in Delhi hold their weekly satsang (on Sunday morning), they invariably do so in the presence of a framed sheet of paper on which are impressed Babuji Maharaj's footprints in red ink. Attending devotees bow before this, symbolically placing their foreheads at or on this guru's feet. (1986:62)

Such symbolic contact is only a substitute for literal contact with the feet of a live guru. "Devotees also avidly sought contact with their gurus' feet. . . . [O]ne of Soamiji Maharaj's most devoted female followers would suck his toes 'for hours,' regarding the 'nectar' that flowed therefrom as 'mother's milk'" (1984:63). By extension, it is common for the water that is used to bath the feet of gurus or temple idols to be consumed as a holy substance.

The use of cow dung for purification is even a more pervasive example of the reversal that occurs in the sacral realm. Moreover, it is clear that people do not use cow dung primarily as a means of showing their humility, nor does it simply wash away impurity. Rather the cow is so holy that its dung—the most impure and lowly of elements—purifies those things with which it comes into contact (Trautmann 1981:287). These outcomes are reversed not because the *principles or form* of status processes have completely changed, but because the *nature or content of the re-lationship* is perceived to be quite different—the social-sacral distance between the devotee and the god is enormous.[11] Unlike that of humans, the status of high gods is not constantly problematic—at least in their relationships with humans; their status is so superior that nothing humans do can degrade them. In turn, because of this qualitatively different level of status, any intimacy the gods allow—even with their dung or jutha—has the power to transform their human devotees.[12]

Differences in Formality: Elaboration and Reversal

The manner in which the three elements of worship are expressed can vary signifi-cantly for different sectarian groups within a given religious tradition. One obvious variation is the degree of formality in worship. Two points can help explain the variations in formality. First, formality in worship can be conceived of as a special form of the elaboration of norms that is characteristic of upper status groups. Second, the effect of the presence or absence of formality is usually to reverse the actor's normal status position and experience in the profane world. For example, upper status actors who often receive formal deference from subordinates are usu-ally attracted to worship styles in which they become the subordinates who give formal deference to a superior, that is, the deity. Lower status actors, who in the profane world usually give formal deference to superiors, are attracted to more informal styles of worship in which intimacy and closeness with the deity are expressed. In Hinduism, such a contrast is found between the Smarta and Sri Vaishnava traditions, and the more emotional bhakti sectarian traditions. In the Church of England, and more generally in modern Christianity, this contrast in formality has become known as high- and low-church traditions.

The religion of upper strata usually emphasizes very formal modes of praise and deference to the deity. Fixed prayers, chants, lectionaries, elaborate religious calendars, and music by trained specialists are characteristic of such traditions. Elaborate formalized body movements are often used to express praise and deference. The emphasis is on the dignity of the deity; when the upper classes approach their own deities, they offer the praise and deference that they normally demand from others. Low traditions, emphasizing intimacy and the accessibility of the deity, see the deity as a friend, parent, or lover who is available to those who seek such a relationship. The language and symbolism used to address the deity tends to be informal and personal. Prayers are more spontaneous, and singing is usually an activity for the congregation of worshippers. These patterns are, of course, a reversal of the typical experience of lower strata, who typically give deference and are rejected or kept at "arm's length" by those of higher status.

Not only norms of behavior, but also modes of thinking can vary in their formality. High and low traditions tend to be associated with religious rationalism and emotionalism respectively. Upper and middle strata are more attracted to rationalized systematic theologies. This proclivity sometimes results in the nature and status of deities being more abstract, ambiguous and tenuous. The god whose status is ambiguous, or insecure demands ritualistic deference and formalistic worship. There may be subtraditions that are pantheistic, agnostic, or even atheistic. In these cases the ritual may become an end in itself, or the essence of what is sacredness. For lower status groups, the existence and power of gods is more taken for granted; the image of the deity is likely to be more concrete and anthropomorphic and it is often seen as an overwhelming transforming power. This power cannot be limited by rules and procedures, but impinges upon people in dramatic, unpredictable ways. It may take control of devotees even against their will: possession, glossolalia, and emotional forms of worship are often the result (see, e.g., Lewis 1986). While worship may be rigidly patterned from an observer's point of view, this patterning is much less explicit and formalized. In his structural analysis of Biblical myths, Leach has expressed this difference as a contrast between those traditions that emphasize the importance of the mediating priest and those that emphasize the mediation of some demi-god like "the holy spirit" (1983:67–71). The first tradition stresses the crucialness of the religious hierarchy in seeking contact with the deity. The second expresses the proclivity of the deity to break through to those who would seek contact with the holy.

These patterns of formality and informality are, of course, only general tendencies. Some higher strata persons participate in low traditions and some lower strata persons take part in high traditions. Moreover, low traditions may have developed certain types of formalism and rationalism, and high traditions some types of informality and emotionalism. Nonetheless, this tendency toward elaboration, systematization, and formality in the worship of upper strata groups is a detectable pattern in most complex religions—and one predicted by our theory. Moreover, the theory also anticipates that the nature of the worshipper's relationship to the deity is likely to be the reverse of his usual status relations in the profane world.

The Limits of the Analysis

In closing, I must emphasize the limits of the analysis carried out in this chapter. As in most other matters concerning India, the significance of variations and exceptions must be stressed. Even within worship as I have narrowly defined it in the preceding chapter, there are considerable variations in how people understand what they are doing. As Fuller says, concerning the issue of whether gods have needs, "the question of divine needs is not simple and there are divergent answers to it, which also suggest that worship, despite its fundamentally uniform structure, can have varying significance for different groups of Hindus" (1992:69). I do not mean to deny this variability; I am simply pointing to what is common across a wide variety of worship traditions.

Second, and even more important, many and perhaps even most rituals conducted by Hindus are probably not worship per se. Most Hindus seldom get to the great temples where the high gods are worshipped. They often conduct rituals focused on a "pile of rocks" or some other modest focal point. Just as often, the main concern is not worship, but to propitiate a fearsome form of the goddess Devi or some demon or ghost. Frequently, ritual activity takes the form of the sacrifice of animals, and Hindus carefully distinguish between puja and sacrifice. As Fuller notes, "With many troublesome little deities and malevolent spirits, propitiation is frequently the sole motivation; give them blood so that they go away" (1992:85). Their power is acknowledged, but they have little status and receive little genuine devotion.[13] This is analogous in the social realm to those who have little positive status but have power and must be reckoned with, for example, a local gangster who runs a protection racket. It is arguable that the majority of ritual activity carried out by Hindus involves relationships of this type: the analogues of what in the previous chapter were described as exchange, coercion, and magical attempts at physical cause and effect rather than worship per se. I do not mean to deny the importance or prevalence of these types of ritual activity. A more complete analysis would have to devote much more attention to these phenomena. Clearly it is a mistake to see all Hindus as sophisticated theologians who clearly understand the difference between religion and magic and systematically reject all forms of the latter. But it is also a mistake to fail to see that even the most humble forms of Hinduism often contain elements of transcendence that are more than the use of magic to pursue worldly benefits.

Religious rituals—even the purest forms of worship—are not, from the actors' point of view, a permanent solution. The separation of the sacred and the profane reasserts itself, and the human experience of contingency and powerlessness continues. The transformation of the person or the world that results is only temporary. This is one of the reasons worship and other rituals must be repeated again and again. Therefore, it is not surprising that some religions have sought a more permanent solution. Usually this involves a notion of salvation, which is the focus of the next chapter.

14

Salvation and Soteriology

The word "soteriology" refers to religious doctrines about salvation, especially the means of salvation.[1] The word "salvation" implies deliverance or release from an undesirable state of being to one that is qualitatively better—usually from the historical empirical world to another world beyond history. Many religions are not particularly concerned about notions of salvation, but it is central to all of the great world religions, including Hinduism.[2] Typically, salvation religions see the present world as at best flawed and imperfect and at worst inherently sinful and evil. In the Hindu view, the essence of human existence is suffering (duhkha). To quote Eliade:

> "All is suffering for the sage" (*duhkameva sarva vivekinah*), writes Patanjali. . . . It is the leitmotiv of all post-Upanisadic Indian speculation. Soteriological techniques, as well as metaphysical doctrines find their justification in this universal suffering, for they have no value save in the measure to which they free man from "pain." (1969:11)

If human existence is by definition suffering, it is not surprising that this culture might be interested in salvation. In Hinduism, ideas of salvation are most often identified with the concept of moksa, usually translated as release or liberation (Obeyesekere 1980:149). Like most key concepts, it has a variety of meanings and implications, but they all concern some notion of escape or transformation, and point to the principles for accomplishing this, that is, to various soteriologies.

The task of this chapter is to show how the theoretical ideas I have proposed can improve our sociological understanding of salvation and soteriology.

Status Attainment in the World-to-Come

Salvation can be conceived of as the ultimate form of social mobility or status transformation. As Obeyesekere notes, salvation is "fundamentally a rite of passage. . . . It is a final or ultimate status" (1968:13). In the terminology of the contemporary literature on social stratification, salvation (or damnation) can be conceived as a form of status attainment. If this perspective is analytically useful, our knowledge about the sources of social status should give us some insight into the sources or means of salvation. If salvation is a form or an analogue of social mobility, then the means of mobility should also be means of salvation.

The earlier theoretical discussion identified two primary means or sources of status: conformity to norms and associations. Ideologies that purport to explain people's placement in a worldly stratification structure vary in which of these they emphasize. For example, kinship associations should have little to do with who becomes president of the United States and everything to do with who becomes the king of England; the idea of equality of opportunity was virtually unheard of in Virginia in 1860, but was a frequently mentioned notion in Virginia in 1980. Just as the ideologies about social placement vary in their emphasis on conformity and association, so do doctrines of soteriology. Most of the variations in doctrines of soteriology can be seen as debates over whether salvation depends on conformity or association. The disagreement over the relative importance of conformity and association is usually expressed as a debate over works versus grace: Is salvation attained by good works and conformity to divine law, or as a gift from God? Corollary debates arise over the appropriate content of conformity and association: the differences over the content of conformity often take the form of a debate over the relative importance of asceticism, ritual, and the faithful performance of one's worldly social roles. The differences over the content of associations usually focus on which deity or mediator has the power and inclination to bring about one's salvation, and the nature of the appropriate relationship between the savior and the devotee.[3]

A caveat is required. As indicated in Chapter 12, the relationships humans have with the sacred can be modeled after physical or mechanical causation rather than social interaction.[4] In many respects, these doctrines are similar to those that emphasize conformity; in both, salvation depends primarily on the actions of humans. They vary from the social conformity model, however, in that the outcome does not depend on the response of a sacred other. Salvation is not a positive sanction, but an outcome or effect. Accordingly, such perspectives tend to deemphasize the importance of deities and can even be atheistic. Of course, the distinctions being drawn here are analytical ideal-types. Most concrete historical religious traditions draw on some mixture of these concepts.

With this in mind, let us see to what degree these notions can help us understand the variations in Hindu soteriology.

Hindu Soteriologies

The task is not to provide a definitive empirical analysis, but to demonstrate the utility of the theoretical scheme. Thus a limited survey of the variations in soteriology will suffice. I shall focus first on the *Bhagavad Gita* as the classic synthesis and summary of Hindu notions of soteriology. This text identifies three paths (*margas*) to salvation: *jnana-yoga*, *karma-yoga*, and *bhakti-yoga*.[5] Implicitly, the

Bhagavad Gita creates a synthesis by acknowledging a legitimate role for each of these soteriologies.

Next, four subtraditions within Hinduism will be considered; three of these are broad categories of religious tradition: Pantanjali's Yoga, the Smarta tradition, and sectarian bhakti. Each of these tends to emphasize one of the three paths identified in the *Bhagavad Gita*. A fourth case, Sri Vaisnavism, is then examined; it is a smaller, historically more specific sectarian tradition.[6] The first three cases represent major traditions within Hinduism. They show the range of variation in soteriologies with respect to their emphasis on conformity and association. Thus the ability of the theory to explain variations across such broad differences will be illustrated. The last case tests the ability of the perspective to explain narrower variations within relatively specific, concrete and limited historical movements.

Soteriology in the Bhagavad Gita

The *Bhagavad Gita* (or simply the *Gita*) is one section of the immense epic poem known as the *Mahabharata*. This segment is arguably the most influential religious text of Hinduism. Its central concern is the legitimacy and effectiveness of alternative soteriologies: Which paths to salvation are efficacious?

The story begins with the great warrior Arjuna about to enter a battle against many of his relatives and mentors; he is greatly anguished at the prospect of having to slay them. He questions Krishna about what constitutes appropriate conduct (dharma) and what is the appropriate path to salvation. Despite Arjuna's plea that the answer be "definite and clear" (ii:7), Krishna's reply is complex and subtle.[7] He outlines the three paths (margas) or methods (yoga) leading to salvation (moksa). Beginning with a discussion of jnana-yoga, he moves on to explain karma-yoga, and concludes with an explication of bhakti-yoga. The exposition is constructed so that with shifts in emphasis the logic of one method suggests the next one.

Jnana-yoga is the way or path of knowledge, that has been characteristic of renouncers and ascetics. Within the jnana-yoga tradition, Krishna acknowledges the legitimacy of both the philosophical-theoretical approach (*Samkhya*)[8] and the more practical meditation techniques of classical yoga. A key component of either of these is the realization that the true self (atman) is immortal. Hence Krishna tells Arjuna he should have no concern about either his own death or causing the death of others, as long as duty (dharma) is being served (ii:22).

This suggests the notion of karma-yoga. In the Brahmanas, "karma" refers to ritual sacrifices. In the Upanisads, sacrifice is internalized in the form of personal asceticism and meditation, and all karma (that is, all external action) is bad. In the *Bhagavad Gita*, however, "karma" refers to all action, but it is good if such action conforms to one's svadharma and is indifferent about the worldly outcome. In this way sacrifice can be not only internalized in meditation but also expressed through one's daily activity. The key idea is that humans should be unconcerned about the consequences or fruits of all of their actions—whether or not these lead to anyone's death—as long as they are carrying out their prescribed duties (ii:47; iii:35). The crucial point is that the legitimacy of action (karma) is separated from its consequences, and yet inaction ("worklessness") is rejected (iii:7, 19). This means the householder can both carry out the actions required by his social roles and, by being indifferent about the results, be detached from worldly concerns. As a member of the Kshatriya warrior caste, Arjuna can and should engage in battle as skillfully and energetically as possible, but he should be indifferent about whether his side wins or loses, whether he or others live or die. Hence, karma-yoga, the path of action or works, becomes not only an acceptable means to salvation, but a preferred one.

Yet a crucial question has remained implicit. To whom should such sacrifices— whether by the actions of karma-yoga or by the disciplines of jnana-yoga—be directed? At this point Krishna begins to reveal that he is the Supreme God and to teach Arjuna the way of bhakti-yoga. At first the discussion of bhakti focuses on the appropriate behavior for renouncers. The emphasis is not on ascetic or yogic accomplishment, but on devotion to Krishna (vi:31). A little later emphasis is placed on communion with the deity (vi:47). Moreover, as the conversation continues the tone becomes more sectarian; the most appropriate devotion is directed exclusively toward Krishna (vii:17–18). Devotion to other gods is acceptable, but ultimately they are only representatives of Krishna (vii:21–22). All kinds of sacrifices and offerings are acceptable, if they are made with true devotion (ix:26). All actions should be carried out as an offering to Krishna (ix:27). Such devotion will ensure salvation (ix:31). Not only does devotion outweigh all other considerations in ensuring salvation, this path is open to all, including women and serfs (ix:32).

Having surveyed the three classic paths outlined in the *Bhagavad Gita*, let us now focus more explicitly on their differing emphases on conformity and association. Both jnana-yoga and karma-yoga emphasize careful conformity to rules, though they differ markedly in what constitutes conformity. Admittedly, in jnana-yoga conformity is in part a matter of following causal laws rather than moral norms, but the latter are by no means unimportant to this tradition. Karma-yoga, which is particularly characteristic of Brahmanical orthodoxy, is almost completely preoccupied with moral conformity to social norms. This is the soteriological perspective most closely linked to the Dharmasastras (literally the treatises on dharma, but implying the "moral laws of social duty") and the Smarta tradition. In contrast, bhakti-yoga involves a major shift in emphasis from conformity to association as the means of salvation. What is crucial is the nature of one's relationship to some deity; in the theoretical terms used earlier, what is required for salvation is intimate association with the deity. For the *Bhagavad Gita,* the nature of this association is primarily as a devout worshipper (ix:14). Nearly all the images of the devotee's relationship to the deity are highly asymmetrical and deferential. Nonetheless, the crucial factor is association, not conformity to particular norms. In sum, jnana-yoga and karma-yoga emphasize conformity, while bhakti-yoga emphasizes association.

The differences in these paths are not absolute; in the *Bhagavad Gita,* an implicit logic links the ideas of one of these soteriologies to the next. The literal notion of sacrifice—characteristic of Vedic ritual—was transformed in the Upanisads into the asceticism and meditation of the renouncer; sacrifice is no longer an external act, but an internal state of mind that produces detachment from the profane world. This jnana-yoga notion of detachment is later applied to the relationship between actions and consequences in daily life; hence the karma-yoga, characteristic of householders, in some respects originated from a central element of the renouncer's tradition. Still later, the devotion and commitment required to develop detachment becomes redirected toward a particular saving deity and becomes the devotion of bhakti-yoga. It is, of course, a considerable simplification to think of these relationships and transformations as distinct historical stages; probably each set of ideas has been present to some degree at most stages of Indian history—just as they are all present in the *Bhagavad Gita*.

The *Bhagavad Gita*'s popularity is rooted in the way it both differentiates alternative soteriologies and maintains links between them that give each its legitimate place in terms familiar to the others. The *Gita* manages to state clearly important differences, yet maintain threads of continuity. In a sense, each of these paths blends into the other, and all receive legitimation. Many different interpretations are credible, thus the *Bhagavad Gita* can be all things to all people. Even ritualism and renunciation are legitimate if combined with bhakti. In sum, the *Bhagavad Gita* is central to most traditions within Hinduism because it manages to synthesize without obliterating varying soteriologies. Now we will turn to traditions that give strong emphasis to one of these three alternative strategies for salvation.

Classical Yoga

While the word "yoga" can mean method or path to salvation, more commonly it refers to techniques of meditation. These meditation techniques are often associated with one strand of jnana-yoga. The roots of yoga meditation are very ancient and varied. The definitive formulation of this tradition, which has become known as classical Yoga, appears in Pantanjali's *Yoga-sutra*. Those who attribute the authorship to Pantanjali, the grammarian, date the document as early as the second century B.C.E., while others claim the compilation was as late as the fifth century C.E. The *Yoga-sutra* generally accepts and assumes the metaphysics of the Samkhya school of philosophy. For Samkhya, salvation is acquiring a particular kind of metaphysical knowledge: the sufferings of the self in this world come to be seen as a special kind of illusion. The true self (purusa) is not a part of the matter (*prakrti*) and suffering of this world. We mistakenly perceive the self as bound to the suffering world because of the I of the ego. Liberation is the realization that the true self has never been so bound. Moksa is the recognition of the freedom and purity that one has always had. As might be anticipated, Samkhya thought is atheistic; what is required for liberation is not the intervention of a deity, but human recognition of the true nature of existence. Of course, Samkhya philosophy involves much more than can be indicated here. For our purposes, however, the main point is a simple one. Salvation comes about by human efforts and actions that do away with normal human consciousness through the acquisition of a special kind of metaphysical knowledge.

Classical Yoga accepts the Samkhya assertion that the problem is false consciousness. It is skeptical, however, that human intellectual activity can, by itself, secure one's salvation.[9] The acquisition of metaphysical knowledge is only a first step. One must also seek the suppression of normal states of consciousness through ascetic techniques. Moksa requires not only a different theoretical viewpoint, but a new kind of praxis: techniques of meditation and concentration, including forms of physical discipline. The three core techniques are the yogic posture or position (*asana*), the rhythmic control of breathing (*pranayama*), and concentration on a single point (*ekagrata*). To become a yogin is to learn these and other more advanced techniques from a guru and to gradually progress through the stages of detachment from conventional perspectives. The final stage is *samadhi*: passing beyond knowledge into a new mode of being. The nature of this state cannot be fully grasped except through yoga itself. It includes the acquisition of miraculous and divine powers (*siddhis*). The ultimate accomplishment goes beyond even this; the powers gained through renunciation can be renounced. By forgoing the use of these powers, the yogin proceeds to a state beyond divinity, to the unification of all modes of being. This is not simply a regression to an undifferentiated reality that existed before creation, but the transcendence to a new mode of being.

Our concern is not, however, the nature of liberation but the means of liberation. For classical Yoga, as in Samkhya philosophy, liberation is restricted to a small elite and is primarily a human accomplishment.[10] As Eliade notes, "What is of first importance in the Yoga-sutras is technique—in other words, the yogin's will and capacity for self-mastery and concentration" (1969:74–75). "*Samadhi* is always owing to prolonged efforts on the yogin's part. It is not a gift or a state of grace" (1969:80).

In Samkhya-Yoga, salvation is not a reward from another social actor—either human or divine—but the outcome of a particular line of action. The process is not primarily moral, but causal. In a sense these perspectives are outside the realm of morality, since their view of both the world and liberation is primarily an asocial one (Eliade 1969:95).

This soteriology is the exception that proves the rule. In classical Yoga, the relation to the sacred is modeled after physical causation rather than social interaction. Thus the status attainment model of soteriology I have proposed—which focuses on the social processes of conformity and association—requires modification in order to fit the data: we must relax the assumption that all soteriologies are modeled after social processes. Such an adjustment is easily made, because our theoretical argument anticipated that sacral relationships can fall along a continuum from physical causation to various types of social interaction. Thus, while the case of classical Yoga does not fit within the status attainment model of salvation, the broader theoretical framework enables us to see why this is so. This case does not invalidate the model, but helps to specify more clearly the parameters of the model—that is, the types of cases to which it applies. Now let us proceed to soteriologies more directly modeled after social processes.

Smarta Orthodoxy

The Smarta tradition refers to Hindus who tend toward Brahmanical orthodoxy in both thought and behavior. Smartas are usually committed to a relatively unified Hinduism that rejects extreme sectarianism. In a very rough way, the difference between Smartas and sectarian Hindus parallels the European distinction between church and sect.[11] The Smarta tradition has roots back to the Brahmanical synthesis that emerged between the third century B.C.E. and the third century C.E. in response to the anti-Vedic movements such as Buddhism and Jainism (see, e.g., Hopkins 1971:chap. 5; Brockington 1981:chap. 5; Hiltebeitel 1987). In contemporary India, the Smarta tradition contains or is influenced by at least four identifiable strands. The most ancient is, of course, a commitment to some elements of Vedic ritualism. This is most clearly characteristic of the Mimamsa school of Indian philosophy, which continues to have a small group of adherents in contemporary India. They stress the primacy of the *sruti*, "what has been heard"—that is, the Vedas proper— in contrast to the *smriti*, "what has been remembered"— that is, the tradition. Since "Smarta" means one who follows the smriti, classifying the Mimamsas as part of the Smarta tradition is perhaps controversial. Yet the Mimamsa emphasis on con- formity to the sacred texts is a key element or strand of the Smarta tradition.[12] Especially important for the Smartas is the emphasis on ritual purity and the ritual superiority of Brahmans.

A second important influence is Sankara's (ca. 788–820) Advaita Vedanta non- dualistic philosophy, to which most Smartas officially assent. This adherence is in some respects ironical. Sankara's philosophy and activity was directed toward the tradition of ascetic renouncers, in which salvation was by jnana-yoga. The Smarta tradition has, however, always been dominated not by renouncers, but by Brahman householders. While such householders do not deny the legitimacy of jnana-yoga as a path to salvation, the emphasis has been on karma-yoga: salvation through actions that conform to dharma. The Smarta tradition seems to have accepted the importance and legitimacy of the path of knowledge, but to have down played Sankara's asceticism and monasticism—except as the ideal for the last of the four stages of life.

While the legitimacy of jnana-yoga is embraced in the Smarta tradition, the content of what constitutes saving knowledge is transformed. The legitimacy of nondualistic metaphysical knowledge—that all existence is *brahman*—is recognized. Much more important, however, is the pandit's knowledge of the Dharmasastras, focusing on what Brahman householders must do to be in con- formity with dharma. This is the third major strand of the Smarta tradition. But knowledge of the Dharmasastras is not enough: "men who follow (the teachings of the texts) surpass those who (merely) know (their meaning)" (*Manusmriti* XII:103). Like Mimamsa, the emphasis is on conformity. The details of the Vedic rituals are not, however, the primary concern. Rather, the Dharmasastras and the Smarta tra- dition are preoccupied with the norms of daily life. These include a concern with household and public religious ritual, but are much broader in that they outline the appropriate characteristics of the ideal social order. An especially strong theme in this literature is the avoidance of intermarriages between castes, which is looked on as one of the worst of sins. People are also enjoined to perform their tradition- ally assigned caste roles (svadharma). In short, at the core of this strand are norms supporting the caste system.

The fourth key strand of the Smarta orthodoxy is the theism and cosmology of the religious texts known as the Puranas. The gradual degeneration over time of the creation in general, and the moral order in particular, is a core feature of this cos- mology. The world is set in motion by Visnu and finally ended by Siva the de- stroyer, to be set into motion again, and so on. In the present Age of Kali (Kali

Yuga)—the last age before dissolution (*pralaya*) of the world—humans have forgotten or abandoned dharma. Out of this notion of degeneration develops the idea of
the divine *avatar*, a god who takes on some special form and comes to restore the
moral order. Krishna and Vamana, the dwarf, are the most obvious examples. An
avatar, however, presumes a relatively distinctive deity rather than the atheism of
Mimamsa or the near pantheism of Advaita Vedanta. The notion of restoration of
the cosmic and social order also implies a deity who cares about what goes on in
this world. In turn, divine attempts to restore the world imply a concept of grace. So
the fourth strand introduces an important element of salvation by grace rather than
solely by conformity and knowledge. That is, bhakti-yoga is introduced into the
Smarta tradition in addition to karma-yoga and jnana-yoga. Devotion to named and
identifiable gods becomes an increasingly accepted part of the Smarta orthodoxy. It
is even legitimate for individuals to choose one deity as the object of special devotion (*ista-devata*). Smartas, however, reject the idea of exclusive devotion to one
particular god. As Hopkins says:

> The characteristic Smarta religious form is *pancayatana-puja* (*puja* of the five
> shrines), developed some time after the beginning of the seventh century as a com-
> promise between early Smarta practices and the new Puranic theism. The Smarta rit-
> ual involves the worship of not one but five representative deities: Vishnu, Siva,
> Surya, Ganesa, and Durga. (1971:120–21)

Probably Smartas reject Tantric elements and radical sectarianism. However, in
part because Tantra is practiced "in secret," some Smartas have played an important
role in the Tantric tradition (see Brooks 1990).

While theism and bhakti-yoga are integrated into the Smarta tradition, their implications of salvation by grace are held in check. In the Smarta tradition (at least
the premodern rural tradition), bhakti is still largely a matter of conforming to the
appropriate rituals, especially through pujas. This point should not be overstated;
undoubtedly some individual Smartas express intense devotion. On balance, however, bhakti is both grafted on to the Smarta tradition, and is partly neutralized
through encapsulation and a subtle shift in emphasis of devotion toward ritual conformity.[13]

In the theoretical terms used throughout this analysis, the soteriology of the
Smarta tradition emphasizes conformity. Compared to the nearly mechanical means
of classical Yoga, the path to salvation is clearly modeled after social processes.
The concluding chapter of the *Laws of Manu*—a central text for Smartas—says:

> [E]xamine without tiring the merit and the guilt of that (individual soul), united with
> which it obtains bliss or misery both in this world and the next. If (the soul) chiefly
> practices virtue and [engages in] vice [only] to a small degree, it obtains bliss in
> heaven, clothed with those very elements. But if it chiefly cleaves to vice and to
> virtue in a small degree, it suffers, deserted by the elements, the torments inflicted by
> Yama. (XII:19–21)

What one is to experience in the next world—whether as reincarnation or final
liberation—is seen as fundamentally a moral, social process. It will be determined
primarily by how consistently one has conformed to dharma. To some degree

moksa itself is deemphasized, and conformity to the tradition is honored for its own sake. Yet this emphasis is only relative. For most Smartas, the goal of moksa is still an important one that is acquired primarily by conformity. Significant elements of bhakti are present within the Smarta tradition. Thus salvation can be influenced by the nature of one's relationship to a particular deity, that is, by association. This idea is given much less emphasis than in sectarian bhakti traditions, to which we now turn.

Sectarian Bhakti

As we have seen, significant elements of bhakti were incorporated into Smarta Hinduism. Nonetheless, within Brahman orthodoxy, the implications of bhakti are blunted in at least four respects. First, a significant emphasis remains on conformity to religious and social norms as a means to improve one's position in the cycles of reincarnation (samsara) and even in obtaining ultimate liberation (moksa). Second, the object of devotion is more diffuse; the concept of focusing all devotion and loyalty to a specific personal deity is absent. Third, birth determines whether one is a Hindu and the particular role and subcommunity to which one belongs; being a member of the religious community is a matter of ascribed social association. Fourth, the mother tongue of the people cannot be used for sacred purposes. Sanskrit, the esoteric language of a religious elite, is required. Because of this restriction, the religious social organization is almost inevitably a segmented hieratic structure rather than a community of peers.

While bhakti sects vary significantly, virtually all shift the emphasis with respect to these four matters. First, salvation is by grace through intimate association with the deity. Second, while the sectarian may continue to participate in community rituals and festivals to other deities, most of one's religious devotion is directed toward the sect's special god. Third, membership is—at least in principle—voluntary; what is crucial is not ascribed social association but unremitting commitment to be associated with the sect's deity—usually through the mediation of a guru. Fourth, at least some of the religious texts and much of the worship is in the mother tongue of the devotees.

A corollary of these features is a relative deemphasis on caste and gender differences. Sects vary enormously, however, in how strongly this is stressed. Generally such social differences are played down in the context of religious worship, but maintained in social matters such as marriage and occupation.[14] This weakening of caste differences and the use of a common mother tongue, as well as at least implied criticism or even protest against orthodoxy, usually increases the sense of community among sectarian devotees.

A second corollary feature is the importance of the guru. As we have just seen, the religious significance of ascribed kinship associations is deemphasized. Probably because of this, the voluntaristic association with one's guru is all the more important. Of course, the institution of the guru is very old in South Asia and is not limited to bhakti sectarianism. This institution becomes more salient, however, when salvation by grace through association is emphasized. The role of the guru is also partially redefined. The Vedic guru is primarily a teacher of sacred lore; this function remains in bhakti sectarianism, but the guru is also much more of a direct mediating link to the divine—in some cases, a virtual demigod (see, e.g., Babb 1986). By intimate association with the guru, one associates with the divine. Moreover, while the kinship lineage of devotees is deemphasized, the lineage of the guru becomes very important. Sectarian genealogies often show that the first guru in the line was taught directly by some divinity. Thus for the devotee the connection with the divine is defined not in terms of worldly kinship and caste, but via spiritual kinship.

A third corollary is a shift of emphasis in worship. For the most part in orthodox and popular Hinduism, pujas are performed as a request to the deity for some relatively concrete blessing or as an expression of thanks for some wish already fulfilled. Most bhakti sects perform pujas to their deity, but the spirit and content is changed. Worship is a matter of giving thanks for God's grace and asking only for his presence. The emphasis is on communion rather than tangible benefits such as favors, boons, and blessings. In line with this notion, other forms of worship, such as the singing of hymns, are also used, and these too stress praise and a sense of God's nearness.

Often the bhakti literature openly proclaims its superiority over other paths to salvation. For example, according to the *Bhakti Sutras*: "Devotion is superior to action, knowledge, or yogic contemplation; for devotion is itself its fruit, and God loves the meek and dislikes those who are proud [of their accomplishments]" (de Bary et al. 1972:333). The same sutra makes explicit the importance of the devotee's association with those who are holy, both humans and gods:

> Now, the means of acquiring devotion are . . . renunciation, . . . adoration of the Lord, . . . listening to and the singing of the Lord; [and] chiefly the grace of the great souls or a particle of the divine grace itself.
>
> The association of the great souls [mahatman] is hard to acquire, hard to be had completely, but is always fruitful. For gaining even that association, one requires God's blessing; for between God and His men there is no difference. So try to acquire the company of the holy souls, and strive for that. (de Bary et al. 1972:333–34)

Association with the holy is secured not by purity attained through one's own efforts, but by humility and devotion. As the *Bhagavata Purana* says:

> Even a low-caste man is superior to a brahman who is endowed with the twelve excellences but who is averse to the lotus feet of the Lord; if the former has dedicated his mind, speech, desire, and objects, and his life itself to the Lord, he sanctifies his whole race, not so the latter who is stuck up in his own enormous pride. (de Bary et al. 1972:346)

True humility requires the recognition of the ephemeral and futile quality of worldly activity. The sixteenth century untouchable poet-saint Ravidas proclaims:

> The day it comes, it goes;
>   whatever you do, nothing stays firm.
> The group goes, and I go;
>   and the going is long, and death is overhead. . . .

> Madman, says Ravidas, here's the cause of it all—
> it's only a house of tricks. Ignore the world.
> (Hawley and Juergensmeyer 1988:32)

Humility also requires the recognition of one's own worthlessness. Such is proclaimed by the eighth-century Shavite poet Manikkavachakar: "I am false, my heart is false, my love is false; but I, this sinner, can win Thee if I weep before Thee, O Lord . . . " (de Bary et al. 1972:354). As Yamuna, one of the eleventh-century founders of Sri Vaishnavism, proclaims: "There is not one despised act in the world which I have not done a thousand times; O Lord! at this hour when my sin is bearing its consequences, I am crying before you, without any other way" (de Bary et al. 1972:350).

In addition to the recognition of the ephemeral and corrupt nature of worldly existence, these prayers imply a related theme: without divine help one is powerless. In the imagery of the sixteenth-century theologian Vadiraja, "O Lord Hari [Krishna]! Does an animal fallen into the well know how to lift itself by its own effort? Throwing about its feet and bellowing frequently, it can only excite pity, O Lord" (de Bary et al. 1972:350). This quality of pity, mercy, and forgiveness is proclaimed by a sixteenth-century Sri Vaishnava text: "like a father seeing with his eyes the mistakes of his wife and sons, He goes on without minding at heart the mistakes of His devotees" (de Bary et al. 1972:344). In short, divine grace is emphasized; without grace humans are nothing. The Virasaiva poet Basavanna has a devotee proclaim, "I'm no worshipper; I'm no giver; I'm not even beggar, O lord without your grace" (Ramanujan 1973:88). But God's grace can transform what is valueless. As Kabir, the most famous North Indian poet, says:

> Even worthless bushes
> Are invaded by a nearby
>   sandal tree.
> Its fragrance
>   makes everything around it
> A likeness of itself.
> (Hawley and Juergensmeyer 1988:58)

These selected lines from the bhakti literature (deliberately drawn from different sects, regions, and periods) show that the general themes are common to most types of sectarian bhakti.

Humility by the recognition of corruption and sin, and the response of mercy and grace, can occur only in a special milieu. The crucial context is an intensely personal associative relationship between the devotee and his God. The nature of the devotee's association with the deity is usually modeled after everyday social relationships. The relationships most commonly used as models are: master and servant, parent and child, friend and friend, and beloved and lover. Sects vary as to which of these relationships is most emphasized. In many groups, the individual can choose which role to model behavior after, but some form of an intimate personalized relationship with the deity is required for salvation. The devotee imagines himself or herself to be in the subordinate role of servant, child, or female lover.

Both men and women conceive of themselves as female lovers of their god. Frequently the sexual imagery is very explicit.[15] This form of devotion happens in many sectarian groups, and is especially characteristic Krishna worshippers. The stories of Krishna's love affairs with the *gopi* ("cowherder") women, and especially with his favorite, Radha, are the most famous example. These are married women who are willing to risk everything because of their love for Krishna. Krishna calls them with his music and as Radha tells her friends:

> How can I describe his relentless flute,
> which pulls virtuous women from their homes
> and drags them by their hair to Shyam
> as thirst and hunger pull the doe to the snare?
> Chaste ladies forget their lords,
> wise men forget their wisdom,
> and clinging vines shake loose from their trees,
> hearing that music.
> Then how shall a simple dairymaid withstand its call?
>   (Dimock and Levertov 1967:29)

If Krishna's power is overwhelming and the costs are great, so are the rewards:

> My friend, I cannot answer when you ask me to explain
> what has befallen me.
> Love is transformed, renewed,
> each moment.
> He has dwelt in my eyes all the days of my life,
> yet I am not sated with seeing.
> My ears have heard his sweet voice in eternity,
> and yet it is always new to them.
> How many honeyed nights have I passed with him
> in love's bliss, yet my body
> wonders at his.
> Through all the ages
> he has been clasped to my breast,
> yet my desire
> never abates.
> I have seen subtle people sunk in passion
> but none came so close to the heart of the fire.
>   (Dimock and Levertov 1967:18)

More importantly, this relationship transforms the devotee and is the source of all his or her worth. A devotee proclaims to Krishna, "Love, I take on splendor in your splendor, grace and gentleness are mine because of your beauty" (Dimock and Levertov 1967:16). Salvation and everything of value comes from association with the deity; this is the core idea of sectarian bhakti.

Sri Vaisnavism

The final case to be considered in our discussion of soteriology is Sri Vaisnavism. Here we move from a general discussion of sectarian bhakti to a discussion of the variations within one specific bhakti sect. This South Indian sect of Vaisnavism has its roots in the thought and work of Ramanuja. As discussed earlier, Ramanuja's theology attempted to synthesize Vedantic orthodoxy with bhakti devotionalism in a qualified nondualism. A synthesis of such divergent religious styles was of course subject to internal strains. In the two hundred years following the death of Ramanuja, two distinct branches of Sri Vaisnavism evolved, the northern, or Vatakalai, school and the southern, or Tenkalai, school. The northern school was more traditional and continued to place a heavy reliance on Sanskrit, while the southern school increasingly used Tamil for religious activities. Not surprisingly, this was associated with a greater and lesser emphasis on Brahmanical traditions.

Two key theological differences also emerged. Since both schools are part of the same sectarian bhakti tradition, both emphasized the importance of devotion. Both adopted the even more radical doctrine of *prapatti*: not just devotion but self-surrender is required for salvation. This doctrine rejected all notions of salvation by karma-yoga or jnana-yoga. The devotee is seen as totally helpless; salvation is due to God's grace. While both schools affirmed the doctrine of prapatti, the northern school was much more tentative in its commitment to it. For example, often elaborate ritual conditions had to be met before self-surrender and grace could be actualized. The differences in the two school's doctrines of salvation became symbolized by the contrast between the baby monkey and the baby cat. For both schools, the devotee is like a baby being carried by its mother: it is the mother's action that produces locomotion, and it is God's action which produces salvation. For the northern school, the human was like a baby monkey who must cling to its mother in order to be carried. In contrast, for the southern school the human was like a baby cat who is picked up by the scruff of the neck and carried solely by the action of another. In our theoretical terms, salvation requires human cooperation according to the northern school, but is totally ascribed according to the southern school.

The second key theological difference has to do with the role of the *acarya,* or preceptor. The term "acarya" in many respects overlaps with the concept of guru. In the medieval sectarian tradition, however, the former is usually associated with a sectarian monastic order; the concept of guru is less specific. While the role of the acarya is important in both branches of Sri Vaisnavism, it becomes absolutely central to the southern school. Since this school deemphasizes the role of Brahmans, and of caste and kinship generally, the role and authority of the acarya become central. The acarya control entry into the sect, the initiation of devotees, and have virtually absolute religious authority over those whom they admit, especially with respect to the "shares" (of prasadas and other blessings) devotees will receive at the temple. Moreover they take on the explicit role of mediator. Salvation is attained only through the acarya. In my theoretical terms, salvation is attained by two kinds of association: association with the acarya and association with the deity. The former is the means to the latter; the latter is salvation.

A similar distinction in the emphasis on association and conformity is found within the North Indian Ramanandi monastic sect. The Ramanandis have a historic tie to Sri Vaisnavism, though the nature and extent of that tie is debated (Van der Veer 1988). Most of Ramanandis, however, have largely broken off relationships with Sri Vaisnavism. The distinction drawn within the Ramanandis is between the discipline of devotion and the discipline of renunciation (Burghart 1983). The first emphasizes a personal relationship with Lord Rama, and the devotee usually conceives of himself as either a servant in the deity's court or as a kinsman of the deity. This link with the deity is bestowed upon the Ramanandi as an act of grace of the guru. While virtually all Ramanandis are ascetic monks, those who follow the path of renunciation place much more emphasis on personal asceticism and yoga techniques as the means of liberation. A subgroup of this branch refer to themselves as Great Renouncers and avoid the use of woven cloth, using bark or wood to cover their bodies.

Hopefully, the conclusion is obvious at this point: many and probably most of the variations in Hindu soteriology doctrine can be usefully conceptualized as variations in the emphasis on conformity and association. These are means of obtaining what is conceived to be the ultimate form of status, salvation.

Christian Soteriology: A Brief Analysis

To demonstrate the applicability of this mode of analysis to other religious traditions, I will now briefly analyze Christian soteriology.

An ongoing debate within Christian theology has been over the role that human conformity plays in attaining salvation. Classically, this is expressed as a contrast between works and faith, law and grace. In Jesus' dispute with the Pharisees, he clearly calls into question the efficacy of conforming to the Judaic law as a means to salvation. The concept of justification by faith rather than works is at the core of Paul's theology. One of the earliest recorded disputes within the Christian church was between Peter and Paul and their respective followers over whether Christians must conform to the Jewish rules of purification. A central consideration in Augustine's debates with Pelagius over free will was whether people's own efforts toward religious and moral conformity play a role in their salvation. The theological concern that started Martin Luther toward his break with the Roman Church was his emphasis on salvation through association with and trust in Jesus—justification by faith—rather than salvation by works. A main point of contention within the later Puritan tradition was over the relative emphasis on association and conformity. Orthodox Calvinists—at least in explicitly formulated dogma—rejected all hints of earning one's salvation, or even that good behavior was due to one's own efforts. In contrast, the Methodists, as their very name indicates, granted some legitimacy to systematic human will and effort, at least in the process of sanctification. In short, throughout Christian history a central theological question has been: What is required for salvation? Within the Christian tradition, one's association with the deity—usually through Jesus Christ—has always received the dominant emphasis.

Yet the role of human effort in establishing the association (and whether conformity to moral norms was a reliable sign of such a saving relationship) has frequently been in contention. While not all of the subtleties of the historic debates over Christian soteriology are captured by conceptualizing these as differential emphases on conformity and association, it is parsimonious to see this as a basic issue around which the debates have centered.

Thus in the Hindu and the Christian traditions, the major differences in soteriologies can be meaningfully analyzed as variations in the emphases on conformity or association. This is additional evidence for the analytical usefulness of conceptualizing status and sacredness as parallel notions.

15

Eschatology

Chapter 14 focused on salvation and conceptualized it as a form or analogue of social mobility. But salvation, like all mobility, occurs in a context. For worldly social mobility, that context is the societal stratification system. For salvation that context is an other world.[1] Just as an adequate analysis of social mobility, and status transformation must be linked to the social context in which it occurs, an analysis of the means and types of salvation needs to be linked to the broader characteristics of the other world in which it occurs. Hence it is necessary to describe some of the features of this other world and its relation to salvation. For lack of a better term I use the admittedly Western concept of eschatology to refer to this other world.[2]

Soteriology focuses on where individuals and groups wind up in the structure of the other world; eschatology is concerned with what the other world is like. An eschatology sets out the possible outcomes that people face (e.g., reincarnation in varying forms versus moksa) and suggests the general principle that will determine these outcomes (e.g., karma). In some respects, this contrast is similar to the distinction between identifying the structural features of a stratification system (the number of classes, the size of each class, the distance between them, etc.) and identifying what determines the placement of individuals and groups within the stratification system. The distinction between eschatology and soteriology, like the distinction between structure and placement, is not a precise or absolute one; rather, each concept enables us to look at a complex system from different perspectives.

This chapter will, however, attempt to do more than provide a description of various human conceptions of the other world. It will attempt to show that its characteristics are linked to the central structural features of the societies with which religions have been historically associated. Other worlds necessarily include some of the features and characteristics of the historical world. That is, some features are modeled after and parallel the social worlds that people have experienced empirically. The focus of this analysis, however, will be on structural reversals. More specifically, many features of the other world tend to be structural reversals of this world's stratification system. For example, heaven is often in many respects a reverse or mirror image of earth.

The analysis involves three steps. First, a brief recapitulation of the key features of Hindu social structure will be presented. Second, I will attempt to predict or derive the key doctrines of Hindu eschatology, based on the information about the central structural features of Hindu society, and the key assumption that many features of eschatologies are reversals of worldly structures. Third, I will draw on elements of the general theoretical framework to suggest why such reversals tend to occur.

As in most complex religions, the details of these eschatological doctrines vary significantly for different traditions within Hinduism, and some of these will be considered. Our initial task, however, will be to derive the ideal-type features that apply to virtually all traditions.

Hinduism and the Caste System

Key Features of the Social Structure

Since World War II, a number of detailed ethnographic studies and synthetic works have greatly increased our knowledge of the Indian caste system.[3] Generally they have shown it to be much more complex and fluid than the earlier literature indicated.

Nonetheless, as shown in the discussion of the key features of the Indian caste system in Chapter 5, compared to other structures of inequality, mobility is carefully restricted. More specifically three features are particularly striking. First, a person's central social status in the community is inalienable; in principle, mobility across caste boundaries is prohibited. This involves not just one or two key boundaries—aristocracy versus commoners, blacks versus whites, or Greeks versus barbarians—but a very large number of relatively discrete social boundaries. Second, caste position is in principle based solely on inheritance and ascription. Conformity, performance, and merit may affect many things, but these do not determine one's caste membership. Third, enormous social and individual energies are devoted to differentiating and ranking caste groups and maintaining their boundaries and identities. The norms concerning pollution are the primary, but by no means the only, mechanism for accomplishing this.

If our analytical strategy is correct, the key features of Hindu eschatology will be, in large measure, the opposite of these characteristics. That is, they will be inversions or reversals of the worldly patterns. The essence of my argument is that the three key notions of Hindu eschatology—samsara, karma, and moksa—express reversals of the three characteristics of the caste system just listed.[4]

Samsara as Mobility

The first structural characteristic of the caste system that was noted is severely restricted social mobility. As we would expect, in the world-to-come this pattern is reversed. One moves through a long series of positions, and each move may involve a substantial change in status. In this life, one may be an Untouchable; in the next, a Brahman; in the next, a worm or pig.[5] Hence, on the cosmic level, social status is highly alienable and temporary. This is the well-known notion of reincarnation and transmigration referred to in Hinduism as samsara. This Sanskrit word implies flow or flux. More specifically, human existence is conceived of as an endless cycle of birth, death, rebirth, and so on through a series of worldly existences. The essence of the worldly system is no mobility; the essence of the otherworldly system is endless mobility. This emphasis on flux in the other world is not limited to samsara. Since the Puranas and the concept of yugas, Hinduism has perceived the cosmos and the gods themselves as going through repeated cycles in which they alternate between clearly specified identities and states of amorphous undifferentiation (see Biardeau 1989:101).

The mobility of samsara is not given an especially positive evaluation, at least in formal theology; the stress is on the temporary and ephemeral nature of all worldly conditions. Because of reincarnation, the soul (atman) is bound to this world. In theoretical terms, status has become highly alienable. In the context of endless rebirths, any given status is temporary and insecure. It can be snatched away at any moment by misfortune or death. This is, of course, in contrast to the relative inalienability of one's caste status in the context of any given life. Although the samsara doctrine may be a clear example of structural reversal of the patterns of mobility in the empirical world, it is defined in classical indigenous ideologies as yet another warning about the dangers of mobility and the ephemeral nature of worldly status. Therefore, the correlation between the relative immobility of a caste system and the nearly infinite mobility of samsara is not necessarily rooted in psychological compensation.

Karma as Merit

The second key feature of the worldly stratification system concerns ascription. In principle, the biological and social association with one's kin determines one's caste status. No amount of moral virtue or conformity to valued norms entitles you to move into a higher caste (though grievous breaches of caste norms can result in expulsion from your present caste). From a strictly worldly point of view, not the individual's behavior, but birth and ascription determine this key social status.

In contrast, the status one will acquire in the next life through samsara is determined by one's current behavior—by one's conformity (or lack of it) to the moral and cosmic law—that is, dharma. So, in principle, status in subsequent lives is based solely on merit and achievement. This is, of course, the law of karma. In both sacred texts and popular religious thought, the matter is considerably more complicated, but the basic notion is clear. As Mahony says, "As diverse as the culture of India may be, one common assumption undergirds virtually all major systems of South Asian religious thought and practice: a person's behavior leads irrevocably to an appropriate reward or punishment commensurate with that behavior. This, briefly stated, is the law of *karman*" (1987:261). Kane, the most renowned modern scholar of the Dharmasastras, writes:

The principle of the doctrine of Karma is that every act, whether good or bad, produces a certain result or return which cannot be escaped. In the physical world there is the universal law of causation. The doctrine of Karma extends this inexorable law of causality to the mental and moral sphere. The doctrine of Karma is not a mechanical law; it is rather a moral or a spiritual necessity. . . . In the absence of the theory of karma and rebirth it would have to be assumed that the world is arbitrary. . . . Under the doctrine of Karma there is no such thing as chance or luck. (1977:1560)

White succinctly summarizes the relationship between reincarnation, karma, and dharma: "In the cycle of rebirths, the body into which a transmigrating soul is born in a given existence is one's due, on the basis of the sum total of one's past deeds (*karma*) with respect to *dharma*" (1991:88). In other words, in its pure and most extreme form, the law of karma produces perfect justice; sooner or later, all actions produce their appropriate fruits. Thus the worldly system epitomizing ascription is linked to a cosmic system that is the epitome of achievement. Karma is important not only as the determinant of one's social position in future reincarnations; its consequences are more general: all events in this life and subsequent ones are the consequence of previous actions.

In the worldly system, caste status is determined solely by association— that is, the association with one's parents and relatives. In the worlds-to-come, one's status is determined solely by whether one did or did not conform to the norms appropriate to one's social location— that is, svadharma. From one perspective, social status is based completely on association and ascription, from another perspective it is determined solely by conformity and merit. Of course, the notion of karma was developed in a number of different directions and has evolved into a whole complex of religious ideas. I will take up some of these complications later. Nonetheless, as Mahony indicates, above the core idea is one of just deserts.[6]

Here again we seem to have a clear structural reversal.[7]

Moksa as the Overcoming of Separateness

The third characteristic of the caste system just mentioned is the preoccupation with the formation and maintenance of differentiated, ranked social identities. Enormous efforts are invested in defining and defending the boundaries of local caste groups (jatis). The identity and boundaries of these local jatis are never completely unambiguous, and are frequently in contention. This conflict is an indication of the importance attributed to these distinctive social identities.[8] A hierarchy based on purity and pollution is the primary criterion and idiom of differentiation and caste identity. A central cultural preoccupation is identifying the impure, keeping it separate from the pure, and thereby defining the identity of the pure. This is not to suggest that either identities or differences—what is pure and what is impure—are completely precise or unambiguous. Nor is it to say that Indians are unconcerned about inter-caste integration and unity. It is to suggest that creating and maintaining differences and separated identities based on ritual status is a primary concern of the culture. Generally the more orthodox and Brahmanical the actors are, the more this is so.

Given this cultural preoccupation with the differentiated identities and maintenance of social separation, we would anticipate notions of salvation that focus on overcoming differentiation and separateness. This is, of course, precisely the central content of classical Hindu soteriology as expressed in the concept of moksa— release or liberation from the endless cycles of reincarnation. More accurately, moksa is the core concept of the orthodox Brahmanical tradition represented by the thought of Sankara (ca. 788–820). His Advaita Vedanta philosophy is rooted in the Upanisad tradition of knowledge (jnana) as the means to salvation and is noted for its uncompromising monism: salvation consists in recognizing the unity of the self (atman) and the ultimate reality (*brahman*). Sankara recognizes the legitimacy of other paths (marga) to salvation (e.g., karma-yoga and bhakti-yoga) as means to partial knowledge, but to fully grasp of the unity of the self and the *brahman*, one must follow the path of jnana-yoga and become a wandering holyman (sannyasin). The very process of becoming a holyman or renouncer (sannyasin) involves giving up one's own social identity and ignoring the differentiated social identities of others; in principle, though not always in practice, renouncers are beyond caste and kinship, beyond purity and pollution. Thus, for this tradition, the elimination of differentiating social identities begins in the last stage of this life. As we have seen, the destruction of differentiated identity does not stop here; all differentiated identities are an illusion (maya) due to ignorance (*avidya*); there is only *brahman*.

Other monistic traditions (e.g.,the Vaisnava Vaikhanasa sect) are also associated with social conservatism (Brockington 1981:116, 122). That is, they emphasize caste distinctions and Brahmanical cultural dominance. In theoretical terms, they stress the differentiation and maintenance of social identities in this world and the unity of all identity in the world-to-come. While Sankara's monism is the ideal-typical example of orthodox Hindu eschatology, other subtraditions are numerous. We will briefly examine two other ideal-typical examples of such variations.

Perhaps the tradition at the other end of the continuum from Vedanta monism is bhakti devotionalism. This tradition is made up of many sects with significant differences, but with important commonalities as well. These movements began in Tamil-speaking areas of South India in the sixth century C.E., but spread rather rapidly to many parts of India. Many of these sects emphasized the availability of salvation to lower caste groups and women, and were in varying degrees protests against Brahman orthodoxy—though Brahmans often played a crucial role in their development.[9] Some rejected the caste system per se. Bhakti sects are also concerned with overcoming separateness, but they do not usually define moksa as the merger of human and divine identities. Most bhakti sects emphasize the difference between humans and gods. Gods are relatively all-powerful and pure beings; humans are relatively powerless and sinful. Salvation still involves overcoming separation, but it is not primarily the recognition that God and the self are one and the same. Rather, it is perpetually being in the presence of one's deity as a worshipper and devotee. In fact, for some sectarian groups the notion that the devotee and the deity are one and the same borders on blasphemy. Thus, in contrast to orthodox Brahmanism, bhakti sects deemphasize the differentiation of worldly social identities and place more emphasis on the differentiation of otherworldly sacral identities. There is a tendency to reinterpret moksa so that it consists of some notion of heaven, rather than merger with the deity. A postscript is needed. Some bhakti groups would emphasize the union of humans and the divine, though these groups also tend to be more socially conservative. More fundamentally, however, orthodoxy itself was often significantly shaped by bhakti and vice versa. This does not, however, negate the basic contrast, anymore than would the recognition that socialism has produced transformations in capitalism negate a contrast of the ideologies of these two world views.

A third intermediate case is the theology of Ramanuja (traditionally 1017–1137). Ramanuja's purpose was to create a synthesis between the orthodox Vedanta traditions and the bhakti devotionalism of the masses. While his Sri Vaisnava sect was in principle open to the lower castes, he basically accepted the legitimacy of varnasramadharma—the traditional four stages of the life cycle and the caste system. Only the upper castes (i.e., the twice-born) were capable of fully practicing his version of bhakti-yoga, which was rooted in the concepts of the *Bhagavad Gita*. So with respect to social relationships in this world he was reformist, but not revolutionary. Accordingly, his concept of the relationship between the otherworldly identities is an intermediate one. *Brahman* and the created world have separate real identities. In Ramanuja's commentary, *Vedarthasamgraha*, he describes the nature of the Supreme Person (*Purusottama*): "His essential nature is distinct from all entities other than Himself by virtue of His opposition to all evil and His being wholly infinite perfection [kalyanata]. He has a host of such auspicious qualities [kalyanagunas], which are countless and of matchless excellence" (quoted in Carman 1974:70). Yet an element of monism remains; *brahman* and the individual soul are related like parts to a whole. Later in the same text he notes:

> He has as instruments of his sport [*lila*] an infinite number of intelligent beings, both those bound in samsara and those released from it, all of whom are parts of Himself. Likewise, He possesses all material things, which are subject to infinite, wonderful, and varied changes and which form the object of enjoyment for intelligent beings. Since He is the Inner Controller of His whole creation, He has all things as His body and His modes. (quoted in Carman 1974:70)

In sum, Ramanuja's theology combines a qualified monism with relatively orthodox forms of devotionalism rooted in the *Bhagavad Gita*. There is both an identity and a difference between the deity and the devotee. Consequently, Ramanuja's theology gives additional support to our hypothesis.

Thus salvation usually implies overcoming separateness, but an emphasis on the merger of human and sacred identities usually reflects an emphasis on maintaining worldly social differentiation, especially caste differences. In this sense, there tends to be a structural reversal.

Contemporary Religious Movements

The above comparisons involve very broad streams of Indian thought that evolved over hundreds of years. Since it is usually more difficult to explain small variations than large ones, a more demanding test of our hypothesis would be to look at variations between very specific sect groups over a limited period of time. Lawrence

Babb's book *Redemptive Encounters* (1986) makes this possible. He examines three contemporary Indian religious movements: the movement led by the famous magician Sathya Sai Baba, the millenarian Brahma Kumari movement, and the Radhasoami movement based in Agra. The most famous of these movements is that by Sathya Sai Baba. He is, among other things, a renowned magician who claims to be Siva and Sakti in embodied form. Most Indian followers are prosperous and well educated, and speak English as a second language. While the movement sponsors a considerable amount of philanthropy and social work, it is quite conservative in most social matters and stresses a cultural nationalism. As Babb notes, "The emphasis on social service provides an opportunity for devotees to do good in the world, but Sathaya Sai Baba's profound conservatism on fundamentals like caste and gender ensures that doing good is unlikely to challenge his devotees' more basic sense of propriety and order" (1986:200–21). Of the three movements, this one is the most concerned with worldly benefits and the least soteriologically oriented. Nonetheless, through various meditation techniques "one realizes one's identity with God, who has been within. The final goal, therefore, is merger with God, who is in fact Baba. The result will be the eradication of harmful motives and tendencies, and feelings of deep inner peace (*prashanti*)" (1986:172). Such a view of salvation is clearly a close relative to the monistic Vedanta tradition. Thus this first case supports our hypothesis of a correlation between the maintenance of traditional social identities and salvation conceived of as a merger of all identities.

At the other pole is the Brahma Kumari movement, which initially was viewed as quite radical and highly threatening to the existing social order. In addition to an urgent millenarianism and the rejection of caste distinctions, the major thrust of the movement has been equality for women. Women not only make up the majority of the devotees, they also seem to control the movement. Because the sect expects the end of the world, all members—men and women—are urged to become celibate and concentrate their energies on preparing themselves for the world-to-come. In Hinduism, celibacy has always been a respected option for men as a step toward salvation; what the Brahma Kumaris demand is soteriological equality for women.[10] While those influenced by Western feminism may not find this strategy for gender equality very appealing, in the context of South Asia it is a radical demand, highly threatening to the traditional social and religious order. A serious pursuit of this way of life demands a strict separation from existing social relationships and a quasi-monastic life. While the movement has, to some degree, moderated its rhetoric and is seen as less threatening than in earlier periods, it is undoubtedly the most socially radical of the movements Babb considers. As our hypothesis would predict, it is also the least monistic. For the Brahma Kumaris, salvation is conceived of as a new world in which not only will the identities of humans be continued, but the purist devotees of the movement will serve as the elite who rule paradise. As in the Sathya Sai Baba movement, Siva is considered to be the supreme deity, but for the Brahma Kumaris, there is a radical separation of the deity and the material world and the historical process. While the theology of the Brahma Kumaris does not focus on the issue of monism versus dualism, it is clear that it falls toward the dualistic end of the continuum, which is what our hypothesis would predict.

The third case Babb describes is the Radhasoami movement, headquartered in the Soami Bagh in Agra. It represents an intermediate position with respect to both social radicalism and theological monism. Most of the adherents are middle class government and business employees, many highly successful. Yet the movement is deeply alienated from the existing world. The alienation is, however, largely spiritual and demands little departure from traditional social patterns. While caste distinctions are rejected for spiritual purposes, the world is beyond social reform. In fact all social relationships are a spiritual trap, escaped only by unqualified devotion to the movement's guru. In short, while the movement is highly critical of the existing world, its theology and ethics offer little threat to the existing social identities. Similarly, its theology implies a qualified monism. Salvation occurs when the devotee comes to see the world as the deity sees it. This involves union, but not complete absorption by the deity.

These three contemporary movements, and the three broad traditions discussed earlier, offer considerable opportunities for the hypotheses to be rejected, and this has not occurred. It seems reasonable, then, to conclude that there is substantial tentative support for the theoretical argument. It is very important, however, to make clear that much of the analysis is on a very high level of abstraction; many exceptions and qualifications are apparent on more concrete levels. Throughout this book an attempt has been made to highlight dominant patterns and features, but also to occasionally point to some of the counter-processes and recessive structures present in all complex cultures. Let us now consider some of these complexities with respect to the features of eschatologies.

The Complexities of Alternative and Counter-Structures

We have been identifying the dominant themes in Hindu eschatologies and tracing out their links to features of the social structure. Most religious doctrines, though, attempt to cope with human dilemmas and paradoxes that are, in any final sense, insoluble within the historical empirical world. Predictably, many doctrines contain ambiguities, and alternative interpretations emerge; sometimes these are in significant ways contradictory. Or one doctrinal theme may be emphasized at the expense of some other. Not surprisingly, this often results in alternative or counter-doctrines. At other times, the emphasized themes are honored in the breach. More accurately, they are applied with considerable flexibility and inconsistency—giving counter-values and themes the opportunity to be expressed. With respect to samsara, karma, and moksa, each of these counter-processes exists.

From Samsara to Moksa

The most obvious example of a counter-doctrine is, of course, the development of the notion of moksa that alleviates the fate of endless reincarnation. The counterposing of samsara and moksa creates an eschatology that emphasizes both the continuation of individual identity, and the desirability of ending individual identity;

continual transformation of one's status, and ultimately the merger of one's status into primal quiescence. These doctrines are not logically contradictory, because the one process supposedly precedes the other in sacral time.

The process of transformation does not stop here. As we have seen, the content of moksa also varies, with many bhakti groups emphasizing some notion of heaven and perpetually being in the presence of the deity rather than the Vedanta notion of merger with the divine.

Karma and the Transfer of Merit and Sin

In the introduction to a landmark collection of essays on karma, O'Flaherty (1983:ix–xxv) notes that much of the debate centers around the notion of merit transfer. Merit transfer is primarily a Buddhist rather than a Hindu concept; it is virtually never used in Hinduism. The content of the notion, however, is implicit in Hinduism. This is evident in the postfuneral sraddha rites in which the son transfers merit to his dead father. The idea is also central to the relationship between Brahmans and other castes (see especially Parry 1980, 1985a, 1985b, 1986, 1989b). Marriott's transactional approach to understanding Hinduism implies that karma— thus merit, sin, impurity, and other qualities—can be transferred from one person to another. Buddhism, of course, elaborates the theme, and some traditions make the transfer of merit from the monk (*bhikku*) to the laity a central feature of its religious life. According to Karl Potter, this is only part of the story. He identifies two traditions within Hinduism, and while one of these allows for the transfer of karma, the other tradition—what he calls the philosophical tradition—specifically rejects and denies this possibility. Within the Hindu tradition, this is most obvious in the philosophical schools (*darsanas*) of Samkhya-Yoga and Advaita Vedanta. As Potter says, "In either system one's bondage or liberation is something he himself has to earn; he cannot give away his karma to someone else, even to God. The texts sometimes comment on the untenability of any view which implies that one person might experience the results of another person's actions" (1983:263). In the broader Indian tradition, the Jains are even more adamant that karma is due solely to one's own actions and cannot in any sense be transferred.

According to O'Flaherty (1983:4), this and other ambivalences are present in the very earliest religious texts, so the question of which tradition came first is moot. It is probably most accurate to treat these as dialectically related. The notion of individual responsibility without the transfer of karma and sin can be seen as the ideologically dominant theme for most orthodox Brahmans, but the notion of transfer is quite legitimate within many traditions and de facto is central to Hindu life.

The relationship between these two ideas is not dissimilar to the relationship between grace and works in Christian theology. In virtually all Christian traditions, grace is the dominant concept at the most basic ideological level. Nonetheless, some level of conformity to what is defined as basic morality is central to the day-to-day life of those who are active members of a Christian church. Salvation depends on grace and faith rather than works (e.g., Romans 3), but "faith without works is dead" (James 2:17). Within the Christian tradition churches and movements vary enormously in the degree to which they emphasize the significance of works and moral conformity. Often the ideas of grace and works become intertwined and even confused—with the latter becoming a key sign or component of the former. The same seems to be true within the Hindu tradition with respect to karma and merit transfer.

Karma and Fate

In our previous discussion, karma was a process that, in Weber's (1968:chap. 6) and Obeyesekere's (1968, 1980) terminology, ethicized the totality of existence. In the long run, each action produces its just reward or punishment, or more accurately its appropriate fruit (*phal*). Of special significance, the worldly status one will have in subsequent incarnations is in large measure determined by the actions of one's past lives. The concept is more general, however, for in some versions of the doctrine all aspects of good fortune and, especially, misfortune are also the result of one's previous actions. From this perspective, the law of karma provides a rigorously moralistic view of human existence that makes an individual totally responsible for his or her own destiny. Such a view can be interpreted as the ideal-type concept of free will and human responsibility.

No society attributes the individual's fortunes and misfortunes solely to his or her own actions. Outcomes in the empirical world are too complex and uncertain to make such a world view credible or tolerable. Free will and individual responsibility are to some degree always qualified. In contemporary language, behavior is the outcome not only of individual human agency, but also of social structure and contingency. Thus, when the doctrine of karma approaches the ideal-type example of individual responsibility and free will, other concepts will be used to qualify this view. Concepts develop to give some credence to structure and contingency—that is, to the determining effects of human relationships and to what might be variously viewed as chance, luck, fate, divine providence, or the play (lila) of the gods. While the precise concepts used to represent these ideas in South Asia vary by region and time period, the key issues can be identified by relating the doctrine of karma to the notions of fate (*daiva*).

In my theoretical terms, karma is analogous to status by conformity to norms; the analogy of fate is less straightforward, for it involves elements of both contingency and determinism. Similarly, most social science theories are probablistic and assume an element of contingency and indeterminacy, which is a key element in the notion of fate. What sociologists would call structural effects parallel the aspects of fate that stress impersonal determinism; for example, in traditional Hindu culture, Untouchables are assumed to be inferior. The contingency element of fate is often expressed in South Asia by the concept of lila, the play of the gods—something beyond comprehension or prediction. The determinacy element is often expressed in South India by the notion of head writing (*talai eruttu*).[11]

The matter is, however, considerably more complex. The notion of karma as free will and ultimate justice is not only qualified by the introduction of additional concepts such as merit transfer, fate, and head writing; the concept of karma itself has multiple meanings and interpretations, many of which significantly qualify the implication of free will. Some, in fact, imply nearly complete determinism. O'Flaherty notes, "As is apparent from the Puranic materials, too, karma and fate (*vidhi, niyati,* or *daivam*) are sometimes equated and sometimes explicitly contrasted" (1983:xxiii). To complicate matters even more, the actors in a given situation often define and use these terms and ideas in significantly different ways depending on the social context. As Sheryl Daniel concludes, after her exploration of the Tamil concepts related to such notions as karma, fate, and head writing, "although I began with an apparently simple problem—to explicate the villager's beliefs concerning fate—I discovered not just one composite cultural understanding of 'fate' but diverse perspectives and variations on these perspectives" (1983:60). Her informants picked and chose between the various concepts to suit the particular purposes of the moment. Equally significant, their nonchalance about consistency reflected the larger Hindu world view and especially the concept of lila—the play of the gods.

Generalizations and Qualifications

Initially I discussed Hindu eschatology and soteriology in terms of generalized definitions of samsara, karma, and moksa and attempted to show how they could be understood as structural reversals of the central features of the caste system. In the preceding section I have tried—in a still very summary fashion—to qualify and elaborate the content of these three notions. Obviously, the same process could be carried out for what I termed the "central features of the caste system." I have attempted to do this with respect to variations in patterns of marriage alliances in Chapter 11. The extensive list of literature on caste cited earlier provides ample evidence of elaborations and qualifications for all of the central features that I mentioned.

However, the crucial point is that these qualifications do not invalidate the generalizations I have outlined—for example, the general characterizations of karma cited earlier (Kane 1977; Mahony 1987). The apparent discrepancies involve different levels of analysis. Perhaps an analogy that was drawn on earlier will clarify the nature of the argument. In the contemporary United States, equality of opportunity is a central ideological doctrine, that is proclaimed as a legitimate principle by conservatives and liberals alike. Moreover, compared to most societies, past and present, the social structure in the United States provides a relatively high level of equality of opportunity. To make such an argument is not to say American social structure matches the ideology of equality of opportunity; ascribed characteristics and class structures are obviously highly significant in creating differential life chances. Nor is it to argue that "equality of opportunity" means only one thing. Different individuals and groups are often bitterly divided over what concretely constitutes equality of opportunity. In fact, the concept can be used to mean precisely the opposite thing for contending groups. The contemporary debates in the United States over affirmative action or in India over reserved school and government positions for disadvantaged castes are good examples; in both cases, some people claim that meaningful equality of opportunity requires the assignment of positions on the basis of ascribed characteristics, which traditionally have been considered the essence of inequality of opportunity. A similar example of ambiguity involves the inheritance of private property by children. Such inheritance is clearly the perpetuation of privilege based on ascription. Rarely, however, do Americans consider this a violation of equality of opportunity. Stated in general terms, there are ambiguities and contradictions, as well as alternative and counter-structures, with respect to our cultural ideas about equality of opportunity and property.

Despite these significant qualifications, it is still accurate to say that, in broad historical and comparative perspective, equality of opportunity is a central ideological tenet and structural feature of the United States, and that it is much more important there than in South Africa or seventeenth-century France. In Dumont's (1980) terminology, in the United States equality of opportunity encompasses other concepts at the ideological level.

It is this type of generalization that is being made when I characterize samsara, karma, and moksa as central religious tenets of Hindu eschatology. This is also the case when the central features of the caste system are summarized as prohibition of mobility, ascription, and a preoccupation with differentiating identities. Finally, a similar generalization is implied when these two sets of phenomena—the key doctrines of Hinduism and the key structural features of caste—are identified as structural reversals of one another. To use such abstractions is not to deny the complexities, but to create the intellectual tools needed to see patterns of deep structure.

Christian Eschatology and Social Structure

Even if the arguments just made about Hinduism are correct, the question remains whether such reversals are also characteristic of other religious traditions. To address this question in a very preliminary way, I will now attempt a brief analysis of Christian eschatology, more specifically of the dominant features of Calvinism, medieval Catholicism, and Lutheranism.

Calvinism and Bourgeois Capitalism

In *The Protestant Ethic and the Spirit of Capitalism,* Weber argued that Calvinist theology played a role in the development of modern bourgeois capitalism. Since the publication of Weber's essay in 1904, his thesis has been more or less continuously debated. The unique role of Calvinism has been questioned (Tawney 1960). When a close association between Calvinism and early bourgeois capitalism has been granted, debate has continued over both the causal direction and the mechanisms that mediate the relationship (Little 1969; Poggi 1983). The analysis that follows does not speak to the adequacy or inadequacy of the various arguments suggested by Weber and his commentators; it brackets the question of the precise mechanisms that might connect Calvinism with bourgeois capitalism. Instead, the focus is on how such a correlation might be predicted on the basis of theoretical ideas about the relationship between social structure and eschatology in general— rather than the specific details of how Calvinism might have contributed to the development of capitalism. Such an approach is not a substitute for the identification of specific historical linking mechanisms, much less a rejection of such analyses. It is a different kind of analysis, that provides a more general context for the analysis of specific mechanisms.

The key features of capitalist social structure, as portrayed in conventional ideology, are almost the opposite of those found in Hindu society. In principle, mobility across class lines is legitimate and held up as an ideal. Second, the assignment of status is in principle based upon conformity and performance—primarily in economic activities—and not on association and ascription. Third, in principle, most social groups have permeable boundaries and are based upon such notions as "free choice," "free labor," and "voluntary associations." This is true in the realm of marriage, occupation, and public organizations. All differentiation of social identities is supposedly secondary to the one common identity, citizenship in a particular nation-state.[12] Moreover, all collectivities are of lesser value than the individual; the last vestiges of holism are replaced by a nearly unqualified individualism.[13] In the contemporary United States, the discourse about these matters is conceptualized primarily as an issue of equality of opportunity. Of course, considerable stratification, ascription, exclusiveness of social associations, and the creation and maintenance of differentiated ranked identities are present in actual capitalist societies; these are, however, counter to key ideological ideals of the system.

When we compare this ideology with Calvinist eschatology, we find almost a precise reversal.[14] The world-to-come is an absolute caste system: there are the eternally damned and the elect, and the former can never become the latter or vice versa. Second, the most famous characteristic of Calvinist theology is the doctrine of predestination: whether one is damned or elected to salvation is totally a matter of God's choice and has nothing to do with one's conformity or merit; at the moment of creation, God decides who is predestined for damnation and who is predestined for salvation. Calvin makes it clear that salvation is totally a matter of ascription when he denies any role to God's foreknowledge: God does not decide who is to be saved because he knows how people will behave during the course of their life (see, especially, Calvin 1960:3.21.5). Salvation is solely a matter of grace.[15] The logic and intent of the doctrine of predestination is to establish and secure a concept of God as totally other and as completely immune to manipulation by humans. This is, of course, the third key characteristic of Calvinist theology in general and Calvinist eschatology in particular: the absolute differentiation and distinction between God and humans. Any notion that salvation involves union or merging with God, that human and divine identities are ultimately the same, is the worst kind of heresy. This emphasis on the absolute differentiation of profane and sacred identities is further indicated by the rejection of any concept of intermediary sacred beings, such as saints.[16] Human roles and identities may be fluid and permeable in the capitalist world, but in the Calvinist heaven they are absolutely fixed and differentiated. In sum, key features of Calvinist eschatology are, in at least some key respects, the reverse image of the ideological ideals of a bourgeois capitalist social order.

Feudalism and Medieval Catholicism

Hinduism and Calvinism represent traditions at opposite poles of the variations observed in complex religions. Moreover, each emerged in their own historical and cultural milieu; the influence of one on the other was virtually nonexistent until well into the eighteenth century. This is obviously not so for Calvinism and medieval Catholicism; the former was one of the cultural offshoots of the latter. Therefore, the analysis of the latter should indicate whether our hypothesis is applicable to variations within a common religious tradition other than Hinduism.

The argument should be easily anticipated: European feudal society and medieval Catholicism form an intermediate case, with respect to both social structure and eschatology. In most periods and areas of feudalism, a relatively formal (but by no means unambiguous) distinction exists between lords and vassals, and between the aristocracy and the peasantry.[17] The elaborateness and formality of everyday social inequalities are not as great as in the Hindu caste system, but they are significantly greater than those characteristic of bourgeois capitalism. The same is true with respect to the possibility and means of mobility. Ascription and association through kinship and vassalage are dominant, but conformity and achievement are not completely rejected as a means of mobility to higher statuses. For example, the priesthood was in principle always open to those of low status origins, which certainly has never been the case in Hinduism. Finally, while the maintenance of traditional social identities was often important, it was never developed to the degree characteristic of Indian civilization. Notions of pure and aristocratic blood were common, but extensive rules of pollution and separation were not characteristic of European feudal society; most strata could, and on occasion did, take the sacrament of communion together as a symbol of their religious equality.[18]

In a similar vein, when we turn to eschatology, we find an intermediate case. Notions of eternal damnation and eternal salvation are present, but the world-to-come also has a "middle class," or more accurately an interregnum: most souls first enter purgatory, where they suffer until they have paid for their sins. While the perpetual mobility of samsara is absent, mobility from purgatory to heaven is a crucial feature of the world-to-come. The greatest poem of this period, Dante's *Divine Comedy*, is centrally concerned with the stratification of the afterlife and more specifically with mobility from purgatory to heaven.

Second, while in principle all salvation is by grace, human conformity and effort are officially recognized as a key determinant of one's final fate. This is clearly indicated by the Thomist distinction between venial and mortal sins; the latter deprives the soul of sanctifying grace. Not only is conformity to moral norms emphasized, but conformity to the ritual requirements laid down by the Church are essential to salvation; outside the Church and its sacraments, salvation is impossible. Human efforts can even affect the length of suffering to be endured by those already in purgatory. Not unlike the sraddha rituals in Hinduism, where the merit of the son is passed back to deceased ancestors, the indulgence system of medieval Catholicism made it possible for the ritual actions of survivors to affect the suffering of the deceased. By praying for the deceased, and even better by paying for the clergy to conduct such prayers, the punishments of purgatory could be shortened. The role of conformity is not as complete here as in a fully consistent doctrine of karma, but it is a far cry from the complete ascription characteristic of the doctrine of predestination.

Finally, the differentiation of the identity of humans and the deity is more ambiguous. The high God and the typical soul are points on a hierarchy of gradation. Heaven is populated with saints, angels, archangels, and the Virgin Mary, as well as

Christ. Humans do not merge with God, but by becoming saints they can attain a degree of divinity, and by doing this become mediators between humans and God. A few subtraditions of Catholic mysticism come close to the notion of the union of human and divine identities. In short, Catholicism does not envision salvation as the union of the human and the divine, but neither does it insist on the absolute distinction so important to Calvinism.

The increasing emphasis on purgatory, and the corollary notion that salvation must be achieved, was paralleled by an increasing emphasis on ascription in the worldly stratification system; in the twelfth to the fourteenth centuries, both purgatory and the transformation of the nobility into a legal class came to fruition (see Bloch 1964:2:xxiv; Le Goff 1984). Inheritance and birth became more important to the worldly stratification system, while one's place in the world-to-come was increasingly tied to elaborate calculations about one's sins and the actions necessary to offset them. Stated another way, the hypothesis seems to hold for changes over time within Catholicism as well as for the contrast between Catholicism and Calvinism. Possibly variations by region also existed.[19]

I have referred to medieval Catholicism as an "intermediate case." By this I mean that significant elements of achievement and ascription affect the rewards of both this world and the next. Such cases have an interesting feature: the structure of the other world seems to closely parallel the structure of this world. It is probably an analytical mistake to see this as simply the reproduction of this world in the next. Even in such cases, significant elements of reversal are present; if nothing else, the location of specific individuals often changes; "the first become last." The structure may be modelled after the existing social world, but the whole intent is to redistribute rewards on the basis of spiritual merit. As McDannell and Lang note, "Simple, undifferentiated equality did not satisfy the medieval . . . sense of justice. Rank in heaven involved reward to those who followed a life not of pride and conquest, but of spiritual purity" (1988:77). Other worlds frequently copy many elements of this world, but rarely do they simply reproduce the inequalities of this world.[20]

Lutheranism and the "Two Kingdoms"

Lutheranism is an intermediate case between medieval Catholicism and Calvinism, both historically and theologically. Explaining why Lutheranism differs from Calvinism and Catholicism is explaining a smaller range of variation and therefore is a still more rigorous test of our hypothesis.

At the core of Luther's theology is the Word of God as found in the Bible; this makes possible the believer's personal relationship with Jesus Christ, which, in turn, provides the gift of grace and salvation. Central to Luther's ethical and social thought is the notion of two kingdoms: one in which the power of the Word is supreme and one in which the sword still reigns. The Christian must live in both realms, but the first is an anticipation of what is to come. This notion of being in but not of the world has obvious antecedents in Christian thought. Paul and Augustine are the two most famous examples, and both had a profound influence on Luther's thinking. For Luther, Christian freedom is largely restricted to the realm of the conscience. As Luther says in *A Commentary on St. Paul's Epistle to the Galatians*:

> This is that liberty whereby Christ hath made us free, not from an earthly bondage, from the Babylonical captivity [an allusion not only to the exile of the ancient Hebrews, but also to papal dominance of Luther's time] or from the tyranny of the Turks, but from God's everlasting wrath. And where is this done? In the conscience. There resteth our liberty, and goeth no farther. For Christ has made us free, not civilly, nor carnally, but divinely. (n.d. [1535]:442)

The primary implication was the right of the individual Christian to read and interpret the Word, not political or worldly freedom per se. Accordingly, each individual had two relatively well-defined identities. As Christians, all were one in Christ. In the world, however, each person had a station that was to be accepted and faithfully performed as part of God's creation and as one's own divine calling. More often than not, this notion of the two kingdoms and two identities resulted in a social and political ethic supportive of the status quo. As Troeltsch argues, this does not mean Lutheran theology and ethics were intended as a defense of the status quo (1931:569–76). In fact when Luther uses the idea (though not the precise label) of the two kingdoms in one of his early works, *An Open Letter to the Christian Nobility of the German Nation* (1943), it is intended as a radical critique of the papacy's usurpation of civil authority. But the historical product of the concept was a passivity compatible with a wide variety of social and political structures. As Troeltsch notes:

> In the Imperial towns it glorified aristocratic-republican rule. In Wuttemberg, where there was no corresponding nobility, although it held the ruling prince in all honor, it did not hinder bourgeois and peasant democratic ideas, but even fused itself with them. In the military national State of Sweden it justified the aggressive policy of Gustavus Adolfus, and in the class struggles in the Austrian territories it justified the rise of Lutheran nobility; in Denmark and Norway a very firmly established peasant democracy is to-day [*sic*] united most closely with a sturdy Lutheranism, which is certainly tinged with Pietism; and in America the most orthodox Lutheranism one can imagine flourishes under the wing of democracy. (1931:574–75)

Troeltsch's book was published in 1911, and subsequent events reveal Lutheranism's compatibility with both Nazi Germany and social democratic Sweden. Within the contemporary United States, Lutheranism is associated with both the social and the political conservatism of midwestern Missouri Synod Lutherans and the liberalism and social democratic inclinations of Minnesota's Democratic-Farmer-Labor party. In short, Lutheranism has had little specific to say about the content of the political and social structure and has in fact been associated with a wide variety of stratification and political systems.

A caveat is required. Luther himself and Lutheranism in general have tended to emphasize the importance of love for one's neighbor in interpersonal relationships. Luther was therefore suspicious of urbanism and the impersonality of market transactions. So Lutheranism has had a special affinity with small-landowner agrarian societies. But where economic or political processes have created other class and economic structures, Lutherans have accepted or at least tolerated them. As Troeltsch says, "Thus Lutheranism is inclined to endure existing conditions humbly

and patiently, even when they are bad and to glorify them when they agree with . . .
earlier ideals" (1931:573).

If Lutheranism has relatively little to say about what constitutes a legitimate
distribution of responsibilities and rewards in this world, and has, in fact, been associated with a wide variety of political systems and patterns of inequality, it is also
relatively silent and indifferent about the details of eschatology.[21] Arguing that a religious ideology's silence and ambiguity on one matter is a predictor of silence and
ambiguity about another matter is, by itself, a rather weak argument. When placed
in our broader theoretical and comparative context, though, predicting silence and
ambiguity is a not unimportant analytical accomplishment.

Lutheranism and Calvinism are more clearly distinguishable in another way.
The core of the difference is found in the doctrine of perseverance.[22] For Calvinism,
those who have been elected to salvation can never fall from grace; they have, as
the Westminster Confession says, "the assurance of grace and salvation."[23] In the
parlance of later theological debates, "Once saved, always saved." In Lutheranism,
on the other hand, though salvation is wholly due to the grace of God and not to
human efforts, humans can reject God's redemptive gift and fall from grace. As the
Augsburg Confessions says, "Rejected here are those who teach that persons who
have once become godly cannot fall again" (Tappert 1959:35). Therefore, salvation
is continually problematic for the Lutheran. The danger is accentuated because the
Lutheran must live in the "two kingdoms." Potentially, a preoccupation with upward mobility or the exercise of power in the worldly kingdom is a threat to one's
salvation; with success and power goes arrogance and with arrogance, the tempta-
tion to reject God's grace. The Word can be heard only by those with a troubled
conscience. Consequently, the safest thing is dutiful acceptance of, but indifference
to, the content of the worldly kingdom.

To conclude, we have another identifiable structural reversal. While
Lutheranism emphasizes God's sovereignty and grace over human free will, ultimately the deity's sovereignty is limited; people can refuse to accept God's redeem-
ing gift and lose their salvation. One's eternal fate is not fixed; spiritual mobility is
possible. The possibility of spiritual mobility is associated with a severe suspicion of
worldly mobility or political rebellion. This contrasts with Calvinism's spiritual immobility and more positive attitude toward social mobility and political activism.[24]

It could be argued that the reversal of an ambiguous and ambivalent attitude
about stratification would be an otherworldly structure that was highly explicit and
precise. The argument, however, is that the *content* of the worldly stratification
system is likely to be reversed. Since the types of stratification with which
Lutheranism has been associated are relatively variable, and Lutheranism has been
largely indifferent about such variations, there is no consistent pattern that can be
reversed. Accordingly, Lutherans have been relatively indifferent about eschatology, thus it tends to be undeveloped and inconsistent.

A postscript is in order: the content of the contrasts between Lutheranism and
Calvinism parallel those between Calvinism and Hinduism, though obviously the differences between the former pair are much more limited and subtle. This is additional
evidence that we are dealing with an underlying process rather than happenstance.

Cultural Analysis, Structuralism, and Generalizations

Recent cultural analysis has tended to emphasize more concrete units of analysis, engage in more complex forms of interpretive analysis, and be suspicious of—if not eschew—efforts to create systematic generalizations.[25] By drawing on a version of structural analysis, I have tried to show that broad comparisons can suggest patterns that more fine-grained analyses might miss. Wuthnow, however, has claimed that (Lévi-Straussian) structural analysis "in no way succeeds in generating positivistic knowledge," is "inevitably interpretive," and that "the kinds of symbolic boundaries on which attention has focused are clearly theoretical constructs rather than intrinsic attributes of the data" (1987:96).

The findings of the preceding analysis seem to call this conclusion into question. My claim is that there are detectable patterns that are not solely the result of the theoretical perspective. In my opinion, like all knowledge, the patterns detected are rooted in *both* theoretical constructs and attributes of the data. It is not, I think, fruitful to draw an absolute distinction between positivistic and interpretive frames of reference, and then force all our sociological knowledge to fit into one or the other.

Sociology does not have to produce iron laws in order to be scientific or create useful—though usually qualified—generalizations. The foregoing analysis is on a high level of abstraction; accordingly, many exceptions and qualifications are apparent on more concrete levels. For example, as already indicated, the detailed analyses carried out in recent years show that karma means many things and is used in many different ways. Nonetheless, the general characterizations cited earlier (Berger 1967; Kane 1977; Mahony 1987) are not incorrect; the apparent discrepancies involve different levels of analysis.

The foregoing analysis has provided considerable opportunity for my hypothesis to be invalidated, and this has not occurred. Thus it seems fair to conclude that the proposition is worthy of further research and investigation. Obviously, additional analyses are needed, especially of other world religions. Undoubtedly eschatologies exist that do *not* follow this precise pattern (Lang 1989).

Two analytic tasks remain. One is to identify the conditions under which this pattern is likely to be found. This must, of course, await the analysis of additional cases. The second is to specify the intervening mechanism connecting the structural reversals. We now turn to that task.

The Question of Why

The Usual Suspects

Why do at least some eschatologies tend to be structural reversals of the ideological images of worldly stratification systems? Two standard interpretations come to mind. According to Lévi-Strauss (1963, 1966) the human mind operates on the basis of dualistic contrasts, such as structural reversals. Supposedly, the patterns identified are simply the playing-out of a kind of cultural algebra rooted in the way the human mind works. The details of what Lévi-Strauss is arguing are open to ambiguity and debate, not to mention the validity of his arguments (see, e.g., Leach 1974). Yet clearly his notions focus on the cognitive aspects of how the human mind works.

The second and most obvious interpretation is that eschatologies provide psychic compensation for the deprivations experienced in this world. This interpretation is still in some respects rooted in psychological processes, but here the emphasis is on emotion rather than cognition. This is the answer suggested by a long line of thought that includes Feuerbach, Marx, and Freud—and, in a more complicated way, Durkheim and Weber—and has been articulated most recently by Stark and Bainbridge (1980, 1985). This explanation is in many respects plausible, but it has been criticized on a number of grounds.[26]

The Nature of Status as a Resource

It seems highly likely that at some point, the reversals we have described involve psychological processes involving the human mind, but such processes are almost certainly conditioned by the structural and cultural context in which people operate. Therefore, without denying the potential significance of psychological processes, I want to point to the more structural considerations suggested by the theoretical perspective that has guided this study.

If we take into account the nature of status as a resource, we would expect other worlds—that is, worlds that are conceived of as something different and beyond the mundane empirical world—to often have characteristics that are reversals of the features of the mundane world. It is, of course, logically possible for people to imagine an afterlife or other world that primarily reproduces the current structure, or one in which all share equally in the delights of heaven.[27] Most complex cultures follow neither of these paths. Typically, people's fates in the afterlife or other world are differentiated—for example, some go to "heaven" and some go to "hell." When this is the case, then the nature of status means that there will tend to be reversals. More specifically, because status is relatively inalienable in any given world—whether natural or supernatural—mobility is most likely to occur during the transition from this world to the other world. In Turner's (1969) terms, this is a key moment of liminality and antistructure, and thus transformation is possible. Because status is relatively inexpansible, such mobility usually means that some move up and some move down. The most extreme form of this implies that "the first shall be last."

Finally, if such mobility is to occur, and there is some sense of people's identity in this world being carried over into the next, then the means of status attainment and mobility usually must change. If the same criteria of stratification are used, the old structure will simply be reproduced. Hence, what typically happens is that the relative emphasis on conformity and association are reversed. For example, societies that are highly moralistic about conforming to the rules of this world are likely to emphasize grace and the connection with some savior as the means of salvation.

I want to stress that this type of structural explanation is not a substitute for the questions having to do with how the human mind operates. Nor does it explain why the more extreme alternatives (simply copying the present world, or totally rejecting any notion of otherworldly stratification) do not occur. But if the other world is conceived of as stratified, either in its admission criteria or in its internal structure, then taking into account the characteristics of status gives us considerable insight into why reversals are to be expected. In sum, while the theory leaves important questions unanswered, it is useful in helping us to understand the patterning of the social phenomena, whether in this world or the next.

Finally, it is certainly true that some features of other worlds will parallel rather than reverse the features of this world; not even other worlds are created de novo. My hypothesis is that where societies are significantly stratified and where religions attempt to develop the commitment of the masses, there will be strong tendencies toward reversals. Moreover, some of the cases that on first glance appear to be parallels rather than reversals—for example, medieval Catholic eschatology—on more careful examination contain elements of reversal or are influenced by pressures for reversal.

Compensation Theory Reconsidered: A Postscript

As I indicated, compensation theory has been criticized on a number of grounds. The analysis carried out here has special implications for two aspects of such theorizing. First, as indicated in the previous chapter, not all of the otherworldly reversals are viewed as a positive outcome. For example, repeated reincarnation, which is the reversal of no mobility, is not viewed as a reward—at least in the writings of religious elites. Even reincarnation into a significantly improved status is still defined as being bound to the suffering inherent in worldly existence. Hence, eschatological reversals are not always compensatory.

Second, and more important, the direction of causation is less clear-cut than is often assumed. From Feuerbach to Stark and Bainbridge, the usual assumption is that conditions in the empirical world cause humans to create in their imagination a world-to-come that provides compensations for the frustrations and deprivations of this world. Supposedly, when major changes occur in this world, the image of the other world changes accordingly—though it may take centuries for these transformations to play themselves out. Undoubtedly, this is often and perhaps even usually the case. The question is whether at times the direction of causation is, in part, reversed. Do the strains and contradictions projected into the other world sometimes create anxieties and frustrations, and do people seek to alleviate and compensate for these by changing their worldly behavior—and does this ever occur on a significant enough scale to produce changes in the patterns of social structure?

Protestantism and Capitalism

The classic attempt to address this question is, of course, Weber's *The Protestant Ethic and the Spirit of Capitalism* (1958a). Earlier we eschewed the debate over the causal mechanisms linking Calvinism and capitalism. Now we must return to the issue, not to attempt to solve the complex historical questions, but as a way of asking whether compensation theories of religion are too unidirectional in their assumptions. Weber's analysis is rather complex (see, e.g., Poggi 1983), but the core of the argument concerns the anxieties and frustrations produced by a particular eschatology and soteriology and, more specifically, Calvin's doctrine of predestination. The individual's ultimate destination—salvation or damnation—is, according to Calvin, determined by God at the moment of creation. A person can do nothing to influence his or her eternal fate. Consequently all moral bookkeeping and calculations about the consequences of human behavior are irrelevant to salvation. Weber claims that

> this doctrine must above all have had one consequence for the life of a generation which surrendered to its magnificent consistency. That was a feeling of unprecedented inner loneliness of the single individual. In what was for the man of the age of the Reformation the most important thing in life, his eternal salvation, he was forced to follow his path alone to meet a destiny which had been decreed for him from eternity. (1958a:104)

In the terminology used here, contingency and powerlessness over the future world produced an anxiety that resulted in compensating behavior in this world. If the other world was a completely ascribed system over which humans had no influence, this world was to become an achievement-oriented system driven by the power of human efforts. If calculation about one's eternal fate in the other world was impossible and irrelevant, the calculation of profit in this world was to become the essence of bourgeois life. In sum, the core of Weber's argument can be conceptualized as compensation theory "standing on its head."

Religious Renunciation and Caste Hierarchy

Such a perspective may also be helpful in understanding the development of the caste system in India. Elements and rudiments of caste are reported in the earliest religious texts of India. Some evidence suggest that Buddhism and other heterodoxies were in part a response to an increase in inequality and rigidity of the social structure. Nonetheless, the "classical" caste system did not become fully developed until the new Brahmanical synthesis that gradually emerged between 200 B.C.E. and 900 C.E. (Hopkins 1971; Brockington 1981). A key antecedent, and possibly stimulus, to this emergence was the thought of the Upanisads and some of the religious heterodoxies, such as Buddhism. Despite the enormous differences between and within these religious traditions, the essence of salvation for them is the superseding of individual identity, the merger of the divine and the profane. The key to attaining such salvation is the development of disciplined detachment from both the social and physical world. The lone renouncer is held up as the religious ideal. Only a small elite has any possibility of attaining salvation—though because of the doctrine of reincarnation (samsara), others may be able to eventually become members of this elite. It is at least conceivable that such visions of the other world could have created pressures for compensating patterns in this world. If the other world was seen as unity and nonidentity, differentiated hierarchy might be found appealing in this world. If salvation required the destruction of social relationships, their importance might take on added significance in the profane realm. If only a small elite had any possibility of escape to the divine, a system that integrates all levels of religious status—however unequally they might be treated—might be found appealing. In short, the fully developed caste system can be conceived of as a reversal of the eschatologies and soteriologies that preceded it in time—as, in part, compensating responses to the anxieties and contradictions of the imagined other world. Of course, this must be considered only a tentative hypothesis, and if such factors played a role, it was almost certainly a supplementary one. Nonetheless, this suggests a revision of compensation theories in order to take into account the possibility of causality operating in more than one direction. Thus the theory of status relations can also help to clarify issues that emerge from other theoretical perspectives.

Appendix: A Note on the Sociology of Religious Ideology

Considerable scholarly literature has appeared in recent years concerning the nature of religious ideology and, more generally, the sociology of culture. A few remarks about the relationships of the argument presented here and this literature are in order.

A classic sociological conundrum is how to adequately portray the relationship between ideas and actions. On the macro level, this concerns the relationship between cultural forms and social structure. This relationship is, of course, a recurring theme in the sociological classics, and has received renewed attention from contemporary sociologists (e.g., Swidler 1985; Wuthnow 1987; Zaret 1989; Hunter 1991). One key example is the link between the otherworldly religious ideology and worldly social structures, for example, the relationship between stratification in heaven and stratification on earth. Feuerbach, Marx, and Freud saw the images of the afterlife expressed in religious ideologies as psychological compensations for the deprivations of worldly existence; they differed over whether the deprivations were inevitable or the result of particular social arrangements or psychological experiences. Weber is most famous for his Protestant ethic thesis suggesting that the content of religious ideology could shape social structure. But in his more general argument in *Economy and Society*, salvation religions often provide psychological compensations to the lower classes and legitimating ideologies for the upper classes—that is, structure shapes ideology (1968:490–92). Durkheim emphasizes the sui generis nature of sociological explanation, he does not explicitly embrace a compensatory theory of religion. Nonetheless, he sees the primary influence running from social structure to culture, more specifically from ritual to beliefs: patterned rituals revitalize sacred beliefs. In his sociology of knowledge, he makes the even stronger claim that cultural concepts in general (including knowledge) tend to be modeled after the patterns of social relationships found in the society. Swanson has elaborated this Durkheimian theme into what might be called a correspondence theory of religious beliefs. In books dealing with primitive and ancient societies (1964) and regimes during the Reformation (1967), as well as related articles, Swanson has attempted to demonstrate that various features of religious ideology are correlated with the type of social structure present in the society. Swanson's work has stimulated considerable research

and discussion (see, e.g., O'Toole et al. 1984), but some of his results have been questioned and qualified by subsequent analyses (e.g., Bouwsma 1968; Underhill 1975;
Simpson 1979).

There is also a tradition within the sociology of religion that is critical of the
strong positivistic assumptions in Swanson's work. Berger (1967) and Bellah (1970)
have been the most prominent advocates of a more interpretive approach to sociology in general, and the analysis of religious ideology in particular. While their work
has been enormously influential, they have been criticized for failing to carry out
systematic empirical research (Wuthnow 1987)—something Swanson clearly has
done. Several scholars influenced by Berger and Bellah have in recent years
attempted to meet this criticism and challenge positivistic analyses of religion by
conducting more empirically based research within the interpretive tradition.

Wuthnow (1985, 1987), for example, criticizes Swanson's work on the
Reformation on theoretical, methodological, and empirical grounds. (Moaddel
[1989] has in turn criticized Wuthnow for not adequately analyzing the effects of
class in the spread of Reformation ideology.) More generally, Wuthnow rejects
Swanson's search for lawlike regularities. He proposes a more complex, eclectic,
and interpretive approach that draws on phenomenological, (Lévi-Straussian) structural, dramaturgical, and institutional analysis. Two features of Wuthnow's argument are of special relevance. According to Wuthnow, "An advantage of this
approach is that hidden psychological affinities need not be posited as the primary
connection between social arrangements and ideologies" (1987:325). More specifically, he questions the utility of psychological theories that explain religious ideologies as compensations for deprivations experienced in worldly affairs (1987:152;
see also Swanson 1967:177).[28] While (Lévi-Straussian) structural analysis does not
rely on the psychological assumptions of compensation theory, Wuthnow, as noted
above, questions the reliability of its results:

> Even though the approach strives for observable data, it in no way succeeds in gener-
> ating positivistic knowledge. The analyst exercises discretion both in selecting the
> cultural elements on which to focus and in imposing categories on these elements.
> The kinds of symbolic boundaries on which attention has focused are clearly theoret-
> ical constructs rather than intrinsic attributes of the data. In short, structural analysis
> is inevitably interpretive. (1987:96)

In short, Wuthnow rejects or seriously questions the fruitfulness of both (Lévi-
Straussian) structural analysis and analysis that posits psychological processes.

Swidler writes, "Culture influences action not by providing the ultimate values
toward which action is oriented, but by shaping a repertoire or 'tool kit' of habits
skills, and styles from which people construct 'strategies of action'" (1985:273).
Moreover, in "settled periods" culture independently influences actions, but in "unsettled periods" structural opportunities largely influence which competing ideologies—an aspect of culture—become dominant and survive. In other words, the causal direction of influence varies for settled and unsettled periods. The Reformation
is, for example, an unsettled period, in which the important effect of Calvinist ideology was not in producing psychological anxieties about whether one was saved,

but in providing an ethos of disciplined action, which provided the method, rather than the motivation, to produce bourgeois capitalism.

Zaret has analyzed the relationship between Puritanism and democracy. He suggests that the adequate analysis of ideological patterns and change requires the consideration of additional complicating factors:

> Building on recent work in the sociology of culture, this study has outlined an analytic strategy for explaining change in ideological systems. The strategy focuses on the episodic and organizational contexts for cultural production, analyzing ideological change in terms of the interaction of intellectual *precedents* and contextual *pressures*. By treating episodic and organizational contexts as variables that mediate between ideological change and its cultural and social structural determinants, this strategy leads to subtler and more sustainable analyses than can be obtained by seeking to establish direct links to cultural and structural factors. (1989:176)

Even this cryptic survey of the literature makes one thing clear: research on the relationship between social structure and culture (and specifically religious ideology) has moved in a more empirical direction. In the process, sociologists have shifted toward (1) more concrete units of analysis and historically situated and specified processes, rather than the analysis of broad civilization-level attributes like the "Protestant ethic" and the "spirit of capitalism"; (2) a suspicion of generalizations relevant across an array of cultures and time periods; and (3) an emphasis on sociological rather than psychological processes as intervening variables between patterns of social structure and patterns of cultural ideas.

It is my methodological thesis that while these developments are in some respects laudable, they run the risk of throwing the baby out with the bath. Undoubtedly, more complex analyses are appropriate for understanding some phenomena. Nonetheless, other problems can be usefully analyzed with broad typological comparisons that are similar to Lévi-Straussian structural analyses.[29]

My substantive thesis was that for some religious traditions, key features of their eschatologies—and their related soteriologies—can be explained as structural reversals. In addition to looking for parallels, as Swanson has done, I looked for reversals or inversions.

In short, it is premature to insist on concrete historical analyses, or to dismiss either Lévi-Straussian structural analysis or psychological assumptions as means for interpreting the relationships between social structure and culture. This is not, of course, to rule out the possibility of developing more strictly sociological explanations of the patterns of reversal I have identified; it is only to report that they are not currently available.

16

Conclusions

This chapter has two purposes: first, to acknowledge some limitations of this mode of analysis; second, to recapitulate and reorganize the major arguments.

Some Limitations

Although long and complex, the analysis has been selective. To indicate all that has been left out or ignored would be a lengthy task in itself—but several limitations require comment.

The analysis that has been presented is to some degree static and ahistorical. This is not because the theoretical perspective is antihistorical, or because it is assumed that stability is more fundamental than change. It is primarily due to a lack of data. While we have a number of excellent studies of the nature of the caste system in particular times and places (e.g., Sharma 1980; Stein 1980; Ludden 1985; Dirks 1987), it is still very difficult to provide a systematic account of changes and variations over the long run. Even for the periods and areas for which we have good studies, it is often difficult to be confident about crucial issues, such as the actual extent of endogamy and commensalism. We simply cannot say with assurance that the caste system was more or less rigid in ninth-century Bihar or nineteenth-century Bihar, much less confidently compare the former with ninth-century Kerala. The key task of any science is to explain variation; this presumes the ability to reliably describe such variations. If we cannot be reasonably sure of the nature and degree of changes over time, it is usually premature to attempt to explain such changes.

In addition to data limitations, there are limits on what can be accomplished in a given book. Since an attempt to also systematically analyze change overtime (even for the limited data available) would have unduly lengthened and complicated the analysis, the focus has been on characteristics that seem to be present in most time periods that we know about. The main implications are about how this form of structuring differs from societies and groups where status is less central as a resource. Such a focus in no way means to suggest that there have been no changes, or that change does not merit analysis, or that stability and order have analytical priority over change and conflict. On occasion I have made some remarks about changes and their possible explanation, but a more extended analysis of these matters will have to await another occasion.

An ancillary limitation is that little attention has been paid to the nature of contemporary urban India. While caste still plays an important role, status is increasingly linked to education, nontraditional occupations, and income. My focus on "traditional India" is not a denial of these changes, any more than a study of race relations in the American South before 1950 would imply that this was an adequate picture of the United States in the year 2000. In both cases, a sound analysis of the "traditional" social structure would be an important aid in understanding contemporary society. My primary intent has been to contribute to this first, preparatory analytic task.

While these limitations are significant, their importance should not be exaggerated. Often "ahistorical" is used as an epithet, implying that any analysis that can be so classified is without intellectual merit. This is simply wrongheaded. To explain to someone how baseball is played, or how the U.S court system currently operates—the formal rules, the more informal stratagems, and the economic or political context—is a meaningful and useful form of explanation. Obviously, one will have a deeper understanding if one is acquainted with the history of the game or the courts, and their changing historical context. But the absence of this kind of historical information does not render the narrower form of explanation invalid; rather it is simply incomplete.

Another limitation is that this study deals almost exclusively with Hindu India. With respect to caste, this is a tolerable limitation, since status stratification is central to most other religious groups in India. The status groups found in non-Hindu India are usually less developed and elaborated than Hindu castes, but they are typically present and have many similarities. Nonetheless, this limitation must be kept in mind.

A Retrospect

The nature of writing and reading requires a linear form of presentation. When ideas are interrelated in complex ways, this necessarily involves some rather arbitrary decisions about the order in which things are introduced. I will now reiterate the key points, reorganized in a way that highlights relationships that might have been missed because of the order of exposition. The analysis has involved several different levels of argument, and it is appropriate to make these more explicit.

Theoretical Strategies

First, an argument was presented about the most fruitful strategy for contemporary sociological theory. I advocated a provisional resource structuralism. I have tried to keep the programmatic parts of the discussion to a minimum, and maximize the space given to the analysis and explanation of empirical phenomena. This means that many of the features and implications of such an approach remain undeveloped. Hopefully, it is clear that I do not mean to rule out all other approaches, but to show how at least some of these can be supplemented and strengthened. Accordingly, I have tried to show how certain parts of this analysis could be conceptualized in terms of a theory of practice and rational choice theory. These do not, of course, exhaust the possible alternatives. Advocating a provisional resource structuralism is not intended to establish a new orthodoxy. Rather, the aim is to clarify and supplement the nature of the existing orthodoxy, which sees structural characteristics and the behavior of actors as dialectically related.

The Nature of Resources and Power

More specifically, I have advocated a structuralism that focuses on variations in the nature of human resources, and especially the need to improve our conceptualization and understanding of nonmaterial resources. In order to do this, I have proposed a typology of resources and power that focuses on the variations in the nature of sanctions: force, goods and services, and expressions of approval or disapproval (Chapter 2). Each of these sanctions is the primary basis of one of the key types of power: political power, economic power, and status power. These distinctions play a crucial role in developing several subsequent parts of the analysis. For example, converting one form of power into another—such as wealth into status—is usually problematic. While such conversions occur frequently, they must usually be disguised. This suggests at least one of the reasons why implicit rather than explicit exchanges are often so central to social life and, more specifically, why gifts often play a vital role (Chapters 7, 10, and 11).

The basic typology of sanctions and power was also used to construct two supplementary typologies. The first was a typology of types of elites and nonelites, which identifies the types of relationships, tensions, and internal differentiation likely to occur in any complex society (Chapter 6). A second supplementary typology suggested the types of relationships that devotees might have with otherworldly entities such as deities: physical causation, coercion, exchange, and worship (Chapter 12). These parts of the analysis were derived from the basic typology of power. These ideas about the importance of human resources, the types of sanctions and power, and the need to improve our understanding of nonmaterial resources comprise a second level of argumentation.

A Theory of Status Relations

The third level of argument focused on what I have called a theory of status relations. (Perhaps "theory" is too grandiose a word to attach to the ideas that have been presented. Such terms as "paradigm," "framework," "conceptual scheme," or whatever would serve equally well.) It is a set of ideas intended to increase our understanding of the patterns of social relationships in situations where status is (1) a relatively important resource and (2) based on criteria other than simply the possession of wealth or political power. Within this level of the analysis, a fourth level of argument is developed. I suggested that for certain purposes, it is useful to consider both legitimacy and sacredness as special forms of status. (There is no claim that this perspective exhausts the rich implications of these two seminal concepts.) The third level, the theory of status relations, supplemented by the fourth level, forms the core of the book.

This level of the analysis has revolved around two sets of ideas. The first focuses on the characteristics of status as a resource: inalienability and inexpansibility. These ideas are actually derived from the second level of argument—that is, the typology of types of power; it is in comparison with other types of resources that status is relatively inalienable and inexpansible. These ideas provide insights into why status groups tend to be relatively stable and to restrict mobility. The notion of inalienability also suggests additional reasons why implicit exchange is important: that which cannot be legitimately appropriated must be transferred surreptitiously.

Perhaps the most fruitful ideas have been the notions of conformity and association as the key sources of status. The first concept suggests why status groups tend to elaborate and ritualize norms, especially those related to lifestyle. This is done, in part, in order to make it very difficult for outsiders to merit or counterfeit membership in the group. Elaboration also contributes to the social control of group members: Central norms and values of the group are reinforced by protecting them with layers of secondary norms and rituals. These secondary norms and rituals are often most effective when they are "coded" and only implicitly linked with the more fundamental values that they protect. Thus analysis requires "decoding."[1] Social associations, especially in intimate expressive relations, also affect status. Associations between actors with different levels of status tend to lower the status of the superior and improve the status of the inferior. This fact helps to explain the strong tendencies toward status homogeneity, the tendency toward various forms of endogamy and commensuality being the most obvious examples. An important secondary idea in the analysis of the two sources of status was that the very tendencies toward elaborate lifestyles and status homogeneity activated "recessive" counter-tendencies to bring in new blood and their wealth; exchanges and associations, including marriages, between those of unequal status thus become attractive in certain circumstances. In short, these concepts helped to explain some of the most characteristic behaviors associated with status groups.

By conceiving of legitimacy as in part the acquisition of a certain type of status and approval, the same two notions of conformity and association have provided important suggestions about the mechanisms used to gain legitimacy. One implication of these concepts is that Weber's famous typology of the types of legitimate authority may have caused sociology to place too much emphasis on conformity to customs (for traditional authority) and on the significance of law and rules (for rational-legal authority). These are, of course, important sources of legitimacy, but this emphasis may have caused us to underestimate the significance of association as a mechanism of legitimacy.

The importance of associations suggested two supplementary arguments. First, what are the alternative types of associations or coalitions that those seeking legitimacy might develop? A tentative answer suggests three ideal-type coalition partners:

superior elites from the same sector (e.g., petty rulers with superior rulers); elites from a different sector (e.g., rulers with priest, intellectuals, etc.); and subordinates (e.g., rulers with their lieutenants). We may improve our understanding of legitimacy by more systematically examining the types of associations that are important in given instances. Second, the conflation of ideas and social processes could be conceived of as a special form of association used to produce legitimacy. For example, conflating political freedom and free markets is one way to add legitimacy to both; such associations are not necessarily fallacious, but the exaggeration and manipulation of such identities is often a mechanism for gaining or maintaining legitimacy. None of these ideas are completely new, but conceiving of them in this way helps to highlight connections and issues that might otherwise be obscured.

Again, the notions of conformity and association have been central to the analysis of sacral relations. When worship is conceived of as a form of temporary status transformation of the devotee, then much of the content of worship can be seen as the momentary manipulation of certain types of conformity in order to gain association and intimacy with higher status beings. This seems to involve, primarily, three processes: various forms of purification; praise and deference toward the sacred; and communion with the sacred. While worship parallels social status processes, they are not identical when there is great social distance between the devotee and the sacred. Such otherness means that behaviors and objects considered degrading in profane contexts may become valued and uplifting in sacred contexts (e.g., eating the "leftovers" of saints and deities). The tendency of higher status devotees to use more formal forms of worship, and the sectarianism that often results, can be seen as a special case of high status groups elaborating and ritualizing their norms. It is also a matter of groups placing themselves in relationships to the sacred that tend to be the reverse of their usual relationships with other people; upper class groups offer elaborate deference to deities, while lower classes seek informal intimacy with them. When salvation is conceived of as a more permanent form of status transformation, the mechanisms of conformity and association again appear as the key alternative means to such transformation. Accordingly, many of the religious debates over soteriologies (the means to salvation) can be conceived of as arguments about the relative effectiveness of conformity and association as sources of status transformation.

In short, seeing conformity and association as the key sources of status has helped to identify a commonality between many social processes that from other perspectives are quite unrelated. These terms are, of course, closely related to the widely used notions of achievement and ascription. The terms "conformity" and "association," however, better describe what people actually do. They also suggest subsidiary processes—for example, the notions of elaboration and the regulation of intimate relationships. Moreover, they are relatively neutral and analytical in their implications rather than the more evaluative and ideological notions of achievement and ascription.[2] So while the creation of new jargon by relabelling old ideas is of little value in itself, I believe this terminological shift has considerable analytical merit.

The analysis of eschatologies drew on several of the notions introduced earlier in the analysis. The other world is seen as the structural context in which a certain type of mobility—salvation—occurs. More specifically, the analysis draws on the theory of status relations for one interpretation of why other worlds and profane worlds are sometimes related by structural reversals. Instead of focusing on psychological processes, attention is given to the nature of the resources that are distributed. The notions of the inalienability and inexpansibility of status suggest why considerable mobility may exist between this world and the next, and why the mechanisms of acquiring status—conformity and association—may be reversed. But this argument is based on the assumption that the profane society is relatively stratified and that the next world is to be significantly "other" than the present one. Obviously, some elements of other worlds parallel rather than reverse features of this world; all transformations draw on what precedes them. Moreover, there are instances of complex societies where these assumptions and the reversals they imply do not seem to operate. Certainly more cases must be studied before the conditions under which this phenomenon occurs can be carefully specified. Nonetheless, the analysis suggested by these assumptions gives us a sometimes startling glimpse of patterns and connections that have not previously been apparent.

Methodological Issues

In addition to these substantive arguments, which are assertions about the way the social world works, there have been a series of subsidiary methodological arguments. These are not about the techniques for data collection and analysis, but rather prescriptions about what kind of data to look for and how to look at it. The first of these concerns the notion of dominant patterns or processes in contrast to recessive or countervailing ones. This is, of course, an old idea. It can be dressed up as a dialectical perspective—and this may add a few additional insights—but in essence it is little more than common sense. It is simply a directive that says, where patterns or processes are especially extreme in some respect, expect there to be deviance and look for more or less opposite tendencies. In Blumer's (1986) terminology, it is a useful "sensitizing concept." Despite its obviousness and simplicity, it has been useful in organizing a wide range of data. First, it helps to anticipate that where status is relatively insulated from material forms of power, there will probably be processes that attempt to qualify or cancel this separation. Objectification is one such process (Chapter 8). Mechanical processes of purification, rather than strictly social processes, become the direct means of gaining status (Chapter 9). Second, the notion of countervailing patterns helps us see that some of the structural sources of Tantrism, with its emphasis on impurities and sexuality, are in part a reaction against the strong emphasis, in more orthodox patterns, on purity and sexual asceticism. Third, this idea helps us see why the strong tendencies toward status homogeneity in the social realm—which are the basis of isogamy and even social strata—might stimulate counter-tendencies that help to explain hypergamy. Conversely, we see why the emphasis on otherness, hierarchy, and extreme forms of deference in the sacral realm might be mitigated by notions of intimacy and communion. Finally, in the realm of religious ideology, this concept suggests why the notion of endless reincarnation might be revised and qualified with a notion of release and salvation; similarly, it suggests why the concept of all human actions producing their just deserts might be qualified by the notions of merit transfer and grace, or notions of fate and the inexplicable "play of the gods."

This form of explanation or concatenation is a rather weak one, if it simply describes two patterns that are in some respects opposites of one another. Such analyses gain strength to the degree that mechanisms and processes that contribute to the production of the reversed pattern can be specified. I have tried to provide such specifications, but the extensiveness and credibility of these kinds of arguments varies. Obviously the notion of structural reversal used to analyze eschatologies is, at least in part, a special case of this more general pattern.

A second methodological argument has been that, at least for human social behavior, there is not a hard-and-fast line between causal analysis and the interpretation of meaning (Chapter 9). This issue is controversial and complex, and a systematic defense is beyond the scope of this work. I have tried to demonstrate this point by example rather than formal argument. This idea is most relevant to the notions of decoding and, more specifically, the analyses of purity and impurity (Chapter 9) and auspiciousness and inauspiciousness (Chapter 10).

A third methodological idea has dealt with the problem of generalization and was discussed in terms of the levels of analysis. This issue is really composed of two subcomponents. The simplest issue is the analogue of variation around the mean: to argue that the typical or dominant patterns take a certain form is not to deny that there may be considerable variation from this pattern, and that it is even possible that no single case matches the hypothetical pattern precisely. This is a problem which those trained in quantitative techniques are well acquainted with, but the idea is often quite foreign to those who usually deal in more qualitative and interpretive modes of analysis. An example is the argument that the tendency toward status homogeneity in intimate expressive relations is the dominant pattern, while the tendency toward forms of heterogeneity such as hypergamy is the recessive pattern for the culture as a whole.

The second subproblem has to do with the relationship between the attributes of some macro unit and its components. An example of this phenomenon is the fact that the prohibition of birth-control devices is a crucial and important characteristic of contemporary Catholicism, and has important impacts on the modern world—even if most Catholics do not believe in or abide by this rule. Similarly, the notion of karma as a process in which everyone ultimately receives their just deserts is a crucial and important characteristic of Hinduism, even if most Hindus do not understand or believe this notion to be true, or hold inconsistent and contradictory ideas about this matter. Of course, for both Catholicism and Hinduism it would be a mistake to consider these macro factors the only relevant attributes in their respective realms; they are both nonetheless valid and important social facts for a given level of analysis.

Agency, Contingency, and Structure

Another issue has cut across the metatheoretical, the theoretical, and the empirical levels of the analysis: the issue of agency, contingency and structure. I do not claim that either my theoretical ideas or the empirical analysis has succeeded in adequately conceiving and portraying the appropriate mix of agency, contingency, and structure. This fundamental and complex issue has always puzzled humans, and it has certainly not been resolved in these pages. I do make two claims: first, that the theoretical perspective I am advocating does not ignore this issue; second, that we may make some progress in further clarifying this puzzle by studying empirically how people go about dealing with it in their own lives. This theme has recurred through much of the analysis.

First, it has been a special concern of the analysis of purity (Chapter 9), inauspiciousness (Chapter 10), and their interrelationship. The social sources of contingency (and danger) have been an important subtheme. Ironically, a sense of contingency may be stimulated by attempts to create high levels of social order. When the social context is elaborately ordered, then relaxing rules, crossing rigid boundaries, and interaction between those who are highly unequal all tend to be more threatening than in less ordered and stratified situations.

Second, and even more important, the issue of agency has been implicit in the distinction between conformity and association. This issue is made more explicit in the closely related notions of achievement and ascription. Supposedly, a central theme of modern history has been the delegitimation of ascriptive criteria: the abolition of legalized aristocracies, the disapproval of racism and sexism as publicly articulated ideologies, the emphasis on achievement and performance as judged by supposedly universalistic criteria. However, there are significant qualifications to this emphasis on conformity to universal performance norms. First, judgments of conformity and deviance usually assume some level of agency. Where people can convince others that they had no agency (i.e., no control over their actions) they may not be held accountable. Chain reaction automobile accidents on crowded expressways have contributed to the development of "no fault" insurance. Changes in our understanding of compulsive and irrational behaviors have resulted in the use of a wide variety of insanity pleas in criminal law. Similarly, younger people are not considered to be responsible agents and are treated under the provisions of special juvenile laws and courts. In short, the assignment of significant negative status is contingent upon the person being defined as a responsible agent.

A second set of qualifications falls under what can be referred to as the rights of citizenship. Here the reverse is the case: a certain level of positive status and associated privileges are assigned almost without regard to one's agency. In Thomas Jefferson's famous phrase, people are deemed to have certain "inalienable rights" that depend primarily on their associations rather than their conformity. People are entitled to equal protection and due process under the law no matter what they have or have not done. As T. H. Marshall (1950) noted, these rights have been expanded into both political and social areas. All people are entitled to vote, no matter how ill-informed or wrongheaded they might be. Many nations provide significant levels of education and health care without regard to the individual's ability to pay. Even their capacity to learn may be considered irrelevant, as indicated by the increasing requirements that the mentally handicapped be provided education at public expense. Many nation-states provide guaranteed employment or minimum levels of income. Most of these rights are contingent upon a specific type of association; that is, one must be a citizen of a particular nation-state. Typically this is acquired by pure ascription at birth. The point is that societies always rely on both achievement and ascription; status is always due to some mixture of conformity and association. This is so because all societies recognize, at least implicitly, that all three factors—agency, contingency, and structure—influence human behavior. Of course, the details and the relative emphasis vary significantly. Human experience is, however, far too complex to simply resolve the tensions between these considerations in any final sense.

As I have indicated, the conundrum of how to accurately express the relative significance of agency, contingency, and structure is, in part, another version of Marx's problem about how history is "made." In keeping with recent trends in contemporary social theory, I have tried to make conceptual room for the notion that humans, both as individuals and organized collectivities, are knowledgeable skilled actors who make choices and thereby go about constructing the social world in which they live. When we look at our own lives, we have a sense that we are answerable for many of the things that have happened to us, and are in some senses responsible for some of the things that have happened to those around us. This is the reason why all people, who are not defined by their contemporaries as mad, operate with some notion of morality—however much their behavior may depart from it. A sociological vision that eliminates this reality is limited and flawed.

Yet this is only half the story, because people also see in their own lives, and even more in the history of their age, many more things that no one anticipated, much less intended. Some of these are truly contingent factors that have little to do with human behavior per se. Natural disasters are the most obvious example.[3] Other events, however, seem very much the result of our past human history. We have some sense that someone is responsible—perhaps even ourselves—but we are unclear about how this is the case. Sometimes the outcomes are more positive than we could have anticipated. More often we are impressed by the frequency of human tragedy. Collectively and even individually we have a sense that we could and should have done better, but we seem ineffective and powerless.

Throughout history, people have testified to this existential reality. Perhaps the most famous of these in Western culture is Paul's frustrated exclamation: "For the good that I would I do not; but the evil which I would not, that I do" (Romans 7:19). Nonreligious ideas point to the same reality. Freud's analysis of the effects of various neuroses and compulsions is perhaps the most influential modern version of this notion. The attention given Robert Merton's (1957) concepts of latent functions and unintended consequences is one reflection of this concern in sociology. The Marxian concepts of alienation and false consciousness, for all their limitations, testify to this reality on the collective level. Lévi-Strauss's ideas of deep structure point to such realities in relatively simple societies. Even Adam Smith's notion of the "invisible hand," though more optimistic, also points to something that happens "behind our backs."

This attempt to understand how we are shaped by what we have often unknowingly created should, in my opinion, continue to be at the heart of the sociological endeavor. At the same time it would be a mistake to become too confident about what we do, or are capable of knowing. We can certainly reduce mystification, decrease contingency, and increase human agency in some respects. But to try or wish to eliminate all sense of mystery is probably to overestimate our ability to control both the material world and our own symbolic activity. To think that we can make history "just as we please" is to enormously overestimate the human capacities for rationality. In all likelihood, it is to perpetuate the same arrogance that is the root of numerous past tragedies, and many of our present predicaments—and quite possibly could result in the destruction of earthly life itself. Once again, one of our most pressing problems, as both actors and analysts, is to give appropriate recognition to agency, structure, and contingency. To underestimate the significance of any of these is to seriously misunderstand the nature of the human condition.

Appendix: Theoretical Implications and Possibilities

I have advocated a provisional resource structuralism as a theoretical framework for the analysis of status and sacral relationships. Here I want to extend this framework into other types of social analysis. I will avoid additional discussions of status and sacral relationships, even where they might be logically implied.

The core of this approach is analyzing how the nature of the resources available shape the patterns of social behavior. To keep the discussion concise, I will restrict the analysis to the characteristics that we have already considered at some length: alienability and expansibility. Drawing on these ideas, I will present a series of arguments in highly condensed outline form, and I will number these to show their logical relationship. The more specific arguments or propositions are not rigorously derived from the more abstract arguments, but rather suggested or implied by them.

Chapter 2 identified three basic types of sanctions: force, goods and services, and status. These three types of sanctions, plus knowledge, comprise the four basic kinds of human resources.

1.0 Resources and Alienability

The types of sanctions vary in the degree to which they threaten one's identity. The types of resources vary in the degree to which they can be stored, and the degree to which they are an integral part of one's identity.

Resources that are "stored" and available to influence the physical and social environment are frequently referred to as "capital resources."[4] For the purposes at hand, it is useful to distinguish three types of capital resources: physical capital, human (knowledge) capital, and status capital. The more a given type of resource is an integral part of one's identity, the more inalienable it is.

1. Physical capital is the most alienable because it is composed of objects completely separable from the identities of other individuals and can be exchanged, stolen, or appropriated by force.
2. Human capital is the least alienable because it is composed of skills embodied in ego's mind and body and cannot be easily appropriated.
3. Status capital has an intermediate level of alienability because it is embodied in the minds of alters (rather than ego).

Conversely, the more a resource is an integral part of one's identity, the more time, energy, discipline, and the suppression of impulses are required for internalization.

1.1 Alienability and the Physical Mobility of Capital

Forms of capital can be ranked in terms of the ease with which they can be physically relocated:[5]

1. Physical capital
   a. Land
   b. Other forms of real estate—for example, buildings
   c. Machinery
   d. Personal chattels
2. Status capital
3. Human capital

The mobility of status capital and human capital is limited by the boundaries of the cultural system. Billy Graham's status is relevant to a much wider area than was Billy Sunday's. A physicist may be able to continue her work in a wide array of industrial societies but not in a simple horticultural society. Usually, however, human capital is more mobile than status capital.

1.1.1 Movable capital and geographical mobility. The more movable a person's capital, the greater the probability of that person being geographically mobile.

1.1.1.1 Refugees. During periods of persecution, the more movable a person's capital, the greater the probability of migration, holding constant the person's rank, level of resources, and reprehensibleness to those in power. For example, top intellectuals are more likely to migrate than top bankers, top bankers more than top merchants, the top merchants more than top landholders, top doctors more than top lawyers.

1.1.1.2 Farmers. Farmers are likely to have low rates of geographical mobility compared to others with roughly comparable levels of capital.

1.1.1.3 Education and migration. The higher the level of education in a society, the higher the rates of geographical mobility. Probably more accurately, the higher the ratio of median education to value of physical capital, the higher the rates of geographical mobility.

1.1.2 Alienability, movability, and conflict-integration. Those with relatively alienable and movable forms of capital are likely to play a key role in social and cultural integration, and conversely, those with immovable capital are especially likely to become involved in conflict.

1.1.2.1 Political decentralization, conflict, and mobility. During periods of political decentralization and high levels of conflict and insecurity, those with low levels of physical capital but high levels of human capital are most able to migrate across political boundaries.

1.1.2.1.1 ACADEMICS. During the Cold War between the Soviet Union and the West, academics could move between the East and the West more easily than entrepreneurs or military personnel.

1.1.2.1.2 MONASTICS. Medieval European and medieval Indian monastics, who had taken vows of poverty and were usually literate, could move between geographical areas more easily than others.

1.1.2.2 Political decentralization and cultural integration. Under conditions of political decentralization, those with low levels of physical capital but high levels of human capital are likely to play an important role in creating or maintaining cultural integration. For example, monastics played a crucial role in the spread and maintenance of Latin Christianity throughout most of Europe, in part because they could more easily move and communicate across political boundaries than other elites.

1.1.2.3 Recalcitrant upper classes. The more immovable the capital—for example, agricultural land—of an upper class, the more likely they are to violently resist a redistribution of wealth, even when their cause is hopeless. For example, "European" farmer-settlers in French Algeria, Southern Rhodesia, and South Africa have typically resisted the end of colonialism or white rule more than "European" merchants or professionals.

1.1.2.4 Conflict-prone industries. Industries that depend on relatively immovable and physically concentrated forms of capital (e.g., mining and port facilities) are likely to experience higher levels of conflict with laborers (e.g., miners and longshoremen) than industries in which capital can be easily relocated—though obviously many other factors also affect rates of industrial conflict.

1.2 Alienability, Movability, and Centralization

More alienable and movable forms of capital are more likely to be associated with centralized forms of authority.

1.2.1 Alienability of physical capital and centralization. Those with influence can both delegate and withdraw authority over physical capital—because it is relatively alienable. Therefore, the greater the significance of physical capital, the more centralized organizational hierarchies. (Obviously, the degree of centralization is also affected by the means of communication, transportation, and pacification that are available, but when these are held constant, the form of capital will have an important independent effect.)

1.2.2 Movability of physical capital and centralization. Land is least likely to be managed by centralized authority because it cannot be concentrated. The corporate control of manufacturing will be greater than in farming.[6]

1.2.3 Alienability and movability of human capital and centralization. Because human capital is relatively inalienable and (from ego's perspective) mobile, the

greater the significance of human capital, the less centralized organizational hierarchies, and the more collegial modes of authority.

1.3 Alienability of Capital and Suppression of Impulse

The more capital is an integral part of one's identity, the more its appropriation requires the suppression of impulses—of what Freud would refer to as the "id."

1. Human capital is usually acquired through long periods of disciplined learning or
   training and, on the average, requires the greatest suppression of one's impulses.
2. Physical capital can be acquired through physical appropriation and does not inherently
   require any suppression of impulses.
3. Status capital requires an intermediate suppression of impulses since it is rooted in behavioral (though not necessarily attitudinal) conformity to social norms.

1.3.1 Freud's *Civilization and Its Discontents* (1962). Higher levels of civilization
are usually closely associated with higher levels of human capital. Hence, the more
important human capital, the longer and longer the period of preparation requiring suppression of impulses, and the greater the likelihood of a sense of "dis-
content."

1.3.1.1 Intellectuals and social criticism. A special case of this is the tendency of
intellectuals to be more critical of the status quo than other elites—which is not to
say that all intellectuals are critics, or that the suppression of impulses is the only
source of such critical tendencies.

1.4 Sanctions and Alienation

Sanctions that threaten one's identity are alienating, while those that affirm one's
identity are not.

1.4.1 Etzioni's compliance typology (1975). Just as capital resources vary in how
inalienable they are from one's identity, sanctions vary in how alienating they are
to one's identity. The categories of Etzioni's compliance typology indicate variations in how alienating a particular type of sanction is:

1. Force and violence are the most alien sanction, and they are the basis of coercive
   compliance structures.
2. Goods and services are moderately alien, and they are the basis of utilitarian compliance structures.
3. Evaluations are moderate to low in alienability and they are the basis of normative
   compliance.

1.4.1.1 Etzioni's Involvement Hypothesis (1975). The level of involvement of subordinate personnel in an organization will be closely related to how alien the typical sanctions are:

1. Coercive compliance structure: when force and violence are the typical sanctions, involvement will be very low.
2. Utilitarian compliance structure: when objects are the typical sanction, involvement
   will be moderate.

3. Normative compliance structure:
   a. Social normative power: when evaluations of others are the typical sanctions, involvement will be high.
   b. Pure normative power: when self-evaluations are the typical sanction, involvement will be very high.

1.4.2 Exceptions that prove the rule. When limited force and violence are used to create or support valued identities—as in initiation rites, mild hazing and sexual play—they are not alienating and do not produce low involvement.[7]

2.0 Resources and Expansibility

Resources vary in the ease with which they can be expanded. For example: status is relatively inexpansible; land is usually less expansible than other types of physical capital; human capital, especially on the collective level, can be expanded almost infinitely.

2.1 The Type of Capital and the Level of Conflict

At least in complex societies, low levels of resources tend to increase the probability of social conflict. Conflict and violence over the control of resources will be highest in those societies that depend primarily on types of capital that are difficult to expand.

2.1.1 Levels of conflict and types of societies. The frequency of conflict and violence over the control of capital will be greater in complex preindustrial societies because the basic types of capital—status and land—are relatively zero-sum resources, while in contrast, physical and human capital can be expanded many-fold.[8]

2.1.1.1 Paige's Agrarian Revolution *(1975).* The more that noncultivators (i.e., elites) are dependent on land for income rather than on other forms of capital, the greater the likelihood there will be violent class conflict with noncultivators.

2.2 The Nature of Capital and the Ideology of Conflict

The type of capital will have an impact on the ideological conception of social conflict. The more inexpansible the capital, the more likely the use of violence is to be seen as a natural and inevitable part of human nature.

2.2.1 Hirschman's *The Passions and the Interests* (1977). When capital is primarily a zero-sum resource—for example, status and land—scarcity and conflict will be defined in terms of the irrational pursuit of brute passions. As expansible forms of capital—for example, machines—become more significant, scarcity and conflict will be defined in terms of the rational pursuit of interests.

2.3 The Social Location of Protest and Alienation

Social protest and deviance is likely when (1) the acquisition of capital requires the suppression of impulses (see 1.3), and (2) public protest does not result in the lowering of privileges. Conversely, protest is less likely where either of these conditions is absent.

2.3.1 Turner's *"The Real Self:* From Institution to Impulse" (1976). As capital formation expanded in the United States in the 1950s and 1960s, the level of resources available to gratify impulses (or passions) increased. There was, however, greater and greater emphasis on the development of human capital, which required the increased suppression of impulses. Therefore, there was a return to a definition of self in terms of impulses among those subpopulations that have experienced extensive suppression of impulses in the process of acquiring human capital, but who have not experienced and do not anticipate scarcity of resources.

2.3.1.1 Student protest and hippies in the 1960s. Protest and deviance were most frequent among those who experienced extended periods of education, and who were relatively economically privileged—for example, children of the upper middle class.

2.3.1.2 Working-class conventionality. Elaborating the logic of the preceding argument, such protest and deviance were least common and most resented among those who had benefited from the expansion of capital and prosperity, but who had neither high levels of education nor a secure economic position—for example, regularly employed blue collar workers.

2.3.1.3 Conservatism and hedonism in the 1970s and 1980s. If prosperity and security become problematic, subpopulations with higher levels of human capital are likely to redefine the self. In the public instrumental–production sphere, they adopt elements of a conventional disciplined institutional self; in the private expressive–consumption sphere, they adopt the hedonistic elements of the impulse self.

2.3.1.4 Alienation of the disadvantaged in the 1980s. In situations where disadvantaged groups (1) live in a context where advantaged groups and mass media increasingly display hedonism, (2) must undergo long periods of relatively poor quality education requiring the suppression of impulses, and (3) receive relatively low status and economic returns for such education, increasing levels of alienation are likely. Such alienation is indicated by lower levels of educational performance and higher rates of crime, drug addiction, divorce, and out-of-wedlock births.

Obviously, these arguments are extremely condensed and simplified. They neglect other factors relevant to explaining the phenomena under consideration, and there is no attempt to discuss the data relevant to the arguments. My purpose is not to demonstrate the validity of these arguments; rather, the goal is twofold. First, I want to show how the arguments suggested by this framework might be related to an array of well-known theories or analyses—that is, to show how a resource structuralism might help us to move toward a better integration of existing theories and research. Second, I want to suggest additional lines of research and analysis.

Glossary

Since the glossary is concerned primarily with foreign words, such words will not be italicized except to indicate that they are the titles of texts or to distinguish *brahman* from Brahman.

acarya   master, preceptor; used to refer to the head of a branch of a religious sect, such as Sri Vaisnavism.

adharma   the absence of dharma; chaos, disorder, lawlessness.

advaita   nonduality; Advaita Vedanta is the particular philosophical school associated with Sankara and his followers, which stresses that the only reality is *brahman*; see Vedanta.

ahimsa   without killing; nonviolence.

akal mrirtyu   out of time; refers to a type of death that brings inauspiciousness.

amangala   inauspiciousness; see mangala, asubha.

ananda   bliss, especially the state attained by devout and knowledgeable sannyasins.

anasara   period of illness; a two-week period during the dark of the moon that comes between the bathing of godly images in the Hindu temple in Puri and the beginning of Ratha Jatra.

annadata   literally, to provide food, one of two kingly functions in India; refers to the king's responsibility for the fertility of the soil and for the rains, necessary for agrarian production and prosperity.

anuloma   following the hair or with the grain; Sanskrit term used to describe marriages in which the groom's family is of superior or equal status to the bride's; in contrast to the groom's family being of inferior status, which is pratiloma.

apsakun   omen; an arbitrary, noncausal predictor of the forces of inauspiciousness and auspiciousness.

Arjuna   the great warrior figure in the *Mahabharata*, and especially the *Bhagavad Gita*, who questions Krishna about what constitutes appropriate conduct and about the efficacy of different paths to salvation.

artha   the pursuit of interest, especially material interest; one of the four ends or goals for the Hindu.

arti   worshipping of a Hindu image by offering it lighted lamps; in temple worship, the priest usually takes the lamp into the inner sanctum, offers it to the deity, and then brings it back and allows devotees to pass their hands over the flames as a form of blessing.

asana   a posture or position used to practice yogic meditation.

asat   literally, nonbeing, unclean (in contrast to sat, clean); used in Bengal and some other areas to distinguish lower status from high status Sudra castes.

asauca   without purity, impurity.

asrama   refers to any one of the four stages of life of twice-born men and the responsibilities appropriate for each of these; together with the notion of varna, one of the central concepts of the varnasramadharma system.

asubha   the absence of auspiciousness; inauspiciousness.

atman   the self, but more specifically the soul of human beings that undergoes an extended series of reincarnations.

avatara   (or **avatar**) descent; the incarnated form of a deity; for example, Krishna and Rama are the incarnated forms of Visnu.

avidya   ignorance, misunderstanding; the source of the illusion (maya) that there is an empirical world that has an identity separate from *brahman.*

baluta   a system in western India of dispensing grain to low level village officials who provide services primarily to the village as a whole rather than individual land controllers; this is contrasted to the jajmani system, in which services are provided to the households of individual land controllers.

bhadralok   the respectable people; in the eighteenth and nineteenth century it came to refer to upper class, relatively westernized Indians, especially in Bengal.

Bhagavad Gita   the most famous section of Book IV of the *Mahabharata*, in which Krishna instructs Arjuna about the paths to salvation; probably the most frequently read religious text in contemporary Hinduism.

bhajans   devotional hymns that are chanted in praise of gods and goddesses.

bhakti   devotion; refers to movements within Hinduism that began in the seventh century in South India emphasizing devotion to a personal deity as the means to salvation; this notion has affected most forms of popular Hinduism in contemporary India.

Bhangis   in the caste system, a term for the category of night-soil collectors.

bhikku (or **bhikkhu**)   an ordained Buddhist monk.

bhuta (or **bhut**)   otherworldly ghosts who haunt the boundaries between this world and the next, and in whose actions inauspiciousness is thought to originate.

biradari   brotherhood; used in some areas of northern India to refer to a group of clans within hypergamous caste considered to be of roughly equal status; women should marry within their own biradari or the one above it.

Brahma   one of the three high gods of Hinduism, though (in contrast to Siva and Visnu) there are few cults devoted to the worship of Brahma; within the cyclical yuga scheme, Brahma is the creator of the universe.

brahmacarin   in the varnasramadharma system, the student; an individual in the first of the four life stages, whose responsibility is to study the Vedas under the guidance of a guru.

Brahma Kumari   contemporary radical religious movement in India that rejects caste distinctions and emphasizes celibacy and equality for women.

brahman   the impersonal absolute form of the deity, which encompasses all aspects of reality.

Brahman (or **Brahmin**)   members of the priestly varna, who are religiously and ritually superior to the other three varnas.

Brahmanas   Vedic texts containing an extended set of sacrificial instructions.

Brahmanism (**Vedic Religion**)   refers to the early forms of Aryan religion, which focused upon sacrifices; while dates are uncertain and imply a level of differentiation that can be misleading, Brahmanism or Vedic religion can be said to have run from some time in the second millennium B.C.E. to the end of the first millennium B.C.E.

carhapa   a particular type of dana, or gift, which involves the passing of inauspiciousness on to others.

caturvarga   the four aims or goals of life for the pious Hindu: dharma, artha, kama, and moksa.

chakravartin   the universal emperor considered to be the direct representative or the incarnation of the great god Visnu; where a more-or-less organized hierarchy of Hindu kings exists, this term usually refers to the king at the top of a hierarchy—though any powerful king may try to claim this status.

Chamars   a large, low-status, often Untouchable caste in North India, whose traditional occupation is the removal of dead hoofed animals, tanning their skins, and making leather products; they are usually referred to as "leather workers"; in fact, most earn their living as agricultural laborers.

contrapriests   a term used by anthropologists to refer to low status functionaries such as Barbers, Sweepers, and Chamars, who serve upper castes by removing various kinds of pollution.

daiva (or **daivam**)   fate, destiny, luck.

daksina   prestations or gifts that those who provide ritual services have a right to receive, sometimes contrasted to gifts like dana, which others have an obligation to receive; they are, in a sense, payments for services rendered.

dana (or **dan**)   various types of ritual gifts that usually involve not only something of value but the transfer of inauspiciousness from the giver to the receiver.

danda   literally, the rod; refers to one of two kingly functions in India; danda is the exercise of force and is considered the essence of kingship, both theoretically and practically.

darsan   view; a form of Hindu worship that involves seeing and being seen by a deity or holy person.

darsana   view, perspective, theory; in Hindu philosophy there are six classical "schools" or darsanas.

devadasis   female temple dancers, who are "married" to the temple god, and are traditionally associated with "prostitution," or more accurately, various kinds of sexual liaisons outside traditional Hindu marriage.

Devi   goddess figure referred to as "Mother" in Hinduism; she is identified with power, either destructive or positive in nature, and has both horrific and beneficent incarnations.

dharma   law; refers to both the universal regularities that govern the cosmos and the rules governing human conduct; in the latter context, it is frequently translated as "duty"; arguably the most fundamental concept of Hinduism, the term has many implications and connotations, depending on the context.

Dharmasastras   literally "law book"; Hindu religious texts containing extended treatises that were intended to guide proper behavior; these texts served as the bases of one of the major strands of Hindu thought.

Dharmasutras   Hindu religious texts containing a series of maxims and proverbs intended to guide proper behavior.

duhkha   the experience of human suffering.

Durga   a form of the Goddess worshipped in Bengal and some other parts of Eastern India.

Durga Puja   the name used in eastern India to refer to the festival of Navaratri; see Navaratri.

dvijas   twice born; a characteristic describing men in the Brahman, Kshatriya, and Vaisya categories of the varna system; signifies having gone through an initiation ceremony that provides one with a rebirth and allows one to study the sacred Veda texts.

ekagrata   single-mindedness; concentration on a single point during yogic meditation.

ghee (or **ghi**)   butter that has been boiled and will not spoil at room temperature; it is considered purifying because it comes from the cow, which is considered sacred, and is used to make pakka foods (see **pakka**).

grihastha   in the varnasramadharma system, the householder; an individual in the second of the four life stages, whose responsibilities are to marry, produce children, acquire wealth, and support those in other stages of life.

guna   quality; the substances of which beings are composed—sattva, raja, and tama; for example, supposedly Brahmans are made up mostly of sattva, Kshatriyas mostly of raja, and low castes mostly of tama.

hak   the right to receive a gift or prestation.

hali (or **halis**)   system of indentured servitude in Gujarat; refers to the servant's position in this system.

Holi   a festival, with parallels to Mardi Gras, in which many of the usual norms of good manners and propriety are relaxed, and it is considered appropriate for those of lower status to haze those of higher status; New Year's Day for some Hindus.

idangai   left, as contrasted to right (valangai), castes in South India; these castes are typically artisans, merchants, and others in conflict with the dominant land controllers and their allies; this was an important distinction in South India and was the basis of considerable conflict through the nineteenth century, but its significance has declined drastically.

ista-devata   preferred; a deity chosen by an individual to be the object of special devotion.

Jagannatha   a form of the Hindu god Visnu associated especially with a temple at Puri in Orissa.

jajman   in modern India, individuals, typically of a dominant caste, for whom Brahmans perform religious rites in return for gifts and fees; also refers to those for whom a variety of specialist castes provide various goods and services.

jajmani system   a set of economic and political arrangements at the village level, in which dominant land controllers (jajmans) offer a portion of the grain produced, or some other gift, in exchange for various religious and nonreligious services provided by members of other castes.

jati   literally, species; term that roughly parallels the English notions of caste, subcaste, and other related forms of ritually significant social differentiations. The precise differentiation referred to depends on the context; typically, it refers to categories of individuals who "traditionally" performed the specific types of occupations that in sum compose the hierarchical social structure referred to as "the caste system."

jnana   knowledge; one of the three classic paths or means to salvation, the favored path in the Upanisads.

jutha   leftover food; in most circumstances, considered highly polluted and not usually accepted by others; the exception is when extreme humility is expressed or imposed, as when a wife eats her husband's leftovers or Untouchables eat leftovers.

kacca (or **kutcha**, **kachcha**, **kaccha**, etc.)   a North Indian term referring to staple cooked food that is easily polluted, hence is only eaten with one's family and members of one's own caste—in contrast to pakka food; more generally, vulnerable, shaky, temporary, make-do, poorly constructed.

Kali   the black one; an aggressive, usually malevolent form of the Goddess that is especially popular in Bengal.

Kali Yuga   the age of Kali; in Hinduism, the last (and present) of four stages through which the world is repeatedly cycling; this stage is the most degenerative, and is marked by widespread moral corruption and the abandonment and decline of dharma.

kama   pleasure, desire; especially the sensual and erotic forms; one of the four goals of the Hindu life.

kaman   in the context of the jajmani system, a serving family that is linked to a patron (jajman) family.

kanyadana   literally, "gift of a virgin"; a crucial part of the Hindu wedding ceremony in which the brides father presents the bride as a gift to the groom, who is at this moment considered to be a god.

karma (or **karman**) action, work; in the Vedic period, referred primarily to ritual actions related to sacrifices; later came to refer to all human actions and/or the consequences or "fruits" of those actions; the accumulated "fruits" of one's actions supposedly determine one's future destiny and more specifically, the form and status of subsequent incarnations.

Krishna (or **Krisna**) the central figure of the *Bhagavad Gita*, who has become probably the most popular deity in bhakti Hinduism; he is considered to be the avatar or incarnation of Visnu; in other texts, he is described as a young cowherder, and is most renowned for his erotic relationships with Radha and other milkmaids, whose devotion to him is supposed to serve as a model for devotion by his followers; literally, black, thus he is often depicted as having a dark skin.

ksatra the Hindu king's powers of command; these powers are nearly absolute and give the king independence, or the right to act to suit himself.

Kshatriya an individual belonging to the second of the four varnas; members are considered warriors, and supposedly kings are drawn from this varna.

kula in Bengal, a subdivision of a jati or caste that is roughly a clan, lineage, or extended family.

kuti in certain areas of Sri Lanka, a matrilineal clan subdivision of a jati or caste.

Laws of Manu see **Manusmriti**.

lila play, the play of the gods; that is, the unpredictable and often incomprehensible behavior of the gods.

Mahabharata a long epic poem in part portraying the conflict between two branches of a family, the Pandavas and Kauravas, and containing an array of religious themes, including the foundation for the deification of Krishna; along with the *Ramayana,* one of the two great epics of Hinduism.

mangala auspiciousness, luck, well-being.

mantra a formulaic prayer or incantation that is thought to give supernatural power.

Manusmriti the most influential of the Dharmasastra law books, dating from 200 B.C.E., which contains an elaboration of the ideology of the Indian caste system.

marga (or **marg**) street, way; a path or means to salvation; a particular soteriology.

maya illusion; the ability of various gods to create illusions; in nondualist Indian philosophy, the cosmos itself, which is an illusion, since there is only *brahman.*

Mimamsa   a school of Indian philosophy stressing the primacy of the Vedas and the performance of rituals.

moksa   release, salvation—from worldly suffering and cycles of reincarnation (samsara); the ultimate goal for individuals in virtually all forms of contemporary Hinduism.

namaste   an expression of greeting and deference that involves putting the palms of the hands together and bringing them up to the face as the head and shoulders are bowed slightly; a simplified form of the pranam.

Navaratri   a celebration or festival in which a sacrifice, sponsored and sometimes conducted by a Hindu king, commemorates and reenacts the defeat of a demon-king who threatens the dharmic order; a key concern of this celebration is to identify the king with the deity, who defeats evil and reestablishes justice, and more generally to associate the social order with the cosmic order.

pakka (or **pukkha**, **pukka**, **puchha**, etc.)   food that can be eaten at public events and in public places in contrast to kacca food; it usually consists of foods fried in ghee, which is considered a purifying and protecting substance; more generally the term means "proper, substantial, solid."

pancayatana-puja   characteristic Smarta religious ritual that involves the worship of five deities: Visnu, Siva, Surya, Ganesa, and Durga.

pandit   a learned man, usually used as an honorific term for scholarly Brahmans; the origin of the English term "pundit."

paniachua   in Orissa, Sudras from whom Brahmans will not accept water.

paniasprusya   see **paniachua**.

panichua   in Orissa, Sudras from whom Brahmans will accept water.

panisprusya   see **panichua**.

pap   sin; can be embodied in dana and passed on to others.

patra   receptacle or vessel; the person (e.g., a Brahman, Barber, Sweeper, in-law, etc.) or place that receives inauspiciousness in the form of dana.

phal   fruit; figuratively, the just rewards or punishments for one's actions.

pinda   a small ball of rice used as an offering to ancestors.

pitr   forefathers or ancestors.

prakrti (or **prakriti**)   nature, matter; the aspect of the creation that the self enjoys and becomes bound to; moksa requires various means of release from this involvement.

pranam   a bowing motion that is performed to show respect to deities and to higher status people; the degree to which the bow is elaborated depends on the status difference between the parties involved.

pranayama   the rhythmic control of breathing in yogic meditation.

prasada   grace; in the context of the Hindu puja, something (usually food) that is given to the god as an offering, and then returned to the devotees as a sacred substance that has the power to transform.

pratiloma   hair brushed the wrong way or against the grain; a Sanskrit term used to describe marriages in which the bride's family is of superior social status to the groom's; in contrast to anuloma, a "proper" marriage, in which the groom is of equal or superior status.

prestation   a "gift" or item that is transferred from one person or group to another in the context of ritual exchange.

preta   the souls of the dead who have not been ritually transformed into ancestors (pitr) and who haunt the boundaries between this world and the next; inauspiciousness is thought to originate in the actions of preta.

puja   the central form of Hindu religious ritual; its essence is to honor a deity by offering a set of services and gifts.

pujari   a religious functionary who conducts pujas; usually a temple priest.

punya   merit; often acquired through the giving of gifts.

Puranas   a set of sixteen major Hindu religious texts created between the third and the tenth centuries C.E.; they contain myths concerning the cycles of creation and destruction of the cosmos, and the origin, genealogy, and exploits of various gods and sages; contributed to a greater emphasis on theism and the worship of particular sectarian deities.

purohit   a Brahman who serves as a priest to twice-born households; purohits tend to specialize in "pure" rituals, having to do with the yearly cycles or life stages (such as marriages), that are performed in the home, in contrast to rituals performed at a temple.

purusa   male, man, person, self; a masculine name for the absolute.

purusartha   the aims or goals of "man"; the caturvarga are a set of four classic purusartha of the Hindu man: pleasure (kama), material interest (artha), duty (dharma), and salvation (moksa).

raja (or **raj**)   kingship, king; raja is also one of the three gunas associated with passion and excitement.

rajadharma   the duties of the king; central to kingly legitimacy, and one of the most important subcategories of dharma.

rajaguru   a king's preceptor-guru.

Rama the hero-deity of the Hindu epic the *Ramayana*; considered a reincarnation of Visnu and a principle deity in much of India.

Ramayana a long epic poem containing an array of religious themes, including the foundation for the deification of Rama and the cults that worship him; along with the *Mahabharata,* one of the two great epics of Hinduism.

Ram Lila in Hindi speaking areas of North India, a form or parallel of Navaratri; see Navaratri.

Rig Veda earliest Aryan text (usually dated toward the end of the second millennium B.C.E.) describing the rituals of early Vedic religion; it includes a myth about the creation of the four varnas (ranked social categories) that suggests a prototype of the Indian caste system.

rishi religious sage; usually refers to ancient mythical Brahmans who are founders of various lineages and the revealers of sacred texts.

rta in Vedic religion, the cosmic order.

sadhanna the secret spiritual discipline of Tantrism; it is learned from a guru and seeks to give the devotee extraordinary worldly powers, as well as moksa.

sadhu holyman, mendicant, saint.

sakti (or **shakti**) power; either destructive or positive female force that is the basis of all worldly power; associated with the Hindu goddess Devi.

sakun see apsakun

samadhi the final stage of detachment from conventional perspectives, achieved through yogic meditation; in this stage, the yogin passes beyond knowledge into a new mode of being, which includes the acquisition of divine and miraculous powers.

Samkhya (or **Sankhya**) one of the six schools (darsana) of classic Hindu philosophy; argues that salvation can be acquired through a particular kind of metaphysical knowledge about the true nature of existence, rather than through the intervention of a deity.

samsara repeated cycles of worldly reincarnation.

sannyasin (or **sannyasi**) any individual who has renounced the world and devoted their lives to learning the techniques necessary for release; the fourth and final life stage (asrama) in the varnasramadharma system.

sat literally, being or existing; truth, clean (in contrast to asat, unclean); used in Bengal and some other areas to distinguish upper status from low status Sudra castes.

sauca purity.

siddhi accomplishment; miraculous and divine powers acquired by a yogi.

Siva (or **Shiva**) one of the three high gods of Hinduism associated with ascetic traditions, but also associated with eroticism; within the cyclical yuga scheme, Siva is the destroyer, in addition to other functions and aspects.

Smarta followers of the tradition (smriti); orthodox Brahmanical Hinduism, especially in South India.

smriti literally, what has been remembered—that is, the traditions of the Vedas.

sraddha last rites for the dead; sacrifices offered by the son of a householder to his ancestors (pitr).

Sri Vaisnavism a small but influential bhakti sectarian subtradition within Hinduism that combines worship of Sri (the goddess) and Visnu, and follows the philosophy of Ramanuja.

sruti literally, what has been heard—that is, the words of the Vedas regarded as revealed sacred texts.

subha auspiciousness.

Sudra (or **Shudra**) the fourth and lowest varna of laborers and servants.

svadharma the rules and actions that constitute appropriate behavior for members of a specific caste or other social category.

talai eruttu headwriting; that is, one's destiny or fate, which the gods supposedly write on one's forehead before birth.

Tantras non-Vedic texts that advocate Tantrism.

Tantrism tradition within Hinduism that places special emphasis on the divinity and power of the human person; it is primarily a form of secret sectarian spiritual discipline, learned from a guru, that seeks to give the devotee extraordinary worldly powers, including liberation (moksa).

tapas heat, energy, and by implication, power; generated by various forms of religious ritual and discipline; also the discipline and techniques used to produce such heat and power; typically associated with the ascetic practices of renouncers, including Siva in his ascetic aspects.

tilaka (or **tilak**) a mark or sign placed on the forehead with some form of cosmetic; often this signifies a particular religious or social identity, such as devotion to Siva or Visnu.

Untouchables category of individuals who are members of the lowest status outcast group in the Hindu caste system; formally, they are considered outside the system, but in actuality they are an integral part of it.

upacara (or **upachara**) the various ways in which the image of a god may be approached or attended to, usually during a puja; these include bathing, clothing, awakening, fanning, and singing to the god; these are usually acts of devotion and symbolize the humility of the devotees and the superior status of the god.

Upanisads a set of texts, usually dated between 500 B.C.E. and 500 C.E., which emphasize the transformation of Vedic sacrifices into nonviolent internal forms of meditation and spiritual discipline and emphasize spiritual knowledge (jnana) as the means to salvation (moksa).

Vaisya an individual belonging to the third category of the varna scheme; Vaisya originally referred to farmers, who made up the bulk of the population, but later the category came to include primarily merchant castes.

valangai right or right-handed, as contrasted to left (idangai), castes, in South India; these castes are usually the local land controllers and those who are closely allied or dependent on them (see **idangai**).

vanaprastha forest-dweller; the third life stage (asrama) for the twice-born Hindu man when he has completed his responsibilities as a householder (grihastha) and retreats with his wife to the forest in order to meditate and study.

varna literally, color; one of the four ranked social categories of Vedic religion and Hinduism: Brahman (priest), Kshatriya (warrior), Vaisya (farmer, merchant), Sudra (laborer, worker); these serve as broad categories within which more specific castes are classified.

varnasramadharma system the norms and duties appropriate for each of the four varnas, and the four asrama or life stages of the twice-born man; the core social ideas of Brahmanical Hinduism.

Veda sacred knowledge; one of the four key texts of Vedic religion, which contain the procedures and rationale for the sacrifices that maintain control over the cosmos; more generally, the oldest and supposedly most authoritative texts of Hinduism.

Vedanta literally the end of the Veda; referring to Upanisadic thought, which serves as the basis of most nondualistic Indian philosophy; more specifically, the philosophy subscribed to by the followers of Sankara and most Smarta Brahmans, which stresses salvation by knowledge (jnana-yoga); salvation is overcoming ignorance (advidya) and the illusion (maya) that the empirical world has an identity of its own, and seeing that all of reality is really *brahman*.

Visnu (or **Vishnu**) one of the three high gods of Hinduism, who has a number of important avatars or incarnations, including Krishna and Rama; within the cyclical yuga scheme, Visnu is the preserver, in addition to other functions and aspects.

yoga the most well-known tradition of ascetic and meditation techniques focusing on control of both the human body and mind in order to attain worldly power and/or salvation; the tradition is divided into many different schools and subtraditions.

yogin (or **yogi**)   one who practices yoga.

yuga   one of the four mythical cosmic stages through which the world repeatedly cycles over millions of years; each succeeding stage is increasingly degenerative and ultimately results in destruction, reincarnation, and the beginning of a new cycle; all of human history, in the modern sense, is considered to be part of the fourth degenerative age, known as Kali Yuga, the age of Kali.

Notes

Chapter 1

1. While it would strain even the very broad definition of structuralism used here to label Parsons, Luhmann, and Habermas as structuralist, they do in large measure share the assumptions of structuralism that are of concern here. As Whimster and Lash note, "What the works of Parsons, Luhmann and Habermas all share is a clear separation of the action level from the system level and a belief that the complexity of societal change is intelligible only through an analysis at the level of the system" (1987:17).

2. Both have produced an extensive body of writings which in turn have stimulated a considerable amount of comment and secondary literature. In my opinion the works most central to their general theoretical frameworks are Giddens (1976, 1979, 1984) and Bourdieu (1977, 1984, 1986). For a useful interpretation of Bourdieu's work see Robbins (1991) and Bourdieu and Wacquant (1992).

3. It is an interesting and somewhat puzzling footnote on intellectual history that neither Giddens nor Bourdieu refer at all in their primary theoretical writings to Berger and Luckmann's (1967) work, even though central to all three is a concern to express more adequately both aspects of Marx's formula. This is probably in part due to the subjectivist tendencies in Berger and Luckmann that result from the influence of Schutz's phenomenology and the exposition of their arguments in terms of a sociology of knowledge. I will show that the central categories of Berger and Luckmann can be given a more objectivist and structuralist slant. Perhaps a second consideration is the relatively strong emphasis on the internalization of common values and norms that is implicit in the Berger and Luckmann exposition. I believe that this emphasis is not necessarily incompatible with the notions of practical consciousness so central to Giddens and Bourdieu.

4. Neither Giddens nor Bourdieu adopts a linguistic model in an unqualified or uncritical way. See, for example, Bourdieu (1977:22–30).

5. I am aware that neither Giddens or Bourdieu use the contrast between micro and macro analysis, but they certainly are both interested in integrating the analysis of different levels of social analysis.

6. To some degree such an approach is allowable within Giddens's scheme through what he calls methodological bracketing: the momentary suspension of the analysis of individual

action ("strategic conduct") in order to analyze institutional structures. But even with this allowance, his attempts to synthesize objectivism and subjectivism and the implications of this synthesis for creating generalizations are too burdensome and often an unproductive distraction. It is not clear that Bourdieu would allow even such methodological bracketing. On the other hand, Bourdieu is less negative than Giddens about the possibility and importance of generalization.

A recent example of a provisional structuralism applied to the explanation of gender inequality is Huber (1990).

7. These contributions include Bendix and Lipset's classic reader on social stratification (1966), Runciman's study of relative deprivation (1966) and more general theoretical work (1989), Etzioni's influential typology of forms of organizational compliance (1975), Collins's theory of class cultures (1975, 1988), and Giddens's analysis of the class structures of advanced societies (1975). Jeffrey Alexander's (1982a, 1982b, 1983a, 1983b) emphasis on a multidimensional approach to social theory is a more general and abstract application of the same principle.

8. See, for example, Dumont (1980:app. A, especially 250), and the essays by Badrinath in Kantowsky (1986).

9. In addition to the works listed in note 7, I have in mind Béteille (1971), Collins (1975, 1979, 1988), Patterson (1982), and Mann (1986).

10. Social science and humanistic fields other than sociology have been equally or even more influenced by this tradition. Some of the names that come to mind are Ferdinand Braudel, Marc Bloch, Moses Finley, Raymond Williams, Jacques Lacan, Roland Barthes, Thomas Eagleton, Marvin Harris, Joan Robinson, Jean Paul Sartre, Eric Fromm, and Max Horkheimer.

11. To quote Bourdieu: "Capital is accumulated labor (in its materialized form or its incorporated, embodied form) which when appropriated on a private, i.e., exclusive basis by agents or groups of agents, enables them to appropriate social energy in the form of reified or living labor" (1986:241).

12. The work of Parsons (1951), Goffman (1967), and Collins (1975, 1988) are only the most obvious examples of the concept's influences on general sociological theory. The impacts of Durkheim's concept on the sociology of religion are too numerous to mention.

13. In his "Theses on Feuerbach" (Marx 1978:143–45) he transforms the concept of alienation from an ontological concept to a sociological one. According to Marx, religion is the elemental example of alienation: structures created by human beings that have come to control them in ways that they do not understand. The rest of his career was spent analyzing the structures of capitalism as a parallel case of alienation: historically contingent structures created by humans, which the ruling classes claimed were natural and inevitable.

14. Of course, unlike Marx, I do not mean to imply that other collectivities will follow the same pattern. Even if they should move toward a greater emphasis on status, they will not necessarily have precisely the same characteristics found in India. On the other hand, if a collectivity increases the significance of status as a form of power and does not develop similar characteristics, we should look for the specific historical factors that offset or block the expected tendencies. A concrete example of this form of analysis is set forth in Chapter 11.

15. The title of Inden's book is *Imagining India*.

16. I am aware that, following Richard Rorty (1979) and others, Inden has rejected the representational notions of knowledge that are implied by such metaphors as pictures and maps. I believe this is a mistake; I would emphasize the tentative and selective nature of our representations rather than abandon such metaphors.

17. Obviously the configuration of resources that is available to people at a given point in time is in large measure—but not completely—the result of their own and others' past actions. I will elaborate considerably on my understanding of the relationships between agency and structure in the next chapter.

18. I am not, of course, suggesting that all possible ways of imagining India—or any other "place"—are equally valid. My point is that to make the enemy "essentialism" is to create a false problem.

19. In the earlier discussion on contemporary social theory I did not mention what has become known as critical theory. Since the discussion in this section obviously implies a critique of the materialism of modernity, it is appropriate to clarify the relationship of my analysis to the theoretical perspective that most explicitly carries on the critical tradition of Marxism. This tradition began before World War II with the work of Adorno, Fromm, Horkheimer, Lowenthal, Marcuse, and others at the Frankfurt Institute (Jay 1973). The most notable and visible successor to this tradition is Jürgen Habermas (1971, 1984, 1987). Habermas continues the Enlightenment tradition of attempting to define reason and rationality, and to use them as a basis for judging and criticizing institutionalized social patterns. Habermas's work is wide ranging, covering both philosophy and social science, and he has revised important elements of his perspective from time to time. Three aspects of his work are of special relevance to my endeavor. First, he attempts to move beyond Marx's materialism, by demoting—though not abandoning—the significance of labor and instrumental action, and emphasizing the importance of communicative action. Reason and rationality are the social consensus that are the outcome of unrestrained and unbiased communicative action, an outcome requiring substantial social equality. Social evolution is the result not simply of transformations in the means of production and the forms of laboring, but changes in the nature of human knowledge and learning. Second, and related to this, he attempts to transcend the distinction between causal and interpretive hermeneutical analysis. In his early work he draws on Freud and psychoanalysis as a preliminary model for such efforts. Third, while he is, of course, aware of the ethnocentrism built into all cultures, he remains committed to a universalistic form of rationality. He rejects all extreme forms of relativism, and maintains that for all its evils, modernity represents an overall improvement in the human condition. Accordingly, further increases in human freedom and welfare will come from greater levels of institutionalized rationality.

I am, of course, sympathetic to the attempt to emphasize the importance of nonmaterial resources. As will become apparent in Chapters 9 and 10, I am also interested in breaking down the rigid distinction between causal and interpretive analysis. About Habermas's third point I am more ambivalent. I certainly agree that a prime function of social science is to unmask the ideologies, pretensions, and special privileges of the status quo. A thoroughgoing relativism makes such criticism impossible or meaningless. A relatively universalistic, reasoned discourse can play an important role in social criticism. On the other hand, reason and rationality—not to mention their advocates—have their own ideologies and pretensions. Moreover, they are based on a questionable assumption. Just as traditional Marxism placed too much emphasis on labor as the essence of human activity, critical theory and other forms of rationalism place too much emphasis on human language and, more specifically, on explicit, articulated discourse. Stated negatively, they ignore the significance of what cannot be said, but rather must be communicated implicitly through ritual and other forms of prelinguistic communication. Because of this bias, they envision and seek a world that is completely desacralized. The result, in my opinion, is too often pseudosacralization: treating as sacred human institutions that are even more historically contingent and arbitrary than the perspectives associated with traditional religions. The free market of capitalism and the will of the party in Communist regimes are two obvious examples. This is not, of course, to imply that what is considered sacred in the more traditional sense should be immune to analytical scrutiny; much of this book is directed toward a social science analysis of the sacred. What I am suggesting is that just as it is a mistake to resolve the dialectical relationships between agency and structure in favor of either end of the continuum, it is a mistake to resolve the dialectical relationship between the profane and the sacred, between the rational and the nonrational, in favor of the former.

Chapter 2

1. The remarks that follow concerning the dialectical relationship between the individual and the collectivity, between action and structure, are suggested by a broad array of writings in the social sciences. I am especially aware of the influence of these sources: Marx's "Economic and Philosophical Manuscripts of 1844," Berger and Luckmann's phenomenological version and elaboration of this perspective in their *The Social Construction of Reality* (1967), the various writings of Anthony Giddens (especially 1976, 1979, 1984), Pierre Bourdieu (1977, 1984), and Jeffrey Alexander's (1982a) contrast between action and order. While the parallel concepts, for example, Giddens's agency and structure, Bourdieu's practice and structure, and Alexander's action and order, are not precise analogues of one another, they are attempting to identify similar theoretical issues.

I believe the view portrayed in these writings represents the key elements of a near orthodoxy in sociology that attempts to recognize that social systems and human actors are self-reproducing systems, and hence seeks to synthesize the objective and subjective aspects of human existence. As I have indicated in Chapter 1, what analysts disagree about is how to best study such a dialectical reality, and especially whether to emphasize structure or agency. I have suggested that the provisional emphasis should be on the former. There are, of course, many additional debates over more specific characteristics, for example, the extent and conditions of human rationality—for example the contrast between Habermas (1984), Hechter (1987), Collins (1988), Etzioni (1988), and Coleman (1990).

2. Anthony Giddens (1984:14–16) has argued that consciousness and intentionality are not part of the definition of agency. I am in some respects sympathetic to the intent of his argument (see note 28). My purpose here, though, is to quickly distinguish between objects and subjects. A much more fundamental objection would come from those structuralists who would insist on a complete "decentering" of the subject (see, e.g., Coward and Ellis 1977). I am sympathetic to a critique of the overemphasis on the individual subject, that has been characteristic of the modern period in general and bourgeois society in particular, but the relationship between the individual and the collectivity must be seen as a dialectical one and not resolved in favor of either.

3. The "outside" includes the "inside," that is, the physical characteristics of the human body that impinge on human identity and social behavior.

4. In my opinion, none of the theorists mentioned in note 1—Marx, Berger and Luckmann, Giddens, and Alexander—have given sufficient attention to what I am referring to as contingency. The partial exception is Berger and Luckmann's reference to chaos, but this concept is an ad hoc one in their analysis, not a formal category. Mary Douglas and Aaron Wildavsky (1982) have analyzed how cultures vary in what risk they focus upon, but their work aims to reveal the cultural features of the current debates about the environment, not how risk and contingency are related to the assignment of responsibility. The pragmatist philosopher Richard Rorty (1989) has devoted systematic attention to this concept of contingency, but I find his rather stoic and relativistic approach to it unconvincing and unsatisfying.

5. Giddens's discussion of ontological security (1984:50) provides one conceptualization of this problem.

6. This states the matter as if human individuals preceded social order, which was the assumption of traditional social contract theories. It is equally accurate to say that structured social orders are what made possible the development of individuals who can cope with contingencies by means other than preprogrammed biological codes. The point of relevance here, however, is the emergence of social order and hence the use of quasi social contract language for purposes of exposition.

7. Lévi-Strauss stresses the distinction between social structure and social relations. "The term 'social structure' has nothing to do with empirical reality but with models which are built up after it" (1963:279). Social relations is the term he uses to refer to "the empirical reality" that provides the "raw materials" for these models. Giddens (1984, especially 16–28) develops a set of even more complex distinctions between structures and social systems. The former refers to the rules and resources that sustain patterned social systems, while the latter refers to concrete systems of interaction located in time and space. These usages are in contrast to the much more widely used definition of social structure as the repetitive patterns of interaction that have relative stability through time. I will follow the more traditional usage because I believe the type of distinctions suggested by Lévi-Strauss and Giddens are misleading. Even the most concrete conceptions of patterned systems of interaction are abstract models that attempt to identify relatively stable and generalized patterns. I agree that social analysis can usefully distinguish different levels in this process of abstraction, but my guess is that it is more useful to think of these as differences in degree rather than kind. For social life there is no absolute distinction between being a participant and an observer; even in the midst of the most concrete ongoing interaction, there is reflexive monitoring in which participants detach themselves from the immediate situation and develop expectations that have some degree of abstractness and generality. Therefore, the difference between Giddens's social systems of practice and structures, and Lévi-Strauss's social relations and structure is only a matter of degree. The bracketing and abstracting that scientific observers carry out to identify "deep structure" is only different in degree from what is required to produce patterned practice.

8. This is a key point in Giddens's (1984:169–206) structuration theory.

9. These very old notions appear in implicit form in various creation myths. For two modern discussions of similar ideas, see Heidegger (1969) and Bourdieu (1977:124–30). In the physical sciences, the parallels for the first two concepts are fission and fusion. I have decided to use "separation" and "combination" in order to avoid implying too close a parallel with physical processes and to make use of the clear verb forms of these words, which make the processes involved sound clearer and more concrete.

10. David Lockwood's *Solidarity and Schism* (1992) has made an important contribution to clarifying the centrality of these processes to the sociological tradition. He points out that Durkheim emphasized solidarity: while his concepts of anomie and declassification recognized the possibility of a loss of solidarity, he had no adequate explanation of schism, that is, a polarization of solidarity. In contrast, Marx and Marxism, preoccupied with class divisions and conflict, has been unable to provide a satisfactory explanation for the continuing levels of solidarity in capitalist regimes, except by recourse to arguments about indoctrination, commodity fetishism, or hegemony, which for the most part are impossible to verify empirically. While Lockwood is skeptical about any kind of simple synthesis, his work suggests that an adequate theoretical framework must deal with both solidarity and schism, and he sees as key to it a better understanding of the articulation of the status order and the class system. We consider this subject in Chapters 6 and 7.

11. No assumption has been made about the source of social order. The order referred to up to this point is what Parsons refers to as "factual order" (1937). Hence while a consensus about values and norms may be a source of such order, this is not necessarily or even usually the case.

12. Durkheim sees this as an ongoing dynamic process. At some periods people focus on profane activities and go their separate ways in pursuit of individual interest, a process which erodes what Durkheim calls the collective consciousness. While he does not stress this point, it is implicit that social inequality emerges in the pursuit of private interest. Solidarity and unity are only renewed when people come back together to focus on another kind of ine-

quality and separation: the inferiority of the group as a whole relative to the sacred, and the enactment of this inferiority in ritual. But this inferiority is not absolute; its very acknowledgment to some degree purifies people, hence they can come closer to the sacred and their impurity and profaneness are mitigated. Since, according to Durkheim, the sacred is simply the emblem of society itself, this process renews a society's solidarity.

13. Parsons explicitly revises this essay twice (1954, 1970); while he qualifies and supplements this argument, he does not abandon it. He is, however, very clear that he does not assume complete consensus or solidarity, but only a level sufficient to make the distribution of social evaluations far from random.

14. This summary of Dahrendorf's argument is taken from Milner (1987a:1057); see this article for a broader overview and synthesis of theories of inequality.

15. In Dahrendorf's (1968) words: "So long as norms do not exist, and in so far as they do not effectively act on people . . . there is no social stratification; once there are norms that impose inescapable requirements on people's behavior and once their actual behavior is measured in terms of these norms . . . a rank order of social status is bound to emerge" (reprinted in Béteille 1969:34).

16. In my opinion notions of sacredness can derive from and contribute to either process. The mixture of the two elements varies historically.

17. The conceptualization that follows draws on (and in some respects departs from) the work of Weber (1968, especially chap. 9), Runciman (1966, 1989), Etzioni (1968, 1975), and Poggi (1990).

18. This does not mean that the most complete and explicit communication of what one wants is always the most effective means of exercising power. Some degree of uncertainty may keep others on their toes and encourage them to anticipate what is wanted. More extreme are situations such as concentration camps where the goal is to terrorize or demoralize others by dispensing sanctions in a near-random fashion. This is, however, effective only where one has overwhelming physical force and is willing to expend considerable amounts of it. Such treatment is ineffective as a means of organizing people for collective action, though it may motivate people to escape, riot, commit suicide, and so forth.

19. A note is needed about the relationship between the terms "affect," "influence," and "exercise power over." They are listed in order of their inclusiveness, with each antecedent term encompassing the latter term(s). We can have an affect on someone without at all intending to do so. We may influence someone without necessarily exercising power over them. But if we influence someone, by definition we affect them, and if we exercise power over them, we both influence and affect them. It is interesting that English does not have a verb form of "power." Since "exercising power over" is a rather awkward phrase, I will often substitute the terms "affect" or "influence." But it should be understood that in some contexts these terms will refer to more general categories than the exercise of power.

20. This is not, strictly speaking, social interaction; the other person is not considered to be a competent agent and accordingly symbolic communication is useless. As implied earlier, controlling humans by force, especially nonviolent force, is extremely costly in terms of time and energy, as the parent of any young child or the caregiver of any incapacitated person knows.

The effectiveness of passive resistance, advocated by Gandhi and others, is that those in authority cannot use symbolic communication to influence their opposition. They must instead resort to the alternative of pure physical force. If this force is nonviolent, it is extremely laborious. If violent, it is usually psychologically and morally debilitating to carry out. This is not necessarily the case, however. If those with power can manage to define their enemies as totally other, they can then be treated with the detached efficiency of the slaughterhouses, whether those that provide meat in contemporary societies or those run by the Nazis.

21. A note is required on the relationships between the concepts of labor, force, violence, services, goods, and coercion. I have already indicated that violence is the use of force to produce pain or injury. The distinctions between force, service, and goods are matters of degree. All three are rooted in labor: the human body's ability to physically manipulate its environment. When labor is used for force, the intent is to make a person do something he does not want to do. When labor is used for goods and services, the intent is to transform some part of the environment to make it more valuable. This process can involve directly "working on" someone else's body, as in a massage or haircut, but more typically it involves transforming some objects, substances, or symbols into something more useful. This can range from manufacturing a computer to cleaning a room. Usually when this labor results in some relatively new object, for example, a computer, we refer to it as a good. When such labor primarily maintains existing objects rather than producing new objects, for example, cleaning a room, we refer to it as a service. Obviously the distinction is often blurred. For example, a frozen dinner produced for sale in a supermarket is usually considered a good; the same dinner heated up in a microwave oven and sold in a restaurant is usually considered a service.

22. Expressions of approval and disapproval are not, however, solely an exchange process. We can express disapproval (or approval) of someone whether or not they want to hear it. That is, the exchange is not necessarily directly with the other individual. Hence, by expressing approval or disapproval to third parties, we can create debits and credits in someone's bank of approval without interacting with them.

23. This process is a special case of what has been called status generalization. For an overview of the data and research on this subject by social psychologists, see Webster and Driskell (1978), Berger and Zelditch (1985, especially chap. 3), and Webster and Foschi (1988).

24. As Lockwood says, "From Hobbes to James Mill, the summary list is the same: power, wealth and honour" (1992:102). He refers to this as a "typology of proximate ends, or generalized means." While I claim to make some important refinements on this trio, I do not mean to deny its long ancestry.

25. Perhaps the most extreme example, though, is what we call madness. The very definition of madness might be conceived of as not responding appropriately to social sanctions. The insane have withdrawn from normal social interaction and are influenced by factors that have a reality largely restricted to their own imagination. In extreme cases, such persons can be influenced only by physical restraint or drugs.

People rarely deliberately make themselves mad; that is, madness is not usually an exercise of agency. However, some forms of madness may be a means of gaining the agency one longs for but does not have in the real world, as when one imagines oneself to be famous and powerful figures. On the other hand, paranoid forms of delusion usually involve a sense of being affected and manipulated by hostile others over whom one has little control.

26. For a stimulating discussion that focuses on power as the distribution of knowledge, see Barnes (1988).

27. The word "ideology" is used in a number of different senses in intellectual and political discourse and is a highly contested concept. At one pole, the term refers to two related ideas: propaganda or misinformation and traditional forms of knowledge, such as mythology and religious doctrines; these are contrasted with objective rational scientific knowledge. At the other pole, the term is employed as a virtual synonym for culture (or at least the core values and assumptions of a given culture) and stresses the historical relativity and social foundation of all ideas. I believe the most useful way to use the term falls in between. As I use it, ideology is a set of ideas that one group claims is valid for defining relationships with some other group(s). Most typically the advocating group is some elite. To some degree, such ideas contain the biases of the group that advocates or promulgates them. These biases may involve blatant lies and misrepresentations deliberately aimed at gaining advantages, or may be largely

unconscious. In my usage, ideology does imply an element of intentionality. That is, ideology is not simply misinformation that all are willing to correct when more accurate knowledge is obtained. It is knowledge shaped by vested interests, even though the association may be quite implicit, taken for granted, or even unconscious. The literature relevant to the concept of ideology is enormous; for a brief overview of it see McLellan (1989).

28. The notion of a biased structure parallels Bourdieu's notion that those who possess power have the ability to define the "field" within which conflict occurs.

29. This example illustrates why Giddens (1984) argues that intention, as contrasted to awareness of the consequences of one's actions, is not an essential element of agency.

Obviously the disadvantage of employing less experienced workers is often exaggerated and may be offset by many other considerations.

30. As this book was going to press, Sewell (1992) published an insightful article on the nature of structure and agency and their place in social analysis. Our notions of structure are generally analogous; my concept of knowledge is very similar to his concept of schema, while my concept of sanctions parallels his notion of resources. He rightfully rejects the overly static connotations of Bourdieu's notion of habitus and identifies factors that can lead to the transformation of structure rather than its reproduction. Most of these factors are compatible with the concept of structure I have outlined. For example, the tension that I discuss between status order and economic pressures in India illustrates what Sewell refers to as the "multiplicity of structures." His notions about variations in the "depth" and "power" of structures are broadly compatible with the conception presented here, though I suspect that "depth" and "power" are typically inversely correlated. In two respects I believe the notion of structure I have outlined is superior to Sewell's. First, my typology of the types of sanctions and power provides a clearer and more concrete referent than Sewell's relatively vague concept of "resources." Second, the notions of combination, separation, and linking provide a clearer account of how structuration comes about.

31. In most polities, force is not the most common or primary way of exercising power, but the ability to prevent the successful use of force by others is the crucial precondition to exercising effective political power. Mann (1986) has argued for distinguishing between political and military power. There is some merit to this suggestion, in that political power is usually a combination of the other forms of power. Nonetheless, the classic argument that political power ultimately depends upon force seems valid (see, e.g., Poggi 1990:chap. 1). The term "economic" is actually a misnomer in this context. Strictly speaking, "economic" refers to the process of taking into account the costs and benefits of alternative allocations of resources; it assumes rationality and a propensity toward efficiency. While the use of objects and services as a means to influence other people usually involves economic calculation, this is not necessarily the case—at least in the short run. On the other hand, the use of force and approval–disapproval often involves "economic" calculations. Strictly speaking, the term "material power" is more accurate than "economic power," but because the latter is so widely used in this sense, I adopt it as a rough synonym.

32. The best-known ethnographic analysis of systems where status is central is the collection of essays entitled *Honour and Shame: The Values of Mediterranean Society* (Peristiany 1966). While these essays have been quite influential, they neither offered nor stimulated a systematic theory of status groups.

33. It is not accidental that in the modern period when the state and the nation have tended to coincide, the common status of citizenship has become the crucial definition of membership in both. In societies such as the Soviet Union that did not achieve a high level of integration between community and state, and between status and political power, there were sometimes separate official definitions of citizenship for different political purposes.

34. The definitive sociological analysis of slavery is Patterson's *Slavery and Social Death* (1982). Patterson defines slavery in terms of three key characteristics: direct violence, natal

alienation, and dishonor. The last characteristic indicates that status degradation played a crucial role in slavery, but Patterson makes it clear that force and violence are prerequisites to the development of the other two characteristics.

35. Economics has frequently been criticized because models that are created under the assumption of perfect competition are then applied to situations where the assumption's validity is doubtful. Even worse, the notion of perfect competition has often become a value and norm rather than an analytically useful assumption, and other means of organizing economic activity have become by definition inferior. My analysis of status could be subject to the same problems; the relationships identified in situations where status was especially important as a resource may not hold up in situations where status is less important. Whether this is so, however, is an empirical question and is a premature concern at this point.

I will not consider or refer to generalizations as "laws" for this implies a more stable set of contextual conditions than is the case for social phenomena.

Chapter 3

1. I realize that the more standard term is "expansitivity," but I coin the terms "expansibility" and "alienability" (as well as "inexpansibility" and "inalienability") in order to have parallel word forms.

2. Of course, premodern societies often attempted to increase productivity. Relatively new is the notion that all peoples and classes can and should have steadily expanding material wealth.

3. I am, of course, speaking here of live organs. The penchant of some tribal groups to collect scalps, heads, and so forth and even to use them in trade is quite old. It is telling that where this was the case there was considerable interest in both the amount and the distribution of these items.

4. The Berger and Luckmann perspective is not as inherently antistructuralist, consensualist, or idealist as it is sometimes perceived (see, e.g., Collins 1988:276, 383), though these tendencies are present. My reliance on the perspective is largely limited to the three key categories of externalization, objectivation, and internalization.

5. This quote is taken from Berger's *The Sacred Canopy* (1969). The first chapter is Berger's own summary of the argument he and Luckmann elaborate in *The Social Construction of Reality* (1967).

Other theoretical perspectives have similar notions. For example, Bourdieu's "habitus" certainly involves processes similar to what is meant by internalization. Both Giddens and Bourdieu, however, would emphasize that humans do not simply act out socially given roles, norms, and values that have been internalized at some earlier point in time. Rather, as knowledgeable agents they produce and reproduce social pattern through skilled performances. Nonetheless, Giddens and Bourdieu would not deny that individually held residues of past experience—whether we call these "internalized values," "habitus," "practical consciousness," or whatever—provide important continuities in the actions of any given individual, which in turn have some role in the patterning of social action. In using the concepts of externalization, objectivation, and internalization, I do not mean to adopt all the implications sometimes associated with these terms, but simply to point to broad processes that most contemporary theoretical approaches acknowledge with one term or another.

6. When the possession of wealth and force are themselves given a positive moral value, they can directly increase one's staus. This must be distinguished from the conversion processes just discussed. A classic example of the conversion is the time required—a generation or two—for the family with new wealth to be accepted into the Social Register. In this case wealth must be used to conform to a valued lifestyle. In contrast, some subcultures

make the mere possession of wealth the actual criterion of status. The newly wealthy New York family may not be admitted to the New York Social Register, but the new oil magnate may be able to join the Dallas Millionaire's Club as soon as he has a net worth of $1,000,000. The classic form of status group, which is the focus of Weber's discussion, does not base prestige directly on possession of wealth or force precisely because if one loses these forms of power, one also quickly loses one's status. Status groups in which honor is based directly on force or goods and services are relatively ephemeral and have considerable turnover in membership.

7. A caveat: the status of a group is, of course, dependent on its membership and their actions, and this dependency creates certain contingencies. As Bourdieu points out, "Whereas economic capital is relatively stable, symbolic capital is relatively precarious: the death of a prestigious head of a family is sometimes enough to diminish it severely" (1977:67). Similarly, an academic department's prestige can be drastically affected by the retirement or resignation of two or three key members. This countertendency is in part a function of size; the status ranking of universities is much more stable that the status ranking of departments because the significance of any given individual's status is more diluted. Thus the status of relatively large status groups will tend to be more inalienable and stable than smaller units.

8. The emphasis is on "relatively." This point is refined in Chapter 8, where I distinguish between objectivation and objectification.

9. For a number of historical examples of this process, see Runciman (1989:19).

10. Obviously societies vary in the extent to which individuals can shape the use of their political and economic resources after their death through dynasties, inheritance, trust funds, foundations, and the like. Nonetheless, Plato is more remembered than Pericles, Thomas Jefferson more than Stephen Girard, supposedly the first American millionaire, and the United States celebrates a national holiday in honor of Martin Luther King, not the founders of the Ford and Rockefeller foundations. The following excerpt from a newspaper shows that the alienability of material resources is well recognized in popular wisdom.

> Frank L. Rizzo, the controversial former mayor of Philadelphia turned radio talk show host, said he will run a fifth time for mayor next year. . . . Rizzo complained in the interview about crime in the city and said taxes have gone up while city services have deteriorated. Asked why he wants to take on these problems and forgo his lucrative talk radio salary, Rizzo replied, "I never saw a Brinks [armored] car in a funeral procession." (*Washington Post*, February 7, 1990, A14)

11. This discussion may seem to imply that children cannot inherit their parent's status, an idea that is, at the very least, counterintuitive. The crucial point is that the means of inheritance is quite different. If a child inherits a gun, he can use it to kill someone quite independently of whether the person that is shot has ever heard of him or his parent. The gun has an alienability, transferability, and efficacy that is largely independent of a given social context. Conversely, the parent can no longer influence others through the use of this gun.

In contrast, the child who inherits a parent's status can only do so in a given historical context, and then only to the degree that the child's identity is seen by others as closely associated with the identity of the parent. Moreover, the dead parent's positive or negative reputation and status may continue to have an influence on people. The issue of the sources of status and the transmission of status by association is taken up in considerable detail later.

12. Weber does not explicitly discuss the inexpansibility of status, but he hints at it in at least two ways. He says that the source of status is "usurpation." While his remarks are rather cryptic, one possible implication is that status must be taken away from someone else

(1968:933). Weber also emphasizes that "stratification by status goes hand in hand with a monopolization of ideal and material goods or opportunities" (1968:935). This emphasis on monopolization also implies that if others are allowed the same privileges, the value of one's status is depleted. My argument that status is relatively inexpansible does not, however, stand or fall on antecedents in Weber, but on its own analytical accuracy and usefulness.

13. For a discussion of the general concept of status inflation and its application to U.S. society, see Milner (1972). Also see Collins (1988). For a brief discussion of how such inflationary processes operate within the caste system, see McGilvray (1982:73).

14. In one sense, a collectivity that has high status has more status to distribute to its members. For example, the faculty at Oxbridge on average have more status than those at British Polytechnics, but the expansion of status resources at Oxbridge is in large measure at the expense of those who are in other institutions. If the status of the faculty at Polytechnics is raised, it will erode the status of Oxbridge faculty, though not necessarily on a one-to-one basis.

15. What has been called "expectation states theory" strongly suggests a tendency toward stability once status orders are established (see Berger and Zelditch 1985). Of course, there is still a big gap in our knowledge between the micro observations in mainly small group experiments, which serve as the basis of expectation states theory, and the analysis of long-term macro historical processes like those that are the focus of this analysis.

16. Weber (1968:29, 319) associates expressions of approval and disapproval, hence prestige and status, with the enforcement of "conventions"—in contrast to "custom," which is not explicitly enforced, and "law," which is enforced with more coercive means. While the norms most commonly associated with status processes are perhaps most typically "conventions," I do not mean to imply that this is always the case. Though he is not explicit about the matter, Weber's concepts of "usage," custom, convention, and law are in part additive, that is, each later category includes the key attributes of the preceding (see 1968:29–31). Accordingly, expressions of approval and disapproval are not restricted to "convention" in Weber's limited sense of the word. Hence, I define status in terms of conformity to norms, which is considerably broader than Weber's concept of "convention."

17. Pierre Bourdieu comments on systems in which differences in domination are not well institutionalized but are dependent on sustained interpersonal interaction: "in such a system, the 'great' are those who can least afford to take liberties with the official norms, and . . . the price to be paid for their outstanding value is outstanding conformity to the values of the group, the source of all symbolic value" (1977:193–94). His point is restricted to certain types of status systems. As we shall see, however, even in those systems where status is highly ascribed, conformity remains a crucial source of status.

18. While it has antecedents within contemporary social theory, "indexicality" is a term made famous by Garfinkel (1967). It points out that any meaning comes from a context that is taken for granted. Any word, concept, meaningful pattern, and so forth is like a line in an index: it refers to a much more elaborate set of meanings. Hence, no matter how explicitly one attempts to define or elucidate something, there is always a much broader implicit context that social actors must take for granted in order to carry out meaningful communication and interaction.

19. In Giddens's terms, "discursive consciousness" (1984:374).

20. As Weber notes, "Linked with this expectation [of conformity] are restrictions on social intercourse (that is, intercourse which is not subservient to economic or any other purposes)" (1968:932).

21. Institutionalization involves not only elaboration but also legitimation: the development of rationales to explain and justify the established patterns. These can range in form and generality from "common sense" maxims to myths, to theologies, to philosophies of

history, and so forth. When these patterns and their rationales are transmitted to the next generation, they become even more taken for granted. Teaching children all they need to know and answering their persistent "whys" is difficult enough without trying to communicate the conflicts and ambiguities that were involved in constructing social patterns. Hence the patterns tend to be transformed from the realm of "this is the way we worked it out the last couple of times" to "this is the way we have always done it." The elaborated and transmitted patterns become preexisting facts and objects that are "natural," "God-given," "inevitable," and so on. For a fuller discussion, see Berger and Luckmann (1967:92–128). Legitimation will be the focus of Chapter 7.

Giddens (1984) places a heavy emphasis on the importance of "routine" and routinization." The focus of his discussion, however, is on providing individual identities the stability required for "ontological security." Without discounting the importance of elaboration and routine for this process, my analysis focuses more on stabilizing and legitimizing social patterns rather than personal identities.

22. I do not mean to deny that some of these patterns of behavior are a carry-over from earlier periods when they may have actually been used in combat. But even then their primary purpose was to create discipline and coordination.

23. My discussion has focused on mechanisms which tend to lend stability to the norms of status groups. But there are subsets of norms which can be elaborated by changing them frequently. Fashions are the most obvious example of this social mechanism. Fashions are especially characteristic of status groups that are (1) relatively short-lived, such as teenage cliques, (2) threatened by upstarts, or (3) under pressure for internal differentiation. The insiders can keep the outsiders off balance by frequently changing what is defined as good taste or style. By the time the new norms are learned, they are no longer the norms. This strategy carries with it definite risk, however. Norms are less sacred and less taken for granted when they change frequently. Hence they are more vulnerable to replacement by alternative or counternorms proposed by upstarts and outsiders.

24. In many societies, including India, children (or at least some subset of them, such as sons) have a virtual absolute right to inherit the parents' property, and so concerns about marriage partners are tied to interests in the transmission of property as well as status. However, even in societies where parents have an absolute right to dispose of their wealth as they choose, there is still considerable concern about the status implications of marriages. Moreover, as I have argued, a wide variety of intimate expressive relationships have implications for status. Thus it is a mistake to see concerns about who a family's children will marry as primarily a concern about property per se.

Chapter 4

1. Some scholars also emphasize that Hinduism has roots in the Harappan civilization, which flourished in the Indus River valley from about 2500 B.C.E. to 1500 B.C.E. There are unquestionably parallels between features of this culture and Hinduism, but it is unclear to what extent there was a direct influence.

2. While tapas is mentioned in some of the earliest texts (e.g., *Rig Veda* 10.190.1), it does not become the central term until the late Brahmanas. (I am indebted to David White for this information.)

3. The importance of a deity's grace is recognized at least as early as the *Bhagavad Gita* (probably 100 B.C.E.–100 C.E.), but it receives a greatly increased emphasis with the development of the bhakti movements. This is discussed at greater length in Chapter 14.

4. I use the term "Untouchables" to refer to the lowest status outcast groups that are found in most areas of India. This is a European term that came into vogue in the nineteenth century. The traditional indigenous terms used for these groups vary widely by region, and sometimes there is no one term that refers to the entire category. Gandhi suggested the name Harijan, and the legal codes of India usually refer to these groups as "Scheduled Caste" and "Tribes." Recently, sections of these groups that are politically active have adopted the name Dalits. None of these terms is completely satisfactory, but for the nonspecialist, Untouchables most easily and accurately identifies the category of people to whom I refer.

5. If two strangers meet on a train and one asks the jati of the other, he wants to know the other person's broad occupational category—Brahman, carpenter, goldsmith, sweeper, and so on. If they happen to both be Brahmans, they will probably inquire about each other's subcaste or jati, of which there can be a number of subdivisions. On the other hand, if one Brahman meets another at a local temple and inquires about the other's jati, he probably wants to know about the other's specific local endogamous group and kinship segment. It is logically analogous to asking someone's occupation in the United States; the same person might appropriately answer teacher, college professor, engineer, mechanical engineer, heat transfer engineer, or solar energy engineer depending on who is asking, the context, and how much detail is being requested. For discussion of the concepts of caste and related terms, see Mandelbaum (1970), Béteille (1964), and Fox (1971:17–47). Because of the contextual nature of the indigenous terms, the scholarly terminology is not standardized. For example, Mandelbaum uses the words "jati" for local endogamous groups, "jati-group" for members of a jati who live in the same village, and "jati-cluster" for the more inclusive related categories. Probably the most common usage is to use "varna" to refer to the four classic categories, "caste" to refer to the broad occupational categories, and "subcaste" to refer to a variety of more specific subdivisions, down to but usually not including specific kinship lineages.

6. The question of precisely what constitutes an "explanation" is complex and controversial, and an extended answer is beyond the scope of this book. Here is a brief clarification of what I mean by the term. I do not claim to identify all the necessary and sufficient conditions for each of the phenomena listed, nor do I show that their presence or absence can be predicted with great statistical certainty. Rather, an explanation may be thought of as a concatenated description, in two senses. First, the analysis demonstrates the interconnectedness of the various phenomena being discussed—in essence, how they are part of a common pattern. Second, the concepts and propositions are sufficiently abstract to be relevant to societies other than India.

Chapter 5

1. When Dumont talks about power, he refers to a rather concrete, historically specific version of this concept: the attributes associated with kingship, specifically the Indian *raja*. Nonetheless, his terminology and analysis have produced confusion and controversy. As Owen Lynch has remarked about Dumont's work, "imprecision and equivocal meanings make not only for heated polemics, but for frozen intellectual progress" (1977:262). Wadley comments, "It is in his perception of power that I disagree most strongly with Dumont" (1975:186).

This is not to imply that Wadley would agree with the conceptualization presented here. For Wadley (1975:186–187), power derives from status and status derives from one's karma. Karma in turn is a function of the degree to which one followed one's dharma in previous lives. But such status must become embodied in some substance in order to have an effect in the world. There are two problems with this concept. First, there are sources of power other than status due to past conformity to dharma. Second, while code and substance are an important idiom for expressing how status and power operate in Hindu society, they are not the only such idiom.

2. In this context I mean two specific things by "explain." First, I will show how the key features of the caste system are extreme examples of the tendencies characteristic of most status groups. Second, I will show how a number of specific characteristics of caste, and status groups in general, can be predicted from a limited number of central features of status and status groups. I will not provide an account of the specific historical origins of the system.

3. Almost every village study published since World War II could be construed to support this contention, as well as much of the work that has been done by historians. Four standard works that stress various aspects of change are Bailey (1957), Béteille (1965), Pocock (1972), and Parry (1979). For historical analyses of India that stress the dynamic nature of pre-British economic and political institutions, see Dirks (1987) and Barnett (1993).

4. O'Flaherty writes, "*dharma* appears to be central because it is central. Unfortunately, no one is quite sure what *dharma* is; those who think they are sure clash with others equally convinced of quite different definitions" (1978:xiv). P. V. Kane, the renowned scholar of the Dharmasastras, says, "*Dharma* is one of those Sanskrit words that defy all attempts at an exact rendering in English or any other tongue" (1968:1). While dharma is a complex notion, it is probably no more difficult to define than central concepts in other complex civilizations, for example, the concepts of freedom or power in Western thought. As we shall see, the most common implication is some notion of law, code of conduct, duty, and so forth.

5. Obviously, generic institutions like the family or religion are older; I am referring to an historically specific and identifiable institution. The Roman Catholic church is probably the runner-up as a specific institution with a continuing existence.

6. Considerable uncertainty and controversy surround the dates of the early periods of Indian history. See Klostermaier (1989:415–25) for a brief discussion of some of the problems and an attempt to construct a chronological overview. Other portions of the *Rig Veda* are probably from the second millennium B.C.E. or earlier.

7. Biardeau (1989:13,160) has made a similar point about Hinduism, especially Hindu thought and science.

8. Clearly, by the 1950s the Communist revolution had significantly disrupted the continuity between the past and the present in China. Two things are less clear: (1) whether prior to that time the degree of cultural continuity in China was as great as that in India, and (2) whether the apparent weakening of the Communist regime in the 1980s will lead to a reestablishment of continuities between past and present.

9. The central defining characteristic from the typical Indian point of view is endogamy, which will be considered in a preliminary way later in this chapter and at some length in Chapter 11. This is not so much a difference in opinion about what actually happens, but rather a difference in assumptions about what is important. At least until political independence, most Indians took for granted extreme restrictions on mobility from one caste to another *and* that there were very narrow limits on the wealth and political power that could be acquired by lower castes. The first assumption still holds for most Indians, but the second is increasingly called into question by both ideology and empirical experience.

10. My primary aim is not to describe the different types of status mobility, but rather to explain why it is more restricted than in most societies. For discussions of caste mobility in India, see Silverberg (1968), Mandelbaum (1970:pt. 6), and Kolenda (1984:chap.6). Also see Beck (1972) for an important discussion of different strategies of mobility for "right-handed" and "left-handed" castes in South India. See Chapter 6 for a discussion of this issue.

11. For a discussion of the relative importance of manipulating local caste categories and varna categories, see Fox (1971:44–47). Fox's general argument is that successfully changing

one's caste category is likely to have more concrete effects on social interaction than changing one's varna classification. While this is probably true in most contexts, successfully claiming a change in a specific local caste group is usually much more difficult than arguing that one's particular Sudra caste was "originally" Kshatriya, Vaisya, or even Brahman. It is one thing to succeed in fabricating an ancestry that allows one to join the Daughters of the American Revolution, and quite another to convince people that you are a member of the Rockefeller or Kennedy clan; the latter may be more useful, but is much more difficult.

12. See White (1991:chap. 5) for references to textual examples, and see Blunt (1969:1) for a British colonial perspective; see Mandelbaum (1970) and Kolenda (1984) for summaries of contemporary ethnographic perspectives.

13. Sometimes it is said that the crushing of seeds is a form of taking life, but then of course so is the cutting of grain, and the harvesting and processing of many other plants.

The details of food patterns are complex and an adequate discussion would require considerable elaboration (see, e.g., Khare 1976).

14. At the same time, questions used to elicit the data for interactional measurements of caste rankings are largely hypothetical, since the issue of who accepts food from whom would come up only in relatively rare situations. It is somewhat analogous to trying to determine racial prejudice in the Old South by asking white persons whether they would be willing to sit next to a black person during a meal: the situation did not come up that often, and the answer would in part depend on who was asking whom the question, and whether anyone else would find out the answer. So just as attributional perspectives have their conceptual and measurement problems, so do interactional perspectives. Hertel (1983) has conducted research, in Ballia District of Uttar Pradesh, measuring caste position by both attributional and reputational techniques (not precisely the interactional techniques advocated by Marriott, but closely related). He finds that the method does not significantly affect the rankings.

Chapter 6

1. Undoubtedly, the significance of the categories to be considered has varied over time. For example, the varna scheme probably took on more importance as a result of the British census authorities' attempt to classify and rank each local caste group. What had been a textual scheme primarily of concern to Brahmans became an ideological tool in the contemporary fights for status and privilege. Nonetheless, it is clear that these categories have long been maintained as important elements of indigenous elites' effort to articulate the nature of and rationale for the social organization of Hindu society.

2. By complex societies I mean societies ranging from advanced horticultural societies, through agrarian societies, to modern industrial societies.

3. A slight modification of a line from Rogers and Hammerstein's musical *The King and I*. The original verse reads:

> Shall I join with other nations in alliance?
> If allies are weak, am I not best alone?
> If allies are strong with power to protect me,
> Might they not protect me out of all I own?

4. The seminal discussion of this issue is in Weber's sociology of religion (see especially 1968:chap. 6). My point here is not to summarize or elaborate Weber's discussion but to show how the cross-pressures that produce differentiations here are processes that operate in social formations based on all three kinds of social power.

5. Others have suggested similar models. Weber's (1968:926–40) notions of class, status, and party, Etzioni's (1975:96–126) discussion of organizational elites, and Runciman's (1966:chap. 3) discussion of the three dimensions of stratification are obvious examples. What this model adds to the picture is the underlying basis of the key categories and the internal contradictions that produce a tendency toward additional categories.

6. Additional differentiation of each of the eight categories is quite possible. The argument is not that there will always be four, eight, or whatever; these are simply the minimum number of categories required to illustrate the logic of the model.

7. Of course, what it meant to be a Brahman in the nineteenth century was not the same thing as at the beginning of the first millennium B.C.E. As has often been noted, most of the content of the Vedas has little to do with Hinduism. Nonetheless, a strong thread connects the various stages of this long cultural tradition. By the time of the Dharmasastras (ca. 500 B.C.E.– 500 C.E.), the main elements of the tradition and its implicit political, economic, and moral strategy were in place. Undoubtedly changes in the means of production, the means of coercion, and the ideological competition helped to produce major changes in the tradition itself; the development of devotional Hinduism, that is, bhakti movements and traditions, is only the most striking example. Nonetheless, the Brahmans were able to maintain a recognizable continuity of social identity.

8. As Tambiah has noted:

The brahman in due course seems to have incorporated as part of his code of conduct and religious regime some of the renouncer's aims and teachings, and thereby become "two-faced," one face looking towards the renouncer's ascetic code and borrowing from it the "pure" conduct of restraining the sense doors [*sic*] and abandoning animal sacrifice, the other face looking to the sphere of this-worldly action and officiating at auspicious and "pure" life-affirming rites. Significantly, within the ranks of the brahmans themselves, superiority comes to be accorded those who devote themselves to learning and who withdraw from priestly and temple functions. (1985:106)

Burghart (1983) has pointed out that most discussions of renouncers look at them from the point of view of the Brahman householder rather than the ascetic renouncer. See his analysis for a correction of this tendency.

9. This may not happen immediately. High levels of cynicism toward religious elites are common to many societies and historical periods, and it may not necessarily threaten the basic structures of religious institutions. For example, where religious elites have direct control of significant amounts of economic resources (e.g., are large landholders in an agrarian society), they may be fairly well insulated from "public opinion." But such situations greatly increase the temptations of political elites to appropriate their material resources. Moreover, there are limits to how much venality lay persons will tolerate, as the histories of religious reformations and transformations indicate.

10. The opposite of becoming a renouncer is to take on a lower status non-Brahmanical occupation; if some are tempted to become too fastidious, others are tempted (especially when under economic strain) to abandon the esoteric and costly lifestyle of the Brahmans. They may be attracted to activities that are directly remunerative and require a less problematic relation with the king. Alternative traditional activities are nearly always religiously and ritually degrading. This is one reason why so many Brahmans have become members of modern occupations and professions, especially those associated with learning and technical skills. These are usually neutral with respect to ritual status.

11. Gonda (1969a:11), drawing on classical Sanskrit texts (rather than the South Indian

texts that are Shulman's focus) notes that the king who tries to collect taxes without providing protection is regarded as a thief (*balisadbhagataskara*).

12. Kings are also sometimes tempted to become sannyasins. In all societies the exercise of power, and especially force, is fraught with moral ambiguities. This is particularly true in a culture that places a high religious value on nonviolence. For examples and a discussion of this phenomenon, see Shulman (1985:64–74).

13. I am not arguing that merchants were not numerous and important in India, only that they were not the primary economic elites. As Raychaudhuri points out, there is an apparent paradox about merchant activity in premodern India:

> As the bulk of the population lived in the villages and the bulk of their needs for goods and services was satisfied through production for use and a network of reciprocal obligations, exchange accounted for a relatively small proportion of economic activity. Yet exchange of goods, found at virtually every level and sphere of economic life, was impressive in its magnitude and complexity. (1982:325)

As he points out, the paradox is in part due to the fact that such a high percentage (as much as fifty percent) of the agricultural production was appropriated by political elites, and that obviously much of this was directed toward various kinds of exchanges. But this very paradox further indicates why the notion of economic elites would be ambiguous in India.

14. The subordinate and ambiguous role of merchants (and usually artisans) in premodern societies is an old story in literature (e.g., Shakespeare's *Merchant of Venice*) and scholarly analysis (e.g., Weber 1958a; Tawney 1960). The vulnerable position of merchants, even relatively late in Indian history is shown in Bayly's suggestion that one of the reasons fifteenth- and sixteenth-century Western traders met so little resistance in India was that the coastal kingdoms "did not consider sea trade and the 'business of merchants' to be important matters for kings" (1983:464). To some extent craftspeople, who frequently are also merchants of a sort, have also had an ambiguous status in agrarian societies. Such craft guilds played a crucial role in the development of both premodern and modern cities (see Sjoberg 1960), due in part to the need to have a more concentrated clientele to support specialization, but also to the denigration of nonagrarian modes of production in the countryside.

15. The sources I have found most helpful for understanding the right–left distinction are Beck (1972, 1973), Stein (1980:chap. 5), and Mines (1984:chap 3). Bayly (1983), though largely limited to an analysis of one century, is most useful in understanding the role of parallel groups in North India.

The Tamil terms *valankai* and *idankai* and their cognates in Kanada literally mean "right-handed" and "left-handed." These terms are those most typically used in the South Asian literature to discuss this distinction. As Beck (1973:395–97) points out, though, Tamil does not distinguish between the hands and the arms, so "right-sided" and "left-sided" seem more accurate translations. The opposing argument is that the left hand is associated with defecation and other impure tasks, and at times this lower status seems to be implied. Nonetheless, I believe that Beck is correct, and I refer simply to right and left castes.

16. Mines (1984:14) cites David (1974) as the source of the distinction.

17. While there were numerous and important holy women in India's history, the vast bulk of the renouncers have been men, and from the traditional Brahmanical perspective, should be men. Given this context, a nonsexist term would be anachronistic and misleading.

18. Part of the emphasis on these categories is undoubtedly due to the ethnocentrism of Western knowledge, which is in turn rooted in the biases of "Orientalism" and other types of Western scholarship. However, it remains also true that Westerners have found it strange and

exotic that these three categories should be so prominent. An ethnocentric Orientalism, may have exaggerated this prominence, but the fact remains that these categories are exceptionally important in Indian society.

19. Sudras often become internally differentiated not just into numerous jatis, but into two rather distinct categories: for example, in Bengal, *sat* ("clean") and *asat* ("unclean"); in Orissa, *panisprusya* or *pani chua* (those from whom Brahmans will accept water, literally "touching water") and *paniasprusya* or *paniachua* (those who cannot give water to Brahmans, literally "not touching water") (Marglin 1985:311). The latter category usually includes landless laborers and the providers of demeaning services. As our theory would predict, this differentiation of Sudras seems especially prevalent and important when the dominant land controllers are not recognized as one of the twice-born varnas but are themselves Sudras; understandably, they want to clearly set themselves off from their poorer varna peers.

20. Klostermaier says:

> Hindus possess an irresistible urge to classify and organize everything into neat and logical patterns. The number four serves not only to classify the Veda (into four *samhitas* and into four classes of books, considered Veda in the wider sense) and to divide humanity into basic sections but also to structure the life of individuals themselves. The successive stages of life of the high-caste person was correlated into another tetrad, the caturvarga or the "four aims of life" (purusartha). (1989:320)

21. For discussions of such methodologies of interpretation, see O'Flaherty (1973:11–21), Daniel (1983:27–62), and Swidler (1985). Each author uses the phrase "tool box" in a slightly different way.

Chapter 7

1. The fact that merchant groups frequently supported various sectarian and heterodox forms of religion, such as Jainism, or that in some periods and areas they were armed monastics, indicates that the dynamics between merchants and Brahmans were by no means identical to the dynamics between Brahmans and warriors. I do not mean to deny these complexities. Nonetheless, the most important relationships for religious elites in any agrarian society is with warrior-rulers, and that will be the focus of the analysis.

2. As indicated in Chapter 4, dharma and artha are two of the four elements of the purusartha, the goals or ends of the Hindu life. The purusartha's significance, as well as the relationship of the various goals to one another, and to the different varnas, is complex and not relevant to our immediate concerns. For a compilation of the most influential Hindu texts that discuss these four categories, see Embree (1988:chaps. 8–11). For useful discussions of the relationship of the four categories of the purusartha, see Malamoud (1982) and Biardeau (1989:chap. 2). For a discussion of the significance of dharma and artha in relationship to kingship see Shah (1982). These concepts will be discussed in slightly more detail in Chapter 10.

3. Often the concepts of status and legitimacy have been associated with consensual views of the world because they seem to imply that most people approve of most of the status quo. Clearly this was not Weber's intent, nor is it mine. Often there is considerable disagreement over a particular regime, order, or law. To claim that some patterns are more legitimate than others is not to deny conflict or disagreement. The degree of legitimacy varies between two polar models. At one extreme, a tyrant rules solely because everyone else fears him, and no one approves of any of his actions. At the other extreme, everyone fully approves of all of

the actions of the governing individual or body. Obviously, most situations fall in between these extremes. Few rulers or regimes last very long if they have no legitimacy; at the very least, a small elite or coalition must approve of each others' actions in order to dominate the rest of the population. Even this is seldom enough. However inclined ruling elites might be to rule solely by force and terror, it is extremely costly and inefficient to do so. Close surveillance and extensive violence are hard work and often dangerous. Accordingly, the higher the percentage of the population that will assist rulers in enforcing their will, the easier it is to rule. Thus most rulers seek a significant level of approval of their actions from at least a sizable minority of the population.

4. For an overview of kingly duties, see Gonda (1969a) and *Manusmriti* VII.

5. Of course, coalitions can also be made with equals or peers. Here, however, we are looking at how one gains the legitimacy to rule over others. By definition, then, one has no peers in the relevant context of one's area of domination. This would not be the case for other forms of exercising power, such as intellectual influence.

6. See Inden (1990:165–80) for a summary of these debates, though one that is constructed from a very definite point of view. Inden's own preference is for a benign, as contrasted to a despotic, version of the chakravartin model. He sees the alternatives as distortions due largely to "Orientalism."

7. A useful brief contrast of these alternatives is Biardeau (1989:64–65).

8. Certainly, the empirical reality frequently departs from the textual ideal. Brahman priests are often seen as rapacious in their pursuit of fees (see Parry 1980), but even the Brahmans themselves usually see this as a violation of the ideal. Where Brahmans are the dominant land controllers, their strategy necessarily becomes more ambiguous, even in principle. Where Brahmans or left castes are the dominant land controllers, the cross-pressures are obviously greater. To the degree that their control is secure and unchallenged, the income from the land allows them to avoid low status activities, for example, serving as temple or household priests to lower caste groups. On the other hand, their control is seldom unchallenged, and hence they frequently become involved in coercion and all the ambiguities of worldly power.

9. In principle, sannyasins cannot serve as mediators; what renunciation means is to lose concern about worldly matters, including the religious fate of others. Sannyasins, however, on occasion become gurus who lead religious orders or movements, and they sometimes seem to serve as mediators between the worldly and the divine (see Babb 1986). Such gurus, however, have obviously not fully renounced all relationships with the world. On the other hand, they rarely if ever serve as the key mediators for kings and warriors.

10. As Dirks notes: "Sovereignty which is gifted, or shared, is always partial, and always represented as a part (not the whole) of the specific sovereignty of the overlord. . . . The sovereignty of a subordinate lord, thus, is always dependent on, indeed part of, the sovereignty of the greater lord" (1987:47).

11. Dirks provides the following characterization of such relationships:

The expansion of the political system was such that the king was now able to establish hierarchical relations with individuals who had previously been either rivals or allies. In the inscriptions these chiefs are said to be independently virtuous and deserving of honor. They received honor by participating in the granting of royal gifts (*danas*). In so doing they entered into a relationship with the Pallava king predicated on the sharing of the king's sovereignty. That is, they became active and necessary participants in the central royal ritual; the sovereignty of the Pallavas which was predicated on their divine origin was shared with the chieftains who embodied similar virtues on a lesser scale. In this capacity the ritual of the royal gift proclaimed the basis of sovereignty and then, by sharing the royal perquisites of that sovereignty, established authoritative relations with loyal subordinates. (1987:29)

12. For an extremely useful description and analysis of these rituals, see Fuller (1992:chap. 5). Admittedly, these rituals focus on sacrifice rather than gifts. While these two modes are often treated as distinct in Brahmanical theory, they in fact have considerable overlap. Obviously, giving a gift involves giving up something, sacrifice in a figurative if not literal sense. Conversely, sacrifices are directed toward someone, usually a deity, and in this sense are a form of gift. The key point is that they are both a form of relatively implicit exchange characteristic of associations between those of unequal status.

13. I have benefitted greatly from a conversation with Burton Stein about the state of our knowledge on this matter. Trautmann's (1981) survey of the Dharmasastras and the typology he developed suggests such gifts would not be considered dana.

14. See Milner (1980) for a fuller discussion of this concept. Perhaps a concrete example will clarify the point. A higher status university related hospital allowed a much lower status institution to operate the ambulance service for the area. This occurred despite the fact that the surgery department of the higher status hospital very much wanted to operate such a service in order to increase the number of trauma cases, which usually require the skills of surgeons. It turned out that most of the lower status hospital's paying patients, as contrasted to charity patients, arrived via the ambulances. If the low status hospital had lost the ambulance service, they would have been forced out of business. The chief significance of this for the higher status hospital was that they would probably have had to start caring for the over 200,000 largely indigent outpatients that the lower status hospital served each year. Such an outcome would not only have seriously strained their resources, but would have eroded their status and legitimacy as a first-class teaching hospital. The nature of these exchanges were seldom, if ever, discussed publicly—and for most staff members of both institutions were largely unknown. Explicit public discussion would have seriously called into question the legitimacy of the whole arrangement. As long as the exchanges remained implicit, they played a crucial role in maintaining the viability and legitimacy of the existing institutions. Obviously, this example of implicit exchange is quite different from those we have considered in India, but in both cases implicitness is the key to maintaining the legitimacy of forms of symbiotic inequality.

15. The parallels seems strongest in the relatively late Middle Ages. Earlier guilds involved a wide variety of associations and fraternities for a number of different purposes. Despite the considerable differences in European guilds and Hindu artisan castes, drawing a parallel seems legitimate, as long as we keep in mind that the comparison is with the narrower and later European concept.

16. The more abstract point is that the nature of this social structure cannot be understood if we try to reduce either class to caste or caste to class. It is not simply a matter of who does or does not control the means of production, or who is ritually pure or polluted. Rather, interaction between these two processes produces the observed social structure. As Lloyd and Susanne Rudolph note about contemporary India:

Of the many cleavages that animate Indian politics, class usually matters less than other social formations, such as caste, religious and language communities, and regional nationalisms. Other cleavages rival or surpass class in political saliency because the consciousness and commitment focused on them are usually more transparent and accessible than those focused on class. How interests are defined and pursued, how causes (objective determinants) become reasons (subjective determinants) is more powerfully determined—for most Indian people most of the time—by formations other than class. (1987:396)

Perhaps this overstates the matter, but obviously I think it is a mistake to reduce the overall analysis of India—and for that matter most societies—to an analysis of class, *except* as an analytical strategy that fully acknowledges the partial nature of the analysis.

17. Fuller (1992:chap. 6), drawing on the work of Biardeau and others, has shown that in many areas of India there is considerable homology between the kingly festivals of Navaratri and village goddess festivals. This finding reinforces the argument that common cultural logics operate and contribute to political legitimacy at both the macro and micro level.

18. My analysis has not dealt directly with the debate over the relative importance of the Brahman and the king to the Indian caste system. To simplify considerably, the predominant view has seen the Brahman as the key instigator of the system. However, beginning with Hocart (1950) there have been those who have seen kings and local land controllers as the central figure in the system. As I have indicated, Dirks (1987), Raheja (1988), and Quigley (1993) represent such a position, though they do not, of course, deny the importance of Brahmans.

While Hindu kings and land controllers are central to caste relations, I am doubtful that they are the originators, or even as crucial to the system as Dirks and Raheja claim. Many of the various protest religions, such as Buddhism, apparently originated among Kshatriyas, and this seems unlikely if caste were primarily an institution of kingly power. Various forms of the caste system have existed under a considerable array of regimes, including Asoka's Buddhism, Buddhist kings in Sri Lanka, a wide array of various Muslim rulers, the British, and the contemporary secular Indian state. In addition, of course, there has been enormous variation over time and space in what constitutes Hindu kingship. Hindu kings obviously are not a necessary condition for the maintenance of the caste system over very considerable periods of time. Local economic and political dominance have been exercised at one place or another by individuals, families, or jatis from virtually every varna—not to mention Muslims, Sikhs, Christians, Parsis, and others—without usually threatening the basic features of caste. I believe a key source of the system's resilience has been its ability to adapt to a wide variety of political elites.

A subsidiary argument is that the caste system "as we know it" did not develop until British rule, and is "fundamentally" different from what preceded it, especially from what existed under Hindu kings. This seems to me to overstate the case and depends on what is meant by such words as "fundamentally." Undoubtedly, there have been profound changes, but the key structural characteristics of restricted mobility, endogamy, commensuality, and a concern about pollution have been present for a very long time—though, of course, their intensity and form have varied. None of this is to deny that kings played a very important role in Hindu society and had a significant impact on caste relations.

Quigley's book (1993), which is strongly influenced by Hocart (1950), did not become available until my book was already in press. Consequently, I have not dealt with its arguments in as much detail as I would have liked. While I am, of course, sympathetic to his emphasis on comparative analysis, his argument that caste is a function of the tension between kinship and political centralization does not result in a systematic organization of a wide array of data that, in my opinion, should be the goal of a theory of caste.

Like most of the literature, I have focused this analysis of gift giving on the behaviors of kings or local land controllers and priests. Rudner (1987) has pointed out that merchant groups also were important donors and played a crucial role in gift exchange, but our data about this is still quite limited.

Chapter 8

1. Here the argument obviously draws on some assumptions about what people want and proceeds to describe where that leads. In that sense, this part of the analysis draws on at least some of the assumptions of rational choice theory.

2. As we shall see, Marriott's (1976, 1989) ethnosociology makes this concept central to understanding Indian society, though he would probably not accept the broader theoretical context in which I have placed it.

3. It may also be useful to develop a parallel concept of *subjectification* to refer to situations in which physical objects and processes are defined as being similar to human subjects. The most obvious examples of this are animism, possession-exorcism, and various forms of anthropomorphism. Various forms of magic also tend to assume this form of reification.

4. A note is needed about the relationship between "moral" exchange and mechanical-causal processes. As I have already indicated, status processes in their "pure" form involve the expressions of authentic evaluations without consideration of what one will receive in return; that is, they are moral processes. I have said that objectification involves exchange and mechanical processes. Exchange is involved insofar as there are efforts to acquire various kinds of objects or semiobjects by giving something in return; the exchange may be direct quid pro quo or more indirect and implicit, but it involves some calculation of return—rather than evaluations expressed independently of anticipated returns. Mechanical and causal processes are involved insofar as the status that is associated with these objects is transferred to the actor who has acquired them. This matter will be taken up in more detail in Chapter 12.

5. For discussions of the significance of status symbols and fetishism that are related to the issues raised here, see Dirks (1987:337–41) and Taussig (1980:31–38).

6. Setbacks experienced by groups are seen as due to the hidden actions of other groups: it's the fault of the Communists, the "capitalist roaders," the ruling class, politicians, the CIA, the Israel lobby, the PLO, the Black Panthers, the drug lords, terrorists, the old-boy network, the women's libbers, and so on. This is not to say that these groups are necessarily nonexistent or without fault or power, but only that it is highly unlikely that they are responsible for all the things of which they are accused—though, of course, they may have done unseemly things that are not even suspected.

7. For examples of this debate, see the quotes from Roger Wilkins and Patrick Buchanan in Edsall (1991:78–79).

8. The objective redistribution of risk is possible because of the law of large numbers: while predicting the probabilities of an individual event may be impossible, often predicting the rate of such events for different categories of individuals is possible. Obviously it is more possible with careful records and actuarial analysis, but for many activities conventional wisdom has a fairly accurate knowledge of relative risk. Unsurprisingly, social inferiors are often assigned the riskiest jobs. For example, mine owners seldom have their personal offices in the lower depths of their pits; if they were required to do so, it seems highly likely that safety equipment would be more elaborate and mine accidents less frequent. While the location of such executive offices is in part a matter of convenience and efficiency, the redistribution of risk is undoubtedly an implicit consideration.

9. They may or may not define these as contingent events. In some societies, disasters may be attributed to the people's sinfulness or lapses in ritual procedures, transforming an area of contingency into an area of agency. In Vedic India, the cosmos itself was seen as sustained by ritual activities, and in principle, little or nothing was contingent.

10. When there are high levels of inequality, but the scope of authority differences is elaborately specified and limited by written rules—as in a rational-legal bureaucracy or a

modern legal system—a different kind of ritual response is likely. In this type of social situation, we are likely to find ritualistic conformity to rules and precedents, and the development of "bureaucratic personalities" (Merton 1957:chap. 6). In other words, instead of using magic to protect oneself from great power, the actors rely on formal rather than substantive rationality (Weber 1968, especially 225–26), which may subvert and displace the goals of the organization.

11. This emphasis can be highlighted by comparing the decisions one must make about one's role as a status-group member with the decisions one must make as a participant in markets and bureaucracies: decisions made in relationship to status-group membership are defined by the actors as typically and predominantly moral, while decisions related to markets and bureaucracies are defined as typically and predominantly technical. The latter process is seen most clearly in modern positive legal systems where it is explicitly stated that the task is to decide what is legal, not what is moral or just. This is a key emphasis in Luhmann's work (1982:chap. 6).

Chapter 9

1. The pledge to the flag was first used in 1892, and enacted by Congress as part of the laws governing use of the flag in 1942. The text has been revised several times and now reads: "I pledge allegiance to the flag of the United States of America and to the Republic for which it stands, one Nation under God, indivisible, with liberty and justice for all."

2. To discuss the literature relevant to this debate would require an extensive tangent inappropriate to the present task. See Nagel (1961) and Homans (1964) for an exposition of the argument for causal analysis, and see Rabinow and Sullivan (1987) for a selection of articles explaining and defending the interpretive approach.

3. As Locke (1975:2:xxvi) emphasized, the notion of causation assumes well-defined separate identities. For all of Hume's (1985:2:iii) famous skepticism about the notions of cause and effect, he seems to have taken this point for granted; his whole argument revolves around the discussion of a certain kind of relationship between "objects" that are assumed to have distinct identities.

4. The notion of behavior assumes some entity that has both relatively stable and relatively variable aspects of its identity. The more variable aspects are referred to as "behavior," but such a concept has little meaning if more stable features cannot be identified. Of course, the matter is considerably more complex than this. See Nozick (1981:chap. 1) for a philosophical discussion of the problem of the identity of the self.

5. As I indicated earlier, this is one point of contact with Habermas's critical theory. See note 19, Chapter 1.

6. In Dumont's words: "The [central characteristics of the caste system] rest on one fundamental conception and are reducible to a single true principle, namely the opposition of the pure and the impure" (1980:43).

7. To quote Goffman:

> I have touched on eight territories of the self, all of a situational or an egocentric kind. . . . One general feature of these several forms of territoriality should be noted: their socially determined variability. Given a particular setting and what is available in it, the extensivity of preserves obviously can vary greatly according to power and rank. . . . In general, the higher their rank, the greater the size of all territories of the self and the greater the control across the boundaries. (1971:40–41)

8. We do not complain about impurity if a tradesperson runs short of the quality we ordered and completes the order by adding higher quality items at no extra charge. As we shall see, there are some analogues of this process in the Indian caste system. For example, lower status groups are willing to accept food from higher status groups, but not the reverse. Marglin (1985b), drawing on the work of Tambiah (1974), provides a more technical statement of the asymmetry between the pure and the impure, drawing on the language of structuralism.

9. For a discussion of dirt and pollution in contemporary India in the context of economic development, see Milner (1987b).

10. For example, the subdivision of a jati referred to in medieval Bengal as *kula* (Inden, 1976) and *kuti* or matrician of certain regions in Sri Lanka (McGilvray, 1982).

11. For example, Marriott says:

Indian thought about transactions differs from much of Western sociological and psychological thought in not presuming the separability of actors from actions. By Indian modes of thought, what goes on *between* actors are the same connected processes of mixing and separation that go on *within* actors. Actors' particular natures are thought to be the results as well as causes of their particular actions (*karma*). Varied codes of action or codes of conduct (*dharma*) are thought to be naturally embodied in actors and otherwise substantialized in the flow of things that pass among actors. Thus the assumption of the easy, proper separability of action from actor, of code from substance . . . that pervades both Western philosophy and Western common sense . . . is generally absent: code and substance (Sanskrit *purusa*, and *prakriti*, *dharma*, and *sarira*, and so on) cannot have separate existences in this world of constituted things as conceived by most South Asians. (1976:109–10)

12. The adequacy of the Marriott perspective has been called into question. The general thrust of the criticisms, as summarized by McGilvray, is to "challenge the uniformity and consistency of indigenous 'caste ideologies' [in my terms, cultural codes or categories] in different South Asian field work settings" (1982:1). McGilvray found in his study of a Tamil caste in Sri Lanka that the perspective of Marriott was not useful in understanding caste: "Theories of bodily substance are highly developed, but in the view of local people they clearly belong to the cultural domain of medicine and health, not to an 'ethnosociological' metaphysic of caste identity" (1982:35). Even more deviant, in terms of both the Dumont and the Marriott perspectives, ideas of ritual purity were not particularly crucial to caste rank in this cultural setting. While the notions of purity and impurity were well known, they were relevant mainly in relation to domestic life crises: birth, death, and so on. In contrast, the primary terms in which the ranks of castes and or *kutis* (matrilineal clan groups) were rationalized involved images of feudal political power, authority, and honor—not purity. These images were central to Hocart's (1950) theory of caste. Similarly, Stirrat (1982) found that while caste is a definite phenomenon among Sinhalese Catholics, there is even less emphasis on pollution. Parry (1989b), who has conducted extensive research on death rites, points out that while Marriott's monism does tap an important element of Hinduism, there are also strong strains of dualism. Therefore, characterizing India as monistic and the West as dualistic unnecessarily exaggerates the contrast. Even more significantly, Parry suggests that the fluidity of the body and the person may be related to the relative rigidity of caste categories.

In some of his early work, Marriott (1955) made social scientists aware of the need to carefully study the interrelationship between Great Traditions and Little Traditions. While these two notions have come under criticism (e.g., Fuller 1992) they point to an important point concerning ethnosociologies. In different areas, and among different subgroups in the same area, varying strands of the Great Tradition will be drawn upon to create the local Little Tradition. Thus while a general theory of status groups and a careful analysis of Great Traditions are crucial to understanding patterns in a particular village or period, we should not be shocked to find that these do not explain everything; they will have to be supplemented by careful attention to the local and particularistic elements of the Little Traditions. In other words we must be sensitive to both the universalistic and the particularistic patterns of social structure and be careful not to reduce one to the other. In my opinion, both Dumont's work and Marriott's ethnosociology pay too little attention both to general sociological propositions and to Little Traditions. As important as the analyses of pan-Indic ideologies and traditions may be, they are not a substitute for either general sociological theory or the careful analysis of relatively unique features of particular social groups.

13. The texts Das "selected for detailed analysis . . . [are] the *Dharmaranya Purana*, a mythical history of the Modh Brahmans and Modh Baniyas of Gujarat . . . [and] the *Grihya Sutra* of Gobhila, which provides the earliest detailed instructions for the performance of what are known as domestic rites" (1982:6).

14. Practices such as animal sacrifice, drinking of alcohol by lower caste groups, and periods of relaxed sexual and moral standards such as *Holi* are sometimes identified with Tantrism. This is questionable. As Biardeau says, "to speak of tantrism in the context of the small temples of the village boundary goddess is out of the question; and this is a sign that tantric practice continues to be accompanied by a certain refinement in knowledge, and correlatively by a certain social position, which village shrines cannot offer" (1989:152). Brooks (1990) also emphasizes the elitism of Tantrism.

15. The sources I have primarily relied on for my understanding of Hindu Tantrism are Gupta et al. (1979), Sanderson (1985), Biardeau (1989), and Brooks (1990).

Chapter 10

1. See Srinivas (1965), Carman and Luke (1968), Khare (1976); for a discussion of this material, see Marglin (1985a:282–99).

2. Madan (1985), Marglin (1985a, 1985b), Inden (1985), Raheja (1988, especially 37–48), and Parry (1991) have all discussed the usage and meaning of the various terms translated as "auspiciousness" and "inauspiciousness," as well as related phrases and terms. These authors are not in complete agreement about the significance of linguistic differences. There is probably some variation between the local groups on which they base their observations. I do not discuss these semantic variations, except at one or two points where it is crucial to my argument. My assumption is that while regional and caste variations exist, in most areas of India, notions roughly synonymous with the English terms "auspicious" and "inauspicious" are present. Such variations may be important, but at this point in time we do not have enough data to systematically identify these, much less explain them. This paucity of information about regional variations is a recurring problem in Indian studies, but is less acute for many other features of Indic culture. For example, in Chapter 11, I will attempt to analyze such variations in the patterns of marriage alliances.

3. I am referring here to unauthorized individualistic transvestism that is deviant from the person's core social position. There are, of course, certain groups and certain times when cross-gender dressing is appropriate and even expected. Such momentary and authorized taking on of different roles is not especially threatening to the social structure or the individual, because it is understood that everyone will soon return to their usual and expected roles. This is not the case with either life-cycle transitions or individualized deviance.

4. Marglin notes:

The opposition between auspiciousness and inauspiciousness is not an exclusive binary one, but one that lacks a fixed boundary between the two poles. Such lack of separation or boundary between signs allows them to carry meanings of dynamism such as the flow of time, processes of growth, maturation, and decay, or a dynamic force like *sakti*. (1985a:296)

5. I use these terms from European feudalism as an analogy and do not mean to imply that Indian social structure was feudal in the technical sense.

6. For an explanation of indexicality, see Chapter 3, note 18.

7. Another illustration: all languages have both a grammar and irregularities (in the technical linguistic sense). Anyone who has ever studied a foreign language soon learns that it is fruitless to look for a pattern to these irregularities or to ask why they exist; they simply have to be accepted and learned in order to use or understand that language. It seems to me that there is every reason to expect the same thing in nonlinguistic systems of meaning; in fact, in such systems the differentiation between signs, and the link between signs and what is signified, are often less systematic and more ambiguous. Thus such systems seem likely to have higher rates of irregularities. (The concept of linguistic irregularity used in this note is different from the concept of omens as irregularity used in the main argument of the text. For omens, the irregularities *are* the grammar: they are the pattern behind auspiciousness and inauspiciousness.)

8. For a useful discussion of deification as a means of controlling threatening forces, see Fuller (1992:chap. 10).

9. Raheja's discussion indicates that one key source of inauspiciousness is those who are in ambivalent or ambiguous cultural categories:

There is one further type of prestation that may be made to remove the inauspiciousness of a *bhut* or *dev-pitar*. It concerns those whose deaths have occurred "out of time" (*akal mrirtyu*), those who, because they were not 'satisfied' (*santusti*) and had no offspring, are unable to "take another birth" (*dusri janam nahi le sakte*). Their continued presence in the house may be a source of "afflictions" (*kast*) and "trouble" (*paresani*) to those live in there: they "wander and turn" (*ghumna-phirna*) and bring inauspiciousness with them. (1988:159)

This is compatible with my argument that a key source of inauspiciousness is ambiguity about structural boundaries and the fluidity of the power this creates.

10. *Dan* is the usual transliteration of the Hindi cognate for the Sanskrit word "dana." The Hindi form is used by Raheja (1988) and her informants.

11. See the glossary for a definition of "prestation."

12. Pfaffenberger (1982) has reported a similar finding for Tamil Sri Lanka, though he has not focused on inauspiciousness and dana in the same way Raheja has.

13. There is little question that lower status castes often accepted dana primarily because of coercion. Raheja reports:

[N]owadays, according to villagers, the Barber is often reluctant to accept the *jora* [a cloth placed over the body during burial preparations] because of its extreme inauspiciousness; in the past, he would simply have been ordered to take it by his *jajman*. But "the times have changed" (*zamana badal gaya*), Gujars say, and now the *jora* is usually burnt with the body. (1988:148)

14. The phrase left out by the elipses is: "as in the *anasara* period of Ratha Jatra." *Anasara* means "period of illness," and Ratha Jatra refers to the famous "Car Festival" at the temple in Puri in honor of Jagannatha, a form of Visnu. (The inexorable movement of the huge temple cart bearing Jagannatha's image is the origin of the English word "juggernaut.") The deities of the temple are taken out in procession annually in order that they can be renewed and in turn symbolically renew the king and the kingdom. The "period of illness" is a two-week period, during the dark of the moon, that interrupts the bathing of the temple images in preparation for the festival and the beginning of the procession. I believe that Marglin's words are relevant to a much broader array of phenomena, and that is why I have left out this specifying phrase.

15. There are, of course, contemporary parallels. Religious elites face the dilemma of how to symbolize the legitimacy of their sources of income (and more generally conventional worldly activities), on the one hand, and their advocacy of various forms of otherworldliness, on the other hand. In the United States during the 1970s and 1980s, James and Tammy Faye Bakker developed a highly popular religious television program by carefully balancing an affirmation of conventional economic success and lifestyles with a call for a more "spiritual" life. The basic message was that Christianity will make you successful and does not conflict with consumerism. The format of the program was that of the typical U.S. television talk show: interviews, musical numbers, brief news reports, and the like. That is, the format stood for conventional secular America. In contrast, the name of the show was the "PTL Club"; PTL was the abbreviation of "Praise the Lord."

Perhaps the Bakkers' balancing act between these two poles was best symbolized in the recreational theme park they developed outside Charlotte, North Carolina, called Heritage U.S.A. It combined the commercial consumerism and subdued hedonism characteristic of a Disneyland with a religious retreat center. As the name of the facility indicates, the two aspects were held together, in part, through a heavy stress on patriotism; American flags were in frequent display. Most of the architecture and commercial services were little different from what would be found in any other middle class tourist center, but important secondary symbols were changed. Instead of Muzak, one heard "Gospelpop" in restaurants, hotels, and shops. In addition to the usual array of souvenirs, gift shops contained a wide array of religious items—for example, pictures of Jesus, and a generous supply of religious books. Employees, including waitresses, were expected to be exceptionally friendly. In short, sets of secondary norms and symbols were developed in an attempt to contain the contradictions. Brahmans must both retain semen and reproduce; members of the PTL Club should both be spiritual and enjoy worldly success. Bakker developed an extensive loyal following who, for a fee, became "partners." In effect, the Bakkers attempted to create a quasi-status group. The solidarity of their followers was not rooted primarily on some common relationship to the means of production; while most were apparently working or middle class Southerners with a background in small towns, his following was quite diverse, in terms of both geography and economic base. The common denominator was a particular style of life—or at least an aspiration to that style. The essence of that style was a nouveau-riche mass consumerism and a conventional conservative religious piety. This quasi-status group needed help in reconciling religious asceticism and otherworldliness on the one hand, with hedonistic consumerism and the idea of occupational success as the determinant of self worth, on the other. The first are central to Biblical religion, while the second are central to the American economy.

The Bakkers' balancing act ultimately failed. Because of both financial and sexual improprieties, Jim Bakker was dismissed by his religious denomination and sent to prison; the theme park went bankrupt and was closed. What makes the case interesting is that the evidence seems to indicate that initially Bakker was not simply a cynical manipulator, but was eventually corrupted by his success; a success based on his ability to express and symbolize two themes or tendencies that were in great tension. That Bakker was at first highly success-ful, and then failed, is testimony to the severity of the cultural contradiction he attempted to resolve by largely symbolic means.

None of this is to say that the Bakkers and their followers were the equivalent of would-be Brahmans. It is to say that status groups, and especially religious status groups, typically face severe tensions between affirming conventional economic values and claiming that their status is rooted in something "higher" and more lasting than the possession of wealth—*and* that they frequently use elaborate sets of secondary norms, rituals, and symbols in an attempt to balance these tensions.

16. Of course at various points some southern whites claimed such religious legitimacy for segregation. But blacks and whites used precisely the same religious texts, the King James Version of the English Bible, to justify their domination and resistance. Clearly, on balance, the texts favored the position of the blacks. Biblically based arguments for the racial inferiority of blacks have virtually disappeared from public discourse in the United States. In contrast, lower caste groups in principle had no access to the religious texts which had legiti-macy among higher caste groups, and the texts of most significance to upper caste groups ei-ther assumed the caste system or offered explicit rationales for it.

For a sympathetic discussion of Cox's work, including his discussion of caste, see the introduction to Hunter and Abraham (1987).

17. I do not mean to imply that conflation is necessarily bad or intellectually inferior. The strong tendency in Western cultures to treat as completely separate the biological, mental, and moral spheres is something Western medicine is having to seriously rethink.

18. In some respects, we could use Althusser's term and say that caste structures are "overdetermined" (1990, especially 89–128); the more general status processes are funda-mental, but they take on a specificity and concreteness through the additional layers of cultural symbols. While there is much about Althusser's Marxism with which I disagree, I admire his attempt to struggle toward a more adequate way of conceptualizing and stating complex forms of causal relationships.

Chapter 11

1. For an attempt to deal with these issues, see Klass (1980).

2. This is only a very informal and loose attempt to distinguish different types and levels of causation. A careful specification of the relationship between the different levels— that is, between individual action and macro outcomes—would require a much more forma-listic approach to theory construction, which would not be in the spirit and style of the present endeavor. Coleman's (1990) work is the outstanding example of developing rational choice theory in a formal manner.

3. A theory of status relationships is not the only way to approach the analysis of marriage alliances. Obviously, kinship structures and inheritance of material property also play a crucial role in the creation of marriage alliances. (For analyses that tend to emphasize these other factors, see, e.g., Tambiah 1973, Dumont 1983, Parkin 1990, and Upadhya 1990.) It would be possible to approach the analysis of marriage alliances by developing theories about the operation of these processes and then introduce status considerations as exogenous variables. But, of course, the purpose of this book is to demonstrate the utility of a theory of status relationships. Hence that is the perspective from which marriage alliances will be analyzed.

4. The development of such ideologies might usefully be considered a distinct fourth order phenomenon.

5. Some castes, mainly high status Rajputs and Jats, are infamous for having practiced female infanticide (see, e.g., Parry 1979:213–21; Hershman 1981). But this was a "solution" for them only because they could impose a significant portion of the cost of a shortage of females on groups lower down the hierarchy. I am not denying that female infanticide occurred at substantial rates for some limited subpopulations. It was not, however, the primary cultural response to the dilemmas of being a wife-giver.

6. The dilemma between asymmetrical exchange and reciprocity is a very old one in India, and is not limited to marriage alliances. Heesterman notes that this same dilemma was characteristic of Vedic and classical India:

> The classical system implies that it is each time the same yajamana who spends his wealth on the brahmins, but the pre-classical system called for reciprocity. In order not to remain permanently saddled with the inferiority implied in his accepting the opponent's food and presents, the donee has to reciprocate ("sich Revanchieren"). (1985:31)

7. I have no direct evidence that families of the groom avoid hypogamy and engage in hypergamy in order to better control women. Control of women is, however, clearly a concern. For example, one of the common reasons given for village exogamy is to avoid interference by the wife's family. Moreover, in Kolenda's analysis of sibling set marriages—two brides from one household marrying into the same family—she cites studies indicating such marriages are frowned upon in some regions because the presence of two sisters in the same household might make them less compliant (1978:267–73). Given these concerns, the problems that might arise if a daughter-in-law were from a family of higher status are likely to be relevant. Of course, where hypergamy and the subservient position of women is thoroughly institutionalized, this potential problem may not be explicitly considered by a given family. This does not, however, mean that such considerations did not come into play in the formation of the institutionalized pattern. The issue can be posed in terms of what Weber would have called a "mental experiment": would male authority be as strong and as taken for granted if the ideal pattern was for women to come from higher status families? It seems highly improbable. In sum, patriarchy is not the immediate cause of the inferiority of wife-givers and hypergamy, but is probably an important antecedent and indirect cause.

8. As Fruzzetti says, "The greatest gift a man can bestow, the one from which he acquires the most merit (*punya*), is the gift of his daughter in marriage" (1982:17).

9. John 1:29, incorporated in the Latin Mass as the Agnus Dei in the late seventh century.

10. Trautmann has commented, "Marriage as a form of exchange is a curiously one-sided affair, oriented in one direction only, and its asymmetry has a hypergamous cast to it. The groom's party are the superiors and benefactors of the bride" (1981:292). He notes that after the period of the Vedas, Brahman thought developed in a direction strongly hostile to reciprocity. This is expressed in the notion of kanyadana and "informs the doctrine that daughters must be given up (anuloma) rather than down (pratiloma). It is this rich concept that opposes hypergamy to the ideal of isogamy" (1981:293). But in the context of concerns about proper worship and the transfer of inauspiciousness, this asymmetry is not so "curious" after all.

11. This is customarily rationalized in terms of what are referred to as the four *gotra* rule—a gotra is a clan within a jati—and the prohibitions against marrying *sapinda*—those defined as sharing common "bodily particles" (see Trautmann 1981:239–77; van der Veen 1973:86–95; Parry 1979:221–27). These notions are too complex to be defined and discussed here. The basic idea, however, is that one cannot marry any of the descendants of one's own

ancestors on either the father's or mother's side for four or more generations back.

12. For a systematic theoretical discussion of these issues, see Blau (1977). For an example of how demographic imbalances between males and females shape marriage patterns, see Coleman (1990:22) and the references he cites.

13. The same problem can also operate geographically if brides tend to move in one direction. In the classical Rajput system, brides ideally moved from east to west; to the degree that the system actually operated this way, this should have created a scarcity of brides in the east and a surplus in the west (see Shah 1982:15n.16).

14. For another example of oscillation, see Shah (1982:16).

15. The form of hypergamy discussed in this section is dependent on the inferiority of wife-givers and the ideology of kanyadana. While this is the key source of most hypergamy in South Asia, there are other sources for some matrilocal South Indian groups (see Milner 1988).

16. It has often been argued that the cross-cousin marriage characteristic of South India reduces the degree of patriarchy in that area. Conklin (1973) attempts to directly test this hypothesis and finds little support for it. While his data and analysis are certainly not definitive, they suggest that rural upper caste South Indian marriage patterns cannot be explained in terms of reduced patriarchy alone.

17. The matrilateral pattern is the most common form of cross-cousin marriage. Initially I thought this might be because it least contradicts the ideology of kanyadana. This pattern takes the form of generalized exchange: A gives to B, B gives to C, C gives to A. In contrast, the patrilateral pattern involves the reversal of roles every other generation, while the bilateral pattern involves direct exchange in the current generation. Hence the matrilateral pattern would seem to best disguise direct exchange and be the least incompatible with the notion of asymmetrical gift giving. On the basis of the evidence now available, however (especially Beck 1972), the matrilateral pattern is apparently most common among castes not adhering to the ideology of kanyadana. Brahmans and other relatively orthodox castes are most likely to engage in patrilateral marriages. Hence the motivation to keep marriage alliances within a narrow circle of families whose ritual standing is unquestioned seems to be a much stronger concern than any contradiction between cross-cousin marriage and the ideology of kanyadana.

18. In the case of matrilocal societies where the couple goes to reside with the bride's parents, the sons rather than daughters are exchanged, though the culture involved may or may not define the relationship in these terms.

19. The following discussion of Dravidian kinship is heavily indebted to Trautmann (1981).

20. This quote is in the context of commenting on the contribution of Carter's (1974) work, but it seems clear that this represents Dumont's position.

21. While cross-cousin marriage is particularly characteristic of the Dravidian region, Parkin (1990) has argued that, considered over long historical periods, cross-cousin marriage may have been much more widely dispersed. The implication is that the distinction between North and South India is more one of gradation than of absolute difference.

22. As Hershman says, "it is only within specific ritual contexts that two kin groups, whether lineages or kindreds, may be seen to be aligned in hierarchical status, but that this ritual inequality at least in the present day Punjab has no further implications for ongoing relations of political inequality between the two" (1981:199).

23. As Hershman notes:

[G]iven the negative rule of nonreversal, the more diffused the actual network of marriages made . . . the greater the equality between all of the units which compose the system; while the more concentrated and repetitive the marriages, the greater the inequality and the greater the potential for the formation of hypergamous relationships. (1981:231–32)

In turn, this diffusion of marriage alliances is in part possible because Jats are a very large caste widely dispersed throughout the Punjab.

24. As Fruzzetti and Ostor conclude in their long review of North Indian kinship terminology:

> Not only is the terminology no guide to marriage (in terms of who is a consanguine, who is an affine, who is marriageable and who is not), but it does not lead to any "groups" whether or not these be in wife-giving and wife-taking, shared descent, lineage, or genealogical blood relationships to each other. . . . In the light of our discussion we may state that hypergamy as anthropological construct [*sic*] has nothing to do with the terminology. (1976:93)

25. According to Trautmann (1981:chap. 5), cross-cousin marriage is unlikely to have been widely practiced outside of Dravidian areas—the allusion in classical texts notwithstanding. Parkin's (1990) work calls this assumption into question. As noted earlier, Parkin argues that instead of an absolute distinction between the kinship systems of North and South, the differences may be more a matter of gradation that is probably the result of long-term historical transformation. Nonetheless, there is currently no significant evidence that cross-cousin marriage patterns lie behind the legitimacy of exchange marriages in Bengal. Another possible source of exchange marriage is the influence of Muslim culture in Bengal, though I have found no specific evidence that this is the case. If either of these possibilities proved to be true, it would not significantly affect the interpretation offered here, since the argument hinges on the presence of exchange marriages—whatever their source.

26. But the tendency to selectively draw on the tradition of kanyadana is not limited to the acceptance of exchange marriages. Fruzzetti claims there is a clear conceptual differentiation between the gift of the virgin and the dowry:

> The gift of the virgin is dictated by caste and kinship principles whereas the dowry is dictated by the sheer availability of cash and property. The two cannot be equated and the criteria for one cannot be reduced to the other. The virgin is given amidst rites of the *kanya dan*; the dowry is paid before the marriage. . . . The virgin is not a commodity, as I have already shown by contrasting *sampradan* (gift of the virgin) to *pon* (dowry), the latter being a *dabi*, a rightful demand which is made before accepting the virgin. (1982:39, 41)

Contrast this to Parry's description of the Rajput view:

> The very idea that the two fathers should sit down together and strike a bargain as if they were haggling over some business deal is pure anathema to Kangra people. The ideal is rather that the groom's side should accept whatever comes their way without comment or complaint, and that the bride's father should give as much as he can possibly afford. But in practice the wife-takers seldom remain entirely aloof from such matters; and they are particularly unlikely to do so when the bride's status is appreciably lower than their own. In order to preserve appearances, however, they themselves stolidly maintain the appearance of complete disinterest while a tacit understanding is reached through intermediaries, who subtly communicate the expectations (or even demands) of the groom's side. (1979:241)

The contrast should not be overdrawn; the differences are of degree. Nonetheless, both in theory and in practice, the Bengalis are more open and explicit about dowry demands, and they conceptually and psychologically differentiate the dowry from the kanyadana, and encapsulate each in its own sphere. The conceptions of kanyadana and exchange marriages probably undergo a similar differentiation and encapsulation.

27. For an alternative attempt to contrast patterns in Bengal and the Dravidian south (more specifically, Tamil Nadu), see Fruzzetti, Ostor, and Barnett (1976).

A few remarks are in order about the literature on Bengali kinship and marriage not discussed up to this point. Much of this literature has been heavily influenced by Schneider (1968). His work stresses the analysis of the relationship between indigenous cultural categories, rather than the cross-cultural comparisons of supposedly universal kinship categories. The work of Inden (1976) and Inden and Nicholas (1977) focuses on the concepts of "substances and codes," while the work of Fruzzetti and Ostor focuses on the "concepts of the person" (Fruzzetti, Ostor, and Barnett 1976; Fruzzetti 1982, 1983). The arguments presented here should not be seen as necessarily hostile to the substantive arguments suggested in these analyses. As I have indicated earlier, the systematic analysis of indigenous categories can be crucial to understanding social arrangements. Inden and Nicholas (1977) show how who is considered (in conventional terminology) an affine and who is considered a consanguine can be much more adequately grasped by a systematic analysis of indigenous categories. Fruzzetti and Ostor (1983) illustrate how the reluctance to form marriage alliances with ego's mother's sister's line because of the danger of "bad blood" can be understood as concern about ritual roles at the time of funeral rites. These kinds of insights could not have been developed by focusing on the types of variables that have been of primary concern in this analysis. But it does not follow that all analyses must primarily focus on the content and relationship of indigenous cultural categories. Moreover, limiting ourselves to such an approach restricts our insight and understanding. Inden's (1976) historical analysis of marriage and rank in Bengal in the period from 1500 to 1850 is instructive in this respect. A major feature of the earlier period is the presence of hypergamous (and hypogamous) marriage arrangements. A central theme in the analysis is the notion of marriage as the worship of those of superior "substances and codes." Inden also briefly discusses why the centrality of marriage has changed, and presumably why these patterns of hypergamy and hypogamy might have emerged and then disappeared. Here he resorts to arguments having to do with changing forms of political control under the Muslims, the British, and the modern independent nation-state—an argument only very tangentially dependent on the elaborate analysis of Bengali cultural categories. Nor does he argue that such a hypothesis requires the careful elaboration of the indigenous concepts of kings, the state, and political power, held by the Hindus, Muslims, and British. He implicitly assumes that whatever cultural variations there may be in these notions, they are not crucial to the point he wishes to make. This is, I believe, a legitimate assumption, but one that should be acknowledged as legitimate for other styles and strategies of analysis as well. I believe Inden's later work (1990) makes room for such approaches, though as indicated in Chapter 1, there are other arguments I find problematic. In sum, while I am sympathetic to many of the concerns and findings of the line of research that focuses on the relation of indigenous categories, I believe it is a mistake to eschew other forms of analysis.

28. Beck's (1972) study of right and left castes in Konku (a district of Tamil Nadu) in some respects provides the exception that proves the rule. The right castes consist of the key land-controlling castes and the other castes closely allied with them. The left castes include artisan and merchant castes and the lower castes allied with them. Brahmans are, in principle, neutral and above this division. In fact, left castes emulate the Brahmanical lifestyle. These left castes are excluded from influence and high status based on control of the local agrarian economy. In response, they emphasize their purer lifestyle and their ties to regional and all-India religious concepts and activities. In this region, the marriage pattern of virtually all groups takes the form of isogamy; there are no institutionalized ranked strata within castes or subcastes. Most castes engage in a series of counter-prestations at marriage, and specifically

have a traditionally fixed bride price called a *paricam*. But there are partial exceptions. Beck reports, "Only two groups, the Brahmans and the Coli Acari, claim to have no traditionally 'fixed' paricam sum. . . . It is most interesting, therefore, that these groups place the most stress on dowry" (1972:236–37). These Brahmans and a few left castes not only deny that they accept a bride price, and emphasize the significance of dowries, but more generally adopt the ideology of kanyadana. As Beck notes, "This tendency to distinguish between wife-givers and wife-takers on the part of left-division groups is associated with their special emphasis on dowry and their determination that the receiver of the bride be superior" (1972:13). This tendency of left castes to model themselves after Brahmans is, in turn, rooted in their relative economic independence from local land controllers. As Heesterman notes, left castes do not mediate power for the lower ones, while right castes do (1985:14). That is, left castes depend on conformity to acquire status, right castes depend on association and deference. Likewise, it is the left castes, which have a minimum of relationships with those of different status outside their caste, that tend to develop differentiations within the caste. Hence, as our theory would predict, it is among those middle castes that model themselves after Brahmans that the strains toward hypergamy would begin to appear. It is here, where most important day-to-day associations are with status equals, that the countervailing tendencies toward status heterogeneity start to play a significant role within the caste group.

29. An additional mechanism, found among the Brahman Pandits of Kashmir and reported by Madan (1965), is the ranking of marriages in terms of how closely they match the ideal patterns. Deviation from the various elements of the kanyadana ideology—for example, the prohibition of exchange marriages—is allowed, but the status acquired from such marriages is reduced accordingly (see Milner 1988).

Chapter 12

1. For example, on the empirical level, Durkheim notes that societies constantly transform profane things into sacred things, including deifying heroes and kings (1965:243–44). Even at the conceptual level, he qualifies his rigorous contrast between the sacred and the profane in a footnote, observing that there are degrees and ranks of sacredness, and that sacredness is a relative term: "So the more sacred repels the less sacred; but this is because the second is profane in relation to the first" (1965:340–41n.7). Finally he notes, "Precautions are necessary to keep them [the sacred and profane] apart because, though opposing one another, they tend to confuse themselves into one another" (1965:360). In short, to proceed with his empirical analysis, Durkheim had to significantly qualify his rigid contrast of the sacred and the profane and acknowledge that the concepts form a continuum rather than an unambiguous dichotomy.

2. Perhaps sacredness is often a series of ranked dichotomies. Jonathan Z. Smith has noted that Ezekiel's description of the temple in Jerusalem very much follows this pattern:

> With respect to the temple mount, the land is profane; with respect to the temple, the temple mount is profane; with respect to the throne place, the temple is profane. . . . we should picture the hierarchy of places not as concentric circles on a flat plane but instead as altitude markers on a relief map. Each unit is built on a terrace, partially higher than that which is profane in relationship to it. (1987:56–57)

Smith is specifically influenced by Dumont's conceptualizaiton of purity and impurity as a series of ranked dichotomies.

3. The classic conceptualizations of the sacred are by Durkheim (1965), Otto (1972),

and Eliade (1959). The literature on the conceptualization of the sacred is enormous. For a recent overview of this material, see Colpe (1987). I have been especially influenced by the work of Berger (1967) and Berger and Kellner (1978).

4. For an excellent discussion of the processes involved in identity transformation through sacral relationships, see Babb (1986, especially 214–25).

5. Such knowledge may imply the transcendence of cause and effect. As Locke (1975: 2:xxvi) emphasized, the notion of causation assumes well-defined separate identities. Hence where salvation is seen as merger with the divine or the recognition that such distinctions are ephemeral, causation tends to become an irrelevant concept. The point is not that Hindu philosophy has strict parallels to and negations of seventeenth- and eighteenth-century Western notions of causation, but rather that all attempts at cross-cultural interpretation, such as the typology of relationships to the sacred that I have proposed, have their limitations—but also their legitimate uses.

6. The difference between physical causation and physical coercion may seem obscure. The key difference is whether the object to be influenced is considered to have any agency— that is, any will of its own. Shooting billiard balls into the appropriate pocket is a matter of physical causation; there is no sense in which the balls consciously resist. Herding wild cattle into the appropriate chute or stall is a matter of physical coercion; the cattle often resist and have to be forced or tricked into the desired behavior. No absolute line can be drawn between these two types of relationship, because there are degrees of agency; usually bacteria are considered to have less agency than worms, worms less than cattle, and cattle less than humans. Parallel gradations exist in the degree of agency attributed to gods and other units of the other world.

7. I use the words "covenant" and "law" here in a very loose sense. In the Western civilizations, these concepts are closely associated with the Old Testament. I do not mean to imply that the precise forms characteristic of the Hebrews are present in other situations.

8. These distinctions overlap with the distinctions made by classical theorists of religion between magic and religion. See, for example, Tylor (1883), Frazer (1922), Malinowski (1948), and Weber (1968:422–39). For a sociologist's discussion of this distinction, see Goode (1951:38–55). For Durkheim, the presence of a church, rather than a shift from physical causation to social interaction, distinguishes religion from magic. See Lowie (1924) for a view that rejects any rigid distinction between religion and magic. It is not necessary for our purposes to resolve the debate over the distinction between religion and magic, or over whether there are clear evolutionary trends. Obviously, though, conceptualizing the sacred as a special form of status does assume that a significant proportion of the interaction between humans and the sacred is conceptualized by the actors as a form of social interaction rather than physical causation. See Wadley (1975:86– 87) for a brief discussion of this type of variation in emphasis in Hinduism. As we shall see when we consider the soteriology implied by classical Yoga, some forms of Indian religion more closely approximate the model of physical causation than that of social interaction.

9. Like the typology of the three types of sanctions, the argument about the difficulties of mixing incongruent sanctions has many similarities with the arguments developed by Etzioni (1975) for compliance structures in formal organizations.

10. To say that a pattern has internal contradictions that make it unstable is not to predict that it cannot persist over time. To the degree that such patterns are able to persist, significant social energies and mechanisms are required to contain the contradictions. Most social and cultural patterns contain such contradictions. What varies is their acuteness and the mechanisms that have been developed to contain them. This particular dilemma and the contradictions it creates are very general, if not universal.

11. Weber (1968, especially 521), among others, makes note of this phenomenon. For a recent analysis of religion as compensation, see Stark and Bainbridge (1980, 1985).

12. See Obeyesekere (1968, 1983) and the various references he gives to Weber (especially 1968:chap.6) for a discussion of "ethicization" of complex societies.

More concretely, universalist notions of salvation—the notion that everyone will be saved—will be relatively rare and restricted to groups that are highly rationalistic. Such groups usually deemphasize the difference between the sacred and the profane and conceive of the ideal profane world as one with relatively low levels of social inequality. As has been the case throughout the analysis, the arguments are restricted to relatively complex societies that have significant degrees of stratification. For relatively simple societies with relatively little status differentiation and stratification, such as hunting and gathering societies, the treatment of people in the afterlife may also be relatively undifferentiated.

Chapter 13

1. Another important intellectual lineage goes from Durkheim (1965) through Radcliffe-Brown to Parsons and Merton and sociological functionalism. Goffman was also influenced by Radcliffe-Brown, but emphasized the analysis of micro interaction rather than the macro analysis of social institutions, which was the special forte of functionalism.

2. Even the key contemporary works in the sociology of religion pay relatively little attention to the details of ritual and worship activity. See, for example, Berger (1967), Robertson (1970), Wilson (1982), and Stark and Bainbridge (1985).

3. Of course, as the typology developed in Chapter 12 indicates, there are at least four ideal-type relationships with the sacred, and only one of these is worship.

4. Goffman's discussion of deference, demeanor, honor, and "face" clearly suggests an overlap between the concepts of status and sacredness. Yet the implications of Weber's work on status for understanding the sacred remain undeveloped; a systematic discussion of the connection between these two concepts does not exist. Goode has made important contributions to our understanding of sacredness (1951) and status processes (1978), but he has not made a sustained attempt to see these as parallel phenomena.

5. For brevity, the analysis here focuses on the attitudes and strategies of the lower status person seeking interaction with someone of higher status. The attitudes and strategies of the superior are the reverse: to be suspicious of the inferior's status claims, and to thwart attempts at presumptuous intimacy. When either side must interact with the other against their will, there is likely to be considerable anxiety or hostility. Goffman's (1959) discussion of actors' cooperating so as not to call into question each other's status claims applies primarily to situations where little is at stake and it is relatively easy to avoid future interaction. A celebrity may humor those who briefly offer unwanted attention in a public place; if marriage or permanent friendship is seriously proposed, the reaction will be quite different.

6. In addition, both status and sacral relationships usually involve departure rituals; you do not abruptly walk away from people or gods with whom you want to maintain good relations. These are, however, much less important and they will not be a focus of the analysis.

7. Fuller (1992:66–69) groups the stages described in the South Indian texts known as the *Agamas*, which are used to guide worship of the high gods such as Visnu and Siva, into four categories. But he clearly acknowledges that these are a convenient form of descriptive classification rather than abstract theoretical categories.

8. This discussion of the media of communion requires an aside concerning Marriott's code and substance approach to the analysis of relationships in Hinduism, discussed in Chapters 8 and 9. While relationships conceived in terms of the transaction of substances are extremely common and important, there are other idioms used to express the nature of

relationships. Possibly some Hindus conceive of *arti* and even darsan as the transaction of substances, but it is doubtful that all do in any literal sense. Again this suggests both the usefulness of the code and substance perspective, but also its inadequacy as a fundamental analytical frame of reference.

9. In the Hubert and Mauss (1964:chap. 2) discussion, sacrifice is divided into three phases: the entry, the victim, and the exit. Especially in the first and third categories, a number of rituals are discussed that are related to sacrifice, but which I believe should be kept analytically distinct from sacrifice per se, for example, the washing and purification of the victim and the priest. The essence of sacrifice is the destruction of one thing to create something of higher value. This can take the form of killing an animal, cutting or peeling fruit, crushing grain, breaking bread, and so forth. The sacrifice may or may not be the central element of the religious ritual. Where sacrifice is the core act, it will often be accompanied by other elaborate forms of ritual. Nonetheless, these related rituals, which are often used in other contexts too, should not be confused with sacrifice per se.

10. The exception that proves this rule is the lesser ability of Brahmans, gurus, and holymen to take on the impurities and transform the sins of their followers. These actors receive gifts that in part stand for the sins and impurities of the contributors, transform them into prasada, and return them to their devotees. They in turn are transformed when they consume or otherwise utilize what the guru has blessed. But precisely because the guru's powers are limited, they must be careful not to accept too much. "This is why the guru does not always accept offerings, or accepts them only in degrees. The burden of impurities might be too much for the frail human frame of the guru to bear (though not, of course, for the Supreme Being who, in his true majesty, 'devours all')" (Babb 1986:66). This notion is also the source of the great ambivalence Brahmans have toward gifts. See Parry (1981, 1985b), for a description of this ambivalence among the Benares funeral priests.

11. For a discussion of seeing and perceiving things in a new way, see Babb (1986, especially 74–80, 214–25). For example, he stresses that the leavings of the guru are seen to have value rather than being polluting because devotees see them in a different light than most people. While I agree that this is an important theme in religious experience, I want to stress that what changes is the perception of the "empirical" relationship—the higher status of the guru or the god compared with humans—not the rules about what is sacred or what constitutes pollution. Not all leavings or effluents have become valuable, only those from clearly superior beings.

Some ascetic traditions in various religions may so stress humility and submissiveness that extreme degradation rituals are created. These may involve consumption of normally offensive substances. Such degradation rituals are not, however, the dominant forms of communion with the deity, and are usually practiced only by extreme ascetics. See Bell (1985) for examples from the medieval Christian church.

12. See Babb (1986: chaps. 1–3) for other contemporary examples of atypical behaviors and relics, which normally would be considered impure and revolting, being used as the means to uplift and provide salvation.

13. It is necessary to distinguish another type of "devil." These have characteristics that are roughly the reverse of some dominant deity, but are nonetheless respected and worshipped by their devotees. This is the case where Satan is considered the supreme deity, and devil worship is performed. In this case, the model I have outlined would apply, though many of the concrete behaviors will reverse those found in more conventional forms of worship. An example of this is radical Tantric worship, in which the actions and items that are considered most impure and unholy by Hindu orthodoxy are the means of worship and communion with the deity. This situation parallels what occurs in the realm of status: Roosevelt and Hitler represent opposite values, and the specific content of deference behavior

would vary accordingly. Their respective devotees would, however, offer both genuine defer-ence and seek intimate association by the means I have outlined above.

Chapter 14

1. While the concept is derived from Western cultures, it has been widely used for com-parative purposes, including the analysis of South Asian religions (see, e.g., O'Flaherty 1980).

2. I do not mean to imply that "salvation" means the same thing across different re-ligions and cultures. Moksa for the Hindu renouncer is certainly not the same thing as the at-tainment of heaven for the Puritan Christian. The imagery of the final end in the Upanisads is relatively abstract, stressing insight, knowledge, consciousness, bliss, purity, and union. For example, the last lines of the Katha Upanisad are: "Having received this wisdom taught by the King of Death, and the entire process of yoga, Nachiketa became free from impurities and death and attained Brahman" (Nikhilananda 1964:82). In the Prasna Upanisad the imagery of merger and union is stressed:

> As these flowing rivers, bound for the ocean, disappear into the ocean after having reached it, their names and forms being destroyed, and are called simply the ocean—even so these sixteen parts of the seer, whose goal is the Purusha, disappear into the Purusha after having reached Him, their names and forms being destroyed, and are called simply the Purusha. He becomes free of parts and immortal. (Nikhilananda 1964:157)

In contrast, Bunyan's imagery in *Pilgrim's Progress* is much more concrete and assumes the continuation of individual identities:

> Now just as the Gates were opened to let in the men, I looked in after them; and be-hold, the City shone like the sun, the streets also were paved with gold, and in them walked many men with crowns on their heads, palms in their hands, and golden harps to sing praises withal. There were also of them that had wings, and they answered one another without intermission, saying, *Holy, Holy, Holy, is the Lord.* (1965:204 [emphasis in original])

Of course, the Hindu Puranas and the theology of later bhakti saints, such as Tulsi Das, also have concrete images that more closely parallel Christian concepts of heaven and hell. Yet the basic point cannot be ignored. The nature of salvation is not the same for different re-ligious traditions.

This could be said, however, about most concepts and human institutions—for example, family, marriage, worship, and so on. While the differences and variations should not be de-nied, this does not mean that cross-cultural comparisons are invalid. With respect to salva-tion, a commonality exists on a certain level of abstraction: all notions are concerned with the transformation of present existence into some condition defined as qualitatively better.

3. See Weber (1968:557–76) for an overview of the variations that can occur within the general framework of salvation by faith and grace.

4. Of course, notions of physical causation are often used to explain placement in the social stratification structure also. Many theories purport to explain social position in terms of biological inheritance. Often the line between arguments that assume physical causation and those that assume social interaction is not clear-cut.

5. The word "yoga" has a number of meanings. Here it is roughly synonymous with the

notion of method, path, or way: thus bhakti-yoga means the bhakti method or the bhakti path to salvation. Incidentally, "marga" also means path. Historically, an earlier and still more common meaning of "yoga" refers to sets of meditation techniques that are characteristic of one kind of path to salvation. This narrower meaning will apply when we discuss classical Yoga, one of the six schools of Indian philosophy.

6. With respect to the level of abstraction, a rough analogue in Christianity might be a comparison of Catholicism, Calvinism, Lutheranism, and the Mormons in the United States.

7. The citations in this section that do not cite a particular author refer to verses in the *Bhagavad Gita*. I have usually drawn quotes from Zaehner's (1966) translation of the *Bhagavad Gita*, which is generally more intelligible than Edgerton's (1964) more literal rendering, and less interpretive than Radhakrishnan's (1957) translation. At a few points, however, I have used the last translation.

8. Like "yoga," "Samkhya" has a general and a specific meaning. The broader meaning refers to intellectual approaches to religious knowledge in general. The narrower meaning refers to one of the six classical schools (*darsanas*) of Indian philosophy, which will be discussed below. In this part of the text, "samkhya" seems to include both the general and the specific sense of the word; many of the samkhya darsana concepts are used, but clearly the broader meaning is also implied.

9. Obviously the term "false consciousness" is not used here in the Marxian sense.

10. Unlike Samkhya, Yoga is in principle theistic. The role of the deity is, however, very prescribed and limited. The god—called *Isvara* by Patanjali, but by different names in other yoga systems—serves as the focal point during the process of concentration (ekagrata), and is a model of the perfect yogin. Isvara is not, however, the primary source of salvation. Neither the deity's response to his devotees nor his initiatives on their behalf are the main source of salvation. Liberation is sometimes accomplished through the grace and action of Isvara, but this is both the exception and an inferior outcome.

11. The way these terms are used in the United States is less useful in characterizing the Indian distinction. Perhaps the parallel would be more apt if the Church of England, as the historically dominant tradition, were a minority church that had no hierarchy of authority, and existed in the midst of a large number of active sects. Even then the church–sect contrast is not strictly appropriate for India. (See Rao [1986], in Kantowsky [1986:193–98], for a discussion of sects in the Indian context.)

12. The relationship between Smarta orthodoxy and the Mimamsa school is somewhat parallel to the relationship between orthodox Protestants, (e.g., Lutherans, Presbyterians, and Methodists), and strict fundamentalists who insist on the literal interpretation of the Bible. Like extreme fundamentalist Christians, the Mimamsas are not quite orthodox because they are so conservative. The parallel between the Christian fundamentalists and the Mimamsa school is at best a loose one; perhaps an even better parallel would be the relationship between the conservative Catholics who refuse to accept Vatican II reforms, such as those who were led by Archbishop Marcel Lefebvre in France, and the orthodox Catholic hierarchy. For all of their ritual conservatism, the adherents to Mimamsa developed extremely sophisticated techniques for the interpretation of Vedic scripture that parallel concepts in modern deconstructionism (for a discussion of this parallel, see Clooney 1988).

13. Singer's study of Madras Brahmans found an increasing shift toward bhakti forms even within the orthodox Sanskritic tradition (1972, especially chaps. 4–5). This was especially expressed through groups that met regularly to sing bhakti hymns. Singer in part suggests that this is a means of seeking social integration and blunting the anti-Brahmanical movements characteristic of the region. Fuller (1992:161) largely rejects this argument, pointing out that most of those participating are Smarta Brahmans. He goes on to argue that

the main purpose of these groups is to maintain Brahmanical identity in an increasingly impersonal urban setting. The problem with this interpretation is that it does not explain why the content of such meetings is bhakti-oriented, rather than more specifically Smarta forms of activity. As Singer's discussion indicates, the rationales—not to speak of the social sources—of such changes are complex. Busy professionals in an urban setting may not have time for the elaborate ritualism of the Smarta tradition. Another factor is probably the impersonality and lower social visibility characteristic of urban settings; deviation from traditional rituals goes undetected. This does not explain, however, the adoption of bhakti forms. While deviation without detection may be easier, demonstrating one's superiority is also more problematic; it is harder for others to observe and detect extraordinary, subtle performance and ritual conformity, especially when rituals are carried out primarily in the home. In contrast, bhakti devotion is, or at least can be, a more publicly expressed form of religious behavior. Perhaps this is, in part, why the emergence of bhakti Hinduism is associated with the increasing importance of temple worship. More orthodox Brahmanical rituals were primarily conducted in the home. Obviously such rituals are less useful to the kings who seek wide legitimation than the more public rituals of temples, which allow for the participation of a much broader array of social strata. The inclusion of more strata would create pressures for salvation to be linked to association and grace rather than conformity and ritual purity. Moreover, the personalistic tie to the deity can be seen as compensation for the more impersonalistic setting of the urban situation.

Interestingly, early Christianity, with its notions of salvation through association, was strongest among the urban middle classes. In many cases, these were Jews who were living in more heterogenous and cosmopolitan surroundings than was characteristic of earlier Judaism. Weber (1946:267–301) noted that the religious inclinations of what he referred to as the "civic strata" had been extremely diverse. Nonetheless, he noted, "it is precisely among these strata that elective affinities for special types of religion stand out" (1946:284). One of these prominent forms was predestination. This doctrine makes all kinds of ritual conformity, which is difficult to observe in urban settings, irrelevant to one's salvation. Subsequently, according to Weber's Protestant ethic thesis, ritual declines as an indicator of social status, while economic success increases in importance.

Of course, the impersonality and lower social visibility that often accompanies urbanism certainly does not always result in soteriologies that stress association rather than conformity. In fact, Bendix points out the importance of the strong social control exercised in urban settings; by applying the same norms to both those within the sect and outsiders, it contributed to more universalistic norms that made wider economic exchanges more practical (see Bendix 1962:70–79). It is possible that this is a form of reversal: associational patterns of salvation lead to emphasis on universalistic conformity to norms of the world. In sum, the hypothesis of a possible relationship between urbanism (which often contributes to lower social visibility and social control) and soteriologies emphasizing grace seems worthy of further research.

14. In the terminology of Chapter 11, the egalitarianism of bhakti sects is usually structurally encapsulated in the religious sector and hence leaves social relationships in nonsectarian context largely unchanged.

15. Sexual connotations are not entirely absent from the relationships between devotees and deities in Western religious traditions. For example, as Weber notes, various degrees of eroticism are implied in the mysticism of St. Bernard, the cult of Mary, and Lutheran and Zinzendorfian pietism (1968:571). Such connotations are even more explicit when Roman Catholic nuns are "married" and become Christ's "bride," and, of course, in the Song of Solomon of the Bible.

Chapter 15

1. I will generally use the term "other world" or "world-to-come," rather than the notion of afterlife. This leaves open the question of whether the other world is life after death or a millenarian restructuring of this world.

2. The term "eschatology" is problematic. Strictly speaking, it refers to the final end and is inappropriate for a religion such as Hinduism that conceives of sacred time as cyclical rather than linear. I have found no better English word under which to categorize the characteristics of the trans-historical nonempirical features of the Hindu cosmos relevant to its soteriology. The term is commonly used for comparative purposes (see Weblowsky 1987) and has been used by scholars to discuss South Asian materials (Obeyesekere 1968, 1980). The word is not completely adequate for our purposes, even for the discussion of Christian traditions, because it tends to be limited to speculations about the "last things." Our concerns will be broader than this; we will also focus on the criteria used to decide the fate of people in the next world. In Christian theology, these notions are typically discussed under the topic of soteriology and include such concepts as redemption, election, sanctification, perseverance, etc., and this overlaps with the concerns of Chapter 14. Despite these limitations, "eschatology" seems the best term available to characterize the general focus of this analysis.

3. The ethnographic studies include Bailey (1957), Mayer (1960), Beteille (1971), Beck (1972), Pocock (1972), Srinivas (1976), Moffatt (1979), Parry (1979), Raheja (1988), Dumont (1986a), and Van der Veer (1988). The synthetic works include Mandelbaum (1970), Marriott (1976), Kolenda (1984), and Dumont (1980).

4. These three notions, and especially the first two, have clearly been a focal point of Indian thought. As Bhattacharyya says: "With the sole exception of the Carvaka school, all Indian philosophical systems, Vedic and non-Vedic, accepted certain basic ideas on which they formulated their theories: (1) the law of *karman*, (2) the belief in the process of rebirth, and (3) an emphasis on mystic experience as the panacea for all evils" (1987:164). While the third point mentioned by Bhattacharyya is broader than the concept of moksa, in many respects moksa can be considered both the ultimate mystical experience and the ultimate panacea.

A word is required about identifying samsara and karma as "otherworldly." From the point of view of most Hindu texts, the notion of samsara focuses on involvement in this world, and is contrasted to moksa, which is release from this world. In that sense, samsara is a very worldly rather than otherworldly concept. Nonetheless, a key aspect of samsara is the idea that the soul (atman) is reincarnated across a multitude of lifetimes. In this sense, from the point of view of the typical Hindu going about his day-to-day business, it is clearly an otherworldly concept. Karma is the process that cuts across or ties together the actions in the present mundane world with existences in other reincarnations and ultimately with liberation. From a mundane everyday perspective, it too is in part an otherworldly concept.

5. It has been suggested (e.g., Obeyesekere 1968, 1980) that notions of reincarnation were probably derived from pre-Aryan tribal cultures—though according to Basham (1989:chap. 3) they developed as a secret doctrine among Aryan elites. In these cultures, entry into "heaven," or one's position in the next reincarnations, was presumed not to be dependent on the moral quality of the person's behavior on earth. Notions of sin and merit, and of their effect on the afterlife, are later developments, which supposedly result out of what Obeyesekere, following Weber, calls ethicization of the afterlife. All of this is highly speculative, since there is virtually no evidence about the content of pre-Aryan cultures relevant to this issue.

6. For a sociologist's discussion of karma, see Berger (1967:65–66).

7. Weber (1958b, 1968) and others have suggested that the doctrine of karma plays a crucial role in providing social legitimacy (and perhaps psychological compensations); one's present situation is not arbitrary and unfair, but supposedly the result of one's own past actions.

For such an effect to occur, the actors must accept on faith that they are linked to a series of previous existences and that one's present fortunes are the result of one's actions in these past lives. This is, of course, precisely what cannot be known in any empirical sense. While occasionally someone claims to remember his or her past lives, for most people there is complete amnesia—they know nothing about their past existences except by inference from their present circumstances. Any real visibility or knowledge about the basis of one's current status is unavailable; the connection between past actions and present status must be accepted on faith.

This fact suggests yet an additional structural reversal. In the village, people's claims about their caste and its status are rarely, if ever, taken for granted. Great energies are devoted to substantiating the legitimacy of status claims. When verification is not possible, claims are significantly discounted. For example, when new groups move into a village, the legitimacy of their status claims and the basis of these claims are usually treated with great suspicion. Long-term visibility of both ancestry and behavior is required. In contrast, visibility of one's past lives, by oneself or others, is not possible. Yet Hindus often assume that one's present status and circumstances are rooted in previous behavior. Thus, there is a complete reversal of what is considered an adequate basis for determining the legitimacy of one's status.

8. See, for example, Béteille (1971:chap. 3) and Shah (1982) for a discussion of segmentation, fission, and fusion.

9. The fact that Brahmans often played a central role in the development of sectarian bhakti does not mean that bhakti sects did not contain significant elements of protest against Brahman orthodoxy. The fact that Martin Luther was a pious Catholic monk and that John Wesley throughout his life was an Anglican clergyman does not mean that Protestantism and Methodism, respectively, were not in part protest movements.

10. While women ascetics have existed throughout much of Indian history, their place in the culture has often been anomalous, and they have not usually openly proselytized other women. What makes the Brahma Kumaris radical is that all women are called upon to follow this path, even though it is expected that only a small elite will respond.

11. The parallel notions of *takdir* (fate) and *lekh* (writing) in the North Indian village studied by Raheja (1988:96) imply a combination of the influence of fate and the will of the local goddess deity. The point holds, however, that something more than a completely moralistic concept of karma is involved.

12. One indicator of the relative importance of different status positions is the penalty invoked for disloyalty to a particular social unit. In bourgeois society, treason to the nation-state is punishable by death. Religious apostasy or unfaithfulness in marriage—things punishable by death in many societies—have much less severe penalties. This is, of course, in part because the state now monopolizes the legitimate use of force, but that is precisely the point—it is the status of citizen that defines one's relationship to the highest level of social authority and power.

13. For a discussion of the impact of Christianity in general, and Calvinism in particular, on the development of Western individualism, see Dumont (1986b:23–59).

14. The most systematic statement of Calvin's theology is, of course, his *Institutes of the Christian Religion*. Some ten editions of the *Institutes* were written by Calvin between 1536 and 1560. The content of these varies substantially in detail, if not in the thrust and spirit of the overall argument. I draw on the English edition edited by McNeill (1960), which is based primarily on the 1559 Latin edition edited by Barth and Niesel. This is considered the more or less definitive version by most Calvinist churches. Additional discussions of the world-to-come occur in Calvin's various commentaries on the books of the Bible. For a summary of Calvin's views on eschatology, see Quistorp (1955) and Martin (1963:chap. 1).

15. Within Calvinism, the doctrine of predestination has been more or less continually

debated. The crucial issue is over the extent to which God willed not only that some be elected to salvation, but also that some be damned. So-called double predestination emphasizes that God willed both. Considerable support for this position can be found in Calvin's own writings, though it is clear that the main intent of his doctrine was one of comfort and assurance rather than condemnation. Later Calvinists have usually emphasized the election to salvation, but rejected the notion that God willed that some be damned. The late-sixteenth-century Dutch theologian Jacobus Arminius is perhaps the most famous proponent of the latter interpretation, but both positions have had their advocates throughout most of the history of Calvinism.

16. Of course, Calvin, like all orthodox Christian theologians, sees Jesus Christ as a mediating figure between the sacred and the profane. But since the fifth century, Christian theology has been concerned with affirming both the unity of Christ's person and the distinctness of the divine and human elements. Here Calvin emphasizes—probably more than his contemporaries—the orthodox Chalcedonian tradition:

> [W]e ought not to understand the statement that "the Word was made flesh" [John 1:14] in the sense that the Word was turned into flesh or confusedly mingled with flesh. Rather, it means that, because he chose for himself the virgin's womb as a temple in which to dwell, he who was the Son of God became the Son of man—not by confusion of substance, but by unity of person. For we affirm his divinity so joined and united with his humanity that each retains its distinctive nature unimpaired, and yet these two natures constitute one Christ. (1960:2.14.1)

17. "Lord" and "vassal" are, of course, relative terms; the same individual may be a lord over some, but a vassal of some superior lord. For the complexities of this relationship see Bloch (1964:1:iv, v). There is, predictably, scholarly controversy over these terms and, more generally, the concept of feudalism, per se. For a critique of the concept of feudalism, see Brown (1974). For a more recent and balanced discussion of these concepts, see Reynolds (1984).

18. Of course, only the priests drank the wine. The distinction is one of function in religious ritual, not one of social strata per se; priests did not meet separately and share wine with one another. This is not to claim that notions of pollution or priestly superiority were completely absent from Christianity, but only that they were a relatively minor theme compared with Hinduism. Nor is it to deny that there were locales and periods in which some strata may have been excluded from the Church and its sacraments. This, however, clearly goes against the dominant textual tradition of Christianity, whereas in Hinduism the dominant textual tradition clearly supports such exclusion.

19. Le Goff (1988) sees purgatory as a mechanism that made it possible to conduct the usury so essential to the development of capitalism without foreclosing the possibility of salvation. My hypothesis suggests that an additional factor may have been the reaction against a worldly stratification system that increasingly emphasized ascription. There is general agreement that this formalization and rigidification of the nobility was less developed in England than in France. Accordingly, my hypothesis would predict less emphasis on purgatory. I have been unable to find evidence that bears on this hypothesis.

20. Lang (1989) reports that in imperial China, images of heaven were to a significant degree part of the state's ideology and tended to reproduce the worldly hierarchy. Not surprisingly, religious protest against the existing social structure tended to draw on foreign religions, such as Buddhism.

21. We must, of course, keep in mind that Lutheranism and Calvinism are very closely related, so in some respects their eschatologies are very similar (see, e.g., McDannell and Lang 1988:146–56). Nonetheless, it seems accurate to say that Lutheranism has generally

been more reticent about eschatology than Calvinism. In the *Institutes* of 1559, Calvin provides a rather extended discussion of his views on the world-to-come (see especially 1960:3.9, 25 ix, xxv)—though like Luther he warns against attempts to be concerned about the detailed specifics of the life to come. A century later, the central doctrinal statement of Presbyterianism, the *Westminster Confession of Faith* of 1647, has explicit sections discussing "Of the State of Man After Death, and the Resurrection of the Dead" and "Of the Last Judgment" (1658:XXXII, XXXIII). In contrast, the Lutheran's famous Augsburg Confession of 1530 has very little to say about the nature of the life to come, and the same is largely true of the historically important Formula of Concord of 1577 (for texts of these, see Tappert 1959). While Calvinist documents were conceived as systematic statements of doctrine, and the Lutheran statements were more attempts to settle specific theological disputes, this difference is a matter of degree. The most orthodox and scholastic strands of later Lutheranism attempt to fill the void with more explicit statements on eschatology (see, e.g., Pieper 1953:507–55), but other statements continue to contain considerable ambiguity and ambivalence over the nature of the "last things" (see, e.g., Kinder 1965:798–801); in these latter strands, no one version of what constitutes the "last things" seems to dominate, but a variety of even contradictory images are used.

22. Strictly speaking, the doctrine of perseverance is part of soteriology—"the means of salvation"—rather than eschatology—"the last things." However, as indicated earlier, for our purposes, no strict line can be drawn between eschatology and soteriology. Soteriologies set forth the means of salvation, and by implication the criteria for the most important kind of stratification in the afterlife—the distinction between the saved and the damned. Such doctrines are an integral part of our concern.

23. See the *Westminster Confession of Faith* (1658:XVIII); see also the section entitled "Of the Preservation of the Saints" (XVII).

24. Lutheranism's political passivity may have led it to at times accept the outcome of drastic social changes—for example, the Nazi regime—but Luther and, for the most part, Lutheranism have been very hostile to rebellion or revolution. Calvinism, too, is suspicious of rebellion, but its acceptance of established authority is more qualified; see Calvin (1960: 4.20). For an influential modern interpretation of Calvinism on this issue, see Niebuhr (1949:278–84).

25. See the Appendix to this chapter.

26. See Swanson (1967:177) for a critique of compensation theory. Stark and Bainbridge's formulation of compensation theory is a definite improvement over earlier attempts, and helps to resolve some of the apparent contradictions that were characteristic of other arguments (1980, 1985, especially 10–12). It is, however, still based on the debatable assumptions of utilitarian exchange theory. For a recent critique of such assumptions by a sociologist, see Etzioni (1988). For a detailed critique of Stark and Bainbridge, see Wallis and Bruce (1984).

27. Cases of equal treatment in the other world may also be largely reproductions of the worldly stratification system. Such undifferentiated "heavens" seem to be associated with those who live in relatively undifferentiated societies—for example, hunting and gathering societies—or those who not only believe that everyone is admitted to heaven—for example, "universalists"—but also have hopes for organizing the present world in such a way as to eliminate injustices and minimize inequalities. In both cases, stratification is eliminated from the other world when, in either reality or hopes, it has been minimized in this world. This is proposed as a very tentative hypothesis. Its validity is not crucial to the main argument.

28. This aversion to considering psychological processes as a means of interpreting the relationship between social structure and action (and presumably structure and culture) is widespread in contemporary sociology. Tilly, in his influential programmatic statement for

historical sociology, identifies what he calls "the eight Pernicious Postulates of twentieth-century social thought" (1984, especially chaps. 2–3). The second of these is: "Social behavior results from individual mental events, which are conditioned by life in society. Explanations of social behavior therefore concern the impact of society on individual minds" (1984:11). He advocates "eschewing socially conditioned mental events as the prime ties of individuals to societies" (1984:30).

29. The strategy for accomplishing this type of analysis involved the following elements. First, I returned to the analysis of broad cultural or civilizational units, such as those Weber contrasted in his analysis of the origins of capitalism: Protestantism, Catholicism, Calvinism, Hinduism, and other religions. Second, the focus was on a relatively specific feature of these units; in this case, structures of stratification, broadly conceived. Third, instead of attempting to relate variations in religious ideology to actual variations in concrete social structures, I looked at the relationship between ideologies that describe the world-to-come and ideological descriptions of worldly social structures; obviously, concrete societies vary in the degree to which they actually conform to accepted ideological descriptions, but such variations are beyond the scope of the analysis. Fourth, I looked for structural reversals as well as parallels.

I have used a terminology that is usually associated with "French" structuralism and more specifically Lévi-Strauss (1963:chap. 11, 1966, 1969). While I find the general orientation of this perspective useful for the purposes at hand, I am not suggesting a strict structuralist interpretation of the data in the sense that patterns of culture will be structured in basically the same way that languages are.

Chapter 16

1. The concepts of coding and decoding are suggested by the notion that norms and rituals of status groups are elaborated and layered, but they are not in any strict sense deduced or derived from the theory of status relationships. These concepts obviously have many antecedents in various forms of semiology, symbolic anthropology, and interpretive forms of sociology.

2. In his discussion of the pattern variables, Parsons (1951) uses the notions of performance and quality as alternatives to achievement and ascription. These do not, however, point to the actual behaviors that people engage in to affect status.

3. Obviously, some types of natural disasters are due to the impact of humans on the environment. As human powers over the physical environment have increased, disasters are increasingly the indirect result of human activity. This is, of course, the key idea behind the notion that there is an environmental crisis.

4. The term "capital" can be used in the historically specific sense of resources that enable the owner to appropriate surplus value in a capitalist society. It is also used in the broader sense of resources that are capable of producing other resources, which may or may not be a means of appropriating surplus value. In this sense, noncapitalist societies can be said to make capital investments. I am using capital in the second broader sense.

5. Of course, there are symbolic representations of various forms of physical capital that are highly mobile: money, stocks, bonds, legal titles, and the like. Frequently, these are the primary items that are actually used for economic exchange. The validity, exchangeability, and mobility of these is dependent on the existence of an effective system of social control, ensuring that the possession of the symbolic representation can be transformed into possession of and authority over actual physical capital. The worthlessness of the paper money of collapsed regimes—for instance, Confederate dollars—is the most obvious example of the crucialness of such control systems. While the existence of social institutions that create and

validate such symbolic forms of physical capital are an important social variation, it is not the focus here. For present purposes, the concern is the alienability and moveability of actual forms of capital.

6. The key word is "managed." Ownership may be more concentrated, but it is difficult to centralize actual management.

7. Obviously, some types of initiation rites and sexual "play" are forced on the participants and are highly alienating. Here the focus is on activities in which the participants more or less choose to participate. This is not to deny the possibility of false consciousness on the part of the participants, but Etzioni's argument focuses on the participants' own sense of alienation.

8. This does not necessarily apply to violence and conflict over other issues—for example, marital disputes and petty thievery. Moreover, the damage that results from incidences of violence in industrial societies may be greater, since the means of violence are more powerful.

Bibliography

Alexander, Jeffrey C. 1982a. *Theoretical Logic in Sociology.* Vol. 1, *Positivism, Presumptions and Current Controversies.* Berkeley: University of California Press.

————. 1982b. *Theoretical Logic in Sociology.* Vol. 2, *The Antimonies of Classical Thought: Marx and Durkheim.* Berkeley: University of California Press.

————. 1983a. *Theoretical Logic in Sociology.* Vol. 3, *The Classical Attempt at Theoretical Synthesis: Max Weber.* Berkeley: University of California Press.

————. 1983b. *Theoretical Logic in Sociology.* Vol. 4, *The Modern Reconstruction of Classical Thought: Talcott Parsons.* Berkeley: University of California Press.

Alexander, Jeffrey C., Bernhard Giesen, Richard Münch, and Neil J. Smelser, eds. 1987. *The Micro–Macro Link.* Berkeley: University of California Press.

Althusser, L. [1965] 1990. *For Marx.* Translated by B. Brewster. London: Verso.

Appadurai, Arjun. 1981. *Worship and Conflict Under Colonial Rule: A South Indian Case.* Cambridge: Cambridge University Press.

Babb, Lawrence A. 1975. *The Divine Hierarchy.* New York: Columbia University Press.

————. 1981. "Glancing: Visual Interaction in Hinduism." *Journal of Anthropological Research* 37:387–401.

————. 1986. *Redemptive Encounters: Three Modern Styles in the Hindu Tradition.* Berkeley: University of California Press.

Bachrach, P., and M. S. Baratz. 1962. "Two Faces of Power." *American Political Science Review* 56:947–52.

————. 1970. *Power and Poverty: Theory and Practice.* Oxford: Oxford University Press.

Badrinath, Chaturvedi. 1986. "Max Weber's Wrong Understanding of Indian Civilization." In *Recent Research on Max Weber's Studies of Hinduism*, edited by Detlef Kantowsky. Munich and London: Weltforum Verlag.

Bailey, F. G. 1957. *Caste and the Economic Frontier.* Manchester: Manchester University Press.

Baldwin, David A. 1989. *Paradoxes of Power.* New York: Basil Blackwell.

Baptist Hymnal. 1975. William J. Reynolds, Chairman and General Editor. Nashville, Tenn.: Convention Press.

Barnes, Barry. 1988. *The Nature of Power.* Cambridge: Polity Press.

Barnett, Richard. 1993. "Common and Exceptional Features of Eighteenth-Century States." Manuscript.

Barry, Brian, ed. 1976. *Power and Political Theory: Some European Perspectives.* London: Wiley.

Basham, A. L. 1989. *The Origins and Development of Classical Hinduism.* Edited and annotated by Kenneth G. Zysk. Boston: Beacon Press.

Bayly, C. A. 1983. *Rulers, Townsmen and Bazaars: North Indian Society in the Age of British Expansion.* Cambridge: Cambridge University Press.

Baynes, Kenneth, James Bohman, and Thomas McCarthy, eds. 1987. *After Philosophy: End or Transformation?* Cambridge, Mass.: MIT Press.

Beals, Alan R. 1962. *Gopalpar: A South Indian Village*. New York: Holt, Rinehart and Winston.

Beck, Brenda E. F. 1972. *Peasant Society in Konku: A Study of Right and Left Subcaste in South India*. Vancouver: University of British Columbia Press.

_____. 1973. "The Right–Left Division of South Indian Society." In *Right & Left: Essays on Dual Symbolic Classification*, edited and with an introduction by Rodney Needham. Chicago: University of Chicago Press.

Becker, Gary S. 1964. *Human Capital: A Theoretical and Empirical Analysis, with Special Reference to Education*. New York: National Bureau of Economic Research.

Beidelman, Thomas O. 1959. *A Comparative Analysis of the Jajmani System*. Locust Valley, N.Y.: Augustin.

Bell, Daniel. 1973. *The Coming of Post-Industrial Society: A Venture in Social Forecasting*. New York: Basic Books.

Bell, Rudolph. 1985. *Holy Anorexia*. Chicago: University of Chicago Press.

Bellah, Robert Neelly. 1970. *Beyond Belief: Essays on Religion in a Post-Traditional World*. New York: Harper & Row.

Bendix, Reinhard. 1962. *Max Weber: An Intellectual Portrait*. Garden City, N.Y.: Anchor Books.

Bendix, Reinhard, and Seymour Martin Lipset, eds. 1966. *Class, Status and Power: Social Stratification in Comparative Perspective*. 2nd ed. New York: Free Press.

Berger, Joseph, and Morris Zelditch, Jr., eds. 1985. *Status, Rewards, and Influence*. San Francisco: Jossey-Bass.

Berger, Peter L. [1967] 1969. *The Sacred Canopy*. Garden City, N.Y.: Anchor Books.

_____. 1979. "The Worldview of the New Class: Secularity and Its Discontents." In *The New Class*, edited by B. Bruce-Briggs. New Brunswick, N.J.: Transaction Books.

Berger, Peter, and Hansfried Kellner. 1978. "On the Conceptualization of the Supernatural and the Sacred." *Dialog* 17:36–42.

Berger, Peter, and Thomas Luckmann. [1966] 1967. *The Social Construction of Reality: A Treatise in the Sociology of Knowledge*. New York: Anchor Books.

Berreman, Gerald D. 1960. "Caste in India and the U.S." *American Journal of Sociology* 66:120–27.

_____. 1968. *Hindus of the Himalayas*. Berkeley: University of California Press.

_____. 1972. *Hindus of the Himalayas: Ethnography and Change*. New and extended ed. Berkeley: University of California Press.

Béteille, André. 1964. "A Note on the Referents of Caste." *European Journal of Sociology* 5:130–34.

_____. [1965] 1971. *Caste, Class, and Power*. Berkeley: University of California Press.

_____. 1974. *Studies in Agrarian Social Structure*. Delhi: Oxford University Press.

_____, ed. 1969. *Social Inequality: Selected Readings*. Harmondsworth: Penguin.

Bhattacharyya, Sibajiban. 1987. "Indian Philosophies." In *Encyclopedia of Religion*, edited by Mircea Eliade. Vol. 7. New York: Macmillan.

Biardeau, Madeleine. [1981] 1989. *Hinduism: An Anthropology of a Civilization*. Translated by Richard Nice. New Delhi: Oxford University Press.

Black, Anthony. 1984. *Guilds and Civil Society in European Political Thought from the Twelfth Century to the Present*. London: Methuen.

Black, Donald. 1976. *The Behavior of Law*. New York: Academic Press.

Blau, Peter M. 1977. *Inequality and Heterogeneity*. New York: Free Press.

Bloch, Marc. [1939] 1964. *Feudal Society*. 2 vols. Chicago: University of Chicago Press.

Blumer, Herbert. [1969] 1986. *Symbolic Interactionism: Perspective and Method*. Berkeley: University of California Press.

Blunt, E.A.H. [1931] 1969. *The Caste System of Northern India*. Delhi: Chand.

Book of Common Prayer, The. 1979. According to the use of The Episcopal Church. New York: Seabury Press.

Boulding, Kenneth E. 1956. *The Image: Knowledge in Life and Society.* Ann Arbor: University of Michigan Press.

———. 1990. *Three Faces of Power.* Newbury Park, Calif.: Sage.

Bourdieu, Pierre. 1977. *An Outline of a Theory of Practice.* Translated by Richard Nice. Cambridge: Cambridge University Press.

———. 1984. *Distinction: A Social Critique of the Judgement of Taste.* Translated by Richard Nice. Cambridge, Mass.: Harvard University Press.

———. [1983] 1986. "The Forms of Capital." In *Handbook of Theory and Research of the Sociology of Education,* edited by John G. Richardson. New York: Greenwood Press.

Bourdieu, Pierre, and Jean-Claude Passeron. 1977. *Reproduction in Education, Society and Culture.* Translated by Richard Nice. Beverley Hills, Calif.: Sage.

Bourdieu, Pierre, and Loic Wacquant. 1992. *An Invitation to Reflexive Sociology.* Chicago: University of Chicago Press.

Bouwsma, William J. 1968. "Swanson's Reformation." *Comparative Studies in Society and History* 10: 486–91.

Bowman, Mary Jean. 1962. "Human Capital: Concepts and Measures." [U.S. Office of Education] *Bulletin* 5:69–92.

Brockington, J. L. 1981. *The Sacred Thread.* Edinburgh: Edinburgh University Press.

Brooks, Douglas Renfrew. 1990. *The Secret of the Three Cities: An Introduction to Hindu Sakta Tantrism.* Chicago: University of Chicago Press.

Brown, Elizabeth A. R. 1974. "The Tyranny of a Construct: Feudalism and Historians of Medieval Europe." *American Historical Review* 79:1063–88.

Bruce-Briggs, B., ed. 1979. *The New Class.* New Brunswick, N.J.: Transaction Books.

Buhler, G. [1886] 1964. *The Laws of Manu.* Delhi: Motilal Banarsidass.

Bunyan, John. [1684] 1965. *Pilgrim's Progress.* Edited and with an introduction by Robert Sharrock. Harmondsworth: Penguin.

Burawoy, Michael. 1985. *The Politics of Production: Factory Regimes Under Capitalism and Socialism.* London: Verso.

Burghart, Richard. 1983. "Renunciation in the Religious Traditions of South Asia." *Man,* n.s. 18:635–53.

Burt, Ron S. 1982. *Toward a Structural Theory of Action: Network Models of Stratification, Perception, and Action.* New York: Academic Press.

Calvin, John. [1559] 1960. *Institutes of the Christian Religion.* Edited by John T. McNeill. Vols. 1 and 2. Philadelphia: Westminster Press.

Carman, John B. 1974. *The Theology of Ramanuja.* New Haven, Conn.: Yale University Press.

Carman, John B., and P. Y. Luke. 1968. *Village Christians and Hindu Culture.* London: Lutterworth Press.

Carman, John B., and Frederique Apffel Marglin, eds. 1985. *Purity and Auspiciousness in Indian Society.* Leiden: Brill.

Carter, A. T. 1974. "A Comparative Analysis of Systems of Kinship and Marriage in South Asia." *Proceedings of the Royal Anthropological Insititute for 1973,* 29–54.

Clegg, Stewart R. 1988. *Frameworks of Power.* London: Sage.

Clifford, James. 1988. *Predicament of Culture: Twentieth-Century Ethnography, Literature and Art.* Cambridge, Mass.: Harvard University Press.

Clooney, Francis. 1988. "Why the Veda Has No Author: Language as Ritual in Early Mimamsa and Post-Modern Theology." *Journal of the American Academy of Religion* 55:659–84.

Cohen, B. S. 1964. "The Role of Gosains in the Economy of Eighteenth- and Nineteenth-Century Upper India." *Indian Economic and Social History Review* 1:175–82.

Coleman, James S. 1986. "Social Theory, Social Research and a Theory of Action." *American Journal of Sociology* 91:1309–35.

———. 1987. *Norms as Social Capital in Economic Imperialism: The Economic Approach Outside the Field of Economics*. Edited by Gerard Radnitzky and Peter Bernholz. New York: Paragon House.

———. 1988. "Social Capital and the Creation of Human Capital." *American Journal of Sociology* 94:S95–S120.

———. 1990. *Foundations of Social Theory*. Cambridge, Mass.: Belknap Press of Harvard University Press.

Collingwood, R. G. [1946] 1956. *The Idea of History*. New York: Oxford University Press.

Collins, Randall. 1975. *Conflict Sociology: Toward an Explanatory Science*. New York: Academic Press.

———. 1979. *The Credential Society*. New York: Academic Press.

———. 1981. "On the Micro-foundations of Macro-sociology." *American Journal of Sociology* 86:984–1014.

———. 1982. *Sociological Insight: An Introduction to Nonobvious Sociology*. New York: Oxford University Press.

———. 1988. *Theoretical Sociology*. San Diego: Harcourt Brace Jovanovich.

Colpe, Carsten. 1987. "Sacred and Profane." In *Encyclopedia of Religion*, edited by Mircea Eliade. Vol. 12. New York: Macmillan.

Conklin, George H. 1973. "Urbanization, Cross-Cousin Marriage, and Power for Women: A Sample from Dharwar." *Contributions to Indian Sociology*, n.s. 7:53–63.

Coward, Rosalind, and John Ellis. 1977. *Language and Materialism: Developments in Semiology and the Theory of Subject*. Boston: Routledge and Kegan Paul.

Cox, Oliver. 1948. *Caste, Class and Race: A Study in Social Dynamics*. New York: Doubleday.

Dahl, Robert Alan. 1961. *Who Governs? Democracy and Power in an American City*. New Haven, Conn.: Yale University Press.

Dahrendorf, Ralf. 1958. "Out of Utopia." *American Journal of Sociology* 64:115–27.

———. 1959. *Class and Class Conflict in Industrial Society*. Stanford, Calif.: Stanford University Press.

———. 1968. *Essays in the Theory of Society*. Stanford, Calif.: Stanford University Press.

Daniel, Sheryl. 1978. "Power and Paradox: Marital Roles in a Tamil Village." Paper presented at the panel on Conceptions of Women and Power in Tamil Culture, annual meeting of the Association for Asian Studies, Chicago, March 31.

———. 1983. "The Tool Box Approach of the Tamil to the Issues of Moral Responsibility and Human Destiny." In *Karma: An Anthropological Inquiry*, edited by Charles F. Keyes and E. Valentine Daniel. Berkeley: University of California Press.

Das, Veena. 1982. *Structure and Cognition: Aspects of Hindu Caste and Ritual*. 2nd ed. Delhi: Oxford University Press.

David, Kenneth, 1974. "And Never the Twain Shall Meet? Mediating the Structural Approaches to Caste Ranking." In *Structural Approaches to South Indian Studies*, edited by Harry M. Buck and Glenn E. Yocum. Chambersburg, Pa.: Wilson Books, published by Conococheague Associates.

———, ed. 1977. *The New Wind*. The Hague: Mouton.

Davis, Marvin. 1983. *Rank and Rivalry: The Politics of Inequality in Rural and West Bengal*. Cambridge: Cambridge University Press.

de Bary, William Theodore, et al. [1958] 1972. *Sources of Indian Tradition*. Delhi: Motilal Banarsidas.

Derrida, Jacques. 1987. "The Ends of Man." In *After Philosophy: End or Transformation?* edited by Kenneth Baynes, James Bohman, and Thomas McCarthy. Cambridge, Mass.: MIT Press.

Desai, A. R., ed. 1979. *Peasant Struggles in India*. Delhi: Oxford University Press.

Dilthey, Wilhelm. 1976. *Selected Writings*. Edited, translated, and introduction by H. P. Rickman. Cambridge: Cambridge University Press.

DiMaggio, Paul. 1979. "Review Essay on Pierre Bourdieu." *American Journal of Sociology* 84:1460–75.

———. 1982. "Cultural Capital and School Success: The Impact of Status-Culture Participation on the Grades of U.S. High School Students." *American Sociological Review* 47:189–202.

———. 1987. "Classification in Art." *American Sociological Review* 52:440–55.

DiMaggio, Paul, and John Mohr. 1985. "Cultural Capital, Educational Attainment, and Marital Selection." *American Journal of Sociology* 90:1231–61.

DiMaggio, Paul, and Michael Useem. 1978. "Social Class and Arts Consumption." *Theory and Society* 5:141–61.

Dimmit, C., and W. J. C. van Buitenen, eds. 1983. *Puranic Myths*. New Delhi: Rupa.

Dimock, Edward C., Jr., and Denise Levertov. 1967. *In Praise of Krishna: Songs from the Bengali*. Chicago: University of Chicago Press.

Dirks, Nicholas. 1979. "The Structure and Meaning of Political Relations in a South Indian Little Kingdom." *Contributions to Indian Sociology* 13:169–206.

———. 1982. "The Past of a Palaiyakarar: The Ethnohistory of a South Indian Little Kingdom." *Journal of Asian Studies* 41:655–83.

———. 1986. "From Little King to Landlord: Property Law and the Gift Under the Madras Permanent Settlement." *Comparative Studies in Society and History* 28:307–33.

———. 1987. *The Hollow Crown: Ethnohistory of an Indian Kingdom*. New York: Cambridge University Press.

Domhoff, William G. 1967. *Who Rules America?* Englewood Cliffs, N.J.: Prentice-Hall.

Donnan, Hastings. 1988. *Marriage Among Muslims: Preference and Choice in North Pakistan*. Delhi: Hindustan.

Douglas, Mary. 1966. *Purity and Danger*. London: Routledge and Kegan Paul.

Douglas, Mary, and Aaron Wildavsky. 1982. *Risk and Culture: An Essay on the Selection of Technical and Environmental Dangers*. Berkeley: University of California Press.

Drekmeir, Charles. 1962. *Kingship and Community in Early India*. Stanford, Calif.: Stanford University Press.

Dube, S. C. 1955. *Indian Village*. London: Humanities Press.

———. 1968. "Caste Dominance and Factionalism." *Contributions to Indian Sociology*, n.s. 2:58–81.

Dubois, Abbé J. A. [1906] 1983. *Hindu Manners, Customs and Ceremonies*. 3rd ed. Oxford: Clarendon Press; Delhi: Oxford University Press.

Dumont, Louis. 1967. "Caste: A Phenomenon of Social Structure or an Aspect of Indian Culture?" In *Caste and Race: Comparative Approaches*, edited by Anthony de Reuck and Julie Knight. London: Churchill.

———. 1977. *From Mandeville to Marx: The Genesis and Triumph of Economic Ideology*. Chicago: University of Chicago Press.

———. [1966] 1980. *Homo Hierarchicus: The Caste System and Its Implications*. Translated by Mark Sainsbury, Louis Dumont, and Basia Gulati. Enlarged ed. Chicago: University of Chicago Press.

———. 1983. *Affinity as Value*. Chicago: University of Chicago Press.

———. 1986a. *A South Indian Subcaste*. Translated by Michael Moffatt. Delhi: Oxford University Press.

_____. 1986b. *Essays on Individualism*. Chicago: University of Chicago Press.

Durkheim, Emile. [1915] l965. *The Elementary Forms of Religious Life*. Translated by Joseph Ward Swain. New York: Free Press.

Eck, Diana L. 1981. *Darsan: Seeing the Divine Image in India*. Chambersburg, Pa.: Anima Books.

Edgerton, Franklin. [1944] 1964. *The Bhagavad Gita*. Translated and interpreted by Franklin Edgerton. New York: Harper & Row.

Edsall, Thomas Byrne, with Mary D. Edsall. 1991. "Race." *Atlantic Monthly*, May:53–86.

Eliade, Mircea.1959. *The Sacred and the Profane.* Translated by Willard R.Trask. New York: Harcourt, Brace.

_____. 1969. *Yoga: Immortality and Freedom*. 2nd ed. Translated by Willard R. Trask. Bollingen Series LVI. Princeton, N.J.: Princeton University Press.

Embree, Ainslie, ed. 1988. *Sources of Indian Tradition*. 2nd ed. Vol. 1, *From the Beginning to 1800*. New York: Columbia University Press. [Revision of deBary et al. 1958]

Etzioni, Amitai. 1961. *Modern Organizations*. Englewood Cliffs, N.J.: Prentice-Hall.

_____. l968. *The Active Society*. New York: Free Press.

_____. 1975. *A Comparative Analysis of Complex Organizations: On Power Involvement and Their Correlates*. Rev. and enlarged ed. New York: Free Press.

_____. 1988. *The Moral Dimension*. New York: Free Press.

Fairbank, John K. l983. "Blind Obedience." Review of *Son of the Revolution,* by Liang Heng and Judith Shapiro. *New York Review of Books*. May l2, p. 2l.

Feuer, Lewis. l975. *Ideology and the Ideologists*. New York: Harper Torchbooks.

Foucault, Michel. 1972. *The Archaeology of Knowledge*. Translated by A. M. Sheridan Smith. New York: Harper & Row.

_____. 1977. *Discipline and Punish: The Birth of the Prison*. Translated by Alan Sheridan. Harmondsworth: Penguin.

_____. 1980. *Power/Knowledge: Selected Interviews and Other Writings, 1972–77*. Edited by Collin Gordon. Translated by Collin Gordon, Leo Marshall, John Metham, and Kate Soper. New York: Pantheon Books.

Fox, Richard G. 1971. *Kin, Clan, Raja and Rule: State–Hinterland Relations in Pre-Industrial India*. Berkeley: University of California Press.

Frazer, James George. 1922. *The Golden Bough: A Study in Magic and Religion*. Abridged ed. New York: Macmillan.

Freud, Sigmund. 1962. *Civilization and Its Discontents*. Translated and edited by James Strachey. New York: Norton.

Friedson, E. l971. *The Profession of Medicine*. New York: Dodd Mead.

Fruzzetti, Lina. 1982. *The Gift of a Virgin*. New Brunswick, N.J.: Rutgers University Press.

Fruzzetti, Lina, and Akos Ostor. 1976. "Is There a Structure to North India Kinship Terminology?" *Contributions to Indian Sociology*, n.s. 10:63–96.

_____. [1982] 1983. "Bad Blood in Bengal: Category and Affect in the Study of Kinship, Caste and Marriage." In *Concepts of the Person: Kinship, Caste, and Marriage in India*, edited by Akos Oster, Lina Fruzzetti, and Steve Barnett. Delhi: Oxford University Press.

Fruzzetti, Lina, Akos Ostor, and Steve Barnett. 1976. "The Cultural Construction of the Person in Bengal and Tamilnadu." *Contributions to Indian Sociology,* n.s. 10:157–82. Reprinted in *Concepts of the Person: Kinship, Caste, and Marriage in India*, edited by Akos Ostor, Lina Fruzzetti, and Steve Barnett. Delhi: Oxford University Press, [1982] 1983.

Frykenberg, Robert E. 1979. *Land Control and Social Structure in Indian History*. New Delhi: Manohar.

Fuller, Christopher J. 1976. *The Nayars Today*. Cambridge: Cambridge University Press.

———. 1977. "British India or Traditional India? An Anthropological Problem." *Ethnos* 42:95–121.

———. 1979. "Gods, Priests and Purity: On the Relation Between Hinduism and the Caste System." *Man,* n.s. 14:459–76.

———. 1986. "The Nayar Taravad." *Man,* n.s. 21:135–36.

———. 1989. "Misconceiving the Grain Heap: A Critique of the Concept of the Indian Jajmani System." In *Money and the Morality of Exchange*, edited by Jonathan Parry and Maurice Bloch. Cambridge: Cambridge University Press.

———. 1992. *The Camphor Flame: Popular Hinduism and Society in India*. Princeton, N.J.: Princeton University Press.

Gadamer, Hans George. 1975. *Truth and Method*. New York: Seabury Press.

Gardner, Peter M. 1968. "Dominance in India: A Reappraisal." *Contributions to Indian Sociology,* n.s. 2:82–97.

Garfinkel, Harold. 1967. *Studies in Ethnomethodology*. Englewood Cliffs, N.J.: Prentice-Hall.

Geertz, Clifford. 1966. "Religion as a Cultural System." In *Anthropological Approaches to the Study of Religion*, edited by Michael Banton. London: Tavistock.

———. 1973. *The Interpretation of Culture: Selected Essays*. New York: Basic Books.

———. 1980. *Negara: The Theatre State in Nineteenth-Century Bali*. Princeton, N.J.: Princeton University Press.

Gennep, Arnold van. 1960. *The Rites of Passage*. Translated by Monika Vizedom and Gabrielle Caffe. Chicago: University of Chicago Press.

Gibbs, Jack P. 1989.*Control: Sociology's Central Notion*. Urbana:University of Illinois Press.

Giddens, Anthony. 1975. *The Class Structure of Advanced Society*. New York: Harper Torchbooks.

———. 1976. *New Rules of Sociological Method: A Positive Critique of Interpretative Sociologies*. New York: Basic Books.

———. 1979. *Central Problems in Social Theory: Action, Structure and Contradiction in Social Analysis*. London: Macmillan.

———. 1981. *A Contemporary Critique of Historical Materialism*, Vol. 1. Berkeley: University of California Press.

———. 1984. *The Constitution of Society: Outline of the Theory of Structuration*. Berkeley: University of California Press.

Glucklich, Ariel. 1984. "Karma and Pollution in Hindu Dharma: Distinguishing Law from Nature." *Contributions to Indian Sociology,* n.s. 18:25–43.

Goffman, Erving. 1959. *The Presentation of Self in Everyday Life*. New York: Doubleday.

———. 1967. *Interaction Ritual: Essays in Face-to Face Behavior*. Chicago: Aldine.

———. 1971. *Relations in Public*. New York: Harper Colophon.

Gonda, Jan. 1969a. *Ancient Indian Kingship from the Religious Point of View*. Leiden: Brill.

———. 1969b. *Eye and Gaze in the Veda*. Amsterdam: North-Holland.

Goode, William Joshua. 1951. *Religion Among the Primitives*. Glencoe, Ill.: Free Press.

———. 1978. *The Celebration of Heroes: Prestige as a Social Control System*. Berkeley: University of California Press.

Gough, Kathleen. 1952. "Changing Kinship Usages in the Setting of Political and Economic Change Among the Nayars of Malabar." *J.R.A.I.* 82:71–87.

———. 1959. "The Nayars and the Definition of Marriage." *J.R.A.I.* 89:23–34.

———. 1960. "Caste in a Tanjore Village." In *Aspects of Caste in Southern India, Ceylon, and Northwestern Pakistan*, edited by E. R. Leach. New York: Cambridge University Press.

Gould, Harold. 1958. "The Hindu Jajmani System: A Case of Economic Particularism." *South Western Journal of Anthropology* 45:428–37.

———. 1967. "Priest and Contrapriest: A Structural Analysis of Jajmani Relationships in the Hindu Plains and the Nilgiri Hills." *Contributions to Indian Sociology* 1:26–55.

Gouldner, Alvin. 1965. *Enter Plato*. New York: Basic Books.

———. 1979. *The Future of Intellectuals and the Rise of the New Class*. New York: Seabury Press.

Gray, John N. 1980. "Hypergamy, Kinship and Caste Among the Chettris of Nepal." *Contributions to Indian Sociology,* n.s. 14:1–33.

Guha, Ranajit, ed. 1982. *Subaltern Studies I: Writings on South Asian History and Society*. Delhi: Oxford University Press.

———, ed. 1983. *Subaltern Studies II: Writings on South Asian History and Society*. Delhi: Oxford University Press.

Gupta, Sanjukta, Dirk Jan Hoens, and Teun Goudriaan. 1979. *Hindu Tantrism*. Leiden: Brill.

Habermas, Jürgen. 1971. *Knowledge and Human Interest*. Translated by Jeremy J. Shapiro. Boston: Beacon Press.

———. 1984. *The Theory of Communicative Action*. Vol. 1, *Reason and Rationalization of Society*. Translated by Thomas McCarthy. Boston: Beacon Press.

———. 1987. *Theory of Communicative Action*. Vol. 2, *Life, World and System: A Critique of Functionalist Reason*. Translated by Thomas McCarthy. Boston: Beacon Press.

Habib, Irfan. 1963. *The Agrarian System of Mughal India*. Bombay and New York: Asia Publishing House.

———. 1982. "The Peasant in Indian History." Presidential Address presented to the Indian History Congress. Kurukshetra.

Harker, Richard, Cheleen Mahar, and Chris Wilkes, eds. 1990. *An Introduction to the Work of Pierre Bourdieu: The Practice of Theory*. Basingstoke: Macmillan.

Harper, Edward B. 1959. "Two Systems of Economic Exchange in Village India." *American Anthropologists* 61: 760–78.

———. 1964. "Ritual Pollution as an Integrator of Caste and Religion." *Journal of Asian Studies* 23:151–97.

Hawley, John Stratton, and Mark Juergensmeyer. 1988. *Songs of the Saints of India*. Text and notes by John Stratton Hawley. Translated by John Stratton Hawley and Mark Juergensmeyer. New York: Oxford University Press.

Hechter, Michael. 1987. *The Principles of Group Solidarity*. Berkeley: University of California Press.

Heesterman, J. C. 1985. *The Inner Conflict of Tradition: Essays in Indian Ritual, Kingship, and Society*. Chicago: University of Chicago Press.

Heidegger, Martin. 1969. *Identity and Difference*. Translated and with an introduction by Joan Stambaugh. New York: Harper & Row.

Hershman, Paul. 1981. *Punjabi Kinship and Marriage*. Edited by Hilary Standing. Delhi: Hindustan.

Hertel, Bradley. 1983. "Attributional, Reputational, and Self-Ratings of Ritual Status of Castes in Northern India." *International Journal of Contemporary Sociology* 20:73–93.

Hiltebeitel, Alf. 1987. "Hinduism." In *Encyclopedia of Religion*, edited by Mircea Eliade. Vol. 6. New York: Macmiilan.

Hirschman, Albert. 1977. *The Passions and the Interests: Political Arguments for Capitalism Before Its Triumph*. Princeton, N.J.: Princeton University Press.

Hocart, A. M. 1950. *Caste*. New York: Russell and Russell.

Homans, George Caspar. 1964. "Contemporary Theory in Sociology." In *Handbook of Modern Sociology*, edited by Robert E. Lee Faris. Chicago: Rand McNally.

Hopkins, Thomas J. 1971. *The Hindu Religious Tradition*. Encino, Calif.: Dickenson.

Horton, Robin, and Ruth Finnegan, eds. 1973. *Modes of Thought: Essays on Thinking in Western and Non-Western Societies*. London: Faber.

Huber, Joan. 1990. "Macro–Micro Links in Gender Stratification, 1989 Presidential Address." *American Sociological Review*, February 1990, 55:1–10.

Hubert, Henri, and Marcel Mauss. 1964. *Sacrifice: Its Nature and Function*. Translated by W. D. Halls. Chicago: University of Chicago Press.

Hume, David. [1739, 1969] 1985. *A Treatise of Human Nature*. Edited and with an introduction by Ernest C. Mossner. Harmondsworth: Penguin.

Hunter, Floyd. 1953. *Community Power Structure*. Chapel Hill: University of North Carolina Press.

Hunter, Herbert M., and Sameer Y. Abraham, eds. 1987. *Race, Class, and the World System: The Sociology of Oliver C. Cox*. New York: Monthly Review Press.

Hunter, James Davidson. 1991. *Culture Wars*. New York: Basic Books.

Hutton, J. H. 1963. *Caste in India: Its Nature, Function, and Origins*. Bombay: Oxford University Press.

Hymnbook, The. 1955. Edited by David Hugh Jones. Richmond, Philadelphia, and New York: Published by Presbyterian Church in the United States, The United Presbyterian Church in the U.S.A., Reformed Church in America.

Inden, Ronald B. 1976. *Marriage and Rank in Bengali Culture*. Berkeley: University of California Press.

––––––. 1982. "Hierarchies of Kings in Medieval India." In *Way of Life: Essays in Honor of Louis Dumont*, edited by T. N. Madan. Delhi: Vikas.

––––––. 1985. "Kings and Omens." In *Purity and Auspiciousness in Indian Society*, edited by John B. Carman and Frederique Marglin. Leiden: Brill.

––––––. 1986. "Orientalist Constructions of India." *Modern Asian Studies* 20:401–46.

––––––. 1990. *Imagining India*. Oxford: Basil Blackwell.

Inden, Ronald B., and Ralph W. Nicholas. 1977. *Kinship in Bengali Culture*. Chicago: University of Chicago Press.

Isaac, Jeffrey C. 1987. *Power and Marxist Theory*. Ithaca, N.Y.: Cornell University Press.

Ishwaran, K. 1968. *Shivapur: A South Indian Village*. London: Routledge and Kegan Paul.

Israel, Joachim. 1971. *Alienation: From Marx to Modern Sociology*. Boston: Allyn and Bacon.

Jay, Martin. 1973. *The Dialectical Imagination: A History of the Frankfurt School and the Institute of Social Research, 1923–1950*. Boston: Little, Brown.

Kakar, Sudhir. 1981. *The Inner World*. Delhi: Oxford University Press.

Kane, Pandurang Vaman. 1968. *History of the Dharmasastras (Ancient and Medieval Religious and Civil Law in India)*. Vol. 1, pt. 1. 2nd ed. rev. and enlarged. Poona: Bhandarkar Oriental Research Institute.

––––––. 1973a. *History of the Dharmasastras*. Vol. 3. 2nd ed. Poona: Bhandarkar Oriental Research Institute.

––––––. 1973b. *History of the Dharmasastras*. Vol. 4. 2nd ed. Poona: Bhandarkar Oriental Research Institute.

––––––. 1974a. *History of the Dharmasastras*. Vol. 2, pt. 1. 2nd ed. Poona: Bhandarkar Oriental Research Institute.

––––––. 1974b. *History of the Dharmasastras*. Vol. 2, pt. 2. 2nd ed. Poona: Bhandarkar Oriental Research Institute.

––––––. 1974c. *History of the Dharmasastras*. Vol. 5, pt. 1. 2nd ed. Poona: Bhandarkar Oriental Research Institute.

––––––. 1975. *History of the Dharmasastras*. Vol. 1, pt. 2. rev. and enlarged. Poona: Bhandarkar Oriental Research Institute.

_____. 1977. *History of the Dharmasastras*. Vol. 5, pt. 2. 2nd ed. Poona: Bhandarkar
        Oriental Research Institute.

Kantowsky, Detlef, ed. 1986. *Recent Research on Max Weber's Studies of Hinduism*. Munich
        and London: Weltforum Verlag.

Kaplan, Abraham. 1964. *The Conduct of Inquiry: Methodology for Behavioral Science*. San
        Francisco: Chandler.

Keyes, Charles F., and E. Valentine Daniel, eds. 1983. *Karma: An Anthropological Inquiry*.
        Berkeley: University of California Press.

Khare, Ravindra S. 1970. *The Changing Brahmans: Associations and Elites Among the
        Kanya-Kubjas of North India*. Chicago: University of Chicago Press.

_____. 1976. *The Hindu Hearth & Home*. New Delhi: Vikas.

_____. 1984. *The Untouchable as Himself: Ideology, Identity and Pragmatism Among the
        Lucknow Chamars*. Cambridge: Cambridge University Press.

Kinder, Ernst. 1965. "Eschatology." In *The Encyclopedia of the Lutheran Church*, edited by
        Julius Bodensieck. Minneapolis: Augsburg Press.

Klass, Morton. 1966. "Marriage Rules in Bengal." *American Anthropologist* 68:951–70.

_____. 1980. *Caste: The Emergence of the South Asian Social System*. Philadelphia:
        ISHI.

Klostermaier, Klaus K. 1989. *A Survey of Hinduism*. Albany: State University of New York
        Press.

Kolenda, Pauline. 1978. "Sibling-Set Marriage, Collateral-Set Marriage and Deflected
        Alliance among Annana Jats of Jaipur district, Rajastham." In *American Studies in the
        Anthropology of India*, edited by Sylvia Vatuk. New Delhi: Manohar.

_____. [1963] 1981. "Toward a Model of the Hindu Jajmani System." In *Caste, Cult, and
        Hierarchy*. Meerut: Folklore Institute.

_____. 1984. *Caste in Contemporary India*. Jaipur: Rawat.

_____. 1987a. "Brideprice, Dowry and Marital Exchanges in India." Paper presented at the
        meeting of the Association for Asian Studies, Boston.

_____. 1987b. *Regional Differences in Family Structure in India*. Jaipur: Rawat.

Kristol, Irving. 1972. "About Equality." *Commentary* 54:41–47.

Kuhn, Thomas. [1962] 1970. *The Structure of Scientific Revolutions*. 2nd ed. enlarged.
        Chicago: University of Chicago Press.

Kulhe, Hermann, Anncharlott Eschmann, and Gaya Charan Tripathi, eds. 1978. *The Cult of
        Jagannath and the Regional Tradition of Orissa*. New Delhi: Manohar.

Kumar, Dharma, ed. 1982. *The Cambridge Economic History of India,* Vol. 2, *c.1757–c. 1970*.
        Cambridge: Cambridge University Press.

Laing, R. D. 1971. *The Politics of the Family and Other Essays*. New York: Pantheon Books.

Lang, Graeme. 1989. "The Sociology of Heaven and Hell: Afterlife Imagery as Ideology."
        Paper presented at the annual meeting of the Society for the Scientific Study of
        Religion, Salt Lake City, Utah.

Leach, Edmund R. 1960. *Aspects of Caste in South India, Ceylon, and Northwest Pakistan*.
        Cambridge: Cambridge University Press.

_____. 1974. *Claude Lévi-Strauss*. Rev. ed. New York: Viking Press.

_____. 1983. "Melchisedech and the Emperor: Icons of Subversion and Orthodoxy." In
        Structuralist Interpretations of Biblical Myth, edited by Edmund Leach and D. Alan
        Aycock. Cambridge: Cambridge University Press.

Leach, Edmund, and D. Alan Aycock, eds. 1983. *Structuralist Interpretations of Biblical
        Myth*. Cambridge: Cambridge University Press.

Le Goff, Jacques. 1984. *The Birth of Purgatory*. Translated by Arthur Goldhammer. Chicago:
        University of Chicago Press.

_____. 1988. *Your Money or Your Life.* Translated by Patricia Ranum. New York: Zone Books.

Lenski, Gerhard. 1966. *Power and Privilege: A Theory of Social Stratification*. New York: McGraw-Hill.

Lenski, Gerhard, and Jean Lenski. 1974. *Human Societies: An Introduction to Macro-sociology*. 2nd ed. New York: McGraw-Hill.

Lévi-Strauss, Claude. 1963. *Structural Anthropology*. Translated by Claire Jacobson and Brooke Grundfest Schoepf. New York: Basic Books.

_____. 1966. *The Savage Mind*. Chicago: University of Chicago Press.

_____. 1969. *The Raw and the Cooked*. Translated by John Weightman and Doreen Weightman. New York: Harper & Row.

Lewis, I. M. 1986. *Religion in Context: Cults and Charisma*. Cambridge: Cambridge University Press.

Lewis, Oscar. 1958. *Village Life in North India*. New York: Random House.

Lingat, Robert. 1973. *The Classical Law of India*. Berkeley: University of California Press.

Little, David. 1969. *Religion, Order, and Law*. New York: Harper Torchbooks.

Locke, John. [1691] 1975. *An Essay Concerning Human Understanding*. Oxford: Clarendon Press.

Lockwood, David. 1992. *Solidarity and Schism: The Problem of Disorder in Durkheimian and Marxist Sociology*. Oxford: Clarendon Press.

Lowie, Robert Harry. 1924. *Primitive Religion*. New York: Boni and Liveright.

Ludden, David E. 1985. *Peasant History in South India*. Princeton, N.J.: Princeton University Press.

Luhmann, Niklas. 1982. *The Differentiation of Society*. Translated by Stephen Holmes and Charles Larmore. New York: Columbia University Press.

_____. 1989. *Ecological Communication*. Translated by John Bednarz, Jr. Chicago: University of Chicago Press.

Lukács, Georg. [1927] 1968. *History and Class Consciousness: Studies in Marxist Dialectics*. Translated by Rodney Livingstone. London: Merlin Press.

Lukes, Steven. 1973. *Emile Durkheim, His Life and Work: A Historical and Critical Study*. London: Allen Lane.

_____. 1974. *Power: A Radical View*. London: Macmillan.

_____. 1977. *Essays in Social Theory*. New York: Columbia University Press.

Luther, Martin. [1520] 1943. *An Open letter to the Christian Nobility of the German Nation in Three Treatises*. Philadelphia: Muhlenberg Press.

_____. [1535] n.d. *Commentary on St. Paul's Epistle to the Galatians*. Westwood N.J.: Revell.

Lynch, Owen M. 1969. *The Politics of Untouchability: Social Mobility and Social Change in a City of India*. New York: Columbia University Press.

_____. 1977. "Notes on Theory and Method in Dumont." In *The New Wind*, edited by Kenneth David. The Hague: Mouton.

MacDougall, John. 1980. "Two Models of Power in Contemporary India." *Contributions to Indian Sociology*, n.s. 14:77–94.

Machlup, Fritz. 1962. *The Production and Distribution of Knowledge in the United States*. Princeton, N.J.: Princeton University Press.

Madan, G. R. 1979. *Western Sociologists on Indian Society: Marx, Spencer, Weber, Durkheim, Pareto*. Boston: Routledge and Kegan Paul.

Madan, T. N. 1965. *Family and Kinship: A Study of the Pandits of Rural Kashmir*. Bombay: Asia Publishing House.

_____. 1975. "Structural Implications of Marriage in North India: Wife-Givers and Wife-

Takers Among the Pandits of Kashmir." *Contributions to Indian Sociology*, n.s. 9:217–43

_____. [1982] 1983. "The Ideology of the Householder Among the Kashmiri Pandits." In *Concepts of the Person: Kinship, Caste, and Marriage in India*, edited by Akos Oster, Lina Fruzzetti, and Steve Barnett. Delhi: Oxford University Press.

_____. 1985. "Concerning the Categories 'Subha' and 'Suddha' in Hindu Culture: An Explanatory Essay." In *Purity and Auspiciousness in Indian Society*, edited by John B. Carman and Frederique Apffel Marglin. Leiden: Brill.

_____. 1987. *Non-renunciation: Themes and Interpretations of Hindu Culture*. New York: Oxford University Press.

Mahony, William. 1987. "Karman." In *Encyclopedia of Religion*, edited by Mircea Eliade. Vol. 8. New York: Macmillan.

Malamoud, Charles. 1982. "On the Rhetoric and Semantics of the Purusartha." In *Way of Life: King, Householder, Renouncer: Essays in Honor of Louis Dumont*, edited by T. N. Madan. New Delhi: Vikas.

Malinowski, Bronislaw. 1922. *Argonauts of the Western Pacific*. London: Routledge and Kegan Paul.

_____. 1948. *Magic, Science and Religion: And Other Essays*. New York: Doubleday.

Mandelbaum, David. 1966. "Transcendental and Pragmatic Aspects of Religion." *American Anthropologist* 68:1174–91.

_____. 1970. *Society in India*. Berkeley: University of California Press; Bombay: Popular Prakashan.

Mann, Michael. 1986. *The Sources of Social Power*. Vol. 1. New York: Cambridge University Press.

Marcuse, Herbert. [ca. 1955] 1962. *Eros and Civilization: A Philosophical Inquiry into Freud*. New York: Vintage Books.

Marglin, Frederique A. 1977. "Power, Purity and Pollution: Aspects of the Caste System Reconsidered." *Contributions to Indian Sociology*, n.s. 11:245–70.

_____. 1982. "Kings and Wives: The Separation of Status and Royal Power." In *Way of Life: King, Householder, Renouncer: Essays in Honor of Louis Dumont*, edited by T. N. Madan. New Delhi: Vikas.

_____. 1985a. *Wives of the God-King: The Rituals of the Devadasis of Puri*. Delhi and New York: Oxford University Press.

_____. 1985b. "Types of Oppositions in Hindu Culture." In *Purity and Auspiciousness in Indian Society*, edited by John B. Carman and Frederique Apffel Marglin. Leiden: Brill.

Marriott, McKim, ed. 1955. *Village India: Studies in the Little Community*. Chicago: University of Chicago Press.

_____. 1959. "Interactional and Attributional Theories of Caste Ranking." *Man in India* 39:92–107

_____. 1960. *Caste Ranking and Community Structure in Five Regions of India and Pakistan*. Poona: G. S. Press.

_____. 1965. *Caste Ranking and Community Structure in Five Regions of India and Pakistan*. 2nd ed. Poona: Deccan College Post-Graduate and Research Institute.

_____. 1968. "Caste Ranking and Food Transactions: A Matrix Analysis." In *Structure and Change in Indian Society*, edited by Bernard S. Cohn and Milton B. Singer. Chicago: Aldine.

_____. 1976. "Hindu Transactions: Diversity Without Dualism." In *Transaction and Meaning*, edited by Bruce Kapferer. Philadelphia: ISHI.

_____. 1977. "[Remarks in] Symposium." In *The New Wind*, edited by Kenneth David. The Hague: Mouton.

_____. 1989. "Constructing an Indian Ethnosociology." *Contributions to Indian Sociology,* n.s. 23:1–39.

Marriott, McKim, and Ronald B. Inden. 1974. "Caste Systems." In *Encyclopaedia Britannica.* 15th ed. Vol. 3. Chicago: Encyclopaedia Britannica.

_____. 1977. "Toward an Ethnosociology of South Asian Caste Systems." In *The New Wind,* edited by Kenneth David. The Hague: Mouton.

Marshall, T. H. 1950. *Citizenship and Social Class.* Cambridge: Cambridge University Press.

Martin, James P. 1963. *The Last Judgment in Protestant Theology from Orthodoxy to Ritschl.* Grand Rapids, Mich.: Eerdmans.

Marx, Karl. [1867] 1967. *Capital.* Vol. 1. Translated from the 3rd German ed. by Samuel Moore and Edward Aveling. Edited by Friedrich Engels. New York: International Publishers.

_____. 1968. *Karl Marx on Colonialism and Modernization: His Dispatches and Other Writings on China, India, Mexico, Middle East and North Africa.* New York: Doubleday.

_____. [1844] 1978. "The Economic and Philosophic Manuscripts." In *The Marx-Engels Reader,* edited by Robert C. Tucker. 2nd ed. New York: Norton.

_____. [1845] 1978. "Theses on Feuerbach." In *The Marx-Engels Reader,* edited by Robert C. Tucker. 2nd ed. New York: Norton.

_____. [1852] 1978. "The Eighteenth Brumaire of Louis Bonaparte." In *The Marx-Engels Reader,* edited by Robert C. Tucker. 2nd ed. New York: Norton.

_____. 1983. *Marx on Indonesia and India.* Edited by Irfan Habib. Germany: Karl-Marx-Haus.

Marx, Karl, and Friedrich Engels. [1846] 1978. *The German Ideology.* In *The Marx-Engels Reader,* edited by Robert C. Tucker. 2nd ed. New York: Norton.

Mauss, Marcel. [1925] 1970. *The Gift: The Form and Reason for Exchange in Archaic Societies.* London: Routledge and Kegan Paul.

Mayer, Adrian C. 1960. *Caste and Kinship in Central India.* London: Routledge and Kegan Paul.

_____. 1982. "Perceptions of Princely Rule: Perspectives from a Biography." In *Way of Life: King, Householder, Renouncer: Essays in Honor of Louis Dumont,* edited by T. N. Madan. Delhi: Vikas.

Mayhew, Bruce H. 1980. "Structuralism Versus Individualism: Part I: Shadow Boxing in the Dark." *Social Forces* 59:335–75.

McDannell, Colleen, and Bernhard Lang. 1988. *Heaven: A History.* New Haven, Conn.: Yale University Press.

McGilvray, Dennis B., ed. 1982. *Caste Ideology and Interaction.* Cambridge: Cambridge University Press.

_____. 1987. "Bride Givers and Groom Givers in Sri Lanka." Paper presented at the meeting of the Association for Asian Studies, Boston.

McLellan, David. [1986] 1989. *Ideology.* Milton Keynes, Eng.: Open University Press.

McNeill, John T., ed. 1960. *Institutes of the Christian Religion.* Philadelphia: Westminster Press.

Meade, George Herbert. 1956. *The Social Psychology of George Herbert Meade.* Edited by Anselm Strauss. Chicago: University of Chicago Press.

Merton, Robert K. 1957. *Social Theory and Social Structure.* Rev. and enlarged ed. Glencoe, Ill.: Free Press.

Methodist Hymnal, The. 1964. Edited by Carlton R. Young. Nashville, Tenn.: United Methodist Publishing House.

Miller, Barbara Diane. 1986. "Health, Fertility, and Society in India: Microstudies and Macrostudies—A Review Article." *Journal of Asian Studies* 45:1027–36.

Miller, D. B. 1975. *Hierarchy to Stratification: Changing Patterns of Social Inequality in a North Indian Village*. Delhi: Oxford University Press.

Mills, C. Wright. 1956. *The Power Elite*. New York: Oxford University Press.

Milner, Murray, Jr. l972. *The Illusion of Equality*. San Francisco: Jossey-Bass.

_____. l978. "Alternative Forms of Coordination: Combining Theoretical and Policy Analysis." *International Journal of Comparative Sociology* 19:24–46.

_____. l980. *Unequal Care*. New York: Columbia University Press.

_____. 1987a. "Theories of Inequality: An Overview and a Strategy for Synthesis." *Social Forces* 65:1053–89.

_____. 1987b. "Dirt and Development in India." *Virginia Quarterly Review* 63:54–71.

_____. 1988. "Status Relations in South Asian Marriage Alliances: Toward a General Theory." *Contributions to Indian Sociology*, n.s. 22:145–69.

Mines, Diane Paull. 1989. "Hindu Periods of Death 'Impurity.'" *Contributions to Indian Sociology* 1:103–30.

Mines, Mattison. 1984. *The Warrior Merchants: Textiles, Trade, and Territory in South India*. Cambridge: Cambridge University Press.

Moaddel, Mansoor. 1989. "State Autonomy and Class Conflict in the Reformation (Comment on Wuthnow, *ASR*, December 1985)." *American Sociological Review* 54:472–74.

Moffatt, Michael. 1979. *An Untouchable Community in South India*. Princeton, N.J.: Princeton University Press.

Moore, Barrington, Jr. 1967. *Social Origins of Dictatorship and Democracy: Lord and Peasant in the Making of the Modern World*. Boston: Beacon Press.

Moore, Melinda. 1985. "A New Look at the Nayar Taravad.," *Man*, n.s. 20:523–41.

_____. 1986. "Reply to C. J. Fuller," *Man*, n.s. 21:136–37.

Myrdal, Gunnar. 1944. *An American Dilemma: The Negro Problem and Modern Democracy*. New York: Harper and Brothers.

Nagel, Ernest. 1961. *The Structure of Science: Problems in the Logic of Scientific Explanation*. New York: Harcourt, Brace & World.

Nandy, Ashis. 1983. *The Intimate Enemy: Loss and Recovery of Self Under Colonialism*. Delhi: Oxford University Press.

Neale, Walter C. 1973. *Economic Change in Rural India: Land Tenure and Reform in Uttar Pradesh, 1800–1955*. New York: Kennikat Press.

Needham, Rodney, ed. 1973. *Right & Left: Essays on Dual Symbolic Classification*. Chicago: University of Chicago Press.

Niebuhr, H. Richard. [1929] 1965. *The Social Sources of Denominationalism*. Cleveland: World.

Niebuhr, Reinhold. 1949. *The Nature and Destiny of Man*. New York: Scribner's.

Nikhilananda, Swami, trans. and ed. [1963] 1964. *The Upanishads*. Abridged ed. New York: Harper Torchbooks.

Nozick, Robert. 1981. *Philosophical Explanations*. Cambridge: Belknap Press of Harvard University Press.

Oates, Joyce Carol. 1987. "The World's Worst Critics." *New York Times Book Review*, January 18, p. 1.

Obeyesekere, Gananath. 1968. "Theodicy, Sin and Salvation in a Sociology of Buddhism." In *Dialectic in Practical Religion*, edited by E. R. Leach. Cambridge: Cambridge University Press.

_____. [1980] 1983. "Rebirth Eschatology and Its Transformation." In *Karma and Rebirth in Classical Indian Traditions*, edited by Wendy O'Flaherty. Delhi: Motilal Banarsidass.

O'Flaherty, Wendy. 1973. *Shiva: The Erotic Ascetic*. Oxford: Oxford University Press.

_____. 1980. *Sexual Metaphors and Animal Symbols in Indian Mythology*. Delhi: Motilal

Banarsidass. [American edition published as *Women, Androgynes and Other Mythical Beasts*. Berkeley: University of California Press, 1980]

———, ed. 1983. *Karma and Rebirth in Classical Indian Traditions*. Delhi: Motilal Banarsidass.

O'Flaherty, Wendy, and J. Duncan M. Derrett, eds. 1978. *The Concept of Duty in South Asia*. New Delhi: Vikas.

Oommen, T. K. 1970. "The Concept of Dominant Caste: Some Queries." *Contributions to Indian Sociology*, n.s. 4:73–83.

Orenstein, Henry. 1965. *Gaon: Conflict and Cohesion in an Indian Village*. Princeton, N.J.: Princeton University Press.

Ortner, Sherry B. 1984. "Theory in Anthropology Since the Sixties." *Comparative Studies in Society and History* 26:126–66.

Oster, Akos, Lina Fruzzetti, and Steve Barnett, eds. [1982] 1983. *Concepts of the Person: Kinship, Caste, and Marriage in India*. Delhi: Oxford University Press.

O'Toole, Roger, ed. 1984. "Symposium on the Work of Guy E. Swanson." *Sociological Analysis* 45:177–222.

Otto, Rudolph. [1917] 1972. *The Idea of the Holy*. Translated by John W. Harvey. Oxford: Oxford University Press.

Padmanabh, S. Jaini. 1985. "The Pure and the Auspicious in the Jaina Tradition." In *Purity and Auspiciousness in Indian Society*, edited by John B. Carman and Frederique Apffel Marglin. Leiden: Brill.

Paige, Jeffery. 1975. *Agrarian Revolution: Social Movements and Export Agriculture in the Underdeveloped World*. New York: Free Press.

Parker, Robert. 1983. *Miasma: Pollution and Purification in Early Greek Religion*. Oxford: Clarendon Press.

Parkin, Robert. 1990. "Terminology and Alliance in India: Tribal Systems and the North–South Problem." *Contributions to Indian Sociology*, n.s. 24:61–76.

Parry, Jonathan P. 1979. *Caste and Kinship in Kangra*. London: Routledge and Kegan Paul.

———. 1980. "Ghosts, Greed and Sin: The Occupational Identity of the Benares Funeral Priests." *Man*, n.s. 15:88–111.

———. 1982. "Death and Cosmogony in Kashi." *Contributions to Indian Sociology*, n.s. 15:337–65. Reprinted in *Way of Life: King, Householder, Renouncer: Essays in Honor of Louis Dumont*, edited by T. N. Madan. Delhi: Vikas.

———. 1985a. "The Brahmanical Tradition and the Technology of the Intellect." In *Reason and Morality*, edited by Joanna Overing. London and New York: Tavistock.

———. 1985b. "Death and Digestion: The Symbolism of Food and Eating in North Indian Mortuary Rights." *Man*, n.s. 20:612–30.

———. 1986. "The Gift: The Indian Gift and the 'Indian Gift.'" *Man*, n.s. 21:453–73.

———. 1989a. "On the Moral Perils of Exchange." In *Money and the Morality of Exchange*, edited by Jonathan P. Parry and Maurice Bloch. Cambridge: Cambridge University Press.

———. 1989b. "The End of the Body." In *Fragments for a History of the Human Body*. Pt. 2, edited by Michel Feher. New York: Urzone.

———. 1991. "The Hindu Lexicographer: A Note on Auspiciousness and Purity." *Contributions to Indian Sociology* 25:267–85.

Parry, Jonathan P., and Maurice Bloch, eds. 1989. *Money and the Morality of Exchange*. Cambridge: Cambridge University Press.

Parsons, Talcott. 1937. *The Structure of Social Action: A Study in Social Theory with Special Reference to a Group of Recent European Writers*. New York: McGraw-Hill.

———. 1951. *The Social System*. Glencoe, Ill.: Free Press.

_____. 1954. *Essays in Sociological Theory*. Rev. ed. Glencoe, Ill.: Free Press.

_____. 1970. "Equality and Inequality in Modern Society, or Social Stratification Revisited." In *Social Stratification Research: A Theory for the 1970's*, edited by Edward O. Laumann. New York: Bobbs-Merrill.

Patterson, Orlando. 1982. *Slavery and Social Death*. Cambridge, Mass.: Harvard University Press.

Peristiany, J. G., ed. 1966. *Honour and Shame: The Values of Mediterranean Society*. Chicago: University of Chicago Press.

Pfaffenberger, Brian. 1982. *Caste in Tamil Culture: The Religious Foundations of Sudra Domination in Tamil Sri Lanka*. New York: Maxwell School of Citizenship and Public Affairs; Delhi: Vikas.

Pickering, W.S.F. 1984. *Durkheim's Sociology of Religion: Themes and Theories*. Boston: Routledge and Kegan Paul.

Pieper, Francis. 1953. *Christian Dogmatics*. Vol. 3. St. Louis: Concordia.

Pilgrim Hymnal, The. 1935. Edited by Sidney A. Weston. Boston: Pilgrim Press.

Plunkett, Frances Taft. 1973. "Royal Marriages in Rajasthan." *Contributions to Indian Sociology*, n.s. 7:64–80.

Pocock, David F. 1962. "Notes on Jajmani Relations." *Contributions to Indian Sociology* 6:78–92.

_____. 1972. *Kanbi and Patidar*. Oxford: Clarendon Press.

Poggi, Gianfranco. 1983. *Calvinism and the Capitalist Spirit*. Amherst: University of Massachusetts Press.

_____. 1990. *The State: Its Nature, Development and Prospects*. Cambridge: Polity Press.

Polanyi, Karl. [1944] 1957. *The Great Transformation*. Boston: Beacon Press.

Potter, Karl. [1980] 1983. *Karma and Rebirth in Classical Indian Traditions*. Edited by Wendy O'Flaherty. Delhi: Motilal Banarsidass.

Quigley, Declan. 1993. *The Interpretation of Caste*. Oxford: Clarendon Press.

Quistorp, Heinrich. 1955. *Calvin's Doctrine of the Last Things*. Translated by Harold Knight. London: Lutterworth Press.

Rabinow, Paul, and William M. Sullivan. 1987. *Interpretive Social Science: A Second Look*. Berkeley: University of California Press.

Radhakrishnan, Sarvepalli, and Charles A. Moore, eds. 1957. *A Source Book in Indian Philosophy*. Princeton, N.J.: Princeton University Press.

Raheja, Gloria Goodwin. 1988. *The Poison in the Gift*. Chicago: University of Chicago Press.

Ramanujan, A. K. 1973. *Speaking of Siva*. Translated and with an introduction by A. K. Ramanujan. Harmondsworth: Penguin.

Rao, M. Kodanda. 1973. "Rank Differences and Marriage Reciprocity in South India: An Aspect of the Implications of Elder Sister's Daughter's Marriage in a Fishing Village in Andhra." *Contributions to Indian Sociology*, n.s. 7:16–35.

Rao, M.S.A. 1986. "Religion, Sect, and Social Transformation: Some Reflections on Max Weber's Contributions to Hinduism and Buddhism." In *Recent Research on Max Weber's Studies of Hinduism*, edited by Detlef Kantowsky. Munich and London: Weltforum Verlag.

Raychaudhuri, Tapan, and Irfan Habib, eds. 1982. *The Cambridge Economic History of India*. Vol. 1, *c. 1200–c. 1750*. Cambridge: Cambridge University Press.

Reynolds, Susan. 1984. *Kingdoms and Communities in Western Europe, 900–1300*. Oxford: Clarendon Press.

Richards, John F. 1981. *Kingship and Authority in South Asia*. 2nd ed. Edited by John F. Richards. [Madison]: South Asian Studies, University of Wisconsin.

Ricoeur, Paul. 1978. *The Philosophies of Paul Ricoeur: An Anthology of His Works*. Edited by Charles E. Reagan and David Stewart. Boston: Beacon Press.

Robbins, Derek. 1991. *The Work of Pierre Bourdieu: Recognizing Society*. Milton Keynes, Eng.: Open University Press.

Robertson, Roland. 1970. *The Sociological Interpretation of Religion*. New York: Schocken Books.

Rorty, Richard. 1979. *Philosophy as the Mirror of Nature*. Princeton, N.J.: Princeton University Press.

_____. 1984. "The Historiography of Philosophy for Genres: Essays on the Historiography of Philosophy." In *Philosophy in History*, edited by Richard Rorty, J. B. Schneewind, and Quinton Skinner. Cambridge: Cambridge University Press.

_____. 1987. "Pragmatism and Philosophy." In *After Philosophy: End or Transformation?* edited by Kenneth Baynes, James Bohman, and Thomas McCarthy. Cambridge, Mass.: MIT Press.

_____. 1989. *Contingency, Irony and Solidarity*. Cambridge: Cambridge University Press.

Rudolph, Susanne Hoeber. 1987. "Presidential Address: State Formation in Asia— Prolegomenon to a Comparative Study." *Journal of Asian Studies* 46: 731–46.

Rudner, David West. 1987. "Religious Gifting and Island Commerce in Seventeenth-Century South India." *Journal of Asian Studies* 46:361–71.

Runciman, W. G. 1966. *Relative Deprivation and Social Justice*. Berkeley: University of California Press.

_____. 1989. *A Treatise on Social Theory*. Vol. 2, *Substantive Social Theory*. Cambridge: Cambridge University Press.

Said, Edward W. 1979. *Orientalism*. New York: Vintage Books.

Sanderson, Alexis. 1985. "Purity and Power Among the Brahmins of Kashmir." In *The Category of the Person: Anthropology, Philosophy, History*, edited Michael Carrither, Steven Collins, and Steven Lukes. Cambridge: Cambridge University Press.

Schneider, David. 1968. *American Kinship: A Cultural Account*. Englewood Cliffs, N.J.: Prentice-Hall.

Schultz, Theodore W. 1963. *The Economic Value of Education*. New York: Columbia University Press.

Schutz, Alfred. 1964. *Collected Papers*. Edited and with an introduction by Maurice Natanson. The Hague: Nijhoff.

_____. 1970. *On Phenomenology and Social Relations*. Edited and with an introduction by Helmut R. Wagner. Chicago: University of Chicago Press.

Sen, Amartya. 1981. *Poverty and Famines: An Essay on Entitlement and Deprivation*. Oxford: Clarendon Press; New York: Oxford University Press.

_____. 1990. "More than 100 Million Women Are Missing." *New York Review of Books*, December 20, pp. 61–66.

Sewell, William H., Jr. 1992. "A Theory of Structure: Duality, Agency and Transformation." *American Journal of Sociology* 98:1–29.

Shah, A. M. 1982. "Division and Hierarchy: An Overview of Caste in Gujarat." *Contributions to Indian Sociology*, n.s. 16:1–33.

Shah, K. J. 1982. "Of Artha and the *Arthasastra*." In *Way of Life: King, Householder, Renouncer: Essays in Honor of Louis Dumont*, edited by T. N. Madan. New Delhi: Vidas.

Sharma R. S. [1958] 1980. *Sudras in Ancient India*. Delhi: Motilal Banarsidass.

Shulman, David Dean. 1984. "The Enemy Within: Idealism and Dissent in South Indian Hinduism." In *Orthodoxy, Heterodoxy and Dissent in India*, edited by S. N. Eisenstadt, Reuven Kahane, and David Dean Shulman. Berlin: Mouton.

_____. 1985. *The King and the Clown in South Indian Myth and Poetry*. Princeton, N.J.: Princeton University Press.

Silverberg, James. 1968. *Social Mobility in the Caste System in India*. The Hague: Mouton.

Simpson, John H. 1979. "Sovereign Groups, Subsistence Activities, and the Presence of a High God." In *The Religious Dimension: New Directions in Quantitative Research*, edited by Robert Wuthnow. New York: Academic Press.

_____. 1983. "Power Transfigured: Guy Swanson's Analysis of Religion." *Religious Studies Review* 9:349–52.

Singer, Milton. 1972. *When a Great Tradition Modernizes: An Anthropological Approach to Indian Civilization*. Foreword by M. N. Srinivas. New York: Praeger.

Singer, Milton, and Bernard Cohn, eds. 1968. *Structure and Change in Indian Society*. Chicago: Aldine.

Sjoberg, Gideon. 1960. *The Pre-Industrial City, Past and Present*. Glencoe, Ill.: Free Press.

Skocpol, Theda. 1979. *States and Social Revolutions: A Comparative Analysis of France, Russia and China*. Cambridge: Cambridge University Press.

Smith, Jane I. 1987. "Afterlife: An Overview." In *Encyclopedia of Religion*, edited by Mircea Eliade. Vol. 1. New York: Macmillan

Smith, Jonathan Z. 1987. *To Take Place: Toward Theory in Ritual*. Chicago: University of Chicago Press.

Spear, Thomas George Percival. 1978. *The Oxford History of Modern India, 1740–1975*. 2nd ed. Oxford: Oxford University Press.

Srinivas, M. N. 1942. *Marriage and Family in Mysore*. Bombay: Asia Publishing House.

_____. 1959. "The Dominant Caste in Rampura." *American Anthropologist* 61:1–16. Reprinted in *Dominant Caste and Other Essays*. Delhi: Oxford University Press, 1987.

_____. 1962. *Caste in Modern India and Other Essays*. London: Asia Publishing House.

_____. [1952] 1965. *Religion & Society Among the Coorgs of South India*. New York: Asia Publishing House.

_____. 1976. *The Remembered Village*. Delhi: Oxford University Press.

_____. 1984. *Some Reflections on Dowry*. Delhi: Oxford University Press.

Stark, Rodney, and William Bainbridge. 1980. "Towards a Theory of Religion: Religious Commitment." *Journal for the Scientific Study of Religion* 19:114–28.

_____. 1985. *The Future of Religion: Secularization, Revival, and Cult Formation*. Berkeley: University of California Press.

Starr, Paul. 1982. *The Social Transformation of American Medicine*. New York: Basic Books.

Stein, Burton. 1980. *Peasant State and Society in Medieval South India*. Delhi: Oxford University Press.

Stevenson, H.N.C. 1954. "Status Evaluation in the Hindu Caste System." *Journal of the Royal Anthropological Institute* 84:45–65.

Stirrat, R. L. 1982. "Caste Conundrums: View of Caste in a Singhalese Catholic Fishing Village." In *Caste Ideology and Interaction*, edited by Dennis B. McGilvray. Cambridge: Cambridge University Press.

_____. 1984. "Sacred Models." *Man*, n.s. 19:199–215.

Swanson, Guy. 1964. *The Birth of the Gods*. Ann Arbor: University of Michigan Press.

_____. 1967. *Religion and Regime: A Sociological Account of the Reformation*. Ann Arbor: University of Michigan Press.

Swidler, Ann. 1985. "Culture in Action: Symbols and Strategies." *American Sociological Review* 51:273–86.

Tambiah, S. J. 1973. "Dowry and Bridewealth and the Property Rights of Women in South Asia." In *Bridewealth and Dowry*, edited by Jack Goody and S. J. Tambiah. Cambridge: Cambridge University Press.

_____. 1974. "Varna to Caste Through Mixed Unions." In *The Character of Kinship*, edited by Jack Goody. Cambridge: Cambridge University Press.

_____. 1976. *World Conquerer and World Renouncer: A Study of Buddhism and Polity in Thailand Against a Historical Background*. Cambridge: Cambridge University Press.

_____. 1985. "Purity and Auspiciousness at the Edge of Hindu Context—in Theravada Buddhist Societies." In *Purity and Auspiciousness in Indian Society*, edited by John B. Carman and Frederique Apffel Marglin. Leiden: Brill.

Tappert, Theodore G. 1959. *The Book of Concord: The Confessions of the Evangelical Lutheran Church*. Translated and edited by Theodore G. Tappert. Philadelphia: Fortress Press.

Taussig, Michael. 1980. *The Devil and Commodity Fetishism in South America*. Chapel Hill: University of North Carolina Press.

Tawney, R. H. [1926] 1960. *Religion and the Rise of Capitalism*. London: Murray.

Thapar, Romila. 1966. *A History of India*. Vol. 1. Baltimore: Penguin.

Thomas, Keith. 1971. *Religion and the Decline of Magic*. New York: Scribner's.

Thrupp, Sylvia L. 1972. "Gilds." In *International Encyclopedia of the Social Sciences*, edited by David L. Sills. New York: Macmillan.

Tilly, Charles. 1964. *The Vendee*. Cambridge, Mass.: Harvard University Press.

_____. 1981. *Class Conflict and Collective Action*. Beverly Hills, Calif.: Sage.

_____. 1984. *Big Structures, Large Processes, Huge Comparisons*. New York: Russell Sage Foundation.

_____. 1986. *The Contentious French*. Cambridge, Mass.: Belknap Press of Harvard University Press.

Tocqueville, Alexis de. 1961. *Democracy in America*. New York: Schocken Books.

Trautmann, Thomas R. 1981. *Dravidian Kinship*. Cambridge: Cambridge University Press.

Troeltsch, Ernst. [1911] 1931. *The Social Teachings of the Christian Churches*. Translated by Olive Wyon. New York: Macmillan.

Tubielewiez, Jolanta. 1980. *Superstitions, Magic and Mantic Practices in the Heian Period*. Warsaw: Wydawnictwa Uniwersytetu WarszaWskiego.

Tucker, Robert C., ed. 1978. *The Marx-Engels Reader*. 2nd ed. New York: Norton.

Turner, Ralph. 1976. "The Real Self: From Institution to Impulse." *American Journal of Sociology* 81:989–1016.

Turner, Victor. 1967. *The Forest of Symbols*. Ithaca, N.Y.: Cornell University Press.

_____. 1969. *The Ritual Process: Structure and Anti-Structure*. Ithaca, N.Y.: Cornell University Press.

_____. 1974. *Dramas, Fields and Metaphors. Symbolic Action in Human Society*. Ithaca, N.Y.: Cornell University Press.

Tylor, Edward Burnett. 1883. *Primitive Culture: Researches into the Development of Mythology, Philosophy, Religion, Language, Art and Custom*. New York: Holt.

Underhill, Ralph. 1975. "Economic and Political Antecedents of Monotheism: A Cross-Cultural Study." *American Journal of Sociology* 80:841–61.

Upadhya, Carol Boyack. 1990. "Dowry and Women's Property in Coastal Andhra Pradesh." *Contributions to Indian Sociology*, n.s. 24:29–60.

Van der Veen, Klass. 1973. "Marriage and Hierarchy Among the Anavil Brahmans of South Gujarat." *Contributions to Indian Sociology*, n.s. 7:36–51.

Van der Veer, Peter. 1988. *Gods on Earth*. London: Athlone Press.

Varma, I. A. Ravi. 1956. "Rituals of Worship." In *The Cultural Heritage of India*, edited by Haridas Bhattacharyya. Calcutta: Ramakrishna Institute of Culture.

Vatuk, Sylvia. 1975. "Gifts and Affines in North India." *Contributions to Indian Sociology* 9:155–96.

Wadley, Susan. 1975. *Shakti: Power in the Conceptual Structure of Karimpur Religion*. Chicago: University of Chicago Press.

Wallerstein. 1974. *The Modern World-System.* Vol. 1, *Capitalist Agriculture and the Origins of the European World-Economy in the 16th Century*. New York: Academic Press.

———. 1980. *The Modern World-System*. Vol. 2, *Mercantilism and the Consolidation of the European World-Economy, 1600–1750*. New York: Academic Press.

———. 1989. *The Modern World-System*. Vol. 3, *The Second Era of Great Expansion of the Capitalist World-Economy, 1730–1840's*. San Diego: Academic Press.

Wallis, Roy, and Steve Bruce. 1984. "The Stark–Bainbridge Theory of Religion: A Critical Analysis and Counter Proposal." *Sociological Analysis* 45:11–28.

Wartenberg, Thomas E. 1990. *The Forms of Power: From Domination to Transformation*. Philadelphia: Temple University Press.

Weber, Max. 1946. *From Max Weber*. Translated and edited by Hans Gerth and C. Wright Mills. New York: Oxford University Press.

———. 1949. *The Methodology of the Social Sciences*. Translated by Edward A. Shils and Henry A. Finch. Glencoe, Ill.: Free Press.

———. 1958a. *The Protestant Ethic and the Spirit of Capitalism*. Translated by Talcott Parsons. New York: Scribner's.

———. 1958b. *The Religion of India*. Glencoe, Ill.: Free Press.

———. [1920] 1968. *Economy and Society: An Outline of Interpretive Sociology*. Edited by Guenther Roth and Claus Wittich. New York: Bedminster Press.

Weblowsky, R. J. Zwi. 1987. "Eschatology: An Overview." In *Encyclopedia of Religion*, edited by Micrea Eliade. Vol. 5. New York: Macmillan.

Webster, Murray, Jr., and James E. Driskell, Jr. 1978. "Status Generalization: A Review and Some New Data." *American Sociological Review* 43:220–36.

Webster, Murray, Jr., and Martha Foschi, eds. 1988. *Status Generalization: New Theory and Research*. Stanford, Calif.: Stanford University Press.

Weisbrod, Burton A. 1962. "Education and Investment in Human Capital." *Journal of Political Economy* 70:106–23.

Westminster Confession of Faith. 1658. 2nd ed. London: Printed by E. M. for the Company of Stationers.

Whimster, Sam, and Scott Lash, eds. 1987. *Max Weber: Rationality and Modernity*. London: Allen & Unwin.

White, David Gordon. 1991. *Myths of the Dog-Man*. Chicago: University of Chicago Press.

White, Harrison C., Scott A. Boorman, and Ronald L. Breiger. 1976. "Social Structure from Multiple Networks, 1: Block Models of Roles and Positions." *American Journal of Sociology* 81:730–80.

Williams, Raymond. 1976. *Key Words*. New York: Oxford University Press.

———. 1981. *Culture*. London: Fontana.

Wilson, Bryan R. 1982. *Religion in Sociological Perspective*. New York: Oxford University Press.

Wiser, William H. [1936] 1958. *The Hindu Jajmani System*. Lucknow, India: Lucknow Publishing House.

Wittgenstein, Ludwig. 1958. *Philosophical Investigations*. 3rd ed. Translated by G.E.M. Anscombe. New York: Macmillan.

———. [1958] 1965. *Preliminary Studies for the "Philosophical Investigations."* New York: Harper Colophon. [Generally known as the *Blue and Brown Books*]

Woodward, C. Vann. [1955] 1974. *The Strange Career of Jim Crow*. 3rd ed. New York: Oxford University Press.

Wright, Erik Olin. 1985. *Classes*. London: Verso.

Wrong, Dennis. [1979] 1980. *Power: Its Forms, Bases, and Uses*. New York: Harper Colophon.

Wuthnow, Robert. 1985. "State Structures and Ideological Outcomes." *American Sociological Review* 50:799–821.

_____. 1987. *Meaning and the Moral Order: Explorations in Cultural Analysis*. Berkeley: University of California Press.

Yalman, Nur. 1967. *Under the Bo Tree: Studies in Caste, Kinship and Marriage in the Interior of Ceylon*. Berkeley: University of California Press.

Zaehner, R. C. 1966. *Hindu Scriptures*. Selected, translated and introduced by R. C. Zaehner. London: Dent.

Zaret, David. 1989. "Religion and the Rise of Liberal-Democratic Ideology in 17th-Century England." *American Sociological Review* 54:163–79.

Zukin, Sharon, and Paul DiMaggio. 1990. *Structures of Capital: Social Organization of the Economy*. Cambridge: Cambridge University Press.

Index

Cox, Oliver, 139
Craft groups. See *Jajmani* system
Cultural capital. *See* Capital
Cultural codes, 50–52, 106–42, 231, 300n.1. *See also* Secondary norms and rituals
  "codes on codes," 114–15
  compression and repression, 107
  decoding, 130, 282n.7
  "good mother" and "bad mother" as, 118–19
  methodology of analysis, 120, 130
  and metonyms, 107
  multiple layers of, 114–15
  purity, impurity, and pollution, 110–15
  secondary and primary values, 106–8
  seduction as, 118
  semen retention as, 116–18
  sexuality and asceticism, 115–19
  as social control, 111, 113, 114
Culture, 19. *See also* Capital; Cultural Codes; Ideology
  high culture, 9
  sociology of, 225–27

Dahl, Robert, 26
Dahrendorf, Ralf, 21, 262n.15
Dana, 49–50, 85, 87–88, 94
  and inauspiciousness, 132–35
Daniel, Sheryl, 116, 214, 274n.21
Das, Vena, 79, 115, 280n.13
de Bary, William Theodore, 198–99
Deities. See also *Puja*; Sacredness; Worship
  intimacy with, 179–80. *See also* Communion
  low status and malevolent spirits, 187, 292n.13
  relation to humans, 165–69, 208
  sectarian, 197
  worship of, 175–80
Devotion. See *Bhakti*
Dharma, 43, 52, 270n.4. See also *Rajadharma; Svadharma*
  as elaboration, 58
  kings and, 72, 82
  and *purusarthas*, 274n.2
  and soteriology, 191, 196
  and stability, 55
Dharmasastras, 43, 59, 195
Dharmasutras, 59
DiMaggio, Paul, 9
Dimmit, C., 117
Dimock, Edward C., 200
Dirks, Nicholas, 85–86, 92, 297n.3
Dirt, concept of, 111–12
Domhoff, William, 26
Douglas, Mary, 110–12
Dravidian, 156, 159, 160
Driskell, James E. 262n.23

Dualism. *See* Monism and dualism in Hinduism
Dube, S. C., 55, 89
Dubois, Abbé J. A., 124, 151
Duhkha, 43, 122
Dumont, Louis, 3, 71, 258n.8
  on caste and stratification, 139
  concept of power, 53, 269n.1
  ideology, centrality of, 13
  purity, impurity, and pollution, 110, 124, 279n.6
  South Indian marriage, 156
  on western individualism, 197n.13
Durkheim, Emile
  and magic, 290n.8
  notion of the sacred, 12, 163–64, 158n.12, 261n.12, 289n.1
  ritual and worship, 172
  solidarity and sacredness, 20
  on structure and culture, 225

Eagleton, Thomas, 258n.10
Eating, regulation of, 39, 41, 60–61. *See also* Food
  India compared with U.S. Old South, 140–41
  kacca and *pakka* food, 60–61
Eck, Diana L., 178, 180
Editing of social reality, 37–38
Elaboration of norms, 37, 58–60, 106, 231
  asramas and *yugas* as, 78
  sacred texts as, 58–59
Elementary forms and empirical variations, 20–22
Eliade, Mircea, 189, 194, 289n.3
Elites and nonelites. *See also* Chieftains; Kings and kingship
  economic and commercial, 66, 73, 273nn.13, 14
  general model of, 65–68, 272n.6
  local, 48–49
  non–Hindus as, 50
  political, 65–66, 84–88
  religious and intellectual, 65, 67
  and right and left castes, 74–76
Ellis, John, 260n.2
Embree, Ainslie, 274n.2
Encapsulation
  in *bhakti* sects, 197, 295n.14
  ideological, 158–60
  in marriages, 157–60
  structural, 157–58
  in Tantrism, 160
Endogamy, 47, 143, 231, 270n.9
  departures from, 144, 154, 160
Eschatology, 204–27, 232–33
  Christian, 215–20
  concept of, 204, 296n.2, 299n.22
  Hindu, 205–15

Marriage and marriage alliances (con't)
  status alliances, general theory of, 146–49,
    161, 284n.2
Marriott, McKim, 183, 278n.2. *See also*
    Ethnosociology
  code and substance, 114, 140, 280nn.11,12,
    291n.8
  interactional theory of caste ranking, 61
  otherness of India, 13–14
Marshall, T. H., 235
Marx, Karl, 3, 7, 99
  on making history, 3, 236
  on religion, 21, 225
Marxian tradition, 8
Materialism, 14–17
  Habermas and, 259n.19
  materialist reductionism, 11, 107
Mating, regulation of, 39–40. *See also* Marriage
    and marriage alliances
Mauss, Marcel, 62, 182–83
Maya, 122, 208
Mayer, Adrian C., 89, 296n.3
McDannell, Colleen, 218
McGilvray, Dennis B., 280n.12
Merchants, 75, 274n.1, 277n.19. *See also* Elites
    and nonelites, economic and commercial
Merton, Robert K., 236, 279n.10
Metaphor. *See* Cultural codes
Methodology. *See* Theoretical and methodologi-
    cal issues
Metonyms. *See* Cultural codes
Micro–sociology, 4. *See also* Macro and micro
    analysis
Milner, Murray, Jr., 96, 144, 161, 276n.14,
    280n.9, 286n.15, 289n.29
Mimamsas, 195, 294n.12
Mines, Diane Paull, 73, 273n.15
Moaddel, Mansoor, 226
Mobility, social
  economic and political, 57
  inexpansibility of status and, 34–35, 56–58
  manipulation of caste categories and, 57,
    270n.11
Moffat, Michael, 139, 296n.3
Moksa, 44, 135, 197. *See also* Salvation
  as overcoming separateness, 207–9
  as reversal of social distinctions, 207–9
  and *samsara*, 211–12
Monasticism, 69
Monism and dualism in Hinduism, 208–9, 210–11
Moore, Barrington, Jr., 8
Moral implications of book, 14–17
Morality
  and agency and contingency, 102–5, 279n.11
  versus coercive magic, 167

Muslims, 47, 157, 229, 277n.18, 287n.25
Myths. *See* Cultural codes

Nagel, Ernest, 279n.2
Nandy, Ashis, 119
Navaratri, 86, 276n.12
Nicholas, Ralph W., 288n.27
Nikhilananda, Swami, 293n.2
Nonelites. *See* Elites and nonelites
Norms. *See also* Elaboration of norms; Secondary
    norms and rituals
  accountability and agency, 235
  conformity to, 35–36
  fashions and, 268n.23
Nozick, Robert, 279n.4

Obeyesekere, Gananath, 189, 291n.12
Objectification, 98–102
  auspiciousness and inauspiciousness, 131–35
  external, 100–101
  and human substances, 113–15
  internal, 101–2
  as mechanical causation, 100, 278n.4
  protection of status, 98–100
  relationship to objectivation and reification, 99
  as relaxation of status insulation, 99
  semen retention as, 117–18
  and subjectification, 278n.3
Objectivation, 30, 31, 33
Objectivism, 5–6, 109, 258n.6
O'Flaherty, Wendy, 116, 118, 212–14, 270n.4,
    274n.21
Omens. *See* Auspiciousness and inauspiciousness
"Orders." *See* Causal analysis
Orenstein, Henry, 160
Orientalism, 14, 273n.18
Oster, Akos, 158–59, 288n.27
Other worlds, 204–5. *See also* Eschatology
O'Toole, Roger, 226
Otto, Rudolph, 164
Ownership, concept of, 86, 275n.10

Paige, Jeffery, 241
Pakka, 60–61
Pandits, 289n.29
Parker, Robert, 138
Parkin, Robert, 286n.21
Parry, Jonathan P., 212, 270n.3, 280n.12, 281n.2
  auspiciousness and purity, 134, 136
  hypergamy, 153
  inferiority of wife–givers, 149
Parsons, Talcott, 20, 97, 258n.12, 262n.13
Passeron, Jean–Claude, 8
Passive resistance. *See* Force, nonviolent
Patterson, Orlando, 258n.9, 264n.34